A Kamigata Anthology

Edited by Sumie Jones *and* Adam L. Kern
with Kenji Watanabe

ADVISORY BOARD

HOWARD HIBBETT
SHINJI NOBUHIRO

A Kamigata Anthology

LITERATURE FROM JAPAN'S
METROPOLITAN CENTERS, 1600–1750

UNIVERSITY OF HAWAI'I PRESS

HONOLULU

Library of Congress Cataloging-in-Publication Data

Names: Jones, Sumie, editor. | Kern, Adam L., editor. | Watanabe, Kenji, editor.

Title: A Kamigata anthology : literature from Japan's metropolitan centers, 1600–1750 / edited by Sumie Jones and Adam L. Kern with Kenji Watanabe.

Description: Honolulu : University of Hawai'i Press, 2020. | Includes bibliographical references and index.

Identifiers: LCCN 2019050456 (print) | LCCN 2019050457 (ebook) | ISBN 9780824881764 (cloth) | ISBN 9780824881818 (paperback) | ISBN 9780824882655 (epub) | ISBN 9780824882631 (pdf) | ISBN 9780824882648 (kindle edition)

Subjects: LCSH: Japanese literature—Edo period, 1600–1868—Translations into English.

Classification: LCC PL726.4 .K36 2020 (print) | LCC PL726.4 (ebook) | DDC 895.609—dc23

LC record available at https://lccn.loc.gov/2019050456

LC ebook record available at https://lccn.loc.gov/2019050457

Publication of this book has been assisted by a grant from

THE SUNTORY FOUNDATION

Cover art: Detail from *Okuni Kabuki* screen, late 1590s to 1615. A man and a woman make and sell skewered dumplings at the entrance to a kabuki hut. A designated National Important Cultural Property, Kyoto National Museum.

Contents

Color plates follow page 470

Preface to the Three-Volume Anthology

The popular literature and arts of Japan, as with those of many cultures, first appeared in earnest between the sixteenth and seventeenth centuries, buoyed by a nascent humanism that rebelled against more authoritarian, if not hereditary, forms typically bound with the Middle Ages. Although long rooted in the so-called Kamigata region of Kyoto and Osaka in western Japan, both production and consumption of this emerging popular culture shifted eastward in the mid-eighteenth century to the new capital, Edo. By the mid-nineteenth century, Edo was transformed into Tokyo—though this transformation represents a more radical rupture than a mere change of name suggests—for commoner culture became almost exclusively concentrated in this new metropolis in a way that would become representative of Japan's early modern period. Thus, the three volumes of this anthology are clearly divided along geographical as well as chronological lines: (1) *A Kamigata Anthology: Literature from Japan's Metropolitan Centers, 1600–1750;* (2) *An Edo Anthology: Literature from Japan's Mega City, 1750–1850;* and (3) *A Tokyo Anthology: Literature from Japan's Modern Metropolis, 1850–1920.*

Each volume details the unique story of its respective period, contextualizing creative production, advertising, and modes of dissemination among a new class of reader-spectators in the political, economic, and religious landscape of its time. The cover design of each volume is based on a pictorial work taken from the period it represents, in the genre and style most fashionable at the time: the Kamigata volume is graced with a screen painting; the Edo volume, a polychromatic ukiyo-e print; and the Tokyo volume, a Western-style oil painting. Each depicts ordinary men and women of the time at work.

The idea to compile this anthology originated decades ago in a seminar led by Howard Hibbett that gathered a dozen American scholars for the group study of and mutual training in the little-explored field of Edo-period popular literature. I pursued the compilation of an anthology in English in order to create some kind of basic collection for teaching and conducting research as well as for introducing this type of literature to the general reading public. The project, first funded in 2003, would take more than fifteen years to reach completion. Contributors, drawn from the ranks of newly discovered as well as distinguished specialists, proved to be not only conscientious scholars but also enthusiastic artists in their own right who aimed to produce the best possible translations. The coeditors and editorial board, intensely idealistic in the same way, devised a multistep editing process, which over the years improved the manuscript significantly. Such a massive collaborative work may still leave errors: the frequent exchanges of manuscripts may have caused slips, and compromises in interpretation may have created incongruities. Still, we believe that, through our method, our anthology has reached a level of translation we are proud of. The process has benefited from all of the contributors' dedication to literary craftsmanship and creative tendencies, which has made these volumes far more valuable than their simple scholarly accuracy. I thank Julia Whyde, who contributed her expertise and talent to this process by copyediting the final versions of many of the translations in all three volumes.

I am grateful for the expert advice and encouragement from editorial board members Howard Hibbett and Shinji Nobuhiro, as well as the project's primary consultant and liaison in Japan, Kenji Watanabe. I am fortunate to have worked with coeditors Adam L. Kern and Charles Shirō Inouye, both of whom are known for their writing styles: Kern, for his wit and meticulousness, and Inouye, for his crystalline control over logic and rhythm. I derived just as much pleasure working with the translators—some of whom were generous enough to drastically shorten or completely reorganize their contributions to follow the anthology's spirit and format. Not least, I owe much to my many research assistants who contributed their labor and ingenuity to my editing and writing.

I acknowledge in gratitude the ongoing support from the specialists Richard Bowring, Michael Dylan Foster, Toru Haga, and Koji Kawamoto, as well as their many brilliant suggestions on the choice of texts and pictorial materials. I also thank my family for their less specialized assistance throughout the long years.

I regret the untimely passing of University of Hawai'i Press editor Sharon Yamamoto, who, while working at the University of Chicago Press, persuaded me to take on this gigantic project. I am grateful to Pamela Kelley, who ushered the first two volumes and most of the third—assisted by Stephanie Chun, the new editor since December 2018—through the publication process. I thank the anonymous readers appointed by the press who gave us valuable comments on our first draft of each volume. Inouye, Kern, Watanabe, and I have been cheered on by our colleagues and students at our respective institutions and elsewhere. The readers, whether specialists or generalists, along with the reviewers who commented on the first two published volumes, have also enlightened and encouraged us. On behalf of the entire team, I thank them.

I am particularly grateful to the National Endowment for the Humanities, Toshiba International Foundation, and Indiana University for their generous funding and patience for this project from inception to completion. Indiana University's East Asian Studies Center functioned as our headquarters for the first five years of the project, as did the university's Institute for Advanced Study for the last decade. I thank both for their financial, clerical, and technical support. The ornamental figures used in the graphic design of the book include two of the original materials offered to us by Professor Toru Takahashi from his collection.

To the shock and grief of all of us in the field of Japan studies and translation studies, Howard Hibbett passed away on March 13, 2019. He promoted the study of Edo and Meiji literature, particularly through the decades of his teaching and translation. This three-volume anthology is dedicated to him.

Sumie Jones

Preface to the Volume

The present volume is the first installment, though sequentially the last to be published, in a three-volume anthology of Japanese literature spanning the years 1600–1920. It tells the story of the rise of urban popular arts in the context of people's lives and customs in light of gender and class concerns. The story highlights contemporary responses to earlier medieval models, as well as the competitive and mutually inspiring relationship between the venerable western, or Kamigata, region of Kyoto, Osaka, and vicinity and the eastern region of the newly created metropolis of Edo.

The term "Kamigata" ("the upper region") refers to the superiority of the region in terms of history as well as contemporary culture. The swing eastward from Kamigata to Edo was hardly completed in a day, but 1750 can be taken as a convenient, if admittedly approximate, benchmark.

The Kamigata-centric period is marked first and foremost by the rise of popular culture. Of course, popular culture itself goes back further in historical time to the Middle Ages, if not earlier. Yet the advent of mass commercial publishing during the first decades of this period, along with the interrelated rise of basic visual and verbal literacies and the construction of interconnected metropolitan centers, developed an urban popular culture that flourished on a scale never before imaginable. For the first time in Japanese history—if not world history—works of urban popular culture were produced and consumed throughout the land virtually immediately. The Kamigata-centered period is thus not merely a bridge between earlier and later forms of popular culture, as all historical epochs inevitably are. Rather, it is a foundation, built atop the subsiding glory of the Middle Ages, one from which the popular culture of the late Edo period would rise and soar.

Although Kamigata maintained its centrality for over a century after the establishment of the political capital in Edo, Edo eventually caught up and surpassed its predecessor, mostly by stylizing certain artistic genres and forms to appeal to the larger public. To take a few examples, Kyoto's Shimabara pleasure quarter developed slowly over a long stretch of time, whereas Edo's Yoshiwara quarter was more or less built overnight, precisely because it took Shimabara as its model. Similarly, the monochromatic woodblock print originating in Kamigata was developed into the polychromatic print of Edo. And as a counterpoint to the graceful, almost feminine acting style of Kamigata kabuki, the Edo style took a turn toward masculine bravado.

With an eye toward both this future and the past, then, we have selected works of literature in an effort to balance familiar classics with lesser-known exemplars never before translated into English. Contributions were solicited from distinguished scholar-translators ranging from early to late in their careers. Working closely with each contributor, we checked each manuscript against the original Japanese text. Differences of opinion on specific editorial points were hashed out between the coeditors and the contributors, with occasional input from the editorial board, who sometimes would consult leading experts in the field in Japan. Everyone involved in this project benefited from this process of mutual intellectual exchange, as has the project itself. Our greatest debt of gratitude therefore goes to our consultants and contributors.

The contents of this volume were translated anew, with some exceptions. A kabuki version of "Matabei the Stutterer" from Chikamatsu Monzaemon's *jōruri A Courtesan's Soul within Incense Smoke* (here translated by C. Andrew Gerstle), has been previously put into English under the title of "Matahei the Stutterer" (the name of the character pronounced slightly differently in the kabuki version) by Holly A. Blumner in *Brilliance and Bravado, 1697–1766,* volume 1 of *Kabuki Plays on Stage,* edited by James R. Brandon and Samuel L. Leiter (University of Hawai'i Press, 2002). Adam L. Kern's translation of "The Funeral Director's Blowout-Sale Circular" from Jōkanbō Kōa's *Newfangled Spiels* originally appeared in *An Episodic Festschrift for Howard Hibbett,* edited by John Solt (highmoonoon, 2007). An early version of Shelley Fenno Quinn's translation, *The Male Players' "Takasago,"* appeared as part of her article "The Back Side of Noh Chant: A Yatsushi *Takasago,*" in *Imaging/Reading Eros: Sexuality and Edo Culture, 1750–1850,* edited by Sumie Jones (Indiana University East Asian Studies Center, 1996). As for jokes, good ones tend to breed multiple translations. An older version of the story "A Tightwad Priest Crazy about a Boy" (untitled in the original), from Anrakuan Sakuden's

Seisuishō, has been translated by Howard Hibbett as "Embarrassing Moments" in his *The Chrysanthemum and the Fish: Japanese Humor since the Age of the Shoguns* (Kodansha International, 2002). The same story also appeared in English in Andrew H. Dykstra's *Sexy Laughing Stories of Old Japan* (Japan Publications, 1974) with the title "The Miserly Priest Who Loved a *Wakashu,*" along with six other jokes. In the following list Dykstra's titles appear in parentheses: "A Bather Kicks the Bucket" (An Instant Coffin), "A Certain Style of Face" (A Fashionable Face), "A Radish Fit for an Emperor" (Daikon Offered as Tribute), "A Confession, Guessed Wrong" (The Employee Asks the Mistress a Favor), "Piss-Poor in Arima" (A New Idea for Making a Living), and "A White Mouse with Renal Vacuity" (The White Mouse Who Was *Jinkyo*). Finally, "A Fare Outcome" (untitled in the original) was translated by Howard S. Levy under the title "Affinity" in *Japanese Sex Jokes in Traditional Times* (Warm-Soft Village Press, 1973). "A Confession, Guessed Wrong" appeared in a much older translation by the title of "Guessing Wrong," in R. H. Blyth, *Japanese Humour* (Japan Travel Bureau, 1961).

The planning committee for this volume, which the two of us co-chaired, was composed of Howard Hibbett, C. Andrew Gerstle, Haruko Iwasaki, Kenji Watanabe, and Adam Kabat. The committee convened in May 2004 at Harvard University (and, in the case of one committee member, via teleconference), with the generous support of the Reischauer Institute of Japanese Studies. We thank the committee members for their hard work in providing advice on our selection of texts and contributors. As with the other two volumes, this one could not have achieved its current level of quality without the expert advice from editorial board members Howard Hibbett and Shinji Nobuhiro, as well as our primary consultant and liaison in Japan, Kenji Watanabe. We appreciate the advice from Jurgis Elisonas, who shared with us his extensive knowledge of the period and literary works of the time. This volume also benefited from the advice of individual scholars Hideyuki Iwata, Yaeko Kimura, and Taiichi Wakaki. We are grateful to Ryuki Goto, who did much footwork and negotiation to secure images and permissions from various libraries and museums in Japan. We owe Wen-ling Liu of Indiana University's Herman B. Wells Library and Toshie Marra of the C. V. Starr East Asian Library of the University of California, Berkeley, a debt of gratitude for their information and advice through the years of our preparation of this volume. We also thank the librarians and curators in the United States and Japan who have supported us in similar ways.

The National Endowment for the Humanities and Toshiba International Foundation have generously and patiently supported this volume. Indiana University has supplemented the funding with a Bridge Grant through the Office of the Vice Provost for Research and a New Frontiers Grant through the Office of the Vice President for Research in addition to a sizable contribution by the College of Arts and Sciences. We also acknowledge in gratitude the clerical and intellectual support of Indiana University's East Asian Studies Center, which functioned as the project's headquarters during the early years, and the university's Institute for Advanced Study, which has been its base ever since. We also wish to thank our colleagues and students at Indiana University, Harvard University, and the University of Wisconsin–Madison for encouraging and inspiring us during the completion of this volume.

Finally, we wish to express our heartfelt appreciation for two contributors in particular who are no longer with us: Harold "Hal" Bolitho and David Sitkin. They are both sorely missed.

Sumie Jones
Adam L. Kern

A Kamigata Anthology

Introduction

NEGOTIATING A NEW LITERATURE

THE MINGLING OF HIGH AND LOW IN KAMIGATA AND EDO

SUMIE JONES AND ADAM L. KERN

THE AGE OF CHAOS AND ITS SURPRISING END

For the better part of a millennium, the seat of political and cultural power in Japan resided in the western region of the mainland, called Kamigata. Presently better known as Kansai or Kinki, Kamigata consists of the ancient capitals of Nara and Kyoto, the commercial hub Osaka, and surrounding cities. Home to the Yamato people, this region gave rise both to the hereditary imperial line of sovereigns, male and female—the world's oldest such continuous line still in existence—and to their aristocratic court culture, which reached its zenith during the tenth and eleventh centuries.

This culture, not to mention the greater Kamigata region itself, was torn asunder by a series of seemingly endless civil wars during what is loosely known as Japan's Middle Ages, spanning roughly from the early twelfth through late sixteenth centuries (as per the chronology that follows "Notes for the Reader"). The subsequent Edo period (1600–1868)—the first half of which, up to about 1750, the present volume is devoted to—is glamorized, stereotypically, as the age of almighty shoguns, fierce samurai warriors, sensuous courtesans, and spectacular live-actor kabuki and lifelike puppet plays.

The long Middle Ages can be divided into three distinct phases of political *dis*order. The earliest was the Kamakura (1185–1333), during which time appeared the very first shogun in Japanese history, Minamoto no Yoritomo (1147–1199). The shogun was essentially a supreme military dictator who ruled the realm in the name of the sovereign, though in effect reduced that emperor or empress to the status of nominal figurehead. The second phase, the Muromachi (1336–1573), is noteworthy for the failed attempt of the imperial line, supported by the powerful nobility, to regain control of the state, for the early political intrigues and military campaigns of Emperor Go-Daigo (1288–1339) proved futile. Over the next decades, by the time of the third Minamoto shogun, Yoshimitsu (1358–1408), the shogunate had consolidated absolute power, making possible the only stretch of relative peace and stability during the Middle Ages. It was during this stretch when Yoshimitsu transformed a small villa in Kyoto into the sublime Rokuonji, commonly known as Kinkakuji, or the "Temple of the Golden Pavilion" (today a UNESCO World Heritage Site). The stretch was cut short, however, with the reign of the eighth shogun, Yoshimasa (1436–1490), whose obliviousness to affairs political and military alike occasioned a vacuum in leadership. Hoping to fill this vacuum, a few hundred leading warlords, each of whom ruled a provincial domain with its own dedicated armed forces, sought to grab power for themselves.

Needless to say, what ensued were sheer battles royale. This third and last gasp of the Middle Ages, known as the Azuchi-Momoyama period (1573–1600), saw high-ranking samurai struggle to seize power while somehow securing their family's safety through political marriages, adoptions, shifting loyalties, the exchange of collateral hostages, even executions of their own kinfolk. Women and children were not exempt from being traded as pawns with supposed allies as well as incontestable foes. Men occupying the lower ranks, as with guards and foot soldiers, were not infrequently displaced, disavowed, and discarded, sometimes in what amounted to mass slaughters.

Amid this morass of carnage, one warlord in particular seemed to rise above all others as the clear winner. This was Oda Nobunaga (1534–1582), justifiably dreaded as much for his Machiavellian scheming as for his advanced Western-style weaponry. Still, his most formidable and thus most trusted general, Akechi Mitsuhide (1528–1582), turned treacherous, forcing Nobunaga to kill himself. Once Mitsuhide mopped up the remnants of Nobunaga's extended family, he assumed complete, uncontested, supreme control of Japan—at least for eleven days, after which time *he* was forced to suicide by another of Nobunaga's generals, Toyotomi Hideyoshi (1537–1598). In one fell swoop, Hideyoshi effectively seized control of the country for himself while avenging his master's death.

Declining the military title of shogun in favor of the more courtly designation of imperial regent (*kanpaku*), or counselor to the adult sovereign, Hideyoshi nonetheless ruled by dictating laws that regulated trade with foreigners, forbade Christianity, and banned the possession of swords among all but the samurai, whom he singled out as a superior class. If, after a century of continuous bloodshed, the various domains finally seemed to verge on some semblance of concord, it came at the price of tyranny, for Hideyoshi, who had astonishingly risen to prominence from the ranks of the peasantry, proved exceptionally ruthless. On his orders, the ears or noses of perhaps tens of thousands of enemy combatants were taken in order to tally enemy losses and entombed in the so-called Mound of Ears/Noses. Despite this triumphant monument, which stands in Kyoto to this day, in point of fact Hideyoshi's invasions of Korea, as a stepping-stone toward conquering Ming-dynasty China, failed spectacularly. Hideyoshi also ordered the death of the early grand master of the tea ceremony (*chanoyu*), Sen no Rikyū (1522–1591), supposedly over a difference of opinion about aesthetics. After Hideyoshi's own demise from illness, his familial successors failed to whip up the leadership to maintain control, producing another power vacuum.

Peace came to Japan only when that vacuum was filled. Yet the warlord who ultimately emerged victorious, unifying the country at long last and ending the Middle Ages, was an unlikely hero. By all accounts he outwardly lacked the brilliance of Hideyoshi, or the military prowess of Nobunaga, or the charisma of the warlord Takeda Shingen (1521–1573) in inspiring his followers. Nevertheless, this warlord from Mikawa Domain (in modern Aichi Prefecture), Tokugawa Ieyasu (1543–1616), had two hidden talents: patience and political astuteness. These talents enabled Ieyasu to maneuver deftly amid the rise and fall of powers greater than he. After the death of the warlord Imagawa Yoshimoto (1519–1560), for instance, under whom the young Ieyasu had dwelled as a token hostage, he allied himself with Nobunaga. By defeating the clan of Takeda Shingen, Ieyasu also won the confidence of Nobunaga's clan, and upon Nobunaga's death Ieyasu nimbly pledged allegiance to Hideyoshi. No sooner had Hideyoshi expired than Ieyasu abruptly turned on his master's kinsmen, crushing them along with other rivals at the Battle of Sekigahara in 1600. Simply put, Ieyasu had an uncanny ability to bide his time strategically and, like the greatest of modern-day leaders, to make decisive moves at precisely the right moment.

THE TOKUGAWA SHOGUNATE AND THE CONSTRUCTION OF EDO, THE NATION, AND SOCIETY

A few years after effectively unifying the country, Ieyasu arranged in 1603 to have Emperor Go-Yōzei (1571–1617) bestow upon him the lapsed military title of shogun. This title would be passed down through the Tokugawa family for a quarter of a millennium. Ruling in the name of the imperial line, the

Tokugawa shogunate assumed complete control over the hitherto independent provincial domains. To this end, Ieyasu and his counselors set about designing a governmental structure that granted the various regional overlords (*daimyō*) power to preside over their own domains while collecting taxes from farmers, in the form of rice, on behalf of local government and the central state. The steady stream of revenue over time allowed the shogunate to transform urban centers into genuine metropolises and to interconnect them by building an intricate system of highways, way-station towns, and checkpoints that could manage the inevitable flow of goods and people.

At the same time, the shogun was the ruler of the city of Edo, which was designed as a concentrated model for the entire country. Thus, Edo did not have a daimyo with the accompanying local bureaucracy. Instead, the top ruler was the shogun himself, followed by *hatamoto* (banner bearers), who served the shogun directly and were chosen from among the clans related to the shogun or descending from powerful daimyo of earlier periods. The *hatamoto* played various important roles such as serving as the senior and junior councilors of the shogun's cabinet, as well as magistrates in charge of judicial and religious systems in the city. Below *hatamoto* were various ranks of samurai occupying lesser positions within the shogun's castle, some without any title.

To break free of the gravitational pull of the imperial line and aristocratic culture rooted in Kamigata, Ieyasu took the unprecedented step of establishing his new government in the faraway untamed eastern part of the mainland, in a remote fishing district called Edo. As a further measure to shore up central authority, Ieyasu's successors would in the 1630s institutionalize a system of "alternate-year attendance" (*sankin kōtai*) in which each daimyo, accompanied by his own extensive military retinue, would spend one year in Edo and then the next in his home domain, though leaving his family in the shogun's capital permanently, as comfortably caged collateral hostages. Roads, canals, bridges, and samurai mansions were constructed, as was a commanding castle in the heart of town. A complex urban water system connecting the city's wells to nearby rivers was devised. Multitudes of people streamed into the city from various provincial tributaries, bringing with them their own particular cultures, customs, and dialects. The population exploded. By and by, Edo would become both the supreme metropolitan model for an emerging nation as well as that nation's first authentic melting pot. The general eastward shift of cultural momentum from Kamigata to Edo would have lasting implications for both regions, profoundly shaping Japan ever after. Centuries later, Edo would be renamed Tokyo, meaning "Eastern Capital."

Against all expectations, particularly given the preceding centuries of mayhem and disarray, the Tokugawa shogunate would maintain peace and order for nearly 260 years (until the turbulence of the late nineteenth century resulted in the restoration to power of the imperial line). One of two major pillars of this Pax Tokugawana was a policy of isolation from most other countries. Such limits were nothing unusual throughout Asia at the time. Historically, though, the Japanese had actively looked to the continent for their model of civilization. Recorded history itself had been made possible in Japan by significant cultural, religious, and commercial borrowing, during the second half of the first millennium, from China and the three kingdoms of Korea. It was only then that the Japanese developed a written language, adapting Chinese characters to suit their own particular linguistic needs. Punctuating Japan's relations with the continent, apart from Hideyoshi's failed forays into Korea, were two earlier stabs at invading Japan, made by Kublai Khan (d. 1294) during the Middle Ages. Legend has it that a "divine wind" (*kamikaze*) blew away his massive armadas, bearing tens if not hundreds of thousands of Mongolian and Chinese troops. Later scholarship, however, has identified such wind as a typhoon and showed that the regent, Hōjō Tokimune (1251–1284), based on international intelligence work, was well prepared for the attacks by building defensive walls and mounds and by training soldiers who would keep the invaders at sea.

Nevertheless, the Tokugawa shogunate did not wish to cut itself off from continental culture, at least not completely, particularly not from the culture of China, with which the Japanese had a complex long-term relationship characterized just as much by envy as rivalry. Relations with Asian neighbors, including China, were defined by a new set of wider isolation policies. These policies, following the pattern of Hideyoshi's earlier ban on Christianity, were aimed primarily at limiting contact with the West. The one exception was the Dutch East India Company, whose traders prioritized commerce over religion. Still, to be cautious, the shogunate sequestered the Dutch to Dejima, a man-made islet off the coast of Nagasaki—a major port city on the southwesternmost of Japan's islands, at a considerable distance from Edo. Chinese and Korean traders, scholars, and others continued to reside on the nearby island of Tsushima.

The shogunate required that all representatives of the Dutch East India Company send annual tributary emissaries to the shogun according to an elaborate set of etiquette and rules. And so extravagant processions of Dutch traders made the lengthy journey between Nagasaki and Edo, drawing crowds of gawkers along the way. Woodblock prints of the day showing the Dutch in Nagasaki reflect the Japanese curiosity about Western attire and customs. Beginning in 1607, as an attempt to mend the Japanese-Korean relations damaged by Hideyoshi's attacks, the shogunate welcomed emissaries from Chosŏn Korea who would also go to Edo to present themselves to the shogun, staying for half a year and visiting other cities. The Dutch made 166 of these trips, while the Koreans only made 11 during the Edo period; one such Korean procession, which traveled through various regions to Edo, consisted of hundreds of envoys, including scholars, officials, and performing artists. The UNESCO Memory of the World heritage program has registered records of communication and other documents related to the Korean embassy, held in Korea and Japan.

The second and more fundamental pillar of the Tokugawa peace was devising a social structure in which everyone knew her or his place. To this end, the shogunate made use of a Japanese brand of Neo-Confucianism, particularly as articulated by Hayashi Razan (1583–1657), retainer and adviser to Tokugawa Ieyasu. This ideology advocated a hierarchy of relationships between people based on both bottom-up loyalty toward one's social betters, father, and oldest brother, as well as top-down benevolence toward one's subordinates, children, and younger siblings. Citizens were divided into four major classes according to their usefulness to society (in descending order): (1) samurai, the military class, of which the elites came to serve primarily as administrative functionaries; (2) farmers, who tilled the arable land to produce rice, the most vital agricultural product and the primary medium of taxation; (3) artisans, who apart from providing innumerable services also processed raw materials into usable goods; and (4) merchants, who lived by buying and selling things that they themselves did not produce. Additionally, there were various types of outcasts, akin to India's untouchables, such as "nonhumans," particularly the so-called hamlet people (*burakumin*). The *burakumin* were regarded as irredeemably defiled because their livelihood, as butchers or tanners handling animal flesh and hides, entailed breaking the Buddhist prohibition against taking the life of any creature.

Although these categories were more or less hereditary, with strict prohibitions against marrying beyond one's class, the exponential growth of cities during this period helped improve social mobility in sometimes unexpected ways. There were instances in which impecunious samurai renounced their status to take up a trade or to launch a business, particularly in the latter half of the period. Jobless samurai could become marginalized street performers, with license from the head of an outcast group. Conversely, there were instances in which wealthy merchants purchased honorary samurai status. Unencumbered by sales tax, merchants could and did become filthy rich. In fact, to the extent that money was developing into an early modern sign of power that could potentially outstrip hereditary status, merchants increasingly posed a fundamental threat to shogunal authority, if not to the entire social order.

SOCIETY AND ECONOMICS IN CRISIS:
FEUDALISM VERSUS EARLY MODERNISM

In spite of the Tokugawa shogunate's shiny new administrative organization and advanced countrywide infrastructure, the financial core of the system, like the social order itself, remained fundamentally feudalistic. The system largely depended on taxes. The central government (*bakufu*) taxed its own extensive lands, whereas the domains collected taxes, in the form of rice, to support their own samurai but also to help subsidize periodic "gifts" to the shogun for such things as castle repairs. The domains gave their samurai a kind of chit that could be exchanged for cash or for rice, which was typically stored in granaries. The government licensed official rice brokers and money exchangers who, using some of the capital to make loans on the side, also sometimes amassed great personal fortunes.

In contrast to the samurai, the merchants had for centuries operated on the more forward-looking system of cash currencies and capital gains. Coins did exist earlier, but those in gold, silver, and copper were widely spread during the early Edo period. With the rapid growth of the economy afforded by the Tokugawa peace, commerce among the various provincial domains, largely centered on urban markets, made the flow of money both swift and widespread. Because the coin of the realm in Kamigata was silver, whereas that of Edo was gold, currency exchanges cropped up, functioning a bit like those of contemporary banks, as did a collection of stockbrokers who have been described as the world's first major commodities exchange. The paradox of an economic system that was simultaneously feudalistic and early modern would vex the Tokugawa shogunate until the end of its rule in the mid-nineteenth century, when that system was finally replaced by a structure based solely on a fixed currency.

As might be expected, the first signs of fiscal and social strain became visible early on. The shogunate and many daimyo had become financially strapped by rewarding allies during the unification battles and by paying monumental construction fees. In spite of repeatedly increasing taxes, the government never seemed to have quite enough capital to cover its costs. Exacerbating matters was a series of natural disasters—volcanic eruptions, earthquakes, tsunamis, typhoons, floods, sudden climatic changes—that culminated in widespread crop failures and food shortages. Tens of thousands of people, predominantly rice farmers, starved to feebleness or death in the great famines of 1642–1643 (end of the Kan'ei era, 1624–1644) and of 1732 (during the Kyōhō era, 1716–1735). In the absence of governmental aid, combined with the added insult of heavy taxation, peasant protests and even uprisings broke out across the realm. When people from many provincial domains submitted formal written petitions for relief, victory was inescapably pyrrhic, for the shogunate not only censured the daimyo for neglecting the welfare of their subordinates but also penalized the signatories for criticizing their superiors. In large cities too, protests sometimes boiled over into violence. During the Kyōhō famine, a mob in Edo numbering in the thousands attacked and demolished the house of a prominent rice supplier whom they suspected of hoarding rice for the purpose of price gouging. Similar "house smashings" took place repeatedly throughout the period.

The shogunate sought to mitigate the economic and social crises in a series of fiscal reform movements, the first major one being the so-called Kyōhō Reforms (1716–ca. 1740s) of the eighth Tokugawa shogun, Yoshimune (1684–1751). Previously, in an effort to lessen the financial burden on the government, the fifth shogun, Tsunayoshi (1646–1709), had minted new coins with a lower percentage of gold than normal. These substandard coins inadvertently created an economic bubble that, during the Genroku era (1688–1703), initially seemed to revitalize the economy, chiefly because the government could spend extravagantly on building temples and on supporting the arts that were part of a cultural blossoming, particularly among the lower classes.

When the bubble inevitably burst, inflation soared. Yoshimune stepped in, stabilizing rice prices by increasing production on newly developed lands and enacting strict austerity measures, which included laws against any kind of ostentatious display. The reforms also generally loosened the government's tight grip on its subjects by easing existing laws against Western and Chinese learning and by allowing merchants to organize guilds. Although Tsunayoshi's Kyōhō Reforms helped improve the government's finances, both taxes on farmers and rice prices remained steep, precipitating more rural and urban unrest.

Under the tenth shogun, Ieharu (1737–1786), Grand Councilor Tanuma Okitsugu (1719–1788) provided temporary relief to the populace—and government coffers—by promoting a currency-based economy. Tanuma encouraged the formation of merchant guilds in exchange for fees. He supported land reclamation projects so as to generate new taxes. And he not only expanded international trade at the port of Nagasaki, in order to capture additional revenue, but also called for the development of Hokkaido for future trade with Russia. Tanuma even patronized what was referred to as Dutch studies (rangaku), the study of European technology, science, and arts in an early concerted effort to expand Japan's economy and society.

The second major reform movement sought to undo Tanuma's liberalization policies. One of Yoshimune's grandsons, Grand Councilor Matsudaira Sadanobu (1759–1829), personally planned and supervised this set of ultraconservative measures, collectively known as the Kansei Reforms (1787–1793), that sought to turn back the clock to the time of his grandfather's reforms. Enforcing Yoshimune's Confucian policies of morality and frugality, Sadanobu rescinded any law that advantaged merchants. He enforced the division of classes, issuing orders that those peasants and rice farmers who had relocated to Edo to pursue new occupations, for instance, must return to their native provinces to once again toil in the paddies. Outlawing Dutch studies, Sadanobu promoted the newly introduced thought of Master Zhu ("Zhuxi" in Chinese), who emphasized the rational and practical side of China's Neo-Confucianism. He also elevated the Shōheikō, an academy established earlier by Hayashi Razan, into something approaching a national university for samurai.

Ultimately, Sadanobu's reforms failed to resolve the underlying tensions between, on the one hand, the feudalistic model of the economy and society with its authoritarian moralism and rice-based fiscal policies, and on the other, the emerging early modern model with its development of a merchant class. Santō Kyōden (1761–1816), a tobacco-shop merchant who was also the leading author-illustrator of adult comic books called yellow books (*kibyōshi*), published several works couching thinly veiled satire against the Kansei Reforms. Even though Sadanobu had both Kyōden and his publisher, the great Tsutaya Jūzaburō (1750–1797), roundly censured, criticism continued in other quarters, as did violent rebellions. Subsequent efforts—the Tenpō Reforms of the 1840s and the Keiō Reforms of the 1860s—likewise met with limited success.

TWO DEFINING INCIDENTS

More than fiscal meltdowns or violent uprisings, the supreme danger to urban centers, particularly amid earthquakes, was fire. As the populations of these cities burgeoned, overcrowding heightened the risk. In lower-class sections of town especially, hastily constructed tenement houses not only were tinderboxes of flimsy wood and paper, in effect, but were also packed together closely. One spark, and the entire neighborhood could go up in flames.

The conflagration that swept through Edo in 1657 (during the Meireki era)—known as the Great Meireki Fire—is believed to have started in three separate locations simultaneously. Two days later, after the smoke and cinders and dust had settled, about half the metropolis lay in ruins, including the shogun's castle. An estimated one hundred thousand people perished—a staggering figure, representing nearly a quarter of the city's population at the time. (The Great Chicago Fire, by contrast, claimed no more than three hundred lives, merely displacing one hundred thousand people.) Most who did not die of smoke inhalation were burned alive, perhaps within collapsing buildings, perhaps on streets overtaken by firenadoes. Others were trampled to death in mammoth human stampedes. Still others drowned when, unable to swim, they nevertheless plunged into rivers to escape the searing heat. The unprecedented catastrophe was movingly chronicled in Asai Ryōi's (d. 1691) *Stirrups of Musashi* (*Musashi Abumi,* 1661).*

Subsequently, proactive measures were taken, such as the creation of fire brigades to patrol densely populated districts of the city, be they occupied by commoners or samurai. Little wonder that firemen were portrayed, in woodblock prints, popular fiction, and kabuki plays, as reassuringly well-trained, swashbuckling, romantic heroes, and handsome to boot. Less idealistically, the government also embarked on innovative city-planning projects and street renovations, especially the broadening of main boulevards and the creation of public spaces. Ironically, then, the Great Meireki Fire of 1657 helped forge Edo into a better organized and more resilient early modern metropolis—just as years later, in 1923, the Great Kantō Earthquake would help forge modern Tokyo.

The other defining event, the "forty-seven ronin" incident, comprised a series of episodes that unfolded into Japan's national melodrama. It captured the popular imagination of the time with a vengeance and has continued to hold the attention of the Japanese public through the present. The incident began in 1701 when a fight broke out between two officials of Edo Castle. Asano Naganori (1667–1701), the daimyo of Akō Domain (in present-day Hyōgo Prefecture) who was in charge of receiving imperial messengers on behalf of the shogun, unexpectedly drew his long blade and slashed at Kira Yoshihisa (aka Yoshinaka, 1641–1703), a *hatamoto* from Mikawa (the domain of Tokugawa Ieyasu) who oversaw ceremonial affairs at the castle.

It is not known precisely why Asano snapped. One theory holds that he was psychologically imbalanced. Another, that he, having failed to offer an adequate bribe to Kira, was humiliated by Kira's refusal to give proper instructions, resulting in an inadvertent breach of etiquette. No matter the reason, unsheathing a sword within the shogun's castle was a capital offense. Although it had been a long-standing policy to punish both sides of a dispute equally (such as disciplining petitioning peasants as well as their neglectful daimyo), as far as the shogunate was concerned, the so-called Akō Affair was less a matter of a feud between private individuals than a clear-cut case of a single official violating the law. Thus, whereas Kira was exonerated of any wrongdoing, Asano was ordered to commit suicide.

Upon learning of his master's fate, Asano's chief councilor, Ōishi Kuranosuke (1659–1703), was appalled at the hypocrisy of the ruling. To make matters worse, plans for Asano Daigaku (1670–1734)—brother and adopted son of Asano Naganori, then a *hatamoto* under shogun Tsunayoshi—to succeed Naganori in leading the domain were derailed when he and other members of the Asano family were summarily dismissed from their positions. Ōishi thereupon organized a group of retainers who, when attempts to restore the Asano family failed, resolved to exact revenge, even if it meant sacrificing their lives.

This was an extraordinarily bold decision. Although samurai could apply for permission from the shogunate to legally avenge a parent or other family member, including a "disgraced" wife, avenging a daimyo lord was another matter, particularly when doing so threatened the peace and stability between domains. Unable to carry out an official vendetta and unwilling to go on living as ronin, samurai were expected to follow their lords in death. Nevertheless, the ronin from Akō assumed false identities, ostensibly out of shame for the disgrace of not killing themselves, when in fact they were biding their time until they could find the perfect opportunity to strike.

And strike they did—just before dawn on the fourteenth day of the twelfth month of 1703, some two years after the death of Asano Naganori. Under the cover of darkness and in the thick of snow flurries, Ōishi and his fellow ronin stormed the compound of Kira Yoshihisa, cut down his guards, sliced off his head, and presented it before the grave of their daimyo lord.

Samurai are habitually portrayed in historical fiction, movies, anime, manga, and other types of popular media as fiercely courageous swashbuckling swordsmen. In point of fact, however, during the Tokugawa peace, the vast majority of samurai served as unarmed functionaries in the ever-expanding administrative bureaucracy. The old "way of the warrior" (*bushidō*)—famously epitomized in *Code of the Warrior* (*Budō Shoshinshū*), by Daidōji Yūzan (1639–1730) and published in 1828—had, since the latter part of the Middle Ages, long been defunct, if it ever had been anything more than a romantic ideal in the first place. Somewhat hypocritically, Yūzan did his utmost to establish this ideal as a bona fide tradition, as evidenced in his other major work, *A Collection of Fallen Grains—Addendum* (*Ochiboshū*, 1727).* The mystique generated by such works helps explain perennial misunderstandings about samurai. Even so, the Akō Affair rekindled memories among samurai of their supposedly long-neglected virtues of selfless loyalty and sacrifice. The incident challenged intellectuals of the day to debate its meaning in terms of Confucian values. Some daimyo were impressed enough by the bravery of the Akō ronin to offer them positions within their domains. In the end, however, the shogunate sentenced all forty-seven men to death by their own hands.

So sensational was the incident that it began to be adapted for the stage almost instantly. The first such adaptation, a puppet play titled *Night Attack at Dawn by the Soga Brothers* (*Akebono Soga no Youchi*, 1703), was performed within two weeks of the final self-executions. Four years later, the great Kamigata playwright Chikamatsu Monzaemon (1653–1725) penned another puppet play, *History of Great Peace on a Chessboard* (*Goban Taiheiki*, 1706), which was first performed at the Takemotoza, the main theater in Osaka, the city where the puppet theater itself originated.

Both of these plays were necessarily set in the past: *Night Attack at Dawn by the Soga Brothers,* during the early Kamakura period, and *History of Great Peace on a Chessboard,* the Muromachi period. This was because the shogunate had expressly forbidden any depiction of contemporary events, particularly those involving the affairs of samurai, daimyo, or officials, let alone members of the shogunate. Given these circumstances, Chikamatsu, in his play, wisely couched the Akō Affair in terms of a sweeping historical epic, *The Record of Great Peace* (*Taiheiki,* 1370). Although this particular play has since been overshadowed by other adaptations, most of those follow Chikamatsu's strategy of slightly masking the names of the real-life Akō ronin behind the names of historical figures from the epic tale—En'ya Hangan for Asano Naganori, Kō no Moronao for Kira Yoshihisa, and Ōboshi Yuranosuke for Ōishi Kuranosuke.

Undoubtedly the most durable and popular rendering of the Akō Affair, if also the most extensive, is *The Loyal Ronin for Dummies* (*Kanadehon Chūshingura,* 1748), by Takeda Izumo II (1691–1756) and others. This puppet play was adapted to the kabuki stage the following year. Versions of the latter, with selected episodes, have been staged ever since. Although censored during the postwar American occupation of Japan on the grounds that it glorified samurai values of belligerence, today the play remains the biggest crowd-pleaser among the standards of the kabuki repertoire. Particularly those episodes featuring Edo commoners continue to be celebrated in contemporary popular media.

KAMIGATA'S AWKWARD POSITION

Since its formation as a unified collection of states during the ancient period, Japan had always been effectively ruled by a dual system of government, one symbolic, the other actual. The imperial line, whose authority lay in its supposed descent from mythological ancestors, stood at the pinnacle, as the symbolic personification of power. Actual power, however, resided with high-class noble clans and elite samurai, whose elaborate bureaucratic structures governed the entire country as well as the individual domains of warlords and others. The imperial court similarly maintained its own ancient offices and ranks for religious and other ceremonial purposes. During the Edo period, these two systems were separate but intertwined. On the one hand, the imperial court and its samurai protectors were completely dependent on the shogunate for their finances; on the other hand, the shogunate relied on the imperial court to legitimize its authority by conducting ceremonial functions and officially appointing the shogun.

The dual structure was also reflected in the relationship between the old cities of Kamigata and the new actual metropolis of Edo. Even after the establishment of Edo as the seat of the shogun's administration, Kyoto remained the imperial capital and most Japanese still regarded Kyoto as the apex of urbanity. While Edo was situated slightly north geographically, the Japanese continued to speak of "ascending to" or "descending from" the lofty heights of Kamigata, which literally means "upper region," that being where the sovereign resided. Indeed, Kamigata could boast the venerable histories of its cities as highly developed urban centers at least as far back as the Middle Ages. Kyoto, first designated as the imperial seat during the Heian period in 794, was the symbol par excellence of courtly civilization. Osaka, located at the hub of overland routes and coastal byways, was undeniably the supreme marketplace in the realm. The two metropolises had been venues for the rule of both Nobunaga and Hideyoshi. In the minds of most citizens of Kamigata, these warlords had bestowed upon their cities the finest standards of decorative and performing arts. This proud people, with their heritage of superior culture and commerce, were suddenly expected to kowtow to an upstart military ruler whose government had sprung up in a far-off eastern hinterland.

In its early years, the Tokugawa shogunate focused its efforts on the task of refashioning the traditional courtly system into a bureaucracy appropriate for the nation as well as the metropolis. Edo could hardly be built in a day: it would take at least a century for it to become the nation's cultural epicenter. Moreover, most denizens of Edo needed some time to settle into their urban landscape, securing employment and housing, as well as organizing themselves for the sake of neighborhood security and advantages in trade. In the meantime, they had little time or cultural space to cultivate their own tastes and styles, let alone produce first-class art or scholarship. And so most occupants of Edo held Kamigata in high esteem. They thronged to watch troupes of actors, musicians, dancers, and the like who had "descended" from Kyoto or Osaka to their neck of the woods. And when it came to haute couture and accessories, nothing could rival Kamigata for elegance.

The superiority of official histories and literary classics, however, paled in comparison with the more widely accessible genres of Kamigata, such as travelogues, poetry, and fiction, particularly when illustrated. One of the most widespread early forms of prose narrative during the early Edo period, however, was the often lightly illustrated "easy reading book" (*kanazōshi*). What made this genre easy was (as the Japanese term implies) its use of the Japanese syllabary (*kana*), which was considerably less daunting than Chinese characters. The easy reading book also typically featured commoners as characters and highlighted recreational content, deploying contemporary settings and a relatable narrative and visual style that made it accessible to people with even just a modicum of learning. The loose if not disorganized structure bridged medieval folktales and early modern narratives, accommodating a wide range of how-to books, including travel guides, as well as romantic tales, battle histories, courtesan reviews, and fantasies. Even though written by intellectuals as a pastime, the genre was aimed at a larger readership. One of the pioneers of the genre, Kamigata author Asai Ryōi used the easy reading book to great effect. In Ryōi's hands, the widely read account of the Great Meireki Fire, for instance, was an accessible early modern news commentary, replete with precise details, statistics, and objective descriptions.

After a century of wars, the welcome peace inspired an economic boom encouraging consumers to enjoy a widened range of goods and services. Optimism and exuberance pervaded city life everywhere. The often-voiced slogan was "floating world," which was a homonym for "distressing world" (*ukiyo*), a term used in ancient and medieval literature to characterize the Buddhist view of the shortness and insignificance of life. Also, the term *ukiyo* mimics the term *uki-uki,* used to imitate the feeling of elation. Like the phrase "carpe diem," "floating world" carries at its core the cynical worldview that time is limited and nothing significant can be done. The idea of filling the limited time of life with pleasure is best realized in the entertainments at the "pleasure districts" in all cities. The connotation of the term was expanded to include an image of urban life as being sexy and pleasurable, so that "floating world" represented contemporary society. The use of the term "floating world" in easy reading books often comes with erotic connotations and usually points to both meanings. This genre of writing lasted only eight decades before being overtaken by the more refined and realistic "floating world" fiction (*ukiyozōshi*), which elaborated on similar themes and topics and pointed the way to the modern novel.

The easy reading book thereby redefined literacy itself, which had always been conceived of principally in its relationship to classical works written in Chinese characters that only samurai, scholars, and others with specialized training could decipher. The rise of this new kind of basic verbal literacy, reinforced by the proliferation of schoolhouses for commoners, represented one of the major cultural advances of the Edo period. Although only a small percentage of the adult urban population of Japan was proficient at reading Chinese graphs, the rate of basic literacy—meaning the ability to read the Japanese syllabary—of all classes was arguably the highest in the world at the time. Diaries of well-known Western visitors marveled at the ease with which kitchen maids in Japan read for pleasure.

Osaka, for its part, as a port city along with its neighbor Sakai, had flourished through trade with foreign merchants from Europe as well as Asia. Even when the isolationist policies of the Tokugawa regime had confined international trade to Dejima, Osaka remained the marketplace to the nation. It was there, in Osaka, that Japan's first early modern business conglomerates appeared. These merchants exported necessary commodities—lumber, fabric, food, *sake,* and so on—from Kamigata and other areas of western Japan to Edo, where they continued to open and expand branch stores. To the extent that their noble Kyoto counterparts endured, merchants from Osaka flourished.

Most crucially, in terms of popular culture, such success extended to the arts of the city. Indeed, two of the three authors of the early Edo period who are known outside Japan through translations were either born and raised in Osaka or moved there and made it their home. The first is Ihara Saikaku (1642–1693), a leading producer of witty linked verses and an unparalleled humorist, most famous as the author of "floating world" novellas. The second was the playwright Chikamatsu Monzaemon, who dramatized not only episodes from history but also contemporary tragedies. The third was Matsuo Bashō (1644–1694), widely credited with having perfected the seventeen-syllable verse that today is called haiku. Although chiefly associated with Edo, Bashō originally hailed from Iga and for some time lived and wrote in Kyoto.

Taken together, these three authors, and many others, represent the first genuine efflorescence of popular culture that spread to the masses in the later Edo period. True, the Middle Ages was rich in popular culture, but its authors, editors, and artistic creators were of the educated classes, especially the nobility and the clergy, even when the cultural products were based on some oral tradition. It was only with the rise of the merchant class and the advent of commercial printing during the first half of the Edo that truly popular culture was created by, for, and about commoners, to turn into mass arts in the later Edo period, which were consumed far and wide by just about everybody.

THE STATE AND RELIGION

The tension between the medieval capitals in Kamigata and the upstart metropolis of the shogun also played out in the sphere of religion. Before the eastward shift in cultural momentum during the eighteenth century, the spiritual center of Japan had already begun to swing. Buddhism, which originated in India and made its way to Japan in the sixth century through Tibet, China, and Korea, had long been centered in Kamigata. Upon the creation of the shogun's government in Kamakura, Zen and Hokke sects acquired powers in that city and in the surrounding eastern regions. However, the Edo shogunate looked primarily to another system of thought, Neo-Confucianism, for the ideological foundations upon which to construct the social hierarchy and with which to govern the state, but it, as well, turned to patronize new forms of Buddhism with mass appeal. Such control did not come easily, for there were other systems such as Shinto, Daoism, and rival schools of Confucianism that could not easily be consolidated.

The commoner culture of the Edo period drew from the popular religions of the Middle Ages, when egalitarian forms of Buddhism had gained popularity. Pure Land Buddhism, for example, promoted beliefs in the insignificance of earthly existence, eternal damnation in a torturous hell, and a gilded Pure Land that could provide deliverance to every sentient being, including those consigned to the lower social classes. The notion of universal salvation represented a revolution of sorts against earlier forms of Buddhism, which had consisted largely of conventionalized rituals at court derived from esoteric theology and ascetic training of sects such as Shingon and Tendai. Both sects were established in the ninth century, the former by the priest Kūkai and the latter by the priest Saichō. Indeed, Pure Land thought can be understood as a critique of elite practices that allegedly paid lip service to clichés about the impermanence of life, instead opening up Buddhist salvation to the people in their secular lives.

Another influential form of Buddhism from the Middle Ages was Zen. Originating in China (where it is known as Chan), Zen was first introduced into Japan in 1228 and spread by the Sōtō Zen priest Dōgen (1200–1253). Among the aspects of Zen that many found appealing—in addition to the mindfulness technique of seated meditation (*zazen*) favored by samurai—was Dōgen's egalitarian philosophy about human nature and life. Challenging the dominant notions about the end of the world (*mappō*) and the insignificance of earthly existence, Dōgen believed that *all* human beings are containers for Buddhist law (*buppō*). Whereas Dōgen called for the involvement of each practitioner in theological introspection through *zazen,* the newer sects promoted salvation through the simple invocation of the name of the Buddha while dancing and passionately chanting "Hail Amida Buddha" (*Namu Amida-butsu*). Buddhism during the Middle Ages had suddenly become truly democratic: anyone could be saved, regardless of gender, class, geography, or degree of religious training.

In particular, the monk Hōnen (1133–1212), founder of the Pure Land (Jōdo) sect, propagated the idea that anybody could reach the Pure Land simply by uttering the name of Amida Buddha. With an offshoot sect, Hōnen's disciple Shinran (1173–1263) founded the True Essence of Pure Land (Jōdo Shinshū) and eliminated the rule of celibacy, by being openly married. By contrast, Nichiren (1222–1282), founder of the Hokke sect, believed in the efficacy of a single phrase from a holy text, *The Lotus Sutra* (*Hokkekyō*): "All hail the Great Law of *The Lotus Sutra!*" (*Namu Myōhō Rengekyō*). Penitents would chant this phrase (referred to as *nenbutsu*) to the rhythm of a handheld drum. Similarly, the priest Ippen (1239–1289) inspired the faithful into ardent dancing and chanting. Government officials, not to mention several rival Buddhist sects, tended to look at such practices askance.

Throughout the Edo period, the legacy of these participation-oriented religious practices from the Middle Ages merged with indigenous folk beliefs to occupy a fundamental part of people's everyday lives. Realizing as much, the shogunate exploited Buddhism to its advantage, requiring everybody to register with the local Buddhist temple, which was held responsible for keeping meticulous records of the births and deaths of all parishioners. The Tokugawa regime also insinuated itself into the popular consciousness by projecting its authority through highly polished visual representations in Buddhist pictorial art and architecture, especially sponsoring the construction of temples, some grand in scale and luxurious in appearance.

Chief among them was the massive temple complex of Kan'eiji in the Ueno district of Edo. Serving as one of the funeral temples for the Tokugawa shoguns, Kan'eiji came to replace Enryakuji in Kyoto as the new headquarters of the Tendai sect, suggesting that the cultural movement eastward affected even Buddhism. Another temple in Edo performing shogunal funerary services, Zōjōji, founded in the ninth century, became the Tokugawa family temple during the 1500s. Also serving as a training institution for monks, it flourished throughout the Edo period. Some devotees among the Tokugawa extended family made frequent visits to Zōjōji and other temples, accompanied by large entourages, sumptuous gifts in hand.

Among the more fervent devotees was the fifth shogun, Tsunayoshi (1646–1709). His childlessness—widely scandalized—was rumored to have been karmic retribution for having broken, in a previous existence, the Buddhist injunction against taking any form of life. As a kind of overcompensation, Tsunayoshi issued over one hundred edicts, between 1685 and 1700, strictly forbidding cruelty to animals. These edicts pertained especially to dogs, since Tsunayoshi was born, according to the Chinese zodiac, in the year of the dog. Additionally, professions such as fishing and hunting were outlawed, and consumption of fish or poultry became a punishable offense. Anyone caught breaking these laws could be subjected to imprisonment, confiscation of assets, termination of samurai status, exile, and in at least one case, most ironically, capital punishment.

Shinto, an amalgam of indigenous folk beliefs based on Japan's ancient mythology, had, during the Heian period, been organized by the Yamato people of Kamigata into a state religion. Throughout the Edo period, Shinto continued to provide a framework for ceremonies at the imperial court in Kyoto, including the bestowal of rank upon each shogun, not to mention the members of his family and cabinet ministers. Such courtly ceremonies were conducted in the age-old Shinto manner that included high-ranking priests conferring blessings and chanting the ancient myths.

Foremost among the innumerable Shinto establishments throughout the country were the Ise Grand Shrines enshrining the Sun Goddess, Amaterasu. The court had first dispatched priestesses to these shrines at Ise, located in eastern Kamigata, as far back as the seventh century. Although long revered as a venue of ceremonies for the imperial family, the Grand Shrines had, with the improvements to the infrastructure of travel during the Edo period, become an increasingly trendy destination among commoners. Since devotees would provide alms to pilgrims, even penniless nonbelievers came in droves. Shinto priests fanned the flames of the Ise pilgrimage craze by distributing holy tablets throughout Japan in a kind of publicity campaign, replete with travel brochures.

Since the importation of Buddhism during the ancient period, the Japanese had tended to merge it with indigenous folk beliefs. As the former became widespread and the latter was established as a national religion, the Japanese understanding of one often included elements of the other. During the early Edo period, certain sects of Shinto that were widespread among commoners came to combine actively their beliefs with those of other systems of thought, including Buddhism. Such syncretism influenced even the major temples associated with the shogunate and the shrines that authenticated the emperor and his court. Incidentally, the so-called new religions, which came into view during the 1830s and continued to mushroom during the twentieth century, prominently demonstrated elements of this syncretism.

The combination of Buddhism and Shinto was a prominent feature of Japanese social life throughout the period, even to the extent that the government felt the need to smooth over the apparent paradox of operating under two separate systems of belief. The resultant tendency of "conjoining gods and buddhas" (*shinbutsu-konkō*) is evident in the Tsurugaoka Hachiman Shrine, which was important because it enshrined early sovereigns and was also devoted to protecting the shogun Minamoto's clan. Further, it was a Shinto shrine flanked by Buddhist guardian (*niō*) statues and believed to be protected by bodhisattvas. Several hundred Hachiman shrines are spread throughout Japan, an indication of the importance of commoners' belief in the conjoined gods and buddhas. The most elaborate syncretic monument was the Tōshōgū complex at Nikkō, which integrated Shinto shrines and Buddhist temples, mixing aesthetic styles representing these different faiths. The first Tokugawa shogun, Ieyasu, was enshrined upon his death in a mausoleum there as the Great Incarnation (Daigongen)—a Buddhist manifestation of a Shinto deity, *kami*. The synchronized religions turned into a popular philosophy during the early eighteenth century: *shingaku* (study of the heart), by adding accessible parts of Confucianism to the already popularized Buddhism and Shinto, gave a broad range of common people basic principles of ethics.

Although the shogunate was able to exert some control over Shinto and Buddhism, along with Daoism and rival schools of Confucianism, it was Christianity that stood in stark opposition to the shogunate's authority. The Western religion elaborately presented with the arrival of Francis Xavier (1506–1552), a Spanish-born Jesuit missionary who converted numerous souls there, including several daimyo. In the latter half of the sixteenth century, Nobunaga, who was curious about things Western, particularly military technology, extended his favor to Christian missionaries, like the Portuguese Jesuit Luís Fróis (1532–1597), for theological discussions as well as trade. Nobunaga is even known to have donned a suit of medieval European armor and to have drunk European grape wine. The castle he had built near Lake Biwa, outside Kyoto, was unlike any other in Japan, topped with an octagonal keep tower, equipped with a working dungeon, and perched atop a hill. At the height of Jesuit activity in Japan, the Japanese dispatched a delegation of four young men, aged thirteen and fourteen, for an eight-year sojourn in Rome and other parts of Europe, where they were to have an audience with the pope as well as several European monarchs. This delegation, which was sent with the blessing of Christian priests and the funding of a wealthy daimyo convert, was well documented and handsomely pictorialized. By the end of the delegation's mission, however, and with the death of Nobunaga, the political climate in Japan had changed abruptly.

After Nobunaga's death, Hideyoshi reversed course with respect the Western religion. In principle, the Christian belief in one supreme God conflicted with the notion of the absolute sovereignty of Japan's emperor. On the practical level, Hideyoshi's fear of Christian daimyo amassing wealth and power thanks to their trade with Western countries turned him against any association with those foreign powers. Little wonder, then, that Hideyoshi moved to suppress Christianity, as did the Tokugawa shogunate after him. Europeans wishing to enter Japan had to prove their renunciation of their foreign religion by treading or spitting on a Christian image. Japanese people suspected of Christian leanings were made to undergo similar demonstrations, sometimes on the precincts of Buddhist temples. Those who were found guilty of being true believers were punished mercilessly. One of the young male delegates to Europe, for instance, was immediately put to death upon his return. More drastically, thousands of Japanese Christians were executed, many by crucifixion.

Such persecution contributed to a mass uprising in Shimabara, near Nagasaki, in 1637–1638, known as the Shimabara Rebellion. Unlike earlier Christian daimyo in the region, with the banning of Christianity the new daimyo also levied heavy taxes on the population. Thus, the ones who rebelled were not just Catholics or poverty-stricken peasants. Owners and managers of businesses in agriculture, fishing, crafts, and so on quickly joined in. As the faithful went underground, entire villages of "hidden Christians" sprung up. In secret, believers performed Catholic masses, disguising the figure of the Virgin Mary as the Buddhist deity of mercy, Kannon Bodhisattva. Although these hidden Christians tried to preserve their faith by covertly praying and singing Latin hymns, over time Buddhist elements progressively crept into their practice and theology. One such community, on an island off the coast of Nagasaki, persists to this day.

From these major religions and systems of thought sprung a variety of popular deities. The god of foxes, Inari Ōkami, was among the three most common sights on the streets of Edo, as attested to by a proverb: "Ise stores, Inari shrines, and dog shit" (*Iseya* was a commonplace name for newly opened businesses in the city). Although originally an agricultural deity, in urban centers Inari was transformed into a god of financial success. At a time when merchants, craftsmen, laborers, and the jobless poured into metropolises to make their fortunes, Inari shrines popped up on street corners and in alleyways as well as on the premises of shops, temples, and larger shrines. Today, most high-rise business buildings in Japanese cities have an Inari shrine on the corner of the roof where the employees make visits frequently.

Deriving from folk Buddhism, Jizō is worshipped as the patron saint of children, often depicted with a baby in his arms or in the form of a child himself. There was also Bodhidharma (fl. ca. fifth or sixth century), an Indian priest who founded Zen Buddhism in China. Legend has it that Bodhidharma meditated for nine years—so long that not only did his limbs atrophy but he cut off his own eyelids in order to stay awake. Accordingly, in Japan (where he is known as Daruma), Bodhidharma is popularly regarded as a figure of good luck for undertaking arduous challenges. Beginning in the Edo period, limbless Bodhidharma dolls of papier-mâché were produced with two blank eyes, one to be painted in when setting a goal, the other to be painted in when the desired result was reached. Today, life-size Bodhidharma dolls are still a common sight in election offices throughout Japan.

The so-called Seven Gods of Fortune, including Benzaiten (the goddess of music and wisdom), Ebisu and Hotei (the deities of commerce), and Daikoku (the provider of food and assets), make up popular good-luck talismans. These gods were often woven into shop curtains, drawn into advertisements, or turned into carved figurines (*netsuke*) attached to one's tobacco

pouch. They are featured in folktales and jokes, as in "The God of Fortune"*
and "An Impromptu Performance,"* among the selections in "A Sackful of
Wisecracks."*

Most intellectuals were engaged less with folk belief or religion than with
other kinds of thought. Nativism (*kokugaku,* "national learning"), for instance,
transformed Shinto religion into philosophy. Inspired by commentaries on
classical Japanese literature and poetry such as the *One Hundred Leaves* anthology, Nativist thinkers like Kamo no Mabuchi (1679–1769) and Motoori Nori-
naga (1730–1801) sought to recover an ancient native culture prior to the
intrusion of continental thinking. The initial inspiration came as a rebellion
against formalized and stifling methods of study, in an effort to open up literary texts to a freer, more human appreciation. Later students of Nativism tried
to align old Japanese folk beliefs with new forms of thinking, science, even reportage. Such work helped popularize Nativism among the common folk.

Some intellectuals also reinterpreted Daoism, which had essentially
been a religious faith in China, as a philosophy. The ideas of Chinese Daoist
thinkers—like Laozi's notion of nothingness surpassing existence or
Zhuangzi's concept of the mutability of life and phenomena—appear in
Japanese essays such as "The Transformation of the Sparrow and the Butterfly" (Suzume Cha no Henka) and "The Bullfrog's Shinto" (Hiki no
Shinto) within *The Country Zhuangzi* (*Inaka Sōji,* 1727),* by Issai Chozan
(1659–1741). Similarly, religion increasingly became grist for the mill in
popular literature. Along with Confucianism and Nativism, generally the
more pragmatic and intellectual mind-set of the time tended to encourage
popular writings to go against religion. In addition to widespread collections
of jokes, prose fiction in the categories of "tales of the floating world"
(*ukiyozōshi*) and satirical "sermon books" (*dangibon*) often drew laughter
by exposing the foibles of muckraking monks who broke Buddhist law by
consuming fish, indulging in prostitution, or even taking secret wives.

MONSTERS AND TRICKSTERS

Fantastic beings have occupied a prominent place in the cultural history of
Japan from the beginning of its folk beliefs and religions. The earliest extant
piece of writing in Japan, *Records of Ancient Matters* (*Kojiki,* 712), compiled
by Ō no Yasumaro (d. 723), lays out a Shinto worldview featuring gods, demi-
gods, humans, and monsters—which is to say the countless offspring of the
very first deities, Izanami and Izanagi. The Sun Goddess, Amaterasu Ōmikami,
who gave birth to the first emperor of Japan, is their daughter, while one of
their sons, Susano-o, became a hero by slaying the fabled eight-headed dragon.
Buddhism brought descriptions of Indian and Chinese notions of demonic

deities along with the visual depictions of hideous creatures that punish sinners in Buddhist purgatory. Indigenous folk belief persisted well after Buddhism was embraced during Nara-period Japan and at the Heian court. As exemplified in Lady Murasaki's *The Tale of Genji* (*Genji Monogatari*, ca. 1000), the character of Lady Rokujō is gripped by a jealousy so powerful that it assumes the form of a "living ghost," which takes the life of her romantic rival. The tale and other writings of the period refer to such "possessing spirits" (*mononoke*) that wreak havoc upon their hapless victims.

Uncanny creatures (*yōkai*) increasingly came to populate various forms of Buddhist iconography from the early Middle Ages on. Threateningly massive *niō* statues guarded the entrance to temples. Elaborately illustrated "hell screens" typically portrayed horrifying scenes of torture in purgatory, where the contorted bodies of humans agonize at the hands of demonic henchmen. Picture scrolls relating the histories of temples inevitably included depictions of bizarre beings as cautionary tales for the purpose of religious enlightenment. Such visual representation had a profound impact on literary narrative at the time, as with the many supernatural beings who appear within *Tales Old and New* (*Konjaku Monogatari*), the great repository of folk stories compiled during the twelfth century, mostly from Chinese and Indian sources.

The dramatic power of the dead and the holy drove the characters and plots of many nō plays, undoubtedly setting the precedent for the instant recognizability of such creatures in later periods. More than paintings, nō gave a visceral form to angry fiends, endowing them with signature faces, gestures, and costumes, as well as voices. One of the five major categories of nō, the "demon piece," was typically presented at the end of a day's program. This nō category features historical figures drawn from the great military epics, like the aforementioned *Record of Great Peace* (*Taiheiki*, 1370), which describes the titanic battles between the warrior lineages of the Genji (Minamoto) and the Heike (Taira) that heralded the onset of the Middle Ages.

According to folk belief, a deceased person, unable to attain rest in the next world because of some earthly obsession with love, hate, or fame, would return to this world as a ghost (*yūrei*) or a shape-shifting monster (*bakemono*). Such shape-shifting creatures could also be impish tricksters, such as foxes, raccoon dogs (*tanuki*), and water sprites (*kappa*) that assume human form less to menace or destroy than to seduce or otherwise dupe human beings. Drawn from religion and folk belief, these tricksters became the stuff of stories for a popular readership. *One Hundred Tales from the Various Provinces* (*Shokoku Hyakumonogatari*, 1677)* contains such accounts as "On the Ghost of a Member of the Christian Sect," "How Obsessive Attachment Transformed the Daughter of Ōmi Resident Shirai Sukesaburō into a Giant Snake," "How the Attachments of Love Letters Became a Demon," and "How a Raccoon

Dog Welcomed the Descent of Twenty-Five Bodhisattvas," each one of which illustrates how people came into contact with ghosts, deities, and other mysterious beings in their quotidian lives. Mountain hags (*yamanba*) and mountain men (*yamachichi*) were infamous for maiming and murdering humans, even devouring human flesh. In the cases of Taira no Tomomori and Lady Rokujō, each being the protagonist of a nō play, a ghost turned into a monstrous being until its fury was appeased by a sutra-chanting monk.

Whereas the monstrous ghosts of the nō theatre were typically members of the aristocracy, those of the kabuki and puppet theatres were generally ordinary people who had suffered some grievous offense at the hands of their social superiors. During the early Edo period, at least, few if any larger-than-life ghosts like Tomomori graced the stage. Rather, the ghosts were drawn from the ranks of the lower classes—farmers, artisans, merchants, women, even children—who lacked the power to rebel against their oppressors even when their grievances were more than justified. Plays at times took up the marvelous feats of seemingly ordinary folk. In "Matabei the Stutterer,"* a scene within Chikamatsu's play *A Courtesan's Soul within Incense Smoke* (*Keisei Hangonkō*, 1708),* for instance, an artist wields his brush so skillfully that he can project images on the other side of a stone and can render a tiger that literally springs to life. In the same play, as its title suggests, a courtesan's ghost appears in the smoke when the love letters between her and her lover are burned by the latter. After the mid-Edo period, ghosts and monsters became more spectacular and more central to the plot.

The Japanese also found inspiration in the highly developed monster culture in China. One early triumph was *Liaozhai's Record of Wonders* (*Liaozhai Zhiyi*, completed in 1679), by Pu Song-ling (1640–1715). Korean and Japanese scholars made its nearly five hundred tales accessible to an educated Japanese readership by adding commentary and annotation—a treatment previously reserved for the Chinese classics. Significantly, many of Pu's tales were popularized broadly in a sensational adaptation as an easy reading book, containing sixty-eight stories in thirteen volumes, titled *Bedside Stories* (*Otogi Bōko*, 1666). Its author, Asai Ryōi, not only translated Pu's stories into Japanese but also transposed the fictional characters, settings, and allusions into terms of classical Japanese literature and folklore. Ryōi even rendered the Chinese verses as Japanese ones such as *waka* or haiku. A great part of the appeal of *Bedside Stories* had to do with its immediacy. Ryōi asserted that although his intent was strictly pedagogical for the benefit of children, the stories, unlike the majority of earlier narratives set in the past, were drawn from recent actual events, thereby implying that these events could happen to anyone in the present day. This would become the standard in later works of popular fiction.

So phenomenally popular was *Bedside Stories* that it has continued to inspire fiction, drama, film, and manga familiar to most Japanese people even today. The most immediate effect, however, was to kick off a frenzy of publications featuring fantastic and dreadful creatures. Apparently, these works collected during the Edo period inspired many commoners and samurai alike to test their courage by monster hunting—a bit like modern-day horror movies about teens spending the night at a haunted house on a dare. A fashion of group telling of frightening stories spread: a gathering would occur late at night in a room illuminated only by candles; one by one, each person would tell a spooky tale, then extinguish a candle; and when the very last candle was put out, a real monster would supposedly materialize. The practice resulted in the appellation of "one hundred tales," and printed collections of such stories with the phrase in the title were published in profusion. Although the number "one hundred" meant very little, the anonymously edited *One Hundred Tales from the Various Provinces* actually contained one hundred tales, neatly divided into five volumes. Be that as it may, the fact that these kinds of orally composed ghost stories could be rendered every bit as chilling in print should be counted among the literary accomplishments of the period.

Ghosts, monsters, and tricksters were also the stuff of comic fiction, especially in various genres of comic books and graphic novellas that became massively popular during the mid-Edo period. Published in one to three volumes of ten pages each, these genres included the "red book" (*akahon*), typically retelling folktales for children that originated in Kamigata in the early 1660s but were taken up in Edo by the mid-1730s; the "black book" (*kurohon*), popular in Edo from the 1740s on and typically retelling stories from history or the stage for an older audience with basic literacy, such as *The Bearded Lady of the Haunted House* (*Bakemono Hitotsuya no Higeonna,* 1770),* by Tomikawa Fusanobu (dates unknown); and the "yellow book" (*kibyōshi*), which was vastly popular in Edo from 1775 to 1806 and appropriated the comparatively simplistic-looking visual idioms of these earlier comic books to present biting sociopolitical satires and urbane comedies appealing to sophisticated adult readers. This comic book tradition—carried forth in more serious-minded and far longer graphic novels called combined volumes (*gōkan*)—would merge, in the late nineteenth century, with Euro-American editorial cartoons, eventually giving rise to what has become the modern Japanese manga.

As social problems increasingly came to the fore during the declining years of the Tokugawa shogunate, monsters reemerged with a vengeance in the woodblock prints of Utagawa Kuniyoshi (1797–1862), the vernacular fiction of Kyokutei Bakin (1767–1848), and, perhaps most dazzlingly, the dark, complex kabuki dramas of Tsuruya Nanboku (1755–1829). Receding into the shadows during the Meiji period, these monsters and fantastic creatures would reemerge yet again more recently in such works as the manga by Mizuki Shigeru (1922–2015) and the anime of Miyazaki Hayao (b. 1941).

ECCENTRICITY AND THE RISE OF INDIVIDUALISM

Just as uncanny shape-shifters and other fantastic beings represent a supernatural departure from the realm of the human, within that realm itself difference was often conceived of as an individual's departure from the social norm. This was certainly true of many unconventional Buddhist ascetics who, during the Middle Ages, gave up their worldly lives to lead solitary existences, either as traveling monks or sequestered recluses. In spite of receiving the best training at the most prestigious temples of esoteric Buddhism, these "madcap" individuals made the bold decision to rebel against or even abandon their religious institutions. Many were visionaries who, giving up a life of relative comfort if not renouncing their titles as leaders of their spiritual communities, chose to descend to the ranks of commoners. There they crusaded against highly restrictive theologies and liturgical practices, promoting newer, more accessible forms of devotion, such as chanting while performing some deliberately embodied, highly physical action, often in public spaces. In so doing, these visionaries frequently drew the suspicion and fear of the political as well as religious authorities. With the exception of Nichiren, most were excommunicated if not exiled.

Whereas those visionaries had been the stuff of legend during the Middle Ages, by the early Edo period there emerged an entirely new breed of "madcap" or "eccentric." Such people hailed from all four major social classes and from all walks of life. What set them apart was some unusual skill or talent in a pictorial, literary, or performance art, for instance, or some special knowledge in things Chinese as well as Japanese. The poets, scholars, and essayists who challenged traditionalism were quietly admired, or openly emulated, as the public intellectuals of their day. Those who carried out some social critique on behalf of the general public while risking their reputations—or paying no heed to the consequences—were often elevated to the status of folk hero. For this reason, many so-called literati (*bunjin* in Japanese, *wenren* in Chinese) belong to this category of cultural trailblazer.

Rumors, gossip, and legends about these eccentrics coalesced into a special category of frequently illustrated biographical story, the definitive anthology of which was the two-part *Biographies of Eccentrics of Our Age* (*Kinsei Kijin Den,* five volumes, 1790) and its sequel (five volumes, 1798), written by Ban Kōkei (1733–1806) and illustrated by Mikuma Shikō (1730–1794). These two works presented the charmingly strange lives and amazing talents of nearly two hundred men, women, samurai, merchants, artisans, farmers,

Buddhist monks, Shinto priests, writers, scholars, servants, maids, courtesans, and beggars, not to omit avid collectors of the bizarre. Their biographies often feature some hidden talent—like a common housewife who could compose *waka* poems with uncommon brilliance—or quirky behavior, as with a certain physician who decides to have a huge cherry tree installed in his garden through the low-lying archways of his manor. When the tree is delivered, however, it proves too tall to fit. Rather than send the tree back to exchange it for a shorter one, or plant a sapling and wait for it to grow, or just abandon the scheme entirely, the physician instead improvises in a truly idiosyncratic manner: "Just set the tree down horizontally alongside my house," he directs. "That way, I can enjoy it while lying down!"

The prevailing form of eccentricity during the mid-Edo period was undoubtedly bound up with the socioeconomic condition of the samurai class. Under the Tokugawa peace, samurai became increasingly useless as warriors, the result being that they sought their raison d'être in serving as the model of ethics and learning as well as martial arts. Although most samurai were highly educated, they found themselves either completely unemployed or—perhaps even more soul-crushing—*under*employed, stuck in frustratingly low administrative positions that provided no outlet for their various talents. Works of art and literature by brilliantly overqualified samurai are many, particularly in comic fiction (*gesaku*, or playful compositions) and its precursors. One prime example of a precursor to *gesaku* is the work of Jidaraku Sensei (aka Yamazaki Hokka, 1700–1746), a former samurai turned physician, scholar of classics, respected witty linked-verse poet, and self-proclaimed madcap. His *Book of Everyday Morals* (*Fūzoku Bunshū*, 1744)* epitomizes the literati brand of eccentricity. Jidaraku Sensei published his essays under the pen name "Hokka the Second" as a supposedly posthumous compilation of his master Yamazaki Hokka's own writings after faking a funeral for himself.

In *The Book of Toil and the Four Symptoms of Madness* (*Rōshikyō*, published in 1747), Jidaraku Sensei expounds a philosophy that is nothing if not defiant. This title parodies the Japanese version of the title of *The Book of Laozi* (*Rōshikyō*), though with a zinger: the *shi* here not only means "four," referring to the four major social classes, but also is a pun on "death." Invoking Laozi's *Dao De Jing* (*The Book of the Way*), the work gives credence to Daoist notions critiquing those forces that would oppress the individual. All efforts at climbing the social ladder, at gaining political office, at getting rich, at satisfying one's carnal desires, and so on are condemned bitterly. Jidaraku Sensei's critique of the political and economic conditions of his time focuses on the sharp disparity between the poverty of most ordinary people and the greed of the affluent few who never flag in their efforts to squeeze every last copper coin out of whomever they can.

Such a worldview derived from Jidaraku Sensei's deep indignation at the Tokugawa system of social hierarchies, policies, and ethics, as well as from his personal frustration with the petty bureaucratic positions he occupied. Most damningly, and true to his book's punning title, Jidaraku Sensei argued that following one's heart in life inescapably leads to death. Since the pursuit of pleasure requires effort, the logic ran, one can never achieve ultimate happiness without toiling oneself to the grave. Accordingly, a farmer's cultivation of fields, a monk's chanting of prayers, a priest's reading of sutras, a doctor's medical treatments, a Confucian's scholarship, a nun's crooning, a dancer's prancing, a samurai's service to his lord—all forms of labor—fall disappointingly short of the liberation afforded by death itself. In Jidaraku's case his "madness" was self-proclaimed, but, in general, eccentricity was a pose or performance for public display. Such a stance is a declaration of resistance against orthodoxy. Nevertheless, the neuroses of the eccentrics and the maladies of the sociopolitical system itself seemed to reflect one another.

Although *gesaku* was at first, during the mid-Edo period, primarily written for and by frustrated intellectuals, as it became more profitable, its content tended to be dumbed down to reach a larger readership. One constant, however, was the self-identification of authors as eccentrics. By the early nineteenth century, readers from all classes and educational levels thrilled to attribute some eccentric quality to their beloved writers. Jippensha Ikku (1765–1831), for instance, who penned the comic series *Along the Tōkaidō Highway on Foot* (*Tōkaidōchū Hizakurige,* 1802–1822), was renowned for his skill in the art of incense. And Shikitei Sanba (1776–1822), one of the leading authors of funny books (*kokkeibon*) such as *The Floating World Barbershop* (*Ukiyodoko,* 1813–1814), was widely regarded as a hotheaded roughneck, prone to picking fights. By the late nineteenth century, eccentricity itself had become thoroughly commercialized and massified, if not debased.

Literati eccentricism peaked with Hiraga Gennai (1728–1779), alias Fūrai Sanjin, a brilliant if habitually out-of-work samurai from Kamigata who, having relocated to Edo, claimed expertise in botany, herbal medicine, mineral mining, and salt production, among other early modern scientific fields in loose connection to Dutch studies. Gennai concocted a static-electricity generator, discovered a fire-retardant plant that could be woven into a kind of asbestos cloth, and was perhaps the first Japanese to dabble in Western-style oil painting. Gennai's greatest public acclaim, however, came as the author of light writings in drama, poetry, and fiction. In fact, Gennai can be credited with having transformed Chinese and Japanese precursors into a corpus of works identifiable as comic fiction. His essay *On Farting* (*Hōhiron,* part I published in 1774) is a classic of sociopolitical satire in this vein.

In addition to Gennai's multiple successes and belly flops in the arts and sciences, all of which served as outlets for his seemingly inexhaustible pent-up energy, his eccentricity has often been framed in terms of the blatant sexual and scatological aspects of his writings about everything from his own life to world history. In a historical epoch when heteronormativity was increasingly coming to dominate public life and eroding the acceptance of homoeroticism among even otherwise straight men, Gennai espoused what today would be considered full-fledged homosexuality. This set Gennai apart from the vast majority of his contemporaries. Be that as it may, frustration with his commercial enterprises apparently led to a conviction of manslaughter, whether rightfully or wrongly, and his life and dramatic death in prison have become the stuff of fiction and drama for well over two centuries.

WOMEN AND MEN: GENDER, CLASS, AND POWER

Eccentric individualism was largely limited to men, in accord with the Confucian system of the day, despite Japan's history of women's leadership before the importation of Confucianism. The fact that a female deity stands at the pinnacle of the indigenous Shinto pantheon of deities qualifies Japan as perhaps the only extant major civilization *not* to have worshipped a male god above all others. Some historical anthropologists have suggested that Yamato (the culture that gave rise to what would eventually come to be known as Japan) was primarily a matrilineal society, if not a true matriarchy. In fact, the Japanese imperial line—said to have issued directly from the Sun Goddess, Amaterasu—had half a dozen empresses regnant early on, prior to the Heian period. During the Edo period, there were two more empresses: Meishō (1624–1696), who reigned 1629–1643, and Go-Sakuramachi (1740–1813), who reigned 1762–1771. Although strictly speaking, the reigns of these two empresses were nominal, being under the de facto control of the shogunate, they were no more so than the reigns of the male emperors. Still, even before the age of the shoguns, as continental and specifically Confucian culture was imported, matrilineal authority gave way to full-blown patriarchy. Matters worsened for women when the Tokugawa regime began promoting Neo-Confucianism, an ideology that structures society on the basis of a series of hierarchical relationships, including the subordination of women to men.

The Neo-Confucian patriarchy took the form of a nested pyramid. At the top resided the shogun, to whom the *hatamoto* and daimyo pledged eternal loyalty, while their retainers pledged eternal loyalty to *them*, and so on and so forth down the chain of command, to the lowliest guardsman. The same pattern repeated in local communities as well as individual families, with the grandfather at the top and the youngest child at the bottom. The strong ties between these men were also reciprocal: just as a retainer was expected to

sacrifice his life on behalf of his lord, the lord in return was expected to generously support that retainer and his family. Within the family, the cardinal virtue
was filial piety, or the devotion of a son for his father. As the hereditary system
of social relations that arose during the Middle Ages began to give way to early
modern forms of commercial relations and increased mobility, filial piety was
increasingly eroded. Stories of delinquent sons and disloyal servants litter the
popular literature of the day—for example, Ihara Saikaku's *Twenty Local Paragons of Filial Impiety* (*Honchō Nijū Fukō*, 1686, prologue dated 1687).*

Women were excluded from the pyramid structure of rulers and ruled.
Within samurai families, the wife, as the term *okugata* (the lady in the inner
sanctum) suggests, was kept from any public function in the front part of the
house. Her role was to supervise the female staff and oversee domestic purchases. It is interesting to note that in daimyo's and other high-ranking samurai's mansions it was men who did the cooking in the kitchen. A male child
had the possibility to inherit his father's position, allowing him to occupy a
clearly defined place within the scheme. A girl, on the other hand, was expected in her youth to obey her grandfather, father, and brothers, in her
married life to serve and support her husband, and to depend on her siblings
and children in her old age. Daughters were married off early, ideally for advantageous family connections, though, in the worst case, they were sold into
some kind of indentured servitude to save their family's dwindling fortunes.

Commoner women led surprisingly freer lives than their samurai counterparts. The actual lives of women in farming and mercantile families could
not be so strictly controlled; after all, the ancient matrilineal practices had not
quite died out in the world outside the Confucian samurai culture. Commoners, with the exception of favored merchants, rarely had a stake in their connections with the ruling elite and thus tended not to subscribe wholeheartedly
to its ideology. However, commoners were willing to observe certain gender
norms for pragmatic reasons. Edo was overwhelmingly male: by the middle
of the Edo period, the ratio of men to women was two to one. This effectively
increased the value of women. Marital egalitarianism was thus the norm
among Edo's merchants, and having a wife was a status symbol one did not
risk by displeasing her. Because the husband was busy taking care of the shop's
affairs, such as negotiating and trading with manufacturers, wholesalers, and
customers, the responsibility of managing the shop and the household alike
fell upon the wife. This practice of divided responsibilities continues to this
day, due to certain tax advantages of keeping one spouse as a dependent, with
the husband typically earning the wages and the wife controlling the savings
and expenditures. This practice sometimes allows the wife the luxury of traveling and shopping abroad, taking part in hobby groups, and earning higher
degrees.

Moreover, women during the Edo period were not entirely left out of public office. High priestesses wielded power at the major Shinto shrines, for instance, albeit primarily owing to familial ties with the nobility if not the imperial family. Nuns in many Buddhist institutions enjoyed high-power positions with large stipends and even exerted clout with members of the administration. For ambitious women without such high birth, however, the best chance at upward mobility was Edo Castle's "inner sanctum" (Ōoku), which was the private quarters of the shogun and his family, including his concubines and all-female staff. The hierarchy of this inner sanctum was based on rank and responsibility—mirroring the hierarchy of male officials in the front sections of the castle. At its peak, more than three thousand women populated the quarters, all led by a female executive manager. The woman tapped for this prestigious position was typically one of the most trusted servants to the shogun's wife or a former wet nurse to the shogun's heir and was all the more powerful for being off-limits to the shogun's sexual advances. A distinguished title, such as "Grand Elder" (ōdoshiyori), was bestowed upon the woman occupying this position, again matching a similar title within the male hierarchy. Because the shogun came to depend on this woman, she would also be granted land and income befitting a minor daimyo.

The first such powerful manager was Saitō Fuku (1579–1643), the wet nurse to a child who, largely thanks to her efforts, would go on to become the third shogun, Iemitsu (1604–1651, ruled 1623–1651). In her capacity as manager of the women's quarters, she advised the shogun directly, her influence affecting policies and decisions both inside and outside the castle. During an audience with the emperor, she served as the shogun's envoy, inducing Emperor Gomizunoo (1596–1680, reigned 1611–1629) to resign. It was thanks to this triumph that she received her courtly title, Kasuga no Tsubone (Lady Kasuga)—the name by which she is known today. Lady Kasuga organized the domestic component into a bureaucratic structure and exercised power even over the male hierarchy, setting a precedent for generations to come. Little wonder that Lady Kasuga would become the stuff of modern historical fiction and film—as would one of her successors, whose story was even more dramatic.

Born into the family of a retainer in Kōfu, the territory directly governed by the shogun, Ejima (1681–1741) served the minister of Kōfu, Tokugawa Tsunatoyo (1662–1712). When Tsunatoyo was eventually installed as the sixth shogun, Ienobu (ruled 1709–1712), Ejima served his chief concubine, Lady Okiyo (1685–1752), whose power derived from her being the mother of the next shogun in line, Ietsugu (1709–1716, ruled 1713–1716). Ejima used her position as an influential member of the domestic circle to increase her own authority. This allowed her to bend the rules of proper samurai deportment, as with her custom of bringing her staff along on sumptuous visits to temples and theaters, the two chief venues for pleasure for the women of the castle. She was also known to host extravagant parties where the women would mingle with popular actors.

Unfortunately for Ejima and her staff, her liberality drew the ire of the powerful moralist Arai Hakuseki (1657–1725), a Neo-Confucian of the Zhuzi School ("Shushigaku" in Japanese) and an instructor to none other than Tsunatoyo, both in Kōfu and, after Tsunatoyo's ascendance to shogun, in Edo. If Ejima's power infuriated the members of the ruling patriarchy, her behavior offended their sense of morality. Her enemies thus capitalized on the opportunity to expose her when she was caught trying to sneak back into Edo Castle late one night past curfew. She was placed under house arrest in a remote village for most of the remainder of her life. The punishment extended to the actor Ikushima Shingorō (1671–1743), who was exiled for his suspected affair with Ejima. Only after the short-lived rule of Ietsugu were Ejima and Ikushima finally released from captivity, after the eighth shogun, Yoshimune (1684–1751), as part of the Kyōhō Reforms (1716–ca. 1740s), canceled many of the laws implemented by Hakuseki.

By the beginning of the eighteenth century, women in samurai families were free to go out to shop, visit theaters, and wear the latest fashions. This lavish way of life appalled Kaibara Ekken (aka Ekiken, 1630–1714), a grumpy eighty-year-old Neo-Confucian moralist and herbalist who had authored instructional books on matters of ethics and health. In the section on women in the fifth part of his widely read book *Easy Lessons for Children* (*Wazoku Dōjikun*, 1710), Ekken complains about how "women these days," particularly daughters-in-law, paid little respect to their elders. Almost two decades later, in keeping with the ethical interest of the Kyōhō Reforms (1716–ca. 1740s), this part of Ekken's text was independently republished under the title *The Great Learning for Women* (*Onna Daigaku*, 1729). However, just as the frequency of reform movements throughout the Edo period suggests the failure of all such reform movements to successfully legislate human behavior, let alone desire, so too should the repeated publication of Ekken's work not be taken as an accurate reflection of daily life during the period. If anything, the reissuance of this collected summary of Ekken's work suggests the enduring intensity of the conservative backlash against the ever-improving position of women.

The relatively rare ascent of women in the shogun's inner sanctum or at Shinto shrines notwithstanding, women were increasingly coming to be educated members of society. As commoners prospered economically, they invested in the educations of their daughters in the arts, such as calligraphy, flower arrangement, poetry composition, music, and so forth. Such qualifications might allow a girl to serve at the mansion of a *hatamoto* or daimyo, thereby improving her chances for an advantageous marriage. While the commodification of women in this way was of course nothing new, the scale of it was.

URBAN ENTERTAINMENT AND THE SEX INDUSTRY

It goes without saying that women were the primary objects of exploitation in the sex industry, which was concentrated in the red-light districts (*akusho*, "notorious places") of Kyoto, Osaka, and Edo. Ladies of the night ranged in rank from lowly street walkers—such as "nighthawks" (*yotaka*) and "riverboat dumplings" (*funamanjū*)—who plied their trade with or without a pimp, to bathhouse girls (*yuna*) and various grades of "courtesan" (*yūjo*), such as trainees, attendants, and high-ranking superstars (*oiran*). Although today these women are retrospectively, ahistorically, and erroneously referred to as "geisha" (literally, "entertainers"), the term denoted, throughout the Edo period, both men and women who provided music and singing. Male prostitutes (*kagema*) catering to women and men alike also worked these areas but were located principally in the city's theater districts (where they were known as *wakashū*, "beautiful boys").

The government sought to confine prostitution to special "pleasure quarters" in the major cities. It was a convenient way of sequestering sexually transmitted infections and likely criminal hideouts away from respectable parts of the city. Yoshiwara was the only officially licensed quarters, but the others were largely tolerated. Euphemistically, these were referred to as "enclosures," since they were in effect walled compounds that could keep certain people out—and others effectively trapped within. Unlicensed quarters inevitably popped up as well, like the Fukagawa and Shinagawa districts in Edo. Nakazu (also Nakatsu) was renamed around 1772 on the west bank of the Sumida River (the main waterway in town), not far from Edo Bay, and also flourished. Celebrated for its restaurants, teahouses, fireworks, boathouses, and street spectacles, Nakazu was probably the most popular spot in the shogun's capital in summer to enjoy the evening breeze. In 1789, however, as part of the crackdown that was the Kansei Reforms, the government razed Nakazu.

Each of the three metropolises had its major pleasure quarter. In addition to Edo's Yoshiwara, there were Shimabara in Kyoto and Shinmachi in Osaka. Shimabara was the oldest, tracing its roots back to Ashikaga Yoshimitsu (1358–1408) and later sanctioned by Hideyoshi, though formally established only around 1640, when all brothels in Kyoto were ordered to relocate there. The quarter took its name, according to popular accounts, because the pandemonium that ensued after the relocation called to mind the chaos of the Shimabara Rebellion a few years earlier. As if to offset this association with frenzy, the quarter was nicknamed "Tōgen," that being not only the sinicized pronunciation of the graphs for "Shimabara" but also an ironic pun on the legendarily tranquil "Peach-Blossom Garden" (*tōgen*) of Chinese lore.

Naturally, members of the upper classes, especially those in respectable positions, were at pains to be discreet. Thus, Buddhist priests habitually disguised themselves as physicians, and samurai masked their faces under large sedge hats—thereby spawning a cottage industry of sedge hat rentals at the entrance to the pleasure quarters.

As the population of the major metropolitan centers burgeoned, demand for prostitutes skyrocketed. Since no decent woman would be caught dead working in a lowly brothel, industrious brothel owners resorted to alternative recruiting tactics, such as dispatching agents in search of fresh young girls, ideally six to ten years of age. Sometimes, especially unscrupulous agents would simply abduct girls outright. Most frequently, however, an agent would approach an impoverished rural family and, offering a substantial loan in exchange for one or more daughters, would promise that these girls would be apprenticed in a proper merchant shop. There the girls could learn a trade and eventually repay the principal, plus any incidental living costs and interest that might happen to have accrued. Needless to say, these girls never ended up in respectable professions. Moreover, the supposedly incidental living costs (such as expensive wardrobes, especially for courtesans) and interest took years if not decades to pay off.

The prospects for these indentured sex slaves were bleak. Lucky were the few who, while still young and attractive enough, had their contracts bought out, or "ransomed," by wealthy clients. These women were generally installed as mistresses in new lodgings or, less frequently, taken as wives. The merchant and best-selling author Santō Kyōden actually married two courtesans from Edo's Yoshiwara, the second after the first died unexpectedly. Most women who managed to survive past their prime without being ransomed, however, had no choice but to work off their debt by remaining in the district as managers, domestic servants, or scullery maids. Former courtesans who had received training in reading, writing, singing, dancing, or other arts might hope to land a job teaching privately or in commoners' schools. Before being able to buy out their contracts, however, nearly half of all women in the pleasure quarters perished from sexually transmitted infections. The majority of these women were not even accorded a proper burial.

The structure of a pleasure quarter mirrored the system of Tokugawa bureaucracy. In that system the top one percent had choice over their actions as well as the power to influence those below them. A daimyo, for example, was revered and followed by those who served him, and each of his retainers was followed by his own subordinates. Although the pleasure quarter projected itself as a world outside this pyramid structure by treating all classes of clients equally, the ranking of courtesans was also a pyramid structure. Top-ranked courtesans were known for their skills in calligraphy, poetry composition, and drawing, so that some of them were included in the collaborative collections composed by their well-educated clients. An assistant courtesan was not allowed such subjectivity; she was not allowed to seduce her superior's client, for example. Those in the lower ranks were mere prisoners in the encircled world unless they managed to climb the ranks by their wits, just as all samurai were compelled to, if they wanted any kind of freedom in their system.

Works of popular fiction never fully exposed the sordid details of the sex industry, although stories about a filial daughter of an impoverished samurai father voluntarily selling herself to a bordello in order to support her family were not unheard of. Ihara Saikaku used this paradigmatic plot, in which a commoner daughter allows herself to be sold to offset the heartlessness of an unfilial brother, in his popular work *Twenty Local Paragons of Filial Impiety*.*

Within a few years of its establishment, Shimabara implemented strict rules of client deportment and an elaborate ranking system for prostitutes and courtesans. The top courtesans were called *tayū*—a title previously bestowed upon expert performers—suggesting that these women were masters of the performative arts of dance, instrumental music (on the "zither" [*koto*], shamisen, and "lute" [*biwa*]), and singing. *Tayū* were also experts in the arts of tea ceremony, calligraphy, incense blending, flower arrangement, and poetry composition. Wealthy clients were expected to offer large sums of money to their courtesans during special occasions or ceremonial seasonal events according to the Chinese zodiac. After all, in addition to loans and incidental costs, top courtesans also had to support their extensive retinues. Although the quarter was enclosed in walls with a single gated entrance, courtesans, other employees, and clients were relatively free to come and go as they pleased. However, the combination of restrictive rules of deportment and haughtiness of the *tayū* eventually eroded the popularity of Shimabara, driving clients to other quarters, such as Nijō and Gion, which by the end of the Edo period had replaced Shimabara more or less completely.

In Osaka, the major pleasure quarter was Shinmachi (literally, "new town"). Brothels had long been scattered throughout the bustling metropolis, where Hideyoshi had built his magnificent castle in the last decade of the sixteenth century (later to be sacked by Tokugawa Ieyasu as part of unification). During the first few decades of the seventeenth century, however, the brothels were relocated into a single district, access to which was easily regulated with its several bridges spanning three bounding rivers. The popular literature of the day is studded with references to these and other bridges and waterways in Osaka. The names of famous Shinmachi courtesans are similarly storied, as with the *tayū* Yūgiri, immortalized in kabuki plays for her affair with the son of a wealthy merchant. (Since the names of courtesans—like those of actors—were inherited, it is often difficult to determine precisely which generation of courtesan is being referred to.) Chikamatsu honed his craft by composing puppet plays about the tragic love affairs between merchants and these courtesans. Likewise for Saikaku, Shinmachi served as a dependably relatable setting for many a narrative. The quarter would come to a rather ignominious end when, on a particularly gusty day in 1890, a fire destroyed nearly two thousand buildings. The quarter was later rebuilt within the industrial part of the city.

Edo's foremost pleasure quarter, Yoshiwara, actually was located in two separate places: one old, one new. The first was established in 1618 near the bustling downtown area, Nihonbashi, which also served as the terminus of the East Sea Highway (Tōkaidō) connecting Edo and Kyoto. This was a couple of years after a certain brothel owner named Shōji Jin'emon (1575–1644) from Ieyasu's hometown had petitioned for permission to build a pleasure quarter in exchange for guaranteeing a safe, orderly, sanitary district under shogunal authority. As Edo expanded over the next decades, urban sprawl brought "respectable" neighborhoods of daimyo residences ever closer to the quarter. By 1656, construction on a new location had already begun on the northeastern periphery of the city, in the Nihon Tsutsumi (Japan Embankment) area of Asakusa, close to the temple known as Sensōji (today a famous tourist destination). As it so happens, the Yoshiwara near Nihonbashi burned to the ground during the Great Meireki Fire of 1657. Thus, "Original Yoshiwara" (Moto Yoshiwara), as it was retrospectively termed, was replaced by "New Yoshiwara" (Shin Yoshiwara)—which quickly came to be called just Yoshiwara, as though it had always been the sole Yoshiwara.

True to form for eastern cultural momentum, by the middle of the eighteenth century Yoshiwara had eclipsed its counterparts in Kamigata. For one thing, thanks to monumental construction projects and the system of alternate-year attendance for daimyo and their retinues, the imbalanced gender demographics of Edo guaranteed a constant demand from male clientele. For another, although New Yoshiwara appropriated the efficiencies of the Shimabara system of ranked prostitutes and other employees, it managed to avoid, at least during its developing stage, the corrosive snobbishness and exclusivity that had doomed the Kyoto quarter.

And so Yoshiwara flourished. The spectacular main boulevard, Nakanochō, was lined with incandescent oil lamps by night and with trees bearing exquisite cherry blossoms by spring. Visitors poured into the quarter by the droves: playboys, for sensual pleasures; "window shoppers" (*suken*), for the voyeuristic thrill of gawking at the pretty women behind the latticed windows without paying anything; and many others, for the fine dining, the purveyors of haute couture, the clog cobblers, and innumerable other trendy establishments. The teahouses were venues for parties that included competitions in poetry and art as well as composition of collaborative works. Some districts (particularly those of Osaka) featured outdoor improvised theatricals. In addition to sightseeing destinations, where visitors could catch sight of dazzling courtesans, the pleasure quarters were also a mecca for shoppers looking for boutique stores specializing in kimono and accessories, clogs, and other items of high fashion. The courtesans themselves thus served not only as tourist attractions but also as fashion plates who stimulated shopping.

Most visitors arrived at the Great Gate (Daimon) on foot or by horseback. The more affluent rode in style aboard palanquins (*kago*) from Sensōji or water taxis (*chokibune*) from San'yabori (on the Japan Embankment just across the Sumidagawa from the Mimeguri Inari Shrine). Those who wished to visit a courtesan would enter a "teahouse" of assignation (*chaya*), where they would be entertained with playful banter over light food and drink while waiting for the requested woman to appear. For her part, the Yoshiwara courtesan would promenade in the Shimabara style— gracefully, in high clogs, escorted by an elaborate procession of attendees, trainees, house manager, and various musicians and entertainers. This in itself was a spectacle to behold. Such processions, albeit on a less grand scale, are sometimes re-created today as publicity stunts for the opening of new businesses or as scenes in period dramas for the movies or television.

Assuming the tête-à-tête between courtesan and client went well enough, the client might be lucky enough to be permitted to accompany the courtesan and her retinue back to the brothel for an even more extravagant soirée, replete with singing, dancing, and storytelling. Freelance entertainers and comedians would be summoned to perform magic tricks, shadow puppet plays, shamisen music, and various kinds of comic revue. Some of these performers became famous in their own right, making cameos or even being featured at length in popular literature and art of the day. Improvised theatricals (*niwaka*) of performers and clients together invented at Shinmachi were latter appropriated in Edo's Yoshiwara self-deprecatingly as "tea-server skits" (*chaban kyōgen*), after the practice of casting third-rate kabuki actors as tea servers or for other such inconsequential roles. These skits were sometimes developed into more elaborate performances for public consumption on street corners or the stage; such performances, in turn, were depicted in splashy woodblock prints or illustrated stories. Shōji Katsutomi (1668–1745), *haikai* poet, brothel owner, and descendant of Original Yoshiwara "founder" Shōji Jin'emon, compiled an anthology detailing, among other Yoshiwara-related matters, such performances. Entitled *A Garden of Words from the Boudoir* (*Dōbō Goen*, 1738),* this work was so successful that it gave rise to a sequel and inspired numerous imitations.

The real trendsetters, however, were the famous playboys and high-ranked courtesans, who served as objects of public envy and desire. Their sartorial and even verbal styles came to be celebrated in best-selling novels and woodblock prints. Whereas the beautiful people of Shimabara and Shinmachi were originally the subjects of innumerable monochromatic prints (*tan-e* and *beni-e*) to which some color was manually added, those of Yoshiwara were glamorized in a later exponential explosion of polychromatic prints (*nishiki-e*). Just as the monochromatic form had previously spread to Edo, the new polychromatic method was soon picked up by Kamigata artists. These works remain among the most sophisticated and alluring works of printmaking throughout the Edo and Meiji periods.

Generally speaking, authors, artists, and publishers in Edo appropriated and improved on earlier genres of art and literature in Kamigata. The "book of manners" (*sharebon*) that served as a kind of conversational handbook for amatory and social occasions, for instance, found its ultimate expression in Edo, not only inspiring the "sentimental fiction" (*ninjōbon*) of a later day, but also laying the groundwork for the Japanese appropriation of modern Western-style realistic writing. Edo authors managed to capture the special argot of Yoshiwara courtesans, who were trained to speak in an artificially created dialect that concealed any sign of the woman's provincial origins. Precisely because this argot was shorn of regional dialect, it universalized the culture of pleasure-seeking while, at the same time, enclosed and isolated such a world from the real one.

MALE HOMOEROTICISM AND THE ARTS

The tradition of male homoeroticism in Japan has been associated with the clergy and nobility since ancient times, with samurai since the Middle Ages, and with kabuki actors since the Edo period. This custom may be difficult for some people in the West to comprehend, given long-standing institutional and religious attitudes toward homosexuality. The Japanese custom faced no social or religious stigma and was never associated with such disparaging terms as "sodomy" or "bestiality." In large measure, homoeroticism was considered a matter of taste and fashion among pleasure-seeking men. In the educated Confucian society of the time, "female color" suggested male romantic dalliances with courtesans and other women, while "male color" suggested male liaisons with younger, dependent, male lovers. The educated engaged in debates on "female color" (*nyoshoku*) and "male color" (*nanshoku*), "color" signifying erotic desire as well as its aura. The debates were intense in the

writings of *nanshoku,* while writings on the subject of associating with courtesans paid little attention to such discourse. In fact, reputable playboys practiced both with style. Significantly, then, eroticism was typically defined
strictly from the grown male perspective directed toward objects of desire,
male or female.

Articulations of same-sex relationships date back to the earliest recorded
history in Japan, following antecedents in China's literati tradition. Homoerotic acts are sometimes mentioned in the writing of aristocrats, such as one
incident in Murasaki Shikibu's *The Tale of Genji* in which the eponymous hero,
known as the Shining Prince, is unable to bed a certain noblewoman and
makes do instead with her younger brother. Similarly, among the Buddhist
clergy, priests were prohibited from taking wives, let alone indulging in sex
with prostitutes, found a loophole of sorts in other priests or, perhaps better
yet, virile young acolytes or pageboys (*chigo*). The practice gained momentum, becoming a kind of monastic custom. During the Middle Ages, some
warriors looked back to such precedents fondly. Some of their pageboys even
became celebrated in popular historical accounts for their physical charms as
well as their prowess on the battlefield. One paragon was Mori Ranmaru
(1565–1582), pageboy to none other than Oda Nobunaga.

Little wonder, then, that samurai culture, which was bound to the denial
of fundamental human physicality, also gravitated away from heterosexual
romantic entanglements and toward *nanshoku.* State ideology, as articulated
by the Hayashi School of Neo-Confucianism, left no room for sexuality among
the respectable classes, relegating those who earned their livelihoods from
sensual acts, like prostitutes or kabuki actors, to the category of subhuman.
In his writings, school founder Hayashi Razan declared that although human
beings are virtuous by nature, sexual desire interferes with the exercise of this
virtue. The remedy, according to Razan, was daily study of the Confucian
classics. Such primness was enshrined in the so-called bushido, or Way of the
Samurai, which provided a philosophy of living in order to die beautifully.
Fragments of the celebrated *In the Shadow of Leaves* (*Hagakure,* dictated in
1709–1716, published in 1716), by Yamamoto Tsunetomo (1659–1719),
testify to this philosophy memorably. To the extent that such ideals were embraced, they often became the stuff of fiction, sometimes involving love affairs
between samurai. At the core of the narratives about samurai *nanshoku* is the
tragic death of a young male lover at the height of his beauty.

Without such pressure, political or philosophical, merchant classes came
to favor a sexual fluidity unavailable to their samurai counterparts. Befitting
the mercantilism of the day, in lieu of stories about the emotional and ethical
ties between high-ranked samurai and their pageboys, commoner stories featured merchant tycoons (*daijin*) who would pour their amorous energies into

adolescent male actors (*wakashū*). Whereas books of manners and sentimental fiction focused on heterosexual relationships, the earlier genres of easy reading book and floating-world novella often depicted *nanshoku*. An easy reading book thought to have been written by Konoe Nobuhiro (1599–1649), *Mongrel Essays in Idleness* (*Inu Tsurezure,* written in 1619, published in 1653),* set the trend. Works depicting either heterosexual relationships or *nanshoku* rarely detailed physical intimacy, since government edicts forbade written depictions of eroticism. To insulate themselves from possible prosecution, authors and publishers routinely presented their works as lessons in how *not* to behave. Typically, such pedagogical claims were declared in the preface of heterosexual writings, then dispensed with in the story proper, whereas in homoerotic works, these claims tended to be laced throughout the entire length of the story.

As a matter of fact, the story is presented as an admonitory tale for young men who are expected to know the proper manner of service to a lord or other superior. It is disturbing to us to know that the beautiful boys were very young: ages fourteen to sixteen constituted the ideal peak for male beauty. This means that the works of fiction taught the boys to subject themselves to the absolute power of their owners, whether daimyo or shogun. It was customary for a respectable samurai family to send their young son to a nearby temple as an acolyte, with the unspoken assumption that the child would be a sex object as he studied Buddhist theology and classics in history and literature. Such an experience was probably considered an initiation process. Another aspect of *nanshoku* is that it stood in opposition to sexuality that was forbidden by Buddhism, desire associated only with women. Many of the stories emphasize the spirituality of the relationship: the young male lovers tended not to be mere objects of desire. Rather, they were portrayed primarily through devotion to their official lovers, at the cost of their lives, or as true lovers who disregarded the danger of punishment by death.

One of the great masterpieces of homoerotic literature was Saikaku's *The Great Mirror of Male Love* (*Nanshoku Ōkagami,* 1687). The work is divided into two halves: the first is a well-researched recent history of *nanshoku* among samurai, and the second presents critically minded reports on contemporary practices among commoners surrounding young male actors. A later collection, *Male Colors Pickled with Pepperleaf Shoots* (*Nanshoku Kinomezuke,* 1702),* by Urushiya Ensai (dates unknown), is more playful. It consists of tongue-in-cheek histories and theories about homoeroticism, as well as verbal jokes and flights of fancy. The collection also features pageboys who turn out to be fowl-like goblins (*tengu*), the goddess of mercy, or the Buddhist monk Kūkai (posthumously Kōbō Daishi, 774–835), founder of the esoteric Shingon sect and purported "originator" of homoerotic practice in Japan. In

addition to the depiction of *nanshoku,* the violent endings of some protagonists, and the purported moral lessons, such works no doubt were also enjoyed
for their humor and horror.

Most conspicuously, perhaps, were *nanshoku* parodies of great literary
and dramatic classics. *Bad Boy Morihisa* (*Akushō Morihisa*)* and *The Male
Players' "Takasago"* (*Yarō Takasago*),* for instance, are anonymous spoofs of
the classic nō plays *Takasago,* by Zeami (ca. 1363–ca. 1443), and *Morihisa,* by
his son, Kanze Jūrō Motomasa. Replete with references to the precise details
of the original plays and allusions to classical poetry, these spoofs were emi-
nently chantable and, in all likelihood, were performed to musical accompaniment at private parties.

The wave of homoerotic literature subsided during the first part of the
mid-eighteenth century. Although *nanshoku* as a social practice persisted, as
a literary theme it became less vigorous, gaining strength only now and then
(particularly during Japan's modern wars). Hiraga Gennai was a latecomer in
the genre but was the most articulate in theorizing and describing male-male
eroticism. Gennai's satirical writings took the form of sexualized and politi-
cized biographies, histories, and geographies. In exposing the ludicrousness
and corruption of Neo-Confucian orthodoxy, Gennai presented his brand of
homosexuality not only as a type of heterodoxy but also as a sign of individu-
ality. Ironically, this advancement of *nanshoku* resulted in its destruction, for
in addition to the reassertion of heterosexual practices in the life and arts of
the city of Edo, the domains enacted new laws against homoeroticism.

THEATRE ARISING FROM THE RIVERBED

Although the pleasure quarters provided the major setting for various performances as well as fleshly indulgences, there were other locales too, particularly
the kabuki theater, one of the great centers of popular culture throughout the
Edo period. Accordingly, just as the shogunate had sought to regulate prostitution by confining it into specially designated pleasure quarters, so too did
it seek to control kabuki by concentrating theaters into special districts. Until
the 1670s, four chief theaters were recognized by the shogunate—namely,
Ichimura-za, Morita-za, Nakamura-za, and Yamamura-za—which were
located not far from Yoshiwara. These theaters, representing three authorized
theatrical companies that had been relocated within Edo's greater metropolitan area (a process that included the commercial takeover of one theater)
flourished until the end of the Edo period.

During the Azuchi-Momoyama period, street entertainment had become
all the rage in the urban centers of Kamigata. The shows expanded their repertoire during the early Edo period. Acrobats, ladder balancers, basket

jumpers, sword swallowers, jugglers, magicians, puppeteers, snake handlers, vocal impersonators, storytellers, soapbox orators, sand painters, soothsayers, blind minstrels, dancing mimes, bamboo flute (*shakuhachi*) players, professional regurgitators, and Buddhist mendicants reciting benedictions, for example, competed with one another. Drawn mostly from the lower echelons of society, the entertainers would stream into the great cities in search of paying audiences in public spaces, much to the delight of the masses and the consternation of the authorities. These spectacles often included exotic creatures, such as a peculiar bird imported from Africa, "real-life" mermaids, or a "giantess."

The most extensive of these public display spaces developed, during the first decades of the seventeenth century, on the dry riverbeds of the Yodo River in Osaka and the Kamo River in Kyoto, particularly in the vicinity of Shijō Street. These spaces became some of the greatest centers of popular entertainment throughout the Edo period. Since the strict laws regulating the streets of the major cities did not apply to these riverbeds, which were constantly shifting and therefore impossible to regulate, it was there that the street arts flourished. In short, popular theatre developed in the periphery, both in terms of geography and social class: for actors, musicians, stagehands, dancers, and the like were drawn mostly from the ranks of outcasts and other undesirables. Yet throughout the Edo period, many of these performers would become affluent cultural idols.

Kōdan stood out from other shows because of its pedagogical purpose, which largely determined its material, vocabulary, and tone. During the late Middle Ages, storytellers had entertained high-ranking warriors by delivering lectures, sharing personal anecdotes, and extemporizing about works of history and other lofty subjects. Public oration was a different enterprise, for it was meant for commoners who wished to be educated, about such things as the history of China or Japan, and to be entertained by the smooth and rhythmical delivery of stories in an elevated style. The orator typically sat at a low table, which he would occasionally strike rhythmically with a wooden clapper or closed fan (in Edo). By the eighteenth century, top narrators, like Baba Bunkō, might have their own walled platforms upon which to perform. One successful orator even had his own small roofed performance hall.

Kabuki, the most elaborate of popular shows that originated in Kyoto, reflected an urban fashion called kabuki. The political stability that brought about a rapid economic success created many affluent merchants and investors as well as a huge gap between the rich and the poor. This phenomenon rendered the young, particularly the children of the wealthy, rebellious and delinquent, displaying a fashion of the weird, similar to the "punks" of the 1970s and 1980s and the "Club Kids" of the 1990s. Men and women in conspicuously colorful clothes, often cross-dressing and occasionally carrying a sword, walked on city streets and suddenly broke into dancing in public spaces, their actions wild, sometimes downright criminal. Kabuki as theatre takes its name from this fashion, nicely characterizing its colorful designs, outrageous actions, gender crossing, and other stagey surprises. Like the nō and other forms of theatre, kabuki developed out of agricultural and religious rituals and came to present, in a fuller scope than before, histories and contemporary lives previously left untold.

What is called kabuki at present may find its remote origins in Azuchi-Momoyama women's dance, which would have been performed in brothel districts. Izumo no Okuni (b. ca. 1572), whom legends designate as the founder of kabuki, was a priestess-performer who probably had connections to the sex industry. It is very likely that women's dance could depict the erotic entertainments offered at such establishments, featuring punk-style absurdity characterized by Okuni herself in the role of a samurai pleasure-seeker at a brothel. Women's kabuki by Okuni's group appealed to urban audiences because of its taste for outrageous colors and designs, rebelliousness against tradition and social order, and blatant sensuality. If such unabashed sensuality, flamboyance, outrageousness, and transgression appealed to urban thrill seekers back then, these qualities, to one degree or another, have remained integral to kabuki to this very day.

The narrowly focused kabuki dance by women, however, soon found competitors in the theater district, where young male actor-prostitutes danced and performed skits. Because the authorities feared its immense influence and its potential to promote a subversive lifestyle, women's kabuki was outlawed by 1629. This led to a decades-long heyday for young men's kabuki, but widespread violent sex crimes perpetrated backstage resulted in 1652 laws prohibiting this type of theatrical enterprise. To fill the vacuum created by the banning of women and young men from the stage, kabuki was now compelled to use fully grown men (*yarō*) to fill the roles of women and young boys. Those actors had to entice audiences through their unique affectations in appearance, manner, posture, gesture, and voice. *Onnagata*, or male actors in women's roles, began to grace the most famous productions in Kamigata, and Kamigata kabuki itself came to be characterized by a nuanced, subdued, almost feminine style of acting. This is when Chikamatsu Monzaemon and Ki no Kaion (1663–1740), among others, made Osaka central to kabuki and other theatrical productions.

As acting became increasingly professionalized, schools were formed, and hereditary lineages established, with actors inheriting the names of their masters—some of whom became popular culture stars, even across generations. As part of the eastward cultural shift, kabuki started moving too. Yoshizawa Ayame I (1673–1729), an Osaka actor, made a hit as courtesan Miura in *The Courtesan and Mount Asama* (*Keisei Asamagatake,* 1698), and his eldest son, Ayame II (1702–1754), brought his career to Edo. Another *onnagata* star, Segawa Kikunojō I (1693–1749), was followed by Kikunojō II (1741–1773) and Kikunojō III (1751–1810), who also enjoyed fame among Edo's favorite actors. The first three generations of Iwai Hanshirō's family—Hanshirō I (1652–1699), Hanshirō II (?–ca. 1710), and Hanshirō III (1698–1760)—specialized in male roles in Kamigata kabuki but moved to Edo and performed *onnagata* roles instead. Inevitably, the superiority of kabuki in Kamigata tipped in favor of Edo.

In contrast to the gentle eroticism and realism of Kamigata kabuki, the Edo scene was characterized by an earthy, overtly stylized, and masculine "tough act" (*aragoto*) befitting heroic, divine, and monstrous characters. The Ichikawa Danjūrō lineage of Edo actors—beginning with Danjūrō I (1660–1704) and Danjūrō II (1688–1758), and leading straight to the current Danjūrō XIII (b. 1977)—embodied the ideal in the eyes of Edokko, or "the native sons of Edo." The line also came to be associated with the almighty god Fudō of the temple in Narita, which came to attract tourists from Edo, thanks to this connection. And when Ichikawa Danjūrō VII (1800–1832) selected "kabuki's eighteen numbers"—thereby establishing for posterity a canon of the greatest plays—he did so in order to enshrine the *aragoto* style of Edo acting associated with his family lineage. *Kagekiyo* (1732),* which highlights the hypermasculinity of a warrior as he breaks out of prison, is one of these eighteen favorites still regularly performed.

By all accounts the two greatest playwrights during the second half of the Edo period, Tsuruya Nanboku IV (1755–1829) and Kawatake Mokuami (1816–1893), were both active in Edo. Nanboku, whose aesthetics of evil has long been taken to reflect the increasingly dark "age of decadence" of the early nineteenth century, staged elaborate productions involving the quick change (*hayagawari*) of costumes onstage, thereby allowing actors to transform from a hero to a demon, say, before the very eyes of amazed audience members. Similarly befitting his times, which extended into the Meiji period, Mokuami glamorized lowlife antiheroes, such as thieves, bandits, gamblers, pimps, and murderers, in part by having them deliver sonorous speeches in the traditional rhythmic scheme (of alternating lines of five and seven syllables) of Japanese poetry.

Although kabuki continued to be composed and performed through World War II, it was briefly banned during the American occupation. Since then, traditional kabuki—now celebrated as a national art form—is performed in Tokyo primarily at two major venues: Kabukiza, in the Ginza district, which offers all-star programs just about every month, and the National Theater (founded in 1966), which regularly puts on accessible productions on its main stage, replete with an "earphone-guide" service that provides translation. In Kyoto, the Minamiza continues to put on kabuki plays, among other shows. In recent decades, some regional kabuki theaters in operation since the Edo period have been receiving attention through the media as well as through occasional appearances from chief Tokyo actors. Theatre Cocoon (established in 1989) in the Shibuya district of Tokyo features, among its offerings, newly composed kabuki plays as well as innovative interpretations of traditional pieces. In fact, over the past several decades, kabuki has been reinvigorated by the addition of cutting-edge technology and storylines. The most conspicuous example is Super Kabuki, founded in 1986 by Ichikawa Ennosuke III (b. 1939). Super Kabuki not only creates new plays on a Wagnerian scale but also transforms traditional works into hi-tech media-oriented displays, sometimes with tongue-in-cheek references to contemporary anime and manga.

Apart from kabuki, the other major form of staged entertainment during the Edo period was the closely related puppet theatre (*ningyo jōruri*), which likewise originated in Kamigata. Although its performance aspect largely developed in response to and in tandem with the success of kabuki, puppet theatre can trace its origins back to chanted sutras and narratives of the Middle Ages. Buddhist monks, who performed in public spaces in exchange for donations, offered a variety of rhythmically narrated stories accompanied by flutes, drums, bells, and gongs. This form of musically accompanied vocal narrative came to be known as *jōruri,* though there was also a form of recitation known as *gidayū* in which the reciter was accompanied by the elegantly twangy shamisen. Both *jōruri* and *gidayū* were used to narrate stories enacted by puppeteers manipulating elaborately constructed puppets (*ningyō*).

Among serialized chanted narratives, tragic stories of Lady Tokiwa, the widow of Shogun Minamoto no Yoshiitomo and of his younger brother Yoshitsune, based on histories of battles, were most popular during the late Middle Ages. Particularly *Tales of Princess Jōruri* enticed the audience with its emotionally powerful performances. The term *jōruri* settled as the name for this type of performing art. Kamigata artist Iwasa Matabei (1578–1650) was commissioned by a daimyo to elaborately illustrate a number of hand scrolls with the text of the chanted work embedded. Entitled *Tales of Princess Jōruri* (twelve scrolls, seventeenth century), the hand scrolls, more than seventy meters long in total, were inscribed and illustrated by Matabei and his studio.

Playwrights such as Chikamatsu Monzaemon and Ki no Kaion eventually began composing narratives exclusively for puppets, thereby imbuing the puppet theatre with a broader range of themes and greater dramatic potential. Chikamatsu's main chanter, Takemoto Gidayū (1651–1714)—after whom the *gidayū* style of chanting is named—fanned audience excitement with his emotionally charged delivery of narration and dialogue, while accompanied by musicians who banged out a heavy, urgent rhythm on a specially designed, thick-stringed shamisen. Although kabuki has always been an actor's theatre, without written scripts in most cases and allowing its stars to improvise with impromptu dialogue, puppet theatre relies completely on the written drama for both the narrative and the dialogue parts. Since play scripts for kabuki tended to be provisional, whereas those for puppet *jōruri* were more or less fixed, a textual canon for the latter was more readily established, beginning with the works of Chikamatsu and Gidayū. Other chanters and playwrights followed, of course, but pride of place is almost always accorded to these two for having elevated the puppet theatre from mere entertainment to genuine art form.

Having originated and blossomed in Osaka, the puppet theatre naturally captured the unique taste of the people of that great metropolis. The common appellation *bunraku* for the genre originated from the name of one of the puppet theatre groups that survived all competition. Today, puppet theatre performances take place throughout the country. Although it is not as popular as kabuki, the puppet theatre is heavily sponsored by the Japanese government. In Tokyo, the National Theater reserves its smaller stage for *bunraku* productions and thus has become the primary venue for its appreciation in the city. A second venue, the National Bunraku Theater, was established in Osaka in 1984 and, given the origins of the puppet theatre in that city, was long overdue. Productions at these two venues are occasionally broadcast on TV with subtitles.

The popular music of the period is also largely derived from the kabuki and puppet stages, pleasure quarters, and street performances. Entertainers in the brothel districts crooned sorrowful ballads on the theme of tragic love, waxing romantic about such things as double suicides of courtesans and their lovers. These ballads not only spread the latest rumors but also provided some of the most up-to-date and salacious material for the theatre. Conversely, stage songs also ended up being performed as stand-alone pieces in the brothels and teahouses. Generally speaking, the central conflict in these songs is not between one's social responsibilities (*giri*) and personal feelings (*ninjō*) or between Confucian ethics and romantic love. It is about the clash between the newly emerging merchant-class morality versus an obsessive love that threatened the primacy of family and business. Treasuring the melancholy of these ballads, city dwellers themselves yearned to perform them by heart. Demand for instruction in shamisen and singing increased sharply. By the beginning of the eighteenth century, masters of these arts founded their own schools, the names of which came to be identified with their most popular ditties.

Miyakodayū Itchū (1650–1724), for instance, working in Kyoto, created a form of music for private entertainment. *Itchū-bushi,* as it came to be known, helped improve *jōruri* music by both departing from the high emotionality of *gidayū* and emphasizing a subdued sadness. This softening soon extended to songs meant to accompany dance scenes in Edo kabuki. *Evening Mist over Mount Asama* (1734),* for instance, is a representative *itchū-bushi* that was played both on- and offstage. Likewise, Miyakoji Bungonojō (1660–1740), one of Itchū's students, invented *bungo-bushi,* which, while derived from *jōruri,* imbued a sentimental yet erotic quality to sad stories of love suicides. Giving voice to the guilt of a suicidal son, "Lovebirds' First Journey" (date unknown)* is one such song. By the 1730s, *bungo-bushi* had become so popular that the government banned this type of music for fear that it would instigate a spate of copycat love suicides.

Also immensely popular was *nagauta* (literally, "long song"), essentially a kind of background or mood music. Whereas *gidayū* was melodious chanted narrative, *nagauta* was atmospheric stage music. Initially associated with Kamigata kabuki, *nagauta* was later shortened to suit the Edo stage, forming a new style called *meriyasu. Meriyasu* accompanied moments of silence onstage, when actors had no dialogue or performed any dramatic action. Such music had to be flexible enough to match the cadence of the actors while conveying eroticism and lyricism. By the mid-Edo period, though, *meriyasu,* like many other styles of popular lyric, had broken free of the stage, becoming a favorite form of singing for many people.

BEARERS OF HIGH CULTURE IN EARLY MODERN TIMES

Throughout the Edo period, just as the political clash between the Kamigata and Edo regions brought about complex negotiations as well as mingling of powers, the arts and social life of the time mirrored similar blending of the nature of each cultural center. Within Kamigata cultural production and consumption, the high, reflecting the old city's tradition, and the low, demonstrating newly rising tastes and styles of the day, similarly confronted and merged with each other. Conceptually, these elements are never diametrically opposed but always exist in an ongoing dialogue with each other. Historically, after all, social climbers in just about every culture have tended to legitimize their newfound power by appropriating the aesthetics of their betters. In reality, this process also involves the erosion of the earlier highbrow culture, because social upstarts inevitably interject their own lowbrow elements into the mix, whether consciously or not. Over time, the lowbrow becomes the highbrow, and the previous highbrow withers away, until the next set of upstarts comes to power. Likewise, between the Middle Ages and the early modern, there were similar elements of influence, rebellion, and rivalry that formed a hybrid culture for a hundred or more years to come.

The history of Edo-period theatre and that of popular songs demonstrate the merging of earlier medieval culture and the new trends as well as of the high and the low. Social climbers often successfully legitimatized their newfound authority by appropriating, like the nouveau riche, the high-class style of a former rival. In this process, the unshakable "low" elements not only survive despite a newly adopted guise of elegance but also end up enriching the existing high culture through their subversion. Essentially, early Edo arts were inspired by late medieval legacies. Whereas the Minamoto—the first samurai clan to rule Japan—had merely aspired to be a part of the aristocratic circle at court, it was the Ashikaga clan that actually did. Its success was due in great part to the clan's closer connection with the imperial aristocracy, and this intimacy encouraged a new samurai-esque aesthetic combined with courtly elegance. The clan's patronage of nō, architecture, and garden design, all based on Ashikaga notions of life and beauty, usurped the ambience of earlier courtly elegance. The third Ashikaga shogun, Yoshimitsu, patronized the actor Kan'ami (1333–1384) and his son Zeami in their invention of the art of nō. Yoshimitsu's interest in architecture and gardens is represented by the Golden Pavilion of what is now called Rokuonji Temple. This structure, gleaming and radiant with its gold leaf reflected in the pond below, is the epitome of Ashikaga taste in its religious sobriety and decorative flamboyance.

The eighth shogun, Yoshimasa, following the suit of Yoshimitsu, erected the Silver Pavilion for Jishōji Temple in Higashiyama, in the suburbs of Kyoto. A more somber work of architecture, this temple symbolized a time of struggle between the samurai and the imperial forces after Yoshimitsu's sudden death. When he finally abandoned political administration and took the tonsure, Yoshimasa indulged in the arts, sponsoring nō plays and patronizing such painters as Kanō Masanobu (1434–1530) and Tosa Mitsunobu (1434–1525), as well as garden designer Zen'ami (fl. 1433–1471). The Ashikaga administration ultimately ended because of its conflict with the imperial court and rivalry within its own system. However, the legacy of classical art as reimagined by the shogunate in this period left a significant mark on samurai art of the early Edo period.

Elements of Western art were first mimicked by Oda Nobunaga, who looked not only to medieval theatre and arts as models but also to Western and Christian civilization as a superior source of imagination. Through his association with Portuguese missionary Luís Fróis and others, he absorbed much in theology but also acquired powerful weapons to subdue Zen Buddhist monks responsible for orchestrating riots. Although not a Christian himself, he tolerated the conversions of his retainers and other daimyo to the foreign faith. The open core of his octagonal Azuchi Castle stretched to the fifth floor, providing a platform for performance that could move to whichever floor the lord was on. Although Christianity was strictly banned during the Edo period, Nobunaga's exoticism and aesthetic persisted in the taste of the Tokugawa clan.

For Hideyoshi, rising from the lowest stratum of society, a high-class self-image became a pressing need. A tea hut lined with gold leaf, designed to Hideyoshi's taste, was certainly uncharacteristic of Zen principles for the tea ceremony, but the glittering authority of his rule had to be symbolized by the precious metal that surrounded him. Hideyoshi's taste for decorative arts was inherited by the Tokugawas. They favored Ogata Kōrin (1658–1716), whose screen paintings were adorned with gold leaf and powder. Following Nobunaga, Hideyoshi continued to cultivate an interest in the tea ceremony but furthered the art by patronizing Sen no Rikyū (1522–1591), who, by politicizing the practice, added power to the art of tea. The tea ceremony became a dominant part of social life and, during the early Edo period, bred a number of professional schools to train practitioners.

Nobunaga and Hideyoshi both pursued a passion for the decorative and performance arts during their regnancy, and Kyoto in particular was known for its supreme quality in architecture, garden design, pottery, silk dyeing, and papermaking. Because samurai emerged late as a ruling class, their desire to emulate their betters was intense, and the age-old samurai ways of thinking influenced their imitation of nobility and its courtly culture. Aristocrats, now deprived of political power, parlayed their classical knowledge and high taste into a living by turning themselves into scholars, artists, and instructors, enriching the culture of the Edo period in general.

The austere and somber side of Kamakura-period art arose not only from Buddhist religious principles but also from a samurai aesthetic that favored simple and straightforward presentation, traits often associated with the masculinity inherent in the samurai culture itself. Buddhist influence is most evident in the proliferation of overwhelmingly large sculptures of deities that graced imposing temple buildings and expansive gardens suggestive of Buddhist cosmology; samurai aesthetics modified the Buddhist sense of decor with an astonishingly fresh simplicity in architecture and garden design. Both ornate and austere tendencies came to characterize the high samurai style during the Edo period. For example, *waka* poetry, the chief literary genre handed down from the courtly period, turned, during the Kamakura period, into a more technically polished art form. Following the tradition of poetic competition and imperial anthologies, this period produced *The New Collection of Poems Old and New* (*Shin Kokin Wakashū*, ca. 1205). The practice of poetic theory and criticism arose during this time, often guarded in the form of secret texts passed only among great masters and their followers. Theory and criticism did open themselves through pedagogical group practice during the Edo period, eventually forming the discipline known as Nativist studies.

Since the high styles in architecture, gardening, and interior design during the late Middle Ages were under the influence of samurai innovations inspired by religion, ethics, and especially the glittering Azuchi-Momoyama aesthetics, Edo's high style had a penchant for inventive boldness. The Katsura Detached Palace, a seventeen-acre retreat built for a seventeenth-century prince, is a masterpiece that merges buildings and gardens of the religion-inspired styles from the Middle Ages. What is striking, however, is the more modern, open structure with its elaborately welcoming arrangement of landscapes along winding paths. The interior features depictions of natural scenes and contemporary geometric patterns, not in the traditional ink and gold, but in striking new colors.

Standing screens and scroll paintings, the most conspicuously decorative elements handed down from the late Middle Ages, also provided a template for experimenting with changing tastes. The ruler's penchant for ornate depiction of nature scenes on elaborate gold backgrounds influenced the taste of the Tokugawas and daimyo for similar presentation of their castles and mansions. The same technique was used and, in fact, the same artists patronized by the rulers began to depict street scenes with people from all walks of life mingling, working, and being entertained. Proud focus was on the city. Many screen paintings are entitled *In and out of Kyoto*. These were, for the first time in Japan, a representation of contemporary life. Similar screens produced on the topic of "in and out of Kyoto" never overlooked the pleasure quarters and kabuki theaters. The trend extended to other cities as well, often featuring Osaka's entertainment district. For example, *Pleasure District at the Mouth of the River* (*Kakō Yōraku Zu*, ca. 1640–1655), a pair of ten panel screens, depicted the port town of Sangenya, which was incorporated into Shinmatchi district. Unlike similar illustrations of Shimabara and Yoshiwara, where courtesans and their fashionable clients stand or sit in a rigidly well-mannered fashion, the figures in this scroll are shown touching and embracing one another, laughing, eating, and generally demonstrating the physicality of Osaka culture. These contemporary, real-life city scenes encouraged later productions focused on famous places of Edo and famous places along the Tōkaidō highway, and other such series.

Other examples of forms and techniques from high art accommodating the interest of those at a popular level are found in the work of Kanō Ujinobu (1616–1669). Coming from the family of painters sponsored by the shogun, he created a set of playful pictures and poems to be pasted on a standing screen, commonly called *The Poetic Competition of the Twelve Zodiac Animals.** The poems have been rumored to be an earlier composition by Karasumaru Mitsuhiro (1579–1638), a nobleman of the highest rank at court who was distinguished as a poet as well as a calligrapher. This work belongs to the ancient tradition of the Thirty-Six Great Poets, but only twelve poets are depicted—the number necessarily limited to the number of zodiac animals. The playfulness of the piece evokes humor by parodying the Great Poets convention: the animals are dressed in human finery, and the poems themselves mimic Heian classics.

*Mongrel Essays in Idleness,** a manual for *nanshoku* manners, is a prime example of a nobleman's experiment with a popular subject in high style. Konoe Nobuhiro, whom scholars speculate was its author, belonged to the highest aristocracy and, as was the custom of his class, received ample education to become a distinguished calligrapher, essayist, scholar of classics, and master of the tea ceremony, all the while still maintaining his rank at the imperial court. It is possible to imagine a collaborative effort between Nobuhiro and close friends who had perhaps experienced *nanshoku* as young boys and, having officially passed into adulthood, could now act as the older partner in a relationship. This how-to guide was probably a great occasion for them to show off their knowledge of *nanshoku* conventions from both perspectives. The first printed version was posthumously published in Kyoto in 1653 in the format of an illustrated easy reading book, which turned the privately circulated notes into an item for the popular market.

Daidōji Yūzan (1639–1730) was a ronin, and his writings may fall somewhere between the high and low, or popular, culture. He studied the military strategy of admired warlord Takeda Shingen and spent the rest of his life teaching the subject to a daimyo in Fukui. His chief publication is *Code of the Warrior* (*Budō Shoshinshū*, posthumously published in 1828), but he is also known for *A Collection of Fallen Grains—Addendum* (*Ochiboshū*, 1727),* consisting of essays recalling the days of Tokugawa Ieyasu, reports on social customs, and wartime events. This work historicizes the recent past, suggesting that contemporary experience could become part of an established tradition.

COMMONERS' TASTE AND THE BUSINESS OF PUBLISHING

The rise of the merchant class during the Edo period represents the first time that commoners in Japan had access to the same style of art as the ruling elite. The decorative arts of the earlier Azuchi-Momoyama period found ready buyers among the merchants just as they had among the samurai—whom the merchants increasingly came to emulate in some ways. Yet merchants also used their newfound financial wealth to patronize their own art objects. The so-called Rinpa painting school of Kyoto, beginning with Tawaraya Sōtatsu (d. ca. 1643) and including Ogata Kōrin (1658–1716), whose works depicted landscapes, mythological figures, and animals in bold representation amply glorified by gold leaf and dust, received such patronage. Founded by Kanō Masanobu (1434–1530)—an artist of birds, flowers, and portraits who carried on the legacy of Chinese-style painting—Kyoto's Kanō School came to flourish as the chief provider of decorative art for the upper classes, who sought to collect paintings by his son Kanō Motonobu (1476–1559). Shifting from the austerity of Chinese art and incorporating the narrative tendency of the Tosa School, which followed the more informal Japanese *yamato-e* style, Motonobu strengthened his clan's position as house artists for Kanpaku Hideyoshi, the Tokugawa shogun, daimyo, and other patrons. Emphasizing gold-leaf backgrounds, they created works that displayed brilliant colors and stylized shapes. For this particular group of patrons, the artists produced folding screens, hanging scrolls, and sliding doors. Kanō Tan'yū (1602–1674) departed from this flashy and stylized trend to create subtlety in his depiction of nature, although very few of his works are extant.

The merging of the high and low in visual art culminated in the astonishingly new expression in the scroll paintings of the aforementioned Iwasa Matabei and his studio. Descended from a samurai family, Matabei was orphaned at age two when his family was killed in a brutal attack by Nobunaga's army. This traumatic beginning may explain the foreboding effect of the bright colors used, the garish depictions of violence, and the obsessive desire for narration that made his works, often in ten scrolls, stretch to the length of a football field. In contrast with the pictures on sliding and standing screens that were dominant at the time, hand scrolls afforded more realistic and factually detailed representations of nature, figure, and story. By merging these, Matabei brought the popular culture of violence and the weird into a highly artistic form.

Although he and his studio produced many of the major scrolls on the themes of *The Tale of Genji* and *The Tales of Ise,* as well as depictions of events on the streets in and out of Kyoto, established themes for the artists of the time. Because of his emphasis on the movement of the human body and on facial expressions, Matabei came to be associated with ukiyo-e, or "pictures of the floating world," which featured realistic depictions of quotidian life. These works, often woodblock prints but occasionally paintings, became the reason for the appellation "the founding father of ukiyo-e."

The code of behavior prohibited samurai from enjoying the latest trends in popular entertainment. Commoners had no such restrictions and so became relatively more knowledgeable about, and interested in, current events. Catering to this interest, peddlers roamed the streets hawking one-page woodblock-printed broadsheets (*yomiuri*), often lightly illustrated, that related gossip, scandals, and other fresh "news" on topics such as natural disasters, love suicides, revenge killings, sightings of freakish creatures, and so forth. The realization that matters and incidents surrounding daily life could be put down in print—something hitherto reserved for important personages and historical events—must have inspired the production and appreciation of printed pictures and texts. This revelation also fanned the popularity of prose writers such as Saikaku and playwrights such as Chikamatsu, who found characters, themes, and stories within everyday news items.

Commercial woodblock printing, which enabled these broadsheets to be quickly and easily put into production, had historically originated in Kamigata. Granted, printing itself goes back to the beginning of Japanese recorded history, when the Chinese introduced woodblock technology into Japan during the eighth century—some seven centuries before the Gutenberg Bible, and eight centuries before the advent of chiaroscuro woodcuts in Europe. Still, the technology was monopolized by monastic Buddhists, who used it exclusively to propagate their religious teachings. During the late sixteenth and early seventeenth centuries, the Japanese government experimented briefly with movable wooden-type printing, largely resulting from the use of similar presses with metal type by the Jesuits in Nagasaki to print a simplified version of *The Tales of Hake* (1592) and a Japanese translation of *Aesop's Fables* (1593). These were used as Japanese-language textbooks for missionaries, but the latter represented the first translation into Japanese of a Western, non-Christian literary work. Coincidentally, that year Hideyoshi's army also brought home from Korea a similar metal-type press. Promoting selected Japanese literary and historical classics that they hoped would augment its authority, the Tokugawa shogunate briefly ran its own wooden-type press, though that met with minimal success. As for popular publications, the success of wooden-type printing in the Saga district of Kyoto was overtaken by printers who revived the more efficient and less expensive woodblock printing, effectively launching an entire industry.

One consequential advantage of woodblock printing over movable-type printing during this period was that it allowed for the composition and reproduction of both words, rendered calligraphically, and images within the same visual field. Since Japanese cultural production has, until the modern period, relied heavily upon the seamless integration of words and images, a technology like movable-type printing that could not attain this integration never stood much of a chance. Moreover, block printing allowed a reading gloss (*furigana*) to be readily added to otherwise difficult-to-read graphs, allowing such works to reach a wider readership.

Woodblock printing enabled new narrative trends focused on contemporary events in which common citizens participated. Far more accessible to a greater number of people, the medium encouraged the rapid publication of news about city events and scandals for quick distribution. This also provided a forum for new professionals to advertise their services. Marketing and advertising ploys attempted to harness the audience to maximum effect, and this included providing publicity for newly mushrooming businesses and professions. Many of the first popular publications were created for this exact purpose, as is satirically illustrated in "The Funeral Director's Blowout-Sale Circular," in *Newfangled Spiels* (*Imayō Heta Dangi*, 1752),* by Jōkanbō Kōa.

Movable-type printing, which enjoyed a boom in the beginning of the Edo period, mainly confined itself, with some exceptions in popular writings, to books on religion, history, medical science, and such subjects created and enjoyed by the educated. Producers of popular arts rediscovered the merits of the old method of woodblock printing, which proved to be faster, more flexible, and less expensive. The confluence of new professions in need of customers, a reading public eager for good stories, and the ease of woodblock printing came together in the sex industry's capitalization of print media. Up-to-date reviews of prostitutes and actors were in great demand in all chief cities. In Kyoto and Osaka, publishers spread names and ratings of prostitutes, usually in narratively inclined volumes of easy reading books. Among the very first reviews of Osaka's Shinmachi district was *The Book of Superiors* (*Masarigusa*, 1656), by Hatakeyama Kizan (1626–1704), a Kyoto merchant who was also a *haikai* poet and calligraphy appraiser. Eventually, Kizan extended his observations beyond the local scene in Osaka to review the districts of the major metropolises as a whole. These pleasure-district guides culminated in a voluminous encyclopedia of sorts, *The Great Mirror on the Way on Love* (*Shikidō Ōkagami*, 1678), which included theory and advice about love, as well as the usual stories, maps, events, and ratings of individual brothels and their employees.

In terms of popularity, Yoshiwara took the lead from the very beginning of the Tokugawa rule by putting out pamphlets called *A Guide to Yoshiwara* (*Yoshiwara Saiken*), which during the late seventeenth century were individually sold on the streets within the quarter, turning into biannual booklets by 1732. They continued to be produced until the late Edo period, becoming one of Japan's longest-running regular periodicals. The brochures included simplified maps of the district that listed brothels and the women in their employ, the prices for variously ranked workers, names of teahouses and boathouses, the names of female and male geisha ("music performers"), and a calendar of special celebration days.

Tsutaya Jūzaburō, brothel owner of a small shop by the main gate of Yoshiwara, took over publication from the two previous publishers and turned the guide into a profitable major publication. With an extraordinary eye for modern urban taste and creative talent, he scouted, nurtured, and sponsored many of the luminaries of prose fiction and ukiyo-e art from the mid- to late-Edo period, becoming a hidden hero behind the glorious blooming of Edo's popular culture.

Kabuki reviews were also a hit. Pamphlets with actor ratings, like those of the brothel-district women, used stories and poems to highlight favorites. Ukiyo-e illustrations in black and red began to accompany the texts, the oldest known example being the anonymous *Lover-bugs* (*Yarō-mushi*, 1660), an elaborate combination of commentaries, stories, and pictures. As grown-men's kabuki developed, the actor's value shifted from beauty to acting skills, so that individual actors were necessarily rated in upper, middle, and lower rankings, depending on their performance. The height of such review books was reached by *Riffing on Actors* (*Yakusha Kuchijamisen*, 1699), written by Ejima Kiseki (1666–1735), a Kyoto merchant who became a major writer of *jōruri* and floating-world fiction. The Kyoto-based publisher Hachimonjiya Hachizaemon II (studio name Jishō, d. 1745) also found fame with this book and continued to flourish as the leading press for actor reviews and floating-world fiction.

The personal anecdotes and jokes in these books were not isolated phenomena. Indeed, the Japanese have a venerable tradition of humor, with verbal wit, puns, and other forms of wordplay coursing throughout poetry, prose, and quotidian speech. These are visible in the earliest extant writings in Japan up to works of our own age (as attested to by the publication, in the 1970s, of a twenty-volume anthology of jokes). During the Middle Ages, the Zen sect of Buddhism had developed droll pictures, humorous poems, and comic stories to elucidate its teachings, which often used absurdist humor in the form of paradoxical riddles, or koan. The Zen monk Ikkyū Sōjun (1394–1481) was artistically gifted in this vein, be it poetry, prose, or drawing. Ikkyū's masterpiece, *Skeletons by Ikkyū* (*Ikkyū Gaikotsu*, 1457), was a picture book with essays and poems illuminating the insignificance as well as equality of all human beings in the way of the Buddha. Its illustrations showed skeletons engaging in a variety of human activities. The humorous and satirical *kyōgen*, the interlude in nō performances that gave comic relief to offset the generally grave themes and images of nō, turned, during the Edo period, into kabuki plays and influenced lighthearted scenes of other dramatic works.

Early Edo-period jokes were the work of independent comedians, called *hōkan*, who inserted their acts between dances and other numbers at teahouses in the brothel district. Those entertainers could also dance, sing, and play instruments, but some of them were noted for their ability to tell funny stories. The best ones came to be known by published collections attributed to them, as was the case with Shikano Buzaemon of *Stories Told by Buzaemon* (*Buzaemon Kuden Banashi*, 1683)* and with Tsuyu no Goro of *Jokes Told by Tsuyu*

(*Karukuchi Tsuyu ga Hanashi,* 1691).* Along with their stories established as texts, their performance techniques were handed down, so that the entertainment of seated comic monologues, called *rakugo* today, flourished.

The Edo period saw the phenomenon of graffiti (*rakusho*), not necessarily written on walls but copied and printed for distribution. These were anonymous criticisms of public affairs, ruling-class personages, and current events, many of them skillfully satirical. Of course, the literary genres of mad *waka* (*kyōka*), mad Chinese poems (*kyōshi*), and mad prose (*kyōbun*) that flourished during the early Edo period belonged to the tradition of pastiche and parody, which was rampant in both high and popular arts. The poetic genre of *haikai,* with its derivatives such as *senryū,* contained strong elements of this type of play. In theatre, the term *yatsushi* indicated stylistic parody. The comical rebelliousness of parody is skillfully rendered in *Bad Boy Morihisa* (*Akushō Morihisa,* 1706)* and *The Male Players' "Takasago"* (*Yarō Takasago,* 1707),* both of which were obviously written for teahouse entertainment or other such gatherings.

In addition to those books of information on the pleasure and theater districts, travel guidebooks turned into a major commodity. Throughout the Middle Ages, travel had been limited to those with religious or administrative purposes. Checkpoint guards inspected travelers to ensure that traffic remained restricted to authorized personnel. By the beginning of the Edo period, freeways and station towns were greatly improved, and the roads opened to commoners, making tourism one of the chief forms of entertainment. Information and ratings were in demand as travelers and would-be travelers sought all they needed to know about sightseeing opportunities and local delicacies. Of special interest to Kamigata readers were the roads between their cities and Edo. They were curious about the newly developing metropolis but also proud to read about the famous and familiar spots in their own cities. *Denizens of Kyoto* (*Kyō Warabe,* 1658)* gave Nakagawa Kiun (1636?–1705), a Kyoto physician turned *haikai* poet, occasion to become a travel writer, using easy reading books as his format. In *Denizens of Kyoto,* the reader is guided through various areas by a precocious child.

Chikusai (ca. 1621–1623), by Tomiyama Dōya (1585–1634), was a commercial success featuring a comic duo of a quack doctor and his companion traveling along the Tōkaidō highway. Playing with the idea of a pair of travelers, *Famous Places along the Tōkaidō* (*Tōkaidō Meishoki,* written in 1659),* by Asai Ryōi, is a more developed narrative in which a monk meets and accompanies a young man as they travel from Edo to Kyoto. *Glittering Highlights of Edo: Traces of Famous Places New and Old* (*Edo Sunago Onko Meisekishi,* 1732)*—by Kikuoka Senryō (1680–1747) of Iga, who went to Edo to become a *haikai* poet—was the first major nonfiction guidebook providing trustworthy information, including up-to-date detailed maps organized according to the regions of the city.

We find a curious combination of guidebook and romance in *The Tale of Zeraku* (*Zeraku Monogatari*, ca. 1655),* written anonymously. The description of the short travel from Kyoto to a nearby hot springs, interrupted by lengthy expositions on Chinese history, is tacked onto a love story that parodies classical romance. In addition to giving some useful information on the hot springs and the vicinity, the tale freely mixes fact and fiction, lampooning romantic and religious tales and exaggerating the ghastly aspects of folklore. The loose organization of themes and the patchwork mixture of narrative styles is typical of easy reading books.

Works of floating-world fiction also found inspiration in quotidian events and gossip but appealed to an urban readership by weaving observations on contemporary lifestyles, habits, and attitudes into their stories. Saikaku's *Twenty Local Paragons of Filial Impiety** and Ejima Kiseki's *Characters of Worldly Shop Clerks* (*Seken Tedai Katagi*, 1730),* like many others, constructed more cohesive plotlines than those of easy reading books and provided models for individual characterization through caricatures. Writers of easy reading books and floating-world fiction productively responded to the demand from their readers for newer topics and more interesting characters. These authors probably relied not only on friends and fans who conveyed current news but also on broadsheets. Saikaku, in particular, benefited greatly from this kind of system and was probably Japan's first author whose artistic production was supported by a studio of helpers consciously aimed at marketing their product. The author's reliance on this group effort enabled him to make a brand name for himself in the publishing market during his lifetime and beyond. According to his advice to his publisher and disciples, they were to withhold publication of some of his best manuscripts until after his death, so that the news of his demise would help boost sales.

Despite the popularity of the texts, these new genres often faced a degree of censorship that many of the earlier hand-copied classics had not. A 1657 Kyoto ordinance, the earliest on record, prohibited writings on miracles, deities, goblins, monsters, and magic because of the potential for such stories to agitate the masses and lead them into heterodox understandings of their surroundings. Kyoto publishers, through their branches in Edo, benefited from compiling samurai's family histories, responding to an intense interest in such stories now that the entire military class was struggling for its identity. The demand for these histories prompted the government to control and limit content that could be made available. In Edo, an edict by a magistrate forbade the publication of erotic materials, rumors, and comments on contemporary persons in books, calendars, songs, and other materials. These general prohibitions sometimes resulted in persecution for specific authors. In 1666, Yamaga Sokō (1622–1685) was punished for his book criticizing Neo-Confucianism as understood by the Japanese. In 1672, Utsunomiya Yuteki (alias Ton'an, 1634–1709), a Neo-Confucian scholar, was expelled from Kyoto because of his book *Biographies of Japanese Personages, Historical and Current* (*Nihon Kokin Jinbutsushi*, 1672). The book presented short biographies divided into various critical categories on an ethical scale—including daimyo and others who were Christians, a risky topic for any publication at the time. The case bespeaks the Tokugawas' fear of any content concerning the shogun's family and daimyo that might spread widely among the populace.

This ban on writing about the shogun and the rest of the samurai class remained in place throughout the Edo period. Later shoguns would add to the list of prohibited content, increasing the potential for punishment. Tsunayoshi, the fifth shogun, populated his career with edicts concerning censorship and punishment, though inconsistent, for those who dared to violate his rules. In 1682 he erected five notice boards throughout the city, the third of which included laws specifically against suspicious publications, counterfeiting, and poisoning. This extended to a ban on fashionable songs and any printed materials on unusual tidbits of world news. His ire was particularly directed at the large number of pamphlets and booklets distributed in the city that were spreading rumors of fires, famines, earthquakes, and other disasters.

These edicts affected not only publications but also performances and pictorial creations throughout the Edo period. Banishment from any major city, exile to a remote island, prohibition of publication or performance, confiscation of assets, and fifty days in handcuffs were the standard punishments imposed on some of the most popular painters, actors, songwriters, authors, publishers, and theater owners, destroying their careers and personal lives. The only one who was actually executed was the flourishing *kōdan* narrator Baba Bunkō (1718–1759), who was hanged for disseminating news of a contemporary political scandal. His crime was not that he spoke about it onstage but that he sold handmade copies of his report. Fear of surprise attacks and harsh punishments resulted in self-censorship within the bookmakers' guilds. Writers learned to censor themselves within their writing, claiming pedagogical purposes, for example.

LINKING: ASSOCIATIVE AND COLLABORATIVE CHAINS OF CREATIVITY

Originality and creativity, when pitted against censorship, found escape in two directions: reclusiveness on the part of creators, like those so-called eccentrics, and mass popularity on the part of producers. Even madcap writers and scholarly hermits who made a point of withdrawing from society or otherwise going against the grain were not, after all, completely isolated. They still belonged to an anti-orthodox network of like-minded individuals who composed, performed, wrote, and edited together. Despite protestations to the contrary, one was always part of a larger social network involving personal connections between teacher and student, father and son, husband and wife, elder and younger sibling, one friend and another. The tendency of even radically withdrawn individuals to assume a group identity suggests how dominant collaboration has been in the arts.

Such collaboration was achieved by "linking" otherwise separate literary or artistic elements as well as emotional and imagistic connections between the work and the reader. Allusion by invoking the words, images, characters, and stories of an earlier text—a frequent device in *waka* poetry and common in all art forms in Japan during this period—could enrich the new text as well as the response of the reader. This type of interconnectedness highlights the history of collaborative processes in the Japanese cultural tradition. From the ancient nobility to the medieval samurai, artistic production tended to be embedded in group activities. Competitions in picture collecting, poetic composition, and instrumental improvisation engaged men and women at court. Poetry, in particular, exhibited such linking, as in the earliest example of *The Ten Thousand Leaves* (*Man'yōshū*, mid-eighth century). This text's poetic structure centers upon dialogic exchanges between two persons, drawn from an older tradition in which two people, usually a man and a woman, would respond to each other's poems. *The Ten Thousand Leaves* privileges successive links by one or many persons inspired by the first exchange. It includes many forms, such as the "envoy" (*hanka*), also known as a reflection. This particular form's influence was the most enduring for later literature, though its subsequent usage underwent a name change: first to *tanka,* a short poem, and later to *waka,* which meant Japanese-style poetry in contrast to the Chinese models. The thirty-one-syllable "reflection" consisted of a summary or highlight added at the end of a long poem (*chōka*). The 5-7-5-7-7 syllable scheme opened up an independent form for composing poetry as *waka,* and this was the standard form for social and romantic exchanges in court society.

Before long, older poems were alluded to partially, in the 5-7-5 portion, for example, so that they could be put in a new context in an additional 7-7. Such innovation inspired the invention of a game in which one player composed the first half of a *waka* after which another completed the poem. As the game continued, the result was a long chain of half *waka* composed in a similar style. This practice was called *renga* (linked verse), a form that dominated the late Middle Ages. Sōgi (1421–1502), a priest with connections in high society, polished *renga* into high art, and, under his leadership, his followers composed and compiled *renga* individually or in a group.

Strict rules eventually bound the practice of *renga.* Beginning with the size and the manner of folds of the paper on which the links were to be recorded, rules determined where special images, such as cherry blossoms or the moon, could occur and how each link would contain shared elements or departures in terms of image and setting. Generally speaking, these rules prevented one verse from standing out above the others in terms of the intensity of its imagery or the quality of its composition—except in the cases when convention created an expectation of particularity. Originally, a typical *renga* sequence consisted of one hundred links, though shorter ones also existed in predetermined lengths, such as eighteen or thirty-six verses, which were referred to as "famous poets" (*kasen*), after the popular practice (in poetry and painting) of collecting thirty-six exemplars (that being the set number of famous poets from the Heian period).

Haikai, meaning "ridiculous" or "farcical" *renga,* came to dominate poetic practices during the early Edo period, resulting in a name change for the *renga* genre to *haikai no renga,* or *haikai* for short. These compositions usually involved a number of people who collaborated, or competed with one another, by alternating entries of 5-7-5 syllables and ones of 7-7 syllables. Just as the classical *renga* had complex rules about link numbers, linking methods, topics, and seasons, the comic version also developed regulations specific to its composition. The objective, of course, was to continue the preceding link but also to add certain new turns in terms of setting, story, or season. Here, too, allusions, often ironic or satirical, were highly valued.

By the early Edo period, the popularity of lowbrow *haikai* had already begun to overtake that of highbrow *renga.* The *haikai*'s humorous tone, everyday imagery, and focus on action and events made the genre accessible, drawing a large audience from the fairly educated common classes. There was so much interest in witty linked verse that formal schools developed. Female poets such as Den Sutejo (1633–1698) were early to emerge in composing *haikai,* but the rise of the Teimon School, the earliest major school and the most influential, seems to have discouraged female authorship. Nominally led by Matsunaga Teitoku (1571–1653) and known for its emphasis on the classics, the Teimon originated in Kyoto but quickly caught on in other major cities, including Edo. As public taste turned against classical contexts and contrived humor, however, the school's popularity faded when both the writers and their readers became frustrated by its conventions.

Such frustrations gave rise to the Danrin School, led by Nishiyama Sōin (1605–1682). Although it was centered around Osaka, its popularity expanded quickly to the other large cities. While the Danrin School upheld the tradition of *waka,* its authors declared their originality by incorporating surprising turns of logic and an unexpected course of events. Although the school introduced many talented poets, it lost its vigor at the death of Sōin. Among those who came from that school was Ihara Saikaku, who was one of the most admired of poets before he switched his attention to prose fiction. He was active in the fashionable, rapid-fire *haikai* event in Kyoto known as arrow-shooting *haikai*, in which poets competed by the number of poems they composed within a day or overnight. Saikaku totaled 1,600 poems in the competition of 1677.

It was Matsuo Bashō, who, by rejecting the Danrin School's artificiality, created a more sophisticated poetry filled with profound metaphysical and symbolic potential and a refined aesthetic combining poetic and ordinary languages into something that later would come to be celebrated for its modernity. Bashō revolutionized *haikai* by revising its linking principles and seasonal references, favoring artistic and philosophical implications over ironic humor. When he moved to Edo, where he set up a new school under his own name, the headquarters of poetic movements left the Kamigata cities. The masterpieces of the Bashō School include collections such as *Empty Chestnuts* (*Minashiguri*, 1683),* *The Gourd* (*Hisago*, 1690),* and *The Monkey's Straw Raincoat* (*Sarumino*, 1690).*

One of Bashō's chief disciples, Mukai Kyorai (1651–1704), collaborated with his sister Chine to compose *A Journey to Ise: Some Sibling Scribbles* (*Ise Kikō*, 1686)* during their passage from Kyoto to the Ise Grand Shrines. This exchange between brother and sister is interspersed with short comments by Kyorai. Similarly, Saikaku created a hand-painted scroll of witty linked verses that he composed, illustrated, and annotated himself, somewhat plainly titled *Saikaku's Hundred Linked Verses, Annotated by Himself* (*Saikaku Dokugin Hyakuin Jichū Emaki*, completed in 1692).* Here Saikaku assumes the role of multiple poets, responding to and challenging one another, all the while throwing these into a two-way conversation with the images, and a one-way monologue on the entire ensemble. This present volume follows the format chosen by Saikaku by adding the translator's comments regarding the original poet's observations on the links.

Den Sutejo, mentioned above, was one of the very few women leaders while the influence of Teimon held power. Later, women poets such as Kaga no Chiyojo (1703–1775), later called Chiyoni or Nun Chiyo, and Taniguchi Denjo (1712–1779), leaders in mid-Edo *haikai*, came to be celebrated as judges in popular competitions. By then the public "verse capping" (*maekuzuke*) competitions, described below, were in full swing, and so a greater number of women joined the world of poetic competition. An all-woman anthology was the invention of Yosa Buson (1716–1783), who is known for his rediscovery of the excellence of Bashō and his school. Buson distinguished himself from Bashō by crystallizing the immediate moment into a picture that engages the senses of sound and touch as well as vision. An accomplished artist of traditional Chinese scholarly painting and the so-called *haikai* pictures, he often alludes to classics and history in his poetry, subtly linking the verse, the picture, and the verse's calligraphic rendering. *The Jeweled Water Grass Anthology* (*Tamamoshū*, 1774),* by Buson, consists of nearly five hundred poems written by women. It was not merely the number of women poets that impressed poetry lovers of the day. Graced with contributions from the two stars in the genre—a preface by Kaga no Chiyojo, and an afterword by Taniguchi Denjo—the text glorified the power of women's art. Because the text favored quotidian life with concrete images, the anthology furthered the accessibility of poetic forms for common readers.

By the late Edo period, it seemed as though most people in Japan were producing and consuming some form of witty linked verse, the most common form being public contests of "verse capping," which was a bit like the *New Yorker*'s cartoon captioning contest, in which readers write in with their own captions to a cartoon that has been presented without its original punch line. For the verse-capping contest, judges would publish challenge verses, or *maeku*, and thousands, or even tens of thousands, of people would send in their response verses, along with a nominal submission fee. Winning verses were published and sold in such anthologies as *Two-Needle Pine* (*Futaba no Matsu*, 1690),* compiled by Tachibana Fukaku (Shōgetsudō, 1662–1753). Such contests spread like wildfire from metropolitan centers to the countryside, becoming a national pastime—and a lucrative business for the judges, organizers, compilers, and publishers.

In Edo, Bashō disciple Takarai Kikaku (1661–1707) organized the so-called Edo Coterie (Edo-za) competition that came to dominate the market. Kikaku's disciple Matsuki Tantan (1674–1761), who relocated from Osaka to Edo, distanced himself from collaboration by compiling an anthology of ten thousand verses that he himself composed, adapting the manner of competitive group composition. But the most significant series of verse-capping contests, held by Karai Senryū (1718–1790), culminated in the publication of *Willow Barrels of Haikai* (*Haifū Yanagidaru*) from 1765 into the Meiji period. It became the main repository of the stand-alone seventeen-syllable comic haiku (*senryū*) that has come to bear the name of its judge. *Senryū* remain popular in Japan to this day, with major newspapers publishing weekly the best of competitive *senryū* that comment wryly on contemporary life.

Collaboration, in many ways, was most pronounced in theatre. Puppet *jōruri* featured the combined work of playwrights, musicians, chanters, and puppeteers (up to three operating one major puppet). A single playwright often drew ideas and themes from colleagues, even as his references to history, contemporary events, and, most significantly, town gossip resulted in plays rich in allusion and intertextual linkage to other plays. Japanese performing arts separated themselves from the notion of authorship as well as of that of the self-containment of a work. One play was never completely independent from others, because of the practices not only of allusion and borrowing but also of group compositions that did not specify all authors. Thus, in kabuki, where the written script was often nonexistent or flexible, individual actors freely improvised parts of their lines, and the music, as well as dancing and other movements, was adjusted on the spot. This sort of improvisation allowed the theatre of the period to take on its own evolving creative life.

Essays, prose fiction, illustrations, and many other forms of artistic production throughout the Edo period also exemplify responsive collaboration. In lieu of a linear "plot" taking some kind of narrative to its climax, texts were composed by associative principles. Here, again, solo authorship was rare. During the early Edo period, popular fiction tended to be illustrated, requiring the author to work together with the artist (assuming they were not the same person). Furthermore, carvers, calligraphers, and publishers were involved in the process as well, and during the mid- and late Edo period, the visual arts were likewise collaborative enterprises. Authors, artists, publishers—they worked together, in much the same way that anime and manga are produced in our own time.

In a sense, the story of the Edo period itself is a series of collaborative responses to the challenges of the past. The culture of early Edo was very much a child of the Middle Ages. It was a child dependent in many ways on the benefit of her parents, carrying on their legacy with reverence and developing it based on her own original mind—which was sometimes rebellious and at other times bemused. In another sense, the early Edo period consisted of conflicting and competing values: the old versus the new, Kamigata versus Edo, and the high versus the low. The arts and entertainments of Kamigata, representing the connection between tradition and innovation, had a similar relationship to their Edo counterparts: curious, respectful, contentious, and even oppositional, forming—through negotiation—a discursive history of the development of a remarkably lively civilization. If anything was early modern about the Edo period, it was less the way in which Edo responded to the foundational challenge of Kamigata, and more the way in which both Kamigata and Edo, by interrogating the authority of political, religious, philosophical, and scholarly knowledge, seem to have envisioned a collaborative path forward toward a future together as a modern nation.

Notes for the Reader

1. The use of Japanese terms is kept to a minimum except for those that are commonly used in English. Certain interesting expressions and widely used phrases are introduced in parentheses following their English equivalents.
2. Japanese names, including pen names, are given in the Japanese order, with the family name preceding the given name. Popular writers of the period, however, are customarily referred to by their given name, real or assumed, so Matsuo Bashō is simply called "Bashō," and Ihara Saikaku, "Saikaku." The one exception is Chikamatsu Monzaemon, who is referred to either by his family name "Chikamatsu" or the epithet "Great Chikamatsu."
3. Diacritical marks are used to aid the pronunciation of Japanese names and words. Macrons indicate long vowels. An apostrophe is added to indicate that two letters in the English alphabet, the first one usually being an "n," are to be pronounced separately, as in "Kan'eiji Temple." Sometimes hyphens are used to separate two vowels, as in "Susano-o." In the case of words that are commonly recognized in English, especially proper nouns, the macrons are dropped, as with "Osaka" for "Ōsaka" and "Kyoto" for "Kyōto."
4. In Japanese, the vowels *a, i, u, e,* and *o* are pronounced approximately like "ah," "ee," "ew," "eh," and "oh." Every vowel, even an *e* following a vowel at the end of a word, is pronounced, as shown with a hyphen in the anglicized word "ukiyo-e." There are no diphthongs or sliding from one vowel

to another. For clarity, the word *sake* will be italicized when referring to the Japanese beverage.

5. The spelling of a Japanese word that is established as an English one may be altered to represent the proper pronunciation in Japanese as in "shamisen" instead of "samisen" and "nō" instead of "Noh."

6. In anglicized Japanese, the Japanese sound "n" is sometimes transcribed as "m" when it precedes a "b," "m," or "p." In this volume, however, the sound "n" is represented as "n," as in "tenpura" and "Shikitei Sanba."

7. An asterisk (*) denotes the title of a work that is included in translation in this volume either in full or in part.

8. Traditionally, Japanese is written vertically and from right to left. Therefore, when translating works of graphic fiction from the Edo period, such as *The Bearded Lady of the Haunted House,** adjustments have been made to accommodate the horizontal and left-to-right reading order of English. Similarly, the segments in the picture scroll *Saikaku's Hundred Linked Verses, Annotated by Himself** are reorganized for left-to-right reading.

9. Unlike kabuki plays, which were variable performances based on partial and changeable scripts, puppet *jōruri* were written works of rhythmical narrative delivered by chanters who narrated the story as well as performed the lines for all roles. In this volume, the selection from *A Courtesan's Soul within Incense Smoke** is presented in the format of a play. A scene division is given and the narrative parts are marked by "narrator," while dialogues are attributed to various separate characters.

10. The lunisolar calendar, used in the texts included herein, cannot be translated precisely into the Western Gregorian solar calendar. Since the lunisolar year consisted of twelve months sometimes adjusted with a thirteenth month, the gap between the two calendars is about a month or more. What the Japanese termed the First Month, for instance, does not coincide with the modern January.

11. Generally speaking, the day was divided into periods from dawn and from dusk by two sets of bell strikes: dawn, corresponding roughly to 5–7 a.m., had six bell strikes, as did dusk, corresponding roughly to 5–7 p.m. These periods got longer or shorter, depending on the time of year. Each period, which lasted approximately two hours by the modern clock, was also referred to by a zodiac animal, the names of which in English are a matter of debate.

12. Distance was traditionally measured by *sun* (approximately 1.2 inches), *shaku* (ten *sun,* or approximately one foot), *ken* (six *shaku,* or approximately six feet), *jō* (ten *shaku,* or approximately ten feet), *chō* (sixty *ken,* or approximately half a mile [120 yards] in length and just over two acres as a measure of area), and *ri* (thirty-six *chō,* or approximately two miles).

13. Monetary figures used in Edo-period works cannot be translated reliably

BELL	# OF STRIKES	SOLAR TIME	APPROXIMATE TIME FRAME	ZODIAC ANIMAL
1	6	Dawn	5–7 a.m.	Hare
2	5	Early morning	7–9 a.m.	Dragon
3	4	Late morning	9–11 a.m.	Snake
4	9	Noon	11 a.m.–1 p.m.	Horse
5	8	Early afternoon	1–3 p.m.	Goat
6	7	Late afternoon	3–5 p.m.	Monkey
7	6	Dusk	5–7 p.m.	Rooster
8	5	Early evening	7–9 p.m.	Dog
9	4	Late evening	9–11 p.m.	Pig
10	9	Midnight	11 p.m.–1 a.m.	Mouse
11	8	Late night	1–3 a.m.	Ox
12	7	Before dawn	3–5 a.m.	Tiger

into today's dollars and cents. Currencies based on gold, silver, and copper—the so-called three-coin system—operated depending on the region and market values, as well as the government's policies of the time. For major transactions, silver was used in Kamigata and gold in Edo, whereas copper coins were used for quotidian expenditures everywhere. All types of coins were minted in different sizes and shapes at different times. For gold, the basic coin was the *ryō*, which can be roughly approximated as several hundred US dollars at the time of this writing. There were four *bu* to a *ryō*, and four *shu* to a *bu*, or sixteen *shu* to a *ryō*. For silver, coins were weighed during each transaction, and the denominations were referred to by weight. The basic unit of measurement was one *kan*, which weighed around eight pounds. It was equivalent to one thousand *mon* (or *monme*, as a unit of weight), the most frequently mentioned unit in literary works. The smallest denomination, the *fun*, was one-tenth of a *mon*. A samurai's income was represented by the amount of rice that could be collected in taxes or paid by the superior. Generally, one *koku* was about 330 pounds of grain, or enough to feed one person for a year. A daimyo's name was typically mentioned with his income like an epithet, such as "Lord of Kaga, one million *koku*." Samurai in lower ranks were given income in rice to support the members of the household, which could be enough to support from one hundred persons to possibly one and a half persons.

14. The American spelling of words is maintained throughout with an exception: we use "theatre" to refer to the genre of art and "theater" to refer to the building.

Chronology

The following simple chronology is intended to provide some background information on political, economic, and cultural aspects of the early Edo period discussed in this volume's introduction. The periods before the rise and after the end of the Tokugawa shogunate are represented by only a few items particularly relevant to the contents of this volume.

NARA PERIOD (710–794): Establishment of imperial rule. Compilation of mythology, history, geographical records, and poetry in Japanese and Sino-Japanese. Invention of copper coinage. Introduction of Buddhism and Confucianism into Japan.

PERSONS: Ashikaga Takauji (1305–1358, ruled 1338–1358), first
                Ashikaga shogun
            Ashikaga Yoshimitsu (1358–1408, ruled 1368–1394), unified
                the two imperial lines of the northern and southern courts

HEIAN PERIOD (794–1185): Imperial capital moved to Heian (Kyoto). Golden age of courtly culture: classical poetry and prose, screen painting, textiles, and other aristocratic arts. Fujiwara family rule as regents to the emperor.

PERSONS: Sugawara no Michizane (845–903), an exiled scholar-politician
            Murasaki Shikibu (ca. 973–ca. 1014), composed *The Tale of*
            Genji

KAMAKURA PERIOD (1185–1333): Rise of the military class. Shogunate rule in Kamakura and decline of aristocratic power. Foundation of six new schools of Japanese Buddhism. Development of sculpture, architecture, and garden design.

PERSONS: Minamoto no Yoritomo (1147–1199, ruled 1193–1199), first
shogun
Minamoto no Yoshitsune (1159–1189), defeated the Taira clan
Hōnen (1133–1212), founder of Pure Land (Jōdo) Buddhism
Dōgen (1200–1253), founder of Sōtō Zen Buddhism
Emperor Go-Daigo (1288–1339, reigned 1318–1339), resisted
shogunate rule
EVENTS: Taira clan defeated at the Battle of Dan-no-ura (1185)
Mongol armies deterred by a typhoon, or "divine wind" (1268
and 1281)

MUROMACHI PERIOD (1336–1573): Ashikaga shogunate rules in Kyoto. Construction of several famous temples. Development and refinement of nō theatre and tea ceremony, in addition to Buddhism-inspired ink painting and poetry. Christianity arrives in Japan, and trade with the West begins via Nagasaki port.

PERSONS: Ashikaga Takauji (1305–1358, ruled 1338–1358), first
Ashikaga shogun
Ashikaga Yoshimitsu (1358–1408, ruled 1368–1394), unified
the two imperial lines of the northern and southern courts
Ashikaga Yoshimasa (1436–1490, ruled 1449–1473), patron of
the arts
Zeami Motokiyo (ca. 1363–ca. 1443), actor and nō playwright
EVENTS: The Ōnin War begins, opening up the Warring States period
(1467–1603)
Powerful clans expand their spheres of influence
Christian missionary Francis Xavier arrives in Japan (1549)

AZUCHI-MOMOYAMA PERIOD (1573–1600): Final stage of the Warring States period. Reunification of daimyo territories under powerful warlords. Hideyoshi's invasions of Korea. Western, or "Nanban," style flourishes along with Christianity; both later suppressed. A trend toward decorative arts in furniture making and other interior design as well as castle architecture under the patronage of warlords.

PERSONS: Oda Nobunaga (1534–1582), began Japan's unification
Takeda Shingen (1521–1573), mounted powerful resistance,
though ultimately defeated by Nobunaga
Akechi Mitsuhide (1528–1582), Nobunaga's retainer who
rebelled
Toyotomi Hideyoshi (1537–1598, reigned 1585–1591),
expanded and organized Nobunaga's realm

EVENTS: Tokugawa Ieyasu is victorious at the Battle of Sekigahara (1600)

EDO PERIOD (1600–1868): Establishment of Tokugawa shogunate. Construction of elaborate central government in Edo (now Tokyo). Implementation of isolationist foreign policy and a rigid class system. Rise of metropolitan centers like Edo, Osaka, and Kyoto. Licensed pleasure districts in these centers. Growth and spread of popular arts, including kabuki, music and street performances, ukiyo-e prints, and mass-printed books. Advancements in technology and science. Trade with the Dutch on the isle of Dejima in Nagasaki.

PERSONS: Tokugawa Ieyasu (1543–1616, ruled 1603–1605), founded the
Tokugawa shogunate
Kanō Tan'yū (1602–1674), influential Kanō School painter
Asai Ryōi (d. 1691), author of "easy reading" books and
"floating world" novellas
Ihara Saikaku (1642–1693), poet and author of "floating world"
novellas
Matsuo Bashō (1644–1694), *haikai* poet
Tokugawa Tsunayoshi (1646–1709, ruled 1680–1709), issued
animal protection laws
Chikamatsu Monzaemon (1653–1725), dramatist of puppet
jōrui and kabuki
Ogata Kōrin (1658–1716), screen painter of the Rinpa School
Tokugawa Yoshimune (1684–1751, ruled 1716–1745),
instituted the Kyōhō Reforms (1716)
Hiraga Gennai (1728–1779), literati eccentric
Tokugawa Ieharu (1737–1786, ruled 1760–1786), the tenth
Tokugawa shogun
Tanuma Okitsugu (1719–1788, in office 1767–1786),
instituted coin-based mercantilism
Matsudaira Sadanobu (1759–1829, in office 1783–1812), led
the Kansei Reforms (1787–1817)
Katsushika Hokusai (1760–1849), ukiyo-e artist famous for *The
Great Wave off Kanagawa*

Shikitei Sanba (1778–1822), author of comic fiction (*gesaku*)

Utagawa Hiroshige (1797–1858), ukiyo-e master

EVENTS: Establishment of the three-coin system (1601)

Yoshiwara pleasure district founded (1618)

Shimabara Rebellion (1638–1639)

Meireki Fire. Old Yoshiwara destroyed and New Yoshiwara established (1657)

Genroku era (1688–1703)

Akō Affair (Chūshingura) (1701)

Baba Bunkō, author and raconteur, executed for a seditious lecture (1759)

Commodore Perry's "Black Ships" arrive off the coast of Edo (1853)

MEIJI PERIOD (1868–1912): End of shogunate rule and creation of constitutional monarchy. Increased Western influence, trade, and cultural exchange. Wars with China and Russia.

PERSONS: Emperor Meiji (1852–1912, reigned 1867–1912)

Characters and Manners, High and Low

The Poetic Competition of the Twelve Zodiac Animals

ILLUSTRATED BY KANŌ DAIGAKU UJINOBU

POEMS ATTRIBUTED TO KARASUMARU MITSUHIRO

The impact of medieval arts in early Edo-period culture can be seen in a strong interest in folklore, particularly involving animals. Rabbits, mice, and frogs, as well as shape-shifting foxes and badgers and the like, grace the pictures, stories, plays, and essays of the day. In the books of so-called bedtime stories (*otogizōshi*) widely circulated beginning in the sixteenth century, for instance, such animals were frequently personified, entering the human realm as tricksters or as affectionate companions interceding on behalf of the gods.

Similarly, the practice of the poetry contest, which goes back to the ancient court and became widespread during the Middle Ages, inspired competitions in various poetic forms and parodies throughout the Edo period. These ancient competitions were a serious matter in courtly circles, because poetic achievement had long been a prerequisite for positions in the administrative and political structure. Such competitions were even anthologized, often endorsing the best poems by the best poets from a certain political faction. Ki no Tsurayuki's preface to *Poems Old and New* (*Kokin Wakashū*, tenth century), for instance, contains one of the oldest lists of great poets, including Ariwara no Narihira and Ono no Komachi, who were established as the Six Poetic Immortals (*kasen*) in the Chinese tradition of naming poetic geniuses (*shi xian*). Along with the later tradition of the Thirty-Six Great Poets, the Six Poetic Immortals inspired the addition of a portrait of each poet, establishing a groundbreaking new form in which a poem, rendered in high-style calligraphy, and a colored image of the poet could be combined to adorn standing screens, hand scrolls, fans, or albums.

Poetry contests always centered on set topics, the present one being the moon, one of the major poetic themes in general. Here each poem refers to a distinct phase of the moon and to its effect on the natural landscape as well as the poet's sentiment. Typically, poets would gaze upon the moon while pining away, the moon traditionally representing the uncertainty and sadness of love. At the same time, the moon was also a sign of light, which plays against and with the darkness of feelings and landscapes. The series also borrows from folk stories and fairy tales involving the moon, such as one about how the hare came to reside there for all to see.

The twelve poems and twelve corresponding images presented here, originally alternating on twenty-four sheets of decorative paperboard, date to around 1650. The poems by Karasumaru Mitsuhiro (1579–1638) were probably written down at the hand of a noted calligrapher among his disciples and accompanied by the paintings of Kanō Daigaku Ujinobu (1616–1669). Controlled and visually witty, the calligraphy intentionally plays with the heaviness and thickness of brushstrokes as well as the size and flow of the poem's kanji. Mitsuhiro clearly inscribes each poem with great care, often rendering its characters in intriguing shapes and designs suggesting a style complementary to each of the animal-poets, who themselves are attired in the costumes of the personages they mimic. Ultimately, the charm of the series is the playful combination of word, picture, and calligraphy, which in some cases amusingly conflict with each other and in other cases enhance the joke already present in the combination of the animal and the personage.

Mitsuhiro modeled his untitled work, which might be titled *The Poetic Competition of the Twelve Zodiac Animals*, on a late variation of *A Picture Scroll of Battles between Twelve Zodiac Animals* (*Jūnirui Gassen Emaki*), a sixteenth-century tale. That version tells the story of how one of the animals excluded from a poetry contest challenges the others to war. The present series is an independent work, composed of only the first part in which the twelve poets compete with one another. Players were traditionally grouped into two teams, one on the right and one on the left to mirror the two sides of government. However, for the purpose of this anthology, the twelve poets are instead grouped in the conventional order of the twelve animals of the zodiac.

The names of these zodiac animals in both the Japanese tradition and its

Chinese model have variations in English: Mouse (Rat), Ox, Tiger, Hare (Rabbit), Dragon, Snake, Horse, Sheep (Goat), Monkey, Rooster (Cock), Dog, and Boar (Pig). Be that as it may, the fictional names of the poets play on the names of these twelve animals, lightheartedly echoing ancient courtly titles and ranks. Within the poems themselves, literary puns and other types of wordplay—equivalent to such techniques in Western poetry as assonance, alliteration, and rhyme—exemplify their poetic nature, shedding light on their relationships with the accompanying pictures.

 (TT & JS)

Illustrations reproduced courtesy of the Toru Takahashi Collection

MOUSE
Rice-Field Monk Sogen

The mouse in the painting wears a charcoal-colored monk's robe and sits slumped over two rice barrels—seemingly exhausted—with his elbow bent, reinforcing the words in the poem: "all through the night" and "aging body."

There was a long-standing legend about the Tendai monk Raigō (1002–1084) whose vengeful spirit supposedly transformed into a mouse.

all through the night
when gazing at the autumn sky
my body ages
like the mouse's
on the moon

The mouse is presented as a high-ranked monk, and his name refers to a "rice field hole." His name "*Sogen*"—mouse recluse—not only fits with his occupation but also echoes the names of some of the famously distinguished Buddhist priests, whose names commonly ended with "-gen."

The mouse on the moon, symbolic of the passing of time, plays on the "hare on the moon" in East Asian lore, which appears again in the hare's poem.

OX
Big-Head Kuromaru

Since the ancient period, ox-drawn carriages were a means of transportation for courtiers.

The ox pictured here, wet from rainfall, looks glum. It sits in everyday courtier gear in front of a carriage. The animal-poet is supposedly about to transport himself as a courtier, adding a humorous element to the scene. The green pattern of his kimono matches the carriage's green-trimmed rattan blind, and both contrast with the orange tassel wound around the carriage beam.

The title of this poet, *daikaku no suke*, referring to the animal's large angular head, is a play on *daigaku no suke*, the head position of the university. Since the deified scholar Sugawara no Michizane (845–903) supposedly rode an ox-drawn carriage, a bronze ox head was built at Kitano Shrine in Kyoto centuries ago. Visitors have stroked this statue for good luck in academic achievements so frequently that its head has been worn down to a large indentation. *Kuromaru* means "black-round" like an ox.

the moon
between evening showers
goes sadly unseen
shrouded by
patches of clouds

The poem opens in anticipation of the moon becoming visible between evening show-ers. In the second half of the poem, however, the cloudy sky depressingly blocks the moon, which seems to play a game of hide-and-seek with the cosmos. This poem goes against the grain of others (dragon, boar, horse) in which seeming obstructions are cleared and the moon is seen radiating forth. The clouds, here, seem to correspond to the spotted pattern on an ox's hide.

The word *ushi* (sad, gloomy) is homophonous with "ox."

TIGER
Windblown Okikaze of the Field

The name echoes that of Fujiwara no Okikaze, one of the poets of *Poems Old and New*. It is also a pun on *akikaze* or "autumn wind," associated with wild fields in Chinese and Japanese poetry.

The tiger's gear is presented in the Chinese style of painting, with the animal positioned within a wild field or bamboo grove. Since in the Japanese tradition the tiger is an exotic animal representing China, the poet's attire here complements this connection visually. There was an early association of tigers with fields, wind, and bamboo, as well as with China.

all night long
autumn breezes blow
the tiger crouches in the field
roaring at
the fading moonlight

This scene, depicting the autumn breezes, moonlight, and tiger's roar, is imbued with a sublime majesty. As opposed to the "flying dragon," the "crouching tiger" represented male power and authority in the Chinese tradition.

HARE

Bush Clover Tsukizumi

Hares were associated with bush clover, in which they were apt to hide. The name Tsukizumi is a double entendre: "clear moon" and "living on the moon." The latter reflects the myth about a hare inhabiting the moon.

The hare-poet sits in a bamboo-grass meadow, wearing a black hat and lavish hunting kimono in green with gold-flower pattern. He has his two front paws placed on his cheeks as though hands, looking pensive.

at the crack of dawn
in the moon's glow
a white rabbit
perks up his ears—
wind through the pines

The poem follows the progression of light from sunrise to the remaining glow of the moon, thereby focusing on the whiteness of the hare.

Mention of the rabbit's ears calls the reader's attention to the presence of sound within the poem's imagery.

DRAGON
Water Official Ryūnō

The dragon, as all-powerful mythical ruler of water and sky, is appropriately put in the position of Water and Ice Minister at the imperial court. Rain and clouds naturally came under his administration.

In the painting the dragon looks fierce and majestic in his traditional, formal court dress with courtier hat and sword.

rising clouds
gather around me
but it seems
they won't disturb
this autumn moon

Waves and clouds rising around the dragon highlight its power as the ruler of such natural phenomena.

As the dragon ascends from water to sky, Mitsuhiro designs his calligraphy to imitate the dragon rising diagonally from left to right, unusually placing the second half of the poem on top of the first.

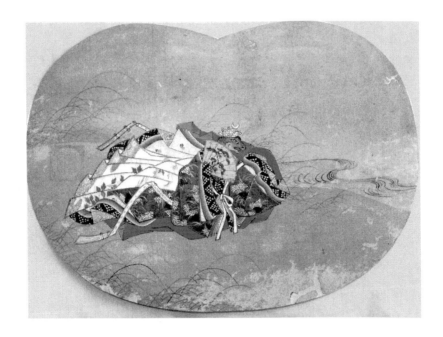

SNAKE
Lady-in-Waiting Mino

The title of the snake suggests the courtly position which required the ability to compose poetry. The serpent's length conjures up the image of the proverbially long autumn night in which one waits longing for one's lover.

The snake-poet wears a colorful kimono and holds a fan of Japanese cypress befitting an elegant lady-in-waiting, recalling great female poets of bygone ages in similar positions, such as Ono no Komachi and Izumi Shikibu. The crescent moon lies atop the snake-poet's gold tiara, as though to represent the moon at which she gazes.

月
み
れ
ば
ち
ぢ
に
物
こ
そ
秋
か
な
し
け
れ
わ
が
身
ひ
と
つ
の
秋
に
は
あ
ら
ね
ど

巳
濃
内
侍

gazing at the moon
on an autumn evening
all gloom is dispelled
but whoever said
an autumn night's too long?

The snake is represented as the only woman poet among the twelve animals, recalling those talented poets depicted in images such as those of the Thirty-Six Poets.

The calligraphy, divided into short words and phrases, is arranged in the shape of a snake zig-zagging over its background.

HORSE
Court Stablemaster Nagatsura

The Court Stablemaster was a formal position involving such things as training and nurturing horses and tending to their feed. Appropriately enough for this official, his given name, Nagatsura, shown with his portrait, means "long faced."

The poet sits in the formal attire of his office, hind hooves drawn together, as in the style of courtly portraits. He wears a courtier hat and monochrome brown kimono with an orange inner lining. Sword girded at his left, what must be his right front hoof leans on his staff of office. He peers off into the distance, presumably at ponies illuminated by the moon.

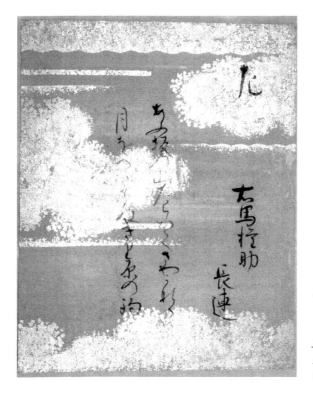

already away from
  Osaka Mountain
but no further
from the clear moon
ponies
upon Foggy Meadow

Horses were associated with the moon in part because they were presented to the throne during the full-moon festival of mid autumn.

The poem plays on the term "foggy meadow" as well as the name Osaka Mountain (or, "Rendezvous Mountain"), where the Court Equestrian came to accept the horses presented to the emperor as part of this festival.

The poem is rendered in two vertical lines presumably to suggest the horse's long face.

SHEEP
Teiyō from China

In a scene suggesting classical Chinese painting, the sheep-poet is depicted as a literary intellectual in the customary white robe. Appropriately, a manuscript is at his side.

The poet's name, Teiyō, meaning "horned sheep," refers to a male sheep. In the Buddhist parable, it was also used to mean a mediocre person who pursues his instinctual desires.

never stopping
the sheep comes and goes
year after year
have I become accustomed
to the autumnal moonlight?

Although the official position of the poet is not specified, he is identified as being "from China." Chinese and Korean scholars and officials graced Japan's court as authorized guests.

The sheep's stride conventionally referred to the passage of time.

The poem, laid out in nine short lines within the upper half of the gilded sheet, suggests the moment-to-moment repetition of time coming and going. The name of the poet is placed in the opening between the clouds in the lower half.

MONKEY
Monk Sarumaru

The name Sarumaru is a takeoff on the poet Sarumaru Dayū, one of the Thirty-Six Saints of Poetry.

Monkeys have a long association with red because of their bottoms. This color-coding is transferred to persimmons, with which monkeys are often coupled, as in this screen painting. The monkey's gaping mouth and wide-open eyes—supposedly staring at the moon—have an intensity that mimics portraits of Daruma and other Zen monks. The monkey, clad in a monk's garb, leans on the tree with his left hand, while holding a twig in his right.

moon in the dead of night
mountain chill blowing down
pierces through my body
pondering autumnal thoughts
a monkey cries out

The mountain wind in autumn that makes the body shiver is an often-repeated metaphor in *waka*, but here it is combined with the cry of the monkey, a set phrase in classical Chinese poetry that conveys the desolation of a mountainous landscape. The monkey in the form of a monk is both the source of that heartrending utterance as well as its listener.

The poem is shaped in a square block consisting of five lines, not unlike standard four-line Chinese poetry.

ROOSTER
Barrier Official Tokitsune

Seki or "barrier" refers to remote checkpoints, typically manned by lonely guards. From ancient times, such guards were used to voice isolation and sometimes to symbolize the barriers hindering the rendezvous of lovers.

The name Tokitsune suggests "time announcer," a phrase mimicking a rooster's cry.

The rooster walks in front of a brushwood fence with bamboo in the background. He wears an everyday kimono of purple (now faded to a brownish hue). On his head is a small hat secured with a strap around his chin, giving the appearance of a nō actor with the mask of a rooster.

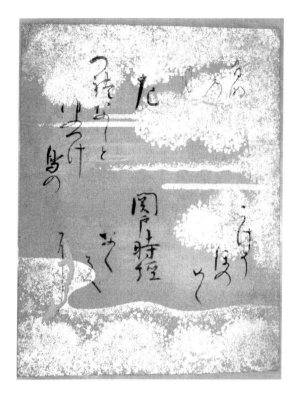

alone
the rooster
crows at dusk
moonlight dimming
at the crack of dawn

The poem achieves a balanced mix of sound (crowing at dusk) and sight (the moonlight dimming as dawn breaks).

This poem observes the *waka* tradition of dawn forcing lovers to part.

The calligraphy scatters the poem into four segments of different shapes as though obscured by clouds. The poet's name comes in the middle.

DOG
House Watchdog Tarō

The poet's title refers to a house watchman. Tarō, a name typically given to the first son, was also not an uncommon name for dogs.

Attired in a crested kimono and small hat appropriate to a house guard, he sits outside a brushwood fence guarding a thatched-roof cottage.

I bark at flowers
but never at the moon
how can people claim
I gaze only at
the stars?

Stargazing implies having "high hopes" beyond reasonable expectations. The dog's attitude is self-deprecating yet prideful, relating a playful complaint about the way he is perceived.

In the original order of the source story, the dog loses against the dragon, shedding an ironic light on the dog's high hopes.

The calligraphy divides the poem into two parts, each in two to three flowing lines.

BOAR
Attack-Samurai Ide Hanakata

An attack-samurai referred either to a young man or to someone serving at court without a formal title. The *i* in the family name Ide is homophonous with the word "boar."

His name, Hanakata, means "solid nose." The boar was characterized by its snout because of its size as well as the animal's acute sense of smell.

Although the poem has the wild boar reclining in bed, the painting depicts him seated outside, in a rice field with raised paths and cut stalks, gazing at the moon. Sword girded at his side, he is clad in the armor of a distinguished samurai. Typical of such outfits, his helmet is crowned with a wild boar sculpture as magic emblem to imbue the wearer with the courage to thrust forward and attack.

Unlike in traditional portraits of poets, this boar is shown from behind.

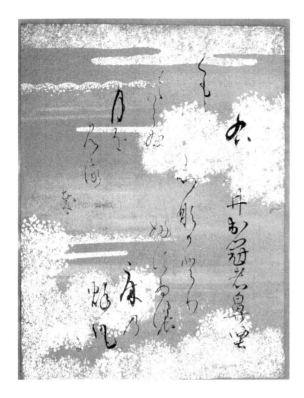

the wild boar
sprawls out on his bed
autumn winds blow through
as he stares at the moon
untouched by clouds

The first word of the poem is an archaic epithet for "boar."

The autumn wind functions as a pivot, first adding to the humor of the wild boar stretched out on a bed, then serving as an instrument of clearing the clouds for a full view of the moon.

The calligraphy is divided into two parts with the second part shown diagonally above the first.

TRANSLATED BY JOHN SOLT

Twenty Local Paragons of Filial Impiety

IHARA SAIKAKU

The unfilial behavior of twenty sons and daughters is the single thread running through the stories in Ihara Saikaku's *Twenty Local Paragons of Filial Impiety* (*Honchō Nijū Fukō*, 1686, prologue dated 1687). Linked by this theme rather than by character, this collection became an enduring template for Saikaku, one he would return to several more times, as with *The Great Mirror of Male Love* (*Nanshoku Ōkagami*, 1687), focusing on male homoeroticism, and *Tales of Samurai Duty* (*Buke Giri Monogatari*, 1688), focusing on samurai honor.

The title of the work is, in fact, a pun on *Twenty-Four Paragons of Filial Piety* (Japanese: *Nijūshi Kō*; Chinese: *Ershisi Xao*), a set of Chinese stories of devotion to parents that was well known in Japan through adaptations in books of bedtime stories (*otogizōshi*) during the Middle Ages and easy reading books (*kanazōshi*) just before Saikaku. Among the most memorable of the paragons are Wang Xiang, who in the dead of winter lay down naked on a frozen river to melt the ice with his body heat so that his stepmother could have fresh fish; Meng Zong, whose tears brought fresh bamboo shoots out of frozen ground for his ailing mother; Wu Meng, who refused to shoo mosquitoes away from his flesh, hoping that the sated insects would leave his parents alone; and pauper Guo Ju and his wife, who were prepared to bury their infant son alive so as to conserve money for the support of Guo Ju's mother—when they dug, they found buried treasure. As these examples indicate, the *Twenty-Four Paragons* stories, full of pathetic self-sacrifice and virtue miraculously rewarded, were calculated to instruct and inspire, the outrageousness of the turns of events naturally encouraging parody.

Saikaku's book was also indebted to *Twenty-Four Japanese Paragons of Filial Piety* (*Yamato Nijūshi Kō*), a 1665 work attributed to Asai Ryōi (d. 1691) that advanced a series of examples of filial piety from the Japanese past by way of showing that this particular virtue was not unknown in Japan. Saikaku's title echoes Ryōi's, and one of the phrases in Saikaku's prologue ("O my fellow creatures in this life") conspicuously mocks Ryōi's straight-faced usage of the phrase.

But in spite of the fun Saikaku has at the expense of the *Twenty-Four Paragons*' solemnity, *Twenty Local Paragons of Filial Impiety* does not deny the fundamental moral principles expressed in the original Chinese stories. Saikaku's impious heroes and heroines sin against their parents, but not in ways that cast virtue itself in any dubious light, nor do they escape unpunished. Indeed, most of them suffer quite severely for their misbehavior. Saikaku avows a didactic purpose in his prologue, and he may not be joking.

What complicates the book, however, is Saikaku's tone. For while the events narrated in the stories are no laughing matter, the narration itself brims over with Saikaku's characteristic verbal verve. His ostensible purpose is instruction, but what he really gives the reader is entertainment. Characters commit moral crimes and are punished, often by death. This makes the book sound vindictive in the extreme, nothing more than a pandering to the reader's worst instincts— either moral superiority or morbid curiosity. And in the hands of a lesser writer it might have devolved into precisely that. But Saikaku is a master, and he is able to find a delicate balance. He satisfies the reader's voyeuristic desire to witness freakishly bad behavior, and in his depiction of antisocial acts engaged in without remorse he provides (at least until the ends of the stories) vicarious liberation for readers caught in restrictive social situations, but the sad ends his characters come to prevent the book from becoming a celebration of evil. On the other hand, he injects the stories with a lightness of tone, a humor and gaiety, that saves the book from too heavy a concentration on guilt and punishment. The horror, the disgust, the titillation, the didacticism, and the vindictiveness are all mutually resolved by the narration's dark humor.

Not that there are no contradictions left behind: there are. In effect, Saikaku is encouraging us to enjoy both his protagonists' defiance and their comeuppance, to root both for his transgressors and against them. Readers who allow themselves to be thus led on by Saikaku might well be accused of moral inconsistency. But we should not be surprised to find Saikaku catering to such inconstancy. He is a past master at exploring the ways in which the urge to pleasure trumps the requirements of propriety. This is perhaps most obvious in *Twenty Local Paragons of Filial Impiety.*

Saikaku was a virtuous prose stylist, but he was a poet before he was a storyteller, and a poet noted for his particularly outlandish, even difficult, imagery. His prose bears the marks of his poetic tastes, emphasizing wordplay that is sometimes nearly impossible to fully untangle, and a tone that veers playfully, even crazily, from high to low, refined to slangy, orthodox to experimental. In addition to that, he tells funny stories. This translation attempts to convey the humor of Saikaku's style while hinting at its complexity. In doing so, it deploys puns, archaic diction, campy (and sometimes sincere) poetic language, and other unorthodox stylistic choices.

The "Ourang-Outang" of the final installment translated here refers to a legendary Chinese creature, called *shōjō* in Japanese, that has bright red fur, seems to speak human language, and has a liking for alcoholic drink. Some theories hold that this *shōjō* may ultimately been inspired by the orangutan of the Indonesian islands, and in modern Japanese, *shōjō* is one word used for the great ape. In having his Nagasaki drinkers name their club after this legendary beast, Saikaku is clearly playing on its penchant for alcohol. But given the association of Nagasaki in the public mind at the time with Dutch traders coming from some of the islands in the East Indies, it is possible that Saikaku was also thinking of the real animal, which would nevertheless have been as unfamiliar to his audience as the legendary beast. The deliberately outmoded spelling "ourang-outang" (used in Edgar Allen Poe's "The Murders in the Rue Morgue") is meant to suggest this mix of the outright exotic and the tantalizingly almost-familiar, so characteristic of works by Saikaku.

PROLOGUE

The greengrocer has your snowbound bamboo shoots; your carp are swimming in tanks at the fishmonger's. Without praying for anything unnatural, even the most average of people can work each at their own trades and, with their wages, arrange everything they need to fully demonstrate their filial piety. And yet the average are rare and evildoers common. O my fellow creatures in this life, if you know not the way of filial piety, you cannot hope to escape Heaven's blame. I have seen and heard examples from every province of our brethren whose impiety has been made manifest in sin. These have I committed to print, and would that they might help exhort you unto filial piety.

The first day of the fourth year of Jōkyō [1687]

BOOK 1, NO. 2

Rain from Pawned Sleeves at Year's End

A BROOM MAKER IN FUSHIMI WHOSE SUBSTANCE WAS SWEPT AWAY

Poor houses always plant peaches, and they flourish in Fushimi, in Yamashiro. But of old, in the village of Sumizome, it was the cherries that bloomed, luring people there even from the capital to begrudge the setting of the sun. Tipplers, to be sure, and even teetotalers would be so moved by spring's fleeing that they would daily exchange cups of parting, the people changing but the trees remaining the same. Unceasingly, drops would drip, in themselves lighter than dew, but as they accumulated, they sank into the sandy soil, beneath it to become a river flowing over the roots. And, alas, the cherries withered, leaving only their name. The Sumizome spring was in the garden among them and provided water for Lord Hideyoshi's tea, but now it is just a well at a crossroads on the way to the capital, and the town itself grows lonelier and lonelier.

In this place there lived, in a ramshackle dwelling, a man called Firepot

Bunsuke, who made his living busily fashioning bamboo brooms. He had no robes with which to endure the windy morns and eves, and kept himself alive on frosty nights only with his little banked fire, and so he was always called Firepot, instead of his proper name.

O sorry state! Come year's end, he made no rice cakes, displayed no pine boughs, his kindling rack was as bare as if swept with a broom, and his rice chest? It was empty. He envied those who could participate in the annual robe-bestowal, who could hang Tango yellowtail in their kitchens, for he and his wife were buffeted by the waves of age, and could do nothing to alleviate their misery but only wish their children might be able to celebrate the New Year with thick willow chopsticks. Disconsolate were they.

One's living is never assured, sad to say. For several years this village had raised something called early peaches: from spring's first budding the villagers would wait anxiously for the arrival of autumn, when with the fruit not yet fully ripe on the boughs they would send it on to the Cicada Street greengrocers in the capital, for a great return on their sales. For several years they had greeted the New Year in ease. But the great winds on the twenty-third day of the eighth month had uprooted all the trees, and there was no harvest this year. And though their sufferings were only such as were common in the world, they felt themselves afflicted above all, with nails all that remained of their roof. When the autumn rains came, by opening the lid of a chest that had gone curiously unsold, the family of five packed themselves in it, a wooden pillow propping open the lid, their breathing restricted even so. "Lost in the darkness of this world, they were. How very distressing." But it was no use complaining.

He owned his house, but he couldn't sell it without buyers. And yet he couldn't very well let a house four *ken* wide go for nothing. "If someone offered me even a little drinking money for it—fifty or even thirty *monme*—I'd take it. If this same house were by the boat landing at Capital Bridge, it'd bring six thousand *monme*—the distance of eighteen *chō* makes all the difference," he said, cursing his location. Hating himself and his life as he lived it, he considered what was to become of him. "Eternally I pine for the shogun, may he live as long the pine, to visit the capital again in all his munificence. I won't leave this house," he said, stubbornly.

This man had three children. His scion was named Buntazaemon, and he had turned twenty-seven this year. He was a long-legged, large man with a naturally bushy beard on his cheeks, and flashing eyes: his expression when he laughed was more frightful than most men's when they fight. He was thick-thewed, to boot, so that were he merely to put his shoulder into it, he could not fail to support his parents. But with his frame such as to scare men, he elbowed his way into the gambling dens, where his body assured him of getting by, if only by cajolery.

This man was a great villain. One summer night in his sixteenth year, his younger sister was fanning him; she was only seven years of age, and her hands had little strength, and so her fanning made but a listless wind. He took her by the neck and flung her: she struck a stone mortar in the garden, forcefully: her breathing stopped, her pulse gave out, and she died on the spot. His mother bawled without restraint and clung to her body, even thinking to end her own life; however, the youngest sister, only five, and with but a child's understanding, clung to her sleeve and wept, and her mother pitied her greatly. As his mother wondered what would become of them, a neighbor came by to ask, "What is it?" She calmed herself and said: "A wound like that—it must have been her time. There's nothing to be done." They held a hurried funeral and concealed the girl's remains.

Then, in his twenty-seventh year, he had his way with another man's woman: nightly he made his way from Kurumamichi to the hamlet of Takeda. His mother heard of this and admonished him: "Have a care for your life!" But one morning, returning at dawn, he kicked his mother, so that from then on she could neither stand nor sit as she would have wished, and she saw out her remaining years in futility. The youngest daughter, now grown up, brought her hot water and tea; she was most filially pious.

Buntazaemon left it to his father to make their living, so as not to interrupt his own pleasant sleep—not once did he see a morning glory in bloom. Then he'd shoot his father a glare and say, "Life's short, Dad." People all hated him, and pointed at him, and called him ignorant of Heaven's decrees—but no good did it do. Karmically governed are parents and children. Letting such a child live on in the same house, letting him insist on eating what they did not have, letting this continue for months and days—finally came the day beyond which Bunsuke could not live, without even firewood enough to heat water. He lay down, prepared for the end.

His wife sorrowed for their daughter. She summoned a woman who could place people, and revealed their circumstances. "Save her life: put us in service to a good merchant family," she begged, and the agent wrung her sleeves and said, "I'll do it—I won't even take my tenth." So she took them—the mother could not stand, so she had to carry her. It's enough to make you cry.

The girl was clever, but small, and could find no master who would pay her enough for two. "What's the use if I alone am saved?" she thought, and returned to her mother. Then she whispered to the agent, "I know I am uncomely, but there's employment for all types—why not sell me to a brothel?" Touched by her kind disposition, the agent replied, "Whatever you do, as long as you do it for your parents…" She took the girl to a brothel called the Ichimonjiya in Shimabara where they listened to her particulars and had mercy on her. "You're not much of a woman, but your heart's in the right place—you'll go far." They advanced her twenty *ryō* for the usual term of service.

She returned to Fushimi and gave this money to her mother, who wept. "It's not unheard of in the world, but still, to let one's daughter sell herself so that one can grow old on the proceeds…" The agent remonstrated with her for a while and then left, after which the girl's mother was gladdened by her daughter's kindness. The next day was the twenty-ninth of the twelfth month, and she set her heart to buying all manner of things. The merchants heard of this, as is their wont, and a bale from the rice seller was brought to the yard; miso, salt, and *sake* were brought; even the fishmonger, from whom they'd been so long estranged, dropped by to ask if they needed anything; so for a little while, it was "there's nothing like money." But that very joyful night, Buntazaemon, the scion of the house, stole the twenty *ryō* in gold and disappeared, no one knew where. Morning came soon after, and the last day of the year found the household in just this state, unable to complete their purchases: everything was repossessed. Like a dream, it was all in the past.

With nothing else to do, the couple stole out of their home and went down by the Six Jizō, thinking to make them their guides to the next world; they went to an open field near Abbot Kōsen's temple, and there they sat. They meditated on far and near: how in the far past of a previous life they must have been guilty of greed and miserliness, so that in the near present they were subject to the Torment of Seeking and Not Obtaining. They repeated the Buddha's name in prayer for that which is to come, and then they bit off their tongues. Their bodies belonged to the wild dogs.

Everybody hated Buntazaemon then, saying, "He must be heading east—don't let him pass the Ōsaka Gate!" They chased him but couldn't find him; empty-handed, they returned by way of Matsubara in Awazu.

Buntazaemon, who, knowing nothing of all this, could do nothing about it, had stolen into the nearby Shumoku neighborhood, where he got carried away with his own New Year's purchases. He assembled numerous prostitutes and until the Day of Seven Herbs showered them with money—until there was none left. Then, at a loss, he retreated, bound for the village of Uji. But on the way he stumbled across the scene of his parents' death—his knees went weak, his body trembled and writhed, his eyes swam, and he fell. The wolves feasting on his parents' corpses came over and gnawed on him the whole night through. Indeed, it was a miserable thing. Numerous wolves ate him, right down to the joints, right down to the bones. And there by the side of the highway in Wolf Hollow lay his bones—arranged neatly in the shape of a man, fully exposing Buntazaemon's shame.

Wolves wage a fitting attack on an unfilial son. (National Diet Library)

What a tale, and what an unfilial son—unparalleled in all the world! Oh, the horror, so swiftly did Heaven punish him! We must watch ourselves indeed!

BOOK 2, NO. 2

"I Am a Priest at the End of My Road"

A GRASS HUT IN KUMANO WITH A NICE LITTLE GIRL

"Blow, snow, blow, and hail, o hail," they sang, the little village girls, gathering it up in their little skirts as the storm gathered in the shadow of the pines, the cold not in the littlest bothering them in their unsewn undersleeves as they begrudged the gathering dusk. A traveling monk, on a pilgrimage to Kumano, having traversed the hardest mountain passes, now finally reached the foothills. He approached the children, calling out in ragged voice, "Is it far to the next house?" Seeing that he could hardly stand, the children ran home.

Among them was Kogin, daughter of Kandayū of the village of Iwane; she had just turned nine, and she said, all grown-up, "Just a little farther and you'll reach our place. We'll offer you a bath." She helped the renunciate, and guided him, until they reached her home. Her parents came out, pleased with the girl's thoughtfulness and full of pity for the traveler. They made a brushwood fire and made him at home.

Delivered from his exhaustion, the teacher of the dharma, with boundless joy and peaceful heart, retied his oilcloth bundle and slung it over his shoulder, saying, "I hail from Fukui, in Echizen country. Last year I was parted from both my parents, and so I rejected the world and put on these inky robes, but always have they been wet with my tears. I travel all lands so that at least I may give their remains repose. Again, I thank you for your kindness." He pressed his palms together and bowed, and then departed into the night. And when he was gone, the girl said: "That holy priest has a pile of coins in a leather sack in his bundle. I saw him put it in. He's alone, so nobody will know. Kill him and take his gold!" As she whispered this, an unexpected lust arose in her father's heart, and he took up his machete and the spear he kept by his pillow and followed the priest's trail.

How evil this little girl, to urge such a thing on her father, at the age of nine! And, also, she was raised in a mountain hut in Kumano, where they think dried bream grows on trees and know not what umbrellas are for—and yet she recognized money. Mysterious indeed!

The renunciate hitched high the skirts of his robe and parted the dry grass as he crossed the wide meadow. It was night on this eighteenth day of the eleventh month, and no moon shone on his road; he pressed forward by guesses. Then there were footfalls on a sideway: suspicious, he stopped in his tracks. A big man unsheathed his spear and flew at him. As the priest fled, he looked back, and, much to his surprise, it was his host who had treated him so mercifully before.

"I have renounced the world, and so I do not begrudge you my life. But what cause have you against me, that you seek to harm me so? If it's my traveling money you'd take, I'll give it willingly in exchange for my life." So saying, he flung down his hundred *ryō* just like that. The man received it, saying, "Think of it this way—money's your enemy in this world," stabbing him through the belly on one side at the same time. The priest raised his voice, painfully: "You! My last thought—and before long—woe, oh, woe!" His breath as he spoke grew weaker until he collapsed there on the shore of the fens. His attacker held him down and finished him off, then sank his corpse beneath the duckweed. Secretly he returned home, and none were the wiser.

After that, his house prospered: he became the sole owner of a bullock and acquired paddies and fields; from the flowering of the cotton to the ripening of the rice, he passed the days and months as he wished. Kogin greeted the spring of her fourteenth year with a complexion the hue of cherry blossoms, and when she made it up, she stood out even more in that little mountain village: suitors beyond number had she. But pride in her looks made her choosy about men and, in the end, she settled on none. She conducted herself untidily and, sad to say, was ill reputed.

Her parents admonished her again and again, but never would she mind them. "Our prosperity is due to my cleverness!" she'd say, touching on the gravest of matters. Although she was their own child, her parents could not control her.

Then once, all by herself, she spotted a man and said, "Now, him I might." "As she wishes, come what may," they thought, and prevailed on someone to get him for her. "Not an ill-gotten groom, when it comes to getting on in the world," they concluded, joyfully. Once the troth had been drunk and concluded, however, she took a dislike to a scar the man had, from a growth behind his ear, hardly to be seen. She ran away to her aunt's house in Wakayama. Her parents didn't dare keep her at home, and so she was sent to a samurai mansion as a maidservant.

But she was wayward and did not scruple to beguile the master even in front of his wife, and before long she had made him hers. For the wife's part, she was a warrior's daughter through and through: she put it down as the way of the world and let it pass, pretending not to know. But Kogin was only incited further and would not stop until the house was thrown into disarray. Then, fearing what the world might say, this inseparable couple discussed the matter: the master apologized for everything, set his heart to rights, and thenceforth steadfastly refused to venture down that road again. Kogin resented the mistress deeply, and one night, chosen for when the master would be on duty and away, she crept to her mistress's pillow, where she lay dreaming. With the wife's own protecting sword, Kogin stabbed her through the chest. Astonished, the mistress cried, "You'll not get away!" and unsheathed her halberd and chased her into the courtyard. But Kogin had prepared her escape and was not to be found. The mistress writhed and struggled, but her wound was deep, and she failed rapidly, having only breath to say "Cut down that Kogin!" two or three times before life left her.

The women sleeping in the next room awoke only after it was over. "What's happened?" they wailed, but in vain. Though they sent pursuers along the road by which Kogin had fled, she'd made good her escape—quite bravely, for a woman.

The order went out that "Until Kogin shows herself, her parents are to be imprisoned," and so their misery was put on display. But never did she

The lady's killer escapes the mansion. (National Diet Library)

come out. And so their sentence was pronounced: "Execution on the eighteenth day of the eleventh month." The official in charge of their imprisonment pitied them, saying, "It is your child who has brought you to this pass. Prepare yourselves to meet your end. Pray for the world to come." All night long he offered them *sake,* and they accepted it graciously, not once bemoaning their fate.

"Others I have seen who, being put to death for their crimes, spoke not of their evil, but only lamented. But you—you are in this sad state in place of your child," he then said. But they told him it was their karma for the killing of a renunciate, saying, "Tomorrow it will be seven years, to the month and day: this is as it should be." And so they made up their minds, and their resignation and the depth of their feelings at that moment, evildoers though they were, deeply moved all those around them.

And so they were hurried down that road we may none of us avoid, and their heads were cut off. The next day, their daughter, having heard about her parents, came out of hiding. She, too, was killed.

Where could she have gone to hide, hunted as she was? And yet she hid. "If only you'd shown yourself, your parents would've got off without a scratch! Never has there been a woman like you!" Everyone hated her.

BOOK 3, NO. 3

In the Shape of a Serpent It Swallowed His Heart

IN UTSUNOMIYA, A LACQUERER STUCK TO HIS GREED

The last month of the year, the thirteenth day. Starting at dawn, everybody was preparing the house for New Year's Day, beating the mats and cleaning away soot; makeshift bamboo-grass brooms were covered in dust, while the people of the house were coated head to toe in dirt. So they heated a bath. "The water's fine," the fine lady of the house announced. The man of the house heard and said: "Fresh bathwater's poison. Have Dad get in first." It had been in his heart, and now he let it slip.

From this we know all there is to know about his lack of filial piety. He lived in a place called Utsunomiya, in Michinoku, and he was a merchant known as Budayū the Lacquerer. In the beginning, he would put a little sulfur and some lampwicks in a sack on his back and go up into the mountains to the huts there. This was how he made his living, but after only four or five years he struck it rich, such that people marveled. But he was an unobjectionable man in most things, and so no one suspected him. They simply whispered that "he must have found the god Daikoku's sack or gotten a fox to grant him good fortune." There's no accounting for other people's luck.

And yet there are all sorts of ways to be rich. If a man does not distinguish himself from the rest of the world but wears raiment appropriate to his station, eats fish and fowl when they're in season, raises up his poor relations, has pity for those below him, celebrates the gods, yearns after the Buddha's way, displays kindness to his parents, never falters in his duty to others, and is humble in all things, then to be rich is the bountiful blessing of Heaven, as well as the true desire of man.

Observe the ways of this world: few are the men in it who live according to this truth. Rather, a man's house prospers for a while, and ruination follows soon after. Whether or not a man can live out his life honestly by his trade depends solely on the disposition of his heart.

This Budayū, suddenly flush, forgot the past and seized the moment. He behaved self-indulgently, and people around him grew to hate him, so that he lost touch with all his relations. But at home he was shogun, living without a care for heat or cold.

How did Budayū come into this fortune? One day, up among the mountain hamlets, he followed the Ōkuma River upstream and then continued along a small tributary of it until he found its source: a deep ravine, enclosed by sharp crags—a waterfall, thundering in his ears. Thick were the trees there, and dark was their shadow; dew from their leaf tips fell incessantly like autumn rains. Even in summer, the water, down deep, was cold enough to shatter ice.

In this river lived mountain trout, and Budayū, a skilled swimmer, would go in and catch them by hand. He often served them to guests. Once, when searching for them in what he took to be a deep pool, he saw something black, looming like a mountain in his gaze: he grasped it and brought it to the surface. It was lacquer sap, which had flowed downriver year after year, hardening there. He secretly made dishes out of it, his own private treasure, which he carried back and sold. It was simply his for the taking—as was the money he made from it, which accumulated until, before long, he had no room to keep it all.

People had become suspicious, and his greed was as deep as it was cunning, so he had a craftsman fashion a dragon, and he placed it in the water. The dragon moved as if alive, and after several days, when he came to look at it, it moved its mouth, stretched out its tail, and bared its claws: terrifying, even though he knew it for what it was.

He went home and told this to his father, who admonished him, saying, "Man's greed knows no bounds! What more could you want? Cease this at once!" So Budayū came to resent his father.

Budayū had one son, named Busuke, age fourteen, and he took him with him to the pool. There he told him everything, bidding him to "learn to gather

The lacquer-guarding dragon turns on Budayū and his son. (National Diet Library)

lacquer, like I do." Father and son entered the water, but the aforementioned dragon now had a spirit: it took Busuke in its mouth and thrashed him about. Budayū saw this and, grieved, dived beneath the duckweed, so that they both died. Forty-eight hours passed, and their bodies came up, and all who saw them detested Budayū as an embarrassment to his parents. Everyone said it was awful.

These events came to official notice, and Budayū's house was discontinued "for the crime of thus arrogating things to himself these several years." His parents were turned out, and though their lives were spared, they lived sorrowfully in this floating world. His wife, who had no relatives, became a beggar straightaway, showing up on people's doorsteps without reflecting on her shame. "She treated her mother-in-law badly," everyone said, and turned her away without giving her so much as used water, so that before long she starved to death.

BOOK 4, NO. 1

The Dual Wheels of Good and Evil

IN HIROSHIMA, PARTNERS IN PROFLIGACY

Good friends are scarce—but not evil companions, no indeed. And these two partners? Hearts alike, deep as the sea, they habitually crossed to the isle of Miyajima in the province of Aki, where they scorched their flesh with the mania for courtesans, five *ri* by swift boat in less time than it takes to burn an inch of match rope, a well-matched party, revelers every night. Inside and out, there could not be two so alike in all the wide world—nay, nor yet in Hiroshima.

One was called Jinshichi of the Bitchūya, and one was called Genshichi of the Kanadaya. Both still dependent on their parents, they knew nothing of making a living in this floating world. They used up gold and silver that had taken years to store up, stealing from themselves. Although they were once known as local grandees, soon their houses decayed, and in a little over ten years they were ruined. Their fathers, who in the prime of youth had mastered many hardships, now found themselves with no provision for old age, nor anyone to depend on, and their twice-daily cookfires faltered.

Jinshichi and Genshichi each had younger sisters of marriageable age. The boys stole the raiment and accouterments prepared by their mothers: they sold them, and the silver proceeds became property of the brothels. No one wants a naked bride, and so the girls were sent out as maidservants, admiring the world's kindly, paternal brothers and hating their own.

Ice in the southern sun is soon only water, and this money, too, soon flowed through their hands. Too poor even to blow coals, they were buffeted

in their breasts by the waves of year-end worries. On the night before the beginning of spring, despite the darkness, Jinshichi and Genshichi donned
paper-cloth headkerchiefs, and in tandem they went out exorcising for alms.

There's no training for begging: they'd endure shame undying for life.
"Dongfang Shuo lived nine thousand years!" they bellowed in droll voices.
But even at this they proved unlucky: by dawn, after all their running around,
they had only eighteen *mon* and two hundred roasted beans between them.
"This'll get us nowhere in the world!" So, instead of the exorcist's cry of "hi-
de-ho, to the West Sea go," it was "hi-de-hey, in the West you stay" for their
parents, as Genshichi and Jinshichi left them there—they left their homes.
But by the time they reached Okayama in Bizen, their travel funds were spent:
they had to plant their feet here, become sleeve-tugging beggars. But still their
past shone through in their well-groomed pates, their fair complexions, their
neatly trimmed temples, and as they stood at gates, they drew wondering stares
and rude cries of "Go on, get moving!" They had no place to put themselves,
and as they recalled their past glory, they wept, men though they were, and
their tears leaked through their rain gear, and they were ashamed before the
gazes of passersby.

In those days, Heart Learning was burgeoning in Bizen: men's hearts were
humble, and those loyal to lords and filial to parents found themselves blessed
by those above; people spontaneously entered into that Way, and thus the
realm was governed. And so our pair, their wits about them, enlisted two
homeless outcasts. Jinshichi made a cripple cart and placed one of them upon
it, an old man of seventy or more: as soon as he entered the streets of the town,
Jinshichi began to shed tears, crying, "My country is Aki, my age twenty-three.
But what is my karma that I can't support my father? Barefaced, I beg you:
have pity on us." His voice seemed so sad, and his cries so sincere, that alms
poured in, coins and rice overflowing from the cart.

Genshichi, too, shouldered an oldster and took a walk around. The people
were all touched and had pity on him. And so they were able to make an enclosure of thin bamboo on the edge of the fields, and to roof it with rotten
wood that they found, until it took the shape of a hermitage, a home of their
own where they could take shelter from the rain and dew. "Consider how until
yesterday we slept looking up at the clouds: can there be any pleasure to exceed
tonight's?" they said, as they scooped marsh water into an earthen pot to cook
together the things they had received. There was unhulled rice, new rice, red
rice, twice-cracked wheat, red beans, and more—myriad colors, as elegantly
matched as a simple rice bowl and a bamboo-lattice window. "While there's
life, there's food," as they say, and with their bellies full, they could scarce wish
for more.

Jinshichi made his old man massage him: all night long he kept him

While Jinshichi mistreats the beggar man, Genshichi honors him like a father. (National Diet Library)

fanning away mosquitoes, making no allowance for weariness. When he fell asleep, Jinshichi kicked him in the ribs, saying, "All you had to do was act crippled!" Jinshichi was hard on his old man, but Genshichi took great care of his. "Now there, you have no reason to treat him like that. You've named him your father—and what's more, it's only thanks to him that you've been spared from starvation for today. You owe him a debt of gratitude—you shouldn't forget that." So conscientiously did Genshichi treat the old man that Jinshichi became resentful. From then on they kept a bamboo-grass divider between them, and not a pine ember would one lend the other.

It would seem that Heaven illuminates all truth and is mindful of good and evil. Before long, Jinshichi stopped receiving people's charity and went utterly broke. Genshichi, though, got more each day, handouts to his heart's desire, so that in the end he need not go out in the rain and wind. He exerted himself in filial piety toward the old man just as if he were his own father. The other old man saw this and bewailed the world and hated Jinshichi. He made up his mind: "Today'll be the end of it: I'll bite off my tongue and die."

This man had not always been so poor. One day when Jinshichi was out, he told a tale of his past to Genshichi: "There were particular circumstances behind my becoming a *ronin*, sequestering myself, and being now thus straitened." Helpless tears spilled down his cheeks. "I have no regrets in dying, but at least hide my body so that the dogs and wolves won't dig it up," he begged. Genshichi pitied him even more, and he said, "Don't worry about that, I beg you, come what may. As long as I am here, you shall not be badly disposed of. Let it not weigh on you in the least." He spoke so sincerely that the old man pressed together his palms and bowed to him, saying, "For joy, for joy!" and bejeweling his sleeve with tears.

Just then a traveler arrived, mounted, but with a palanquin. He stopped and stood, as if to attend to some business, and gazed awhile at the old man's visage. "Sir, are you Hashimoto Takumi?" he said, embracing him. "Kin'ya?" the old man said—the ties of fate binding father to son were yet unbroken. "How boundless my joy at finding you here! I have been down to Musashi, where I strove mightily for employment, but it was long in coming, and I had to look here, there, and everywhere for it. Finally my hope was answered, and an eastern lord appointed me for my former income of five hundred *koku*. Now I have taken my leave to come for you, though I was granted only fifty days, and many of them have already passed. But now here you are, proof that my warrior's fortune has not yet deserted me." He rejoiced, and as the old man told him of his recent difficulties, tears dropped ceaselessly.

Jinshichi came back then and was astonished. Kin'ya took him and bound him. "You—have you no mercy? I should not leave you your life—instead I'll let you ponder what awaits you at the end of it." He destroyed the hermitage until the plain was left as before. As for Genshichi, Kin'ya was moved by his goodwill. "I shall take you on myself," he said. The other old man, too, his legs being aged, he let ride in the palanquin, and so they went down to the east.

What was left? A chipped bowl, a shell ladle, an old mat, and the morning dew and evening wind to torment Jinshichi in his misery. This story became known, and he was run out of the region. There were few places he could go. The snows that year found him on the outskirts of the Shosha Temple grounds in Harima, where he collapsed and died.

BOOK 5, NO. 2

The Ourang-Outang Octet

IN NAGASAKI, AN INKER WHO WAS A STAIN UPON HIMSELF

In the port of Nagasaki, where the waves beat a colorful tattoo, there gathered eight well-known tipplers, setting out two casks, one of sweet *sake* and one of dry, there amidst the *sake* merchants' cedar signs to dance attendance on Matsu-no-o the Great God of Drink, and they bound themselves together as the Ourang-Outang League.

Jinzaburō the Eight-Forked Serpent, Kannai the Sotted Lad, Tōsuke the Japanese Su Shi, Moriemon the Ever-Dreaming, Shihei the Triple-Blissful, Rokunoshin the *Sake* Measuring Cup, Kyūzaemon the Angry Drunk, and Mum-Wine's-the-Word Kikubei—this was the assembly that from the first day of the year to the last never spent a moment unsoused, whose members would dispose of their auld lang synes with their first cup, who while still sober would drop themselves to the bottom of the barrel, there to find every pleasure the world held for them. Amusement-loving men, men with a stomach for a dram, would envy them from afar, and none can tell how many such joined their ranks, only to corrupt their flesh and drink up their lives in strong drink.

At this time, a man from Kokura in Buzen had taken up residence in the city. He was Danbei the Inker, a drawer of import pictures by trade. He had been born into a long line of drinkers, and from the time he'd first been bidden to quaff the face-reddening stuff, he had never known a quaffer greater than himself.

At the age of nineteen he had gone up to the capital to drink in the Sanjūsangendō's drinking contest, modeled after its archery tournament, where the gusto with which he nocked back shots had people saying, "He's the Drinker to the Realm, equal of the great archers Hoshino Kanzaemon and

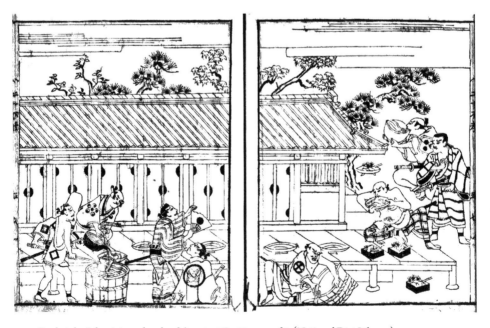

Danbei the Inker joins a drunkards' party at Sanjūsangendō. (National Diet Library)

Wasa Ōhachi!" His fame shot ever higher, and since the great brewer Tachibana had offered gold-leafed dried fish as a prize, Danbei raised it as though it were a golden battle baton. Thenceforth he prided himself on his drinking, and so he advanced to Nagasaki, city of sots, where he opened a cup shop. The weakest of teetotalers there would never lose to the champion drinkers of other lands.

Danbei crashed his way into the Ourang-Outangs, and for thirteen nights and days he drank, but he was among troopers: his weakness began to show, and he began to grow weary. Seeing him so stubborn, his mother admonished him, saying: "This is why I tell you to give up your drunken ways. Your father, Dan'emon, loved his liquor too, without letup, until once at a *go* tournament they drank from dusk to dawn, and he quarreled with an acupuncturist named Uchijima Kyūboku. It began as an argument about something insignificant, but they were both deep in their cups, and their words became so harsh that in the end they pierced each other, quitting this floating world, the laughing-stock of which they both became. Even in the darkness under the sod, his name was so ruined that even I, a woman, am incensed. I tell the story to my children and grandchildren, hoping they will never touch nary a drop of the stuff. But parent though I am, they never listen. You! How many times will you ignore my words? You overreach yourself in drunkenness! You're putting your very life in danger! Give it up, I pray you, and set at ease a mother's heart. And yet, I know you will never quit all at once. Therefore resolve yourself this summer to limit yourself to five cups at a time, three times a day and three times a night. That much will I allow you."

Danbei glared at his mother and said: "And will you be giving up your tea, then, woman? This is all the joy I have in the world. Why should I regret it, though I throw my life away in a bottle? If I die today, bathe my body in *sake* of the highest grade, lay me in an Itami keg for a coffin, and bury me on a blossom'd hillside or in a mapled glade where I can catch drips from the flasks of ramblers each spring and autumn! And since this is what I think of the life to come, how much the less shall I be able to forsake this pleasure in the present world?"

Thus he spoke, emptying another cup and another until he was thoroughly besotted, so that he slept for five, even seven days on end, laying aside entirely the things of the world. Even when this drove his mother to her death, he rose not from his pillow. He missed the hour of her passing. Only much later did he rouse from his dreams, when it was too late to lament her.

TRANSLATED BY GLYNNE WALLEY

Characters of Worldly Shop Clerks

EJIMA KISEKI

Ejima Kiseki (1666–1735) was a younger contemporary of Ihara Saikaku, the recognized giant of Edo-period comic fiction. Kiseki, like many writers of his time, recognized Saikaku's immense talent and copied both conceptually and verbatim from a number of his works. Yet Kiseki managed to take advantage of the rapidly expanding commercial publishing opportunities of his time that opened up only after the master's death, thereby eclipsing him in popularity for the remainder of the Edo period and beyond, until the rediscovery of the half-forgotten Saikaku by progressive writers toward the middle of the Meiji period.

The present translations are gleaned from one of Kiseki's later works, *Characters of Worldly Shop Clerks* (*Seken Tedai Katagi*, 1730), which is often cited as the fourth and last of his masterpieces in the character sketch (*katagimono*) form. A subcategory of "floating world" fiction, which held up entertainingly realistic mirrors to the authors' contemporary world, Kiseki's characters, too, show the world of the "townsman" merchants at the bottom of the official Edo social scale, although they controlled much of the society's wealth.

Kiseki focused on the genre's constant attention to character types rather than unique individuals. He made this the explicit focus of his seemingly endless variations on the form, often using material recycled from Saikaku and other writers. Kiseki's character pieces proved so popular that the form became the mainstay of Kamigata-based popular fiction and remained ascendant for a century or more, until the rise of the Edo-based prose genres at the end of the feudal era.

The stories translated below—"Silver Lost Down a Secret Gold Mine Shaft" (Horinuite Naishō ni Ana no Aku Kanayama no Songin) and "The Love-Town Tune, 'Only Death Can Stop Me,' Sung by a Bad News Son" (Irozato no Nagebushi Shinaza Yamumai Musuko ga Akushō)—are the first two of the second fascicle. They are also two of a total of fifteen stories that make up the work, which is broken into five fascicles—the character sketch's characteristic format. These two stories constitute the conclusion of a series of five interconnected stories concerning the fall and subsequent revival in the fortunes of a Kyoto-based kimono fabric shop, the Minoya.

When headed by the uncompromising old master and owner Shintoku, the shop enjoyed fabulous success and generated tremendous wealth. This was in no small part because of the labors of its honest, hardworking, and streetwise shop clerks, such as Tōsuke and Gohei, who step forward in the shop's time of need to oppose the shop's other star clerk, the talented but avaricious Jūbei. In earlier stories, Jūbei has skimmed a tenth of all the Minoya's income for himself so as to be able to launch his own shop. The conflict between Tōsuke and Jūbei forms one of the major plotlines in these excerpts. Tōsuke, Gohei, and Jūbei have each served as the focus of the three preceding stories, which describe their rise to prominence within the Minoya.

As the first of the two stories below begins, the old master Shintoku is dead, and his successor, a profligate son named Sanshichi who will form the other center of plot interest, is now free to waste his inheritance on revels in the Shimabara pleasure district (a taste and tendency he revealed at the end of the third tale of the first fascicle). Sanshichi's incorrigible and expensive lust for *sake* and women will usher in the crisis that will bring both the Minoya to the brink of bankruptcy and the Tōsuke-Jūbei battle to a head.

A modern reader's interest in these stories would not come from a superficial contemporary "realism," for the world of the Edo-period townsman is a thing of the distant past, even in the confines of the surviving silk merchants still to be found in modern Kyoto. What is as alive to a modern reader as it was to those in the eighteenth and nineteenth centuries, though, is Kiseki's comic sense, his use of situation, timing, and register. Kiseki's multiple plotlines develop and resolve at a quick pace, managing to lighten the mood of recounting awful fates. The insertion of moral disapproval was obligatory in view of government censors. As important as the speed of the narrative are its effortless shifts between high and low registers. One minute the narrator might wax lyrical on the poetic beauty of a scene, filling his prose with allusions to classical poetry and Chinese historical precedent. The next, he might weave into that allusive fabric characters or events that strike a comic contrast, drawing on the seamier side of human desire.

Although basic information on currency of the period is available in "Notes for the Reader," this translation in particular has a notable focus on specific monetary units. *Ryō, kanme, monme, zeni,* and *mon* refer to either monetary units, weights for counting money, or the counter for a kind of coin in the Edo period. In 1871 the yen officially replaced the *ryō* as legal tender in the Japanese monetary system, and at that time both the yen and the *ryō* were valued at 1.5 grams of pure gold. The *monme* was a basic unit of weight for measuring silver and at this time was equal to one-sixtieth of a *ryō*. The *kanme* was a unit of measurement equal to one thousand copper *zeni* coins, and the individual unit counter for *zeni* was *mon*. At this time, four *kanme* (also called *kan*)—and therefore four thousand *mon* of *zeni*—equaled one *ryō*.

(CF)

SILVER LOST DOWN A SECRET GOLD MINE SHAFT

It is as the wise men of old said: a seductive voice and beautiful looks easily lead a man astray; therefore, there is nothing that the young should more as-siduously avoid than the path of lust.

Sanshichi of the Minoya, after the death of his father, faced no great dif-ficulties. Lacking not in the least for money, he spent night and day immersed in debauchery, which spoke only too clearly, chief clerk Jūbei well discerned, of his irredeemable nature. A good time to withdraw, Jūbei surmised, to the confines of his own home and cease all comings and goings to and from the shop. To those who came to confer, he said that the looming disaster for a master such as Sanshichi, whose personal life was a mess, was only too clear, and that no matter how many times he had remonstrated with him, the man simply would not listen. What is more, Sanshichi himself had told Jūbei to stay away and cease coming altogether. There was no way, therefore, that Jūbei himself would make a move in that direction.

"I tell you," he said, "if I avoid that house for a month, the business will collapse. That would be a disgrace to the memory of the late master, but then what can you do?" So went his high-sounding explanation, one that main-tained his pretense of devoted loyalty, but it was just the words of a sycophantic toady.

When the news spread around town that the family fortune was already squandered and the house and holdings were to be put up for sale, many were the comments on the way of the world and how the mighty had fallen, but how sad for the late master! As preparation for his son's generation, he had built a house that would need little future upkeep—a stone well-curb and a metal-lined bucket, copper gutters along the eaves, the shingles shaved from clean knotless cypress—these being just some of the various precautions the old man had taken. But now because of the foul nature of this one child, all these would become the possessions of others. "You know," the village elders at their meeting each worried to one another, "this could well be our fates too."

A potential buyer there had already made an offer of nineteen *kan*, five hundred *me*, and the day for the changing of the title was about to be set when the house's chief clerk in Edo, Tōsuke, traveling night and day, came running. Not bothering even to stop in at his master's home, he came as he was, in his traveler's robes, bringing himself before the elders.

"To allow the late master's mortuary altar to pass into the hands of another would be too much to bear," he cried. "I beg you, please, go to this man to whom you have pledged the property and ask him please to understand. And I beg you as well to sell the master's house to me, for I will add another three hundred to the five hundred *me* that has been offered." The elders found this proposition only too reasonable, so they made their excuses to the would-be buyer and allowed the sale to Tōsuke to proceed.

Because of these doings concerning the main store in the capital, the branch establishment in Edo was closed and the great majority of the clerks there left after finding new masters. Tōsuke's determined retrenchment resulted in a shop a mere fragment of its former size but one that nevertheless continued to display the Minoya banner and insignia. Tōsuke's heartfelt desire was to win over to his cause the most promising among his fellow clerks, to return the firm to its small-shop beginnings to start anew, and in that way to relieve the late master of the load of bitterness no doubt weighing him down along his road to the afterlife. When Tōsuke spoke of what was in his heart to the creditors who had paid off the accumulated debt, they responded warmly to his request for further support, saying that they were moved by his lofty aim and that he could count on them to continue as before to ensure that he would have no lack of stock with which to compete.

Overjoyed, Tōsuke now entered the main house and replaced the young master Sanshichi's silk garments with cotton ones, dressing him on a par with his clerks. Including Sanshichi in all tasks, he sought to win back those patrons of Jūbei's that the latter had lured away from the Minoya. He purposely outfitted the young master in soiled cottons under a short outer coat of unstylish raw silk and the simple striped cotton trousers favored by merchants, seeing to it as well that Sanshichi's hair looked as if it hadn't been combed or coifed in recent memory. Then the two of them started out to make the rounds of their former patrons. As he lamented aloud the various misfortunes that had beset their firm, the potential buyers at their various stops gazed pityingly on the fallen Sanshichi, wondering to themselves about the fortunes of one who previously had worn nothing but new clothes that were unwashed because unworn, but whom the ravages of time had now brought so low as to leave him clothed in the coarsest of padded cottons.

"We beg you most humbly for this kind favor," pleaded Tōsuke and Sanshichi, their hands clasped before them. Everyone looking on felt pangs of pity, and one and all promised their patronage, coming to Tōsuke to put in orders for even as little as foot of this fabric or a sleeve's worth of that. And since Tōsuke took to lowering his prices until they were all slightly below those of Jūbei, it wasn't long before business became quite lively.

"So that's the way that bastard wants to play it," said Jūbei when he heard. He slashed the prices of all his silks, from uncut rolls to precut combinations, sleeves to neckpieces, and deciding that he didn't care if he lost 10 percent across the board, he published his price list and distributed copies to all his customers.

Hearing of this put Tōsuke's chief clerk, Gohei, on his mettle, and he showed his spirit by declaring that if Jūbei would sell at a 10 percent loss, then they should answer him back with a 20 percent loss and thereby try to break him. Tōsuke, however, intervened, saying that though it was the accepted practice of merchants to sell at a loss as a temporary measure, the present affair was likely to last well into the future. With their lengthy list of orders from committed clients, selling at a 20 percent loss would result in a very great loss indeed. Furthermore, there was the matter of the mound of cash that Jūbei, in his great greed, had managed to stash away, likely upwards of two hundred *kanme* it was, while on their side they had barely forty, if that much.

"From the capital that we have managed to lay aside over the years, twenty *kanme* went to pay for the house and the shop, and what remains will be necessary to build up the new shop." It was not like the old days, he said, and since the late master's fortune had been squandered away, no one was going to come along and lend them five hundred *me* of silver. Jūbei, on the other hand, with his healthy fund of two hundred *kanme* could, even if he only got 10 percent annual interest, still count on an income of twenty-four *kanme,* while they themselves with their measly twenty *kanme* at 10 percent annual interest would see but two *kan* and four hundred *me* profit. A price war with archrival Jūbei would result only in great losses for them with nary anything to show for it. If you started a price war with insufficient capital and then got driven into the ground in the end, there was no way to undo the damage, so what could you do then but grit your teeth and bear it? At any rate, in a time when you had to spend money to make money, no amount of hustling on their part was going to enable them to take down that rat Jūbei in the end, Tōsuke reasoned. It was this thought, he continued, that tortured his heart as he cudgeled body and brain night and day in a desperate search for some way to supplant Jūbei and his shop. "Most regrettable" was all the response that Gohei could manage after Tōsuke's declaration that they could not and would not take on Jūbei in an all-out price war.

"All right, if it's only after you've shored up our capital that you'd be of a mind to take him on, pulling out all the stops and giving no thought to losses," Gohei countered, "I offer you this, then, because of the fix we're in." Gohei's father, he related, had been a well-known gold prospector, and in Tada, of his native province, where narrow seams of gold often opened onto gourd-shaped pockets of the stuff, and with a partner from Mikata he had struck it rich. "And because of that," Gohei continued, "from childhood I have always known my way around a gold mine and through my father am privy to the trick of divining the presence or lack thereof of gold in a given stone without ever having to split it open.

"Now, I was in charge of the Osaka store at the time that Master Sanshichi was experiencing his personal downfall, but when our citadel, the house here in Kyoto, was brought down, I had no choice but to close the Osaka branch and at least attempt to restore the fortunes of the master. My training being so very ingrained, I headed off to the west country to spy out a likely spot for a gold mine and then returned. And I tell you, with but a mere ten *kanme* of startup capital, I can guarantee a return within a year of a hundred. I spotted a vein of gold, but since you didn't come from Edo, I sat on my hands doing nothing for the time being. But I ask now that you give me ten *kanme* of your twenty in capital funds," Gohei urged, "and within a year I will return to the capital with a packhorse in tow that bears the weight of one hundred *kanme* of gold, a sum that most certainly will shore up our cash reserves."

When Tōsuke remained unconvinced, Gohei blew up.

"A leader not fit to lead! With thinking like this, we'll never save this shop. And to meekly follow your hopeless lead will just ruin my own fortunes as well. This is too much! I'll find myself a leader who is my equal and then show everyone by striking it rich with this gold mine!" cried Gohei. Now this would have been bad enough even inside and out of sight, but here were Tōsuke and Gohei shouting at each other at the top of their lungs in the street in front of the shop.

Neighbors came running from all directions to see what the ruckus was about while the feud only grew louder until, in the end, Gohei quit in a huff, taking his leave as of that day and returning immediately to his lodging. As a slap in the face directed at Tōsuke, Gohei ran off to Jūbei's shop and begged to be added the latter's ranks of employees, wanting nothing more than to be a thorn in the side of Tōsuke's business.

It was an angry Gohei, then, who entered into Jūbei's employ. He spoke there with a young person, who happened to be Jūbei's son and heir, Jūtarō. Twenty-one that year, Jūtarō was so like his father in taste and appetites that even though he was at the height of his youth, not only did his thoughts never bend longingly toward the Gion pleasure quarter's stone wall enclosure, but he had yet even to set foot on the tatami mats of the Gojōzaka teahouses nearby. At seven he had, in accordance with common custom, received as a present from his maternal aunt in Anekōji his first man's loincloth, and it was this single undergarment of pink silk with which he had made do through all the years, even now wearing that alone.

As he matured, he had gained valuable experience and produced uniformly good results. He could do complicated calculations in his head, and the purse strings in his charge were always pulled tightly shut. Precocious he was, and cunning, with an ability to turn the tables on even the wiliest of rival merchants. The fish or fowl he ate morning or night he bought not by the fin or head but only in carefully measured, to-the-ounce, bargained-down portions, while for "scale" potatoes, normally sold by the pound, he would first ask, "How many would a hundred *me* get me?" and then call out that number to buy.

The abacus was never absent from his thoughts even in dreams, and it was only for moneymaking schemes that he had ears. And that was why Jūtarō's perked up the moment he heard Gohei's report of his argument with Tōsuke and his quitting in disgust at Tōsuke's incapacity to lead, as shown by the latter's refusal to listen to his surefire, get-rich-quick gold-mine scheme. These days, he thought to himself, there was no business deal to be found—absolutely none—that would guarantee a doubling of your money, yet here was talk of a gold mine that would earn a hundred *kanme* for an investment of ten, an alluring prospect that his ears found pleasant indeed, and seeds of greed sprouted in his heart.

Alone late at night he secretly made his way to Gohei's lodging to confer privately, and the plan Gohei outlined to him was even better than he had hoped. It was agreed, then, that an initial trial deposit of ten *kanme* would be entrusted to Gohei, who would put that into the potential gold mine he had found in the west country, so as to help Jūtarō realize his hopes. Dig as the many miners and laborers employed might, however, their labor belied the mountain's prospects and resulted only in a strong geyser of water spouting up from its depths. Immediately a messenger was sent dashing off to Kyoto with a message saying that if the water were not drained off, the string of the all-important gold could never be mined from the shaft; therefore, please remit a hundred *ryō* for fashioning a hundred drainage gutters to be used for this purpose. Having already put in ten *kanme,* Jūtarō knew that if he did not cough up this extra cash, his ten *kanme* of silver would simply have gone to waste, a thought too hard to bear, so he laid out the hundred *ryō.*

From then on, it was something for this and a bit more for that in a steady and endless stream, money about which he put off telling his father. By the time Jūtarō was out twenty-four or twenty-five *kanme,* he had to tell him, and when he did, Jūbei considered that his son had until then never once been rash in his dealings and that if he believed this much in the prospects of this particular venture, then it must be one that would indeed pay off. It'd be one thing, he reasoned, if the project had yet to be started, but since twenty-five *kanme* had already been poured in, why not continue the funding until they had seen a profit? So, as the requests came in for additional funds, he gradually paid out more and more, until something in the neighborhood of two thousand *ryō* had been invested, but out of that hole came nothing but rocks.

The shop's unshakable foundation was eaten away by Jūbei's great greed, a punishment for his having deceived his master in the service of avarice. No words of sympathy, however, were to be heard on street corners about town for the now ruined Jūbei. Indeed, one and all agreed that he had gotten just what he deserved, so roundly disliked by all was he. It is as the saying going goes: only one who serves his master faithfully and honestly, hiding nothing, will receive the grace of the gods.

THE LOVE TOWN TUNE, "ONLY DEATH CAN STOP ME," SUNG BY A BAD NEWS SON

A magic pot of gold just waiting to be found? Not in our times. Even riches and wealth come with a share of pain; with indigence and poverty as well comes a modicum of joy. Human beings one and all plead for social station undeserved, and countless, therefore, are the examples of unhappy fates met.

Jūbei of the Minoya, appointed chief clerk by Master Shintoku, was deemed by the old master supremely wise, one to whom people came for counsel. But even this Jūbei—who possessed, some said, the wisdom of a sage—suffered on the mirror of his heart the fog of desire. Hidden from his master's view, he removed from the shop's ledgers a tenth of the price that each customer paid. So, for example, an item that sold for ten *monme,* in the master ledger would be noted as a sale of nine. In this way he set aside for himself a tenth of each year's sales. Having amassed a great fortune, he established himself as master of his own shop, and though for a time he strutted about as a great man of substance, his former master's wrath and retribution, together with unexpected losses on a gold mine speculation that grew from his own great greed, turned the tide against him, so that everything he tried from then on went south. Though in appearance bursting with wealth, in reality this facade masked but an empty shell. And just when all was slipping completely beyond Jūbei's control, Gohei paid a visit to Tōsuke.

"Thanks to your plan, Jūbei's business is all but caput. *Now* is the time," Gohei whispered, "to lure away, as you have long wished, Jūbei's most valued patrons, one and all."

Well, imagine Tōsuke's elation! "In that case," he whispered back, "let's both start printing up his silk price lists to circulate them all over town!" For three years they waited, then distributed the flyers. When these patrons came to Jūbei's shop inquiring about goods, now, unlike before, he had no wealth of goods, so that no matter what a patron asked for, "We're all out" became his stock response. As a result, all his patrons turned around and found their way to Tōsuke's store!

Tōsuke had glimpsed the avarice in Jūbei's and Jūtarō's hearts. Joining forces with Gohei to reduce Jūbei's vast stock of goods, Tōsuke had Gohei play the traitor to enmesh Jūbei in the hopeless gold mine scheme. Afterwards when people heard of it, all exclaimed, "So that's what it was!" in reasoned understanding. And from that time forward, Tōsuke saw the fortunes of his shop equal the best of even the late Master Shintoku's munificent times. His was the rich joy of the legendary Fan Li of China, having cleared name (and ledger) of a disgraceful stain.

Sanshichi's renewed fortune was entirely the result of Tōsuke's kind efforts, but the former loudly bragged that it was by dint of his own wit and brains. He would go out, making for Shimabara once again. When Tōsuke detained him with a sharply worded remonstrance, only a bitter warning did he receive in response.

"This from a servant is too much, indeed! The libertine's life is my nature, heaven-sent. I couldn't stop it if I tried. If you keep hitting me with that load of disapproving crap," he declared, his face twisting fearsomely, "I'll run you off for good!"

"At present there's nothing I can do," thought Tōsuke, remembering his duties as an employee. "I haven't really pushed all that hard, but if he's veering that far away from the straight and narrow, then this family and its concern won't recover any time soon."

"I purchased this house and these grounds using my own funds, and the stock laid in for starting up the shop again was bought by me as well. What, sir, did you contribute? Did you have even a penny of your own?" said Tōsuke, facing Sanshichi. "The thought of this ancient house passing into the hands of strangers was too much, which was why I bought it and brought it back to its former glory. Had your character, sir, just been of the right sort, then everything would have passed smoothly along from generation to generation, with each new one intent forever on observing the memorials for his parents. I racked my brains night and day to try to come up with another moneymaking trick, meanwhile getting so caught up in thoughts about business, business, and nothing but business that I would forget even to eat or sleep. But after having managed to execute a plan to bring down Jūbei, the master's mortal business foe, and built the shop back up to this extent, I can't allow it to be torn apart by you, sir. That would be to act in bad faith toward the late Master Shintoku. To allow you to stay even one more day will not do. Be off with you—the sooner the better!"

Now Tōsuke figured that the value of the shop and attached home together with the laid-in stock came to a total of forty *kanme,* and though his carefully accumulated funds were all his very own, still everything that he had gained was thanks to the late master; therefore, he made an offer to the young one.

"With this amount of money," he said, taking forty *kanme* out of the storehouse and handing it over to the young master, "you could eat pretty nicely for the rest of your life. Why don't you take it and go?"

Sanshichi thought the offer not wholly adequate. This was the master, after all, being told to get lost. So, would he?

"Forty *kanme* is a trifling sum," answered the young master, "but since staying here means putting up with all your fuss and bother, then go I will!" And still as if he were doing Tōsuke a favor, Sanshichi placed the forty *kanme* in the hands of a manservant. And where did he go? Off to the home of his constant companion in revels known as Uhachi of the Moonlit Nights, a professional jester and paid partier of the pleasure quarter, to rent that very day a room at the rear of Uhachi's home, a mere hop, skip, and jump from Shimabara itself—that's where! From that time forward, now free of fussing clerks, he lived the life of a libertine, carousing with the great hedonists of the world, one who belted out in the quarter the popular ballad "Only Death Can Stop Me!" Was ever a truer statement about Sanshichi likely to be heard?

Jūbei and son had swallowed Tōsuke's bait according to plan and lost a lion's share of their fortune on the hopeless gold mine scheme. Thinking to make it back, they embarked on various ventures—land reclamation for creating new paddy land, the backing of a play that flopped, the purchase of various goods only to have to take losses—and with each new thing they tried, another chunk of their reserves was cut away. Because it was their native village, they bought a parcel of land in the place known as Ogurusu, and thinking that now they had found a lucky retreat, they took up plow and hoe, bending their backs in physical labor, to which neither parent nor child was accustomed. Their labors, though, proved vain, and finally, patience gone, they disposed of their land for a pittance. Though that brought in a little cash, they could for the moment hit upon no ideas for a trade, at which point their inborn dishonesty reared its head, and they made their way to Uji, to the garden of the fabled Byōdōin. On the grass there they marked off a space, laying out straw mats, and cast off their cheap paper cloaks. "A man at the end of his rope turns to the game of devil's luck," said Jūbei, as he placed marker chips numbered from one to fifteen into a circular wooden box, and holding an awl in his right hand to spear out a winning number, he tried to lure in passersby. Using son Jūtarō as an accomplice to drum up business, he managed to fleece some simpletons of their coins, but for gambling at the temple they were soon thrown out on their ears.

How sad the changes in fate of one who, in days of old, knew what seemed an endless stream of coins as golden as the Uji River's kerria-covered shallows but who now faced those shallows gold-starved! What seed of fate sown in a moneymaking scheme had come to rest and flowered here, farther east? What brought them to Makinoshima, where in the morning mists shapes fade faintly in and out to become neither this nor that? Where, despite the presence of both boats and bridges for making one's way, one hesitated at this edge as if there were nowhere to go, fearing all was for naught? Shame, however, was neither Jūbei's nor his son's to feel, so on to Sakamoto they pushed, forcing

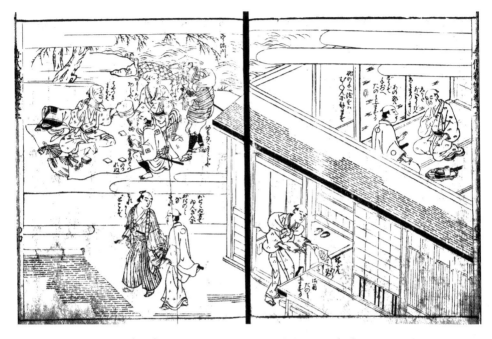

Clerks to the Rescue (*right*): Tōsuke, the Edo branch clerk, having rushed to Kyoto to purchase his deceased master's business, negotiates with the elder in charge. In the lower part (based on the next story, "The Love Town Tune"), Gohei, from the Osaka branch, distributes a new flyer for the Minoya with a more competitive price list. Revenge Afoot, Kamigata-Style (*left*): In the lower part, Tōsuke instructs Sanshichi how to conduct himself toward the former customers. In the upper part (based on the next story, "The Love Town Tune"), on the bank of the Uji River the down-and-out Jūbei and son Jūtarō operate a makeshift gambling joint, hustling temple visitors with a game of numbered wooden chips, before being hustled off themselves farther down the road to ruin. (National Diet Library)

themselves upon an acquaintance they barely knew. Then they headed out onto the Ōtsu Road, where father and son had heart-to-heart and shoulder-to-shoulder work as palanquin bearers. Though some there might have been able to recognize them, having nothing to eat was a greater pain than shame.

They learned the bearers' earthy lingo and thought to entice riders with an offer of a cup of *sake*. But riders these days are sharp.

"Yesterday," Jūbei started to say, "the gentleman we carried—" But before he had gotten out barely a word, "Yesterday," their prospective rider broke in, "the bearers I had were very pleasant fellows indeed. They carried me from Fudanotsuji to the Sanjō Bridge. 'You're a lot lighter than you look,' they said. 'We told you a hundred *mon*, but what say we knock it down to eighty or so?' Common laborers though they were, they still knocked off sixteen for me!

"And what good fellows, too! At a tea shop they said, 'Master, how about a drink?' and put twelve *mon* down for a whole bowlful of tea. I mean, they even covered my drink! Not at all like the old days, eh? Bearers these days are never vulgar, and when I changed palanquins at Hino'oka, I offered to raise their fee as I was climbing down, but they said a deal was a deal and why should they receive anything extra? Just common bearers, mind you!"

Beaten to the punch by their passenger, how could Jūbei and Jūtarō possibly complain? Angry now, they shouldered the palanquin as if hoisting a corpse and sprinted helter-skelter as far as Hashirii, where they lowered their load, their feet now covered in blisters that had broken, making it impossible for them to go any farther. So they took their fare, unloaded their passenger, and made their way back home.

Not used to such labor, their shoulders soon swelled. Changing jobs, they poured sweat into this, bent bones to that, and ground their bodies down to dust. Theirs was a hell in this life—so they donned masks of devils above their threadbare cotton cloaks, and beneath the cold winter skies they ran around outside people's gates crying, "Out with him, out with him, the god of the winds!" beating drums and raising a racket in sickness-quelling exorcisms, the beggar's last resort.

Carrying a begged bag of rice, they dragged themselves back to the hovel in which they dwelled and found next door a man, newly come the night before, who had also hit upon the wind god ploy. Another with a heart like the face of a devil, he wagged his horns about, raging up a storm and shouting, "What punishment is this?" as he returned, drum in hand.

Still in masks, they acknowledged they would be neighbors now. "So why not talk things over in neighborly fashion?" they said, bowing back and forth. How strange they must have looked to others! But from their point of view, their present getups were but a means to make a living and, so, not very embarrassing after all.

"I thought I'd treat myself a little," their new neighbor said, filling an earthenware flask with *sake* he seemed to have purchased along the road, "but no matter what happens, never am I lacking in manners." And as if performing a neighborly duty, he invited in the bemasked devils Jūbei and son.

"Well, then, slip off your masks, why don't you, and make yourselves at home," he said.

"Please, sir, you too. We insist," they answered.

"Oh no, I couldn't! After all, I'm the host here making the offering. I should stay as I am."

"Oh, you are too formal, sir, too formal, indeed! Please, we beg you."

So each removed his mask and faced the others.

"What?" exclaimed Jūbei. "Is that really you, my old Master Sanshichi?"

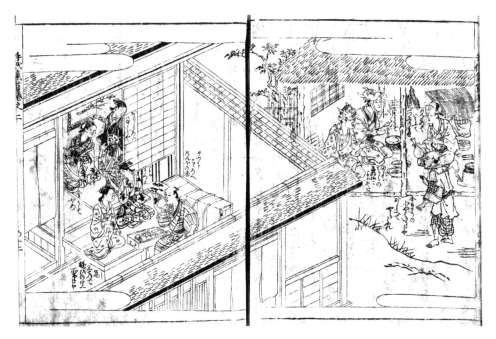

Greed Meets Lust in a Devilish Unmasking (*right*): Jūbei and Jūtarō encounter Sanshichi and their new mentor, Shichiji, at the ruinous road's end. The Irresistible Spiel (*left*): Genroku takes over his brother Chōhachi's pretty ornament business and succeeds in making money by his entertaining art. This image accompanies the next story (not included in this volume), "Jōruri Chanting, the Trader's Capital Gain." (National Diet Library)

"No! It's Jūbei, and Jūtarō his son!"

Flabbergasted, they stared amazedly at the sky.

At this moment of unmasking in this den of indigent toughs, as they each were telling how they came to this plight, in walked another denizen of the hovels, the reigning elder.

"Is this the one who moved in last night?" he asked. "It would appear that he is someone you know, Master Jūbei. Should he be new to the ranks of beggars, then allow me to tell him what it's all about.

"When colds are going around, to hit upon the idea of the wind god is quite good, indeed. While you are young, it's sex, everything sex, so you're disowned by your parents again and again. Finally the apology lifeline snaps, and you end up here in these hovels. Well, let me tell you, not a one of us was born a beggar.

"In my own case, I crossed my master, got turned out by the family, and had nowhere else to go, so I settled in this slum ten years ago. Making like a religious pilgrim, I always managed something to eat. But it never ever pays to go and cheat your master.

"I was apprenticed to a lacquer shop in the Nakagyō ward. When my apprenticeship expired at fifteen, it was time for the ceremonies celebrating my coming of age—and did I ever celebrate! My sights were set on lacquer all right—the brightly colored lacquer of the pleasure quarter! So off I went immediately to Shimabara.

"Shimabara is where money gives you the power to push around the gods at will, and because I aimed to spend money I could never hope to earn, my heart was set upon my master's cash. So, while no one was looking, I slipped off with this, pinched that, and lacquered my way about town.

"But oh, the tenacious perversity of a spirit gone bad! In no time at all I had run up a bill I couldn't pay, a debt of one hundred *ryō*. Through the efforts of family and backers, I got off for fifty *ryō* and an apology. Because he'd known me so long, the master forgave me and let me come back to work for him. This time around, I'd learned my lesson, I said, and for the rest of this life and even the next, I would never forget, I swore. I was damned if I would have anything more to do with the life of a libertine. So scared was I that the sight of a woman had about as much appeal as a snake.

"Well, the master and his wife were relieved to think that someone could make such a complete turnaround, and they thought nothing now of sending me on buying trips from Osaka all the way to Yoshino and giving me two hundred *ryō* in gold to do it. Now, I well knew in my heart of hearts that nothing in the world could destroy a man more quickly than lust, so when another passenger was telling off-color tales of the east on the boat out from Fushimi, I shut my ears and grabbed my rosary, chanting purifying prayers to myself. At just that moment a young wholesaler came along, shouldering a load of satin-covered pillows, which he spread out in the space next to me and then went away. What came along then was a real looker of a woman with a round face wrapped in a padded hood and wearing a gown of black crepe embroidered with a leaved chrysanthemum. When she stepped over from another boat into ours, a river breeze happened to lift her hem, and what did I see if not that which knocked the high-flying Wizard of Kume from the sky—the unforgettable sight of a woman's white inner thigh! That this should be so welcome a sight to someone so leery of such things is the bane of the common man.

"The woman, when she tipped up her hat to see, looked my way, and I swear that it was the face of karma itself staring back at me! We looked at each other, and suddenly she exclaimed:

"'Why, if it isn't Shichiji, the lacquer man!'

"'Aren't you Yakumo of the Shimabara?' I answered.

"Now, one could call this the kind of chance that karma brings, like one bead of the rosary I held hitting up against another, but more likely it was but the fruit of a love seed sown long before. When we cleared aside the bags and boxes that separated her from me, the man who attended her approached, a scowl on his face, and said that even though I seemed like an old friend of the lady's, one with many pleasant memories to reminisce about, I must exercise good judgment and restraint.

" 'Recently,' he said, 'the lady was ransomed by one of the really big spenders of the quarter and was to be set up in his family's suburban villa, but the man's parents were livid when they heard and immediately disowned him for this extravagance.' Now cut adrift, the lady returned to her home, he told me, only to find her father had been named as financial guarantor for a couple that had eloped, which meant he had to come up with 150 *ryō* in gold or be thrown into prison.

" 'When I heard of her predicament,' the attendant Hachibei continued, 'I approached the family as the agent for the Osaka House of Senpū in the Shinmachi pleasure quarter, offering to pay off the debt in return for five years' service from the lady. Just yesterday I carried the money to the capital and paid off every cent to save her family, and today I'm taking her back down to Namba, so no old flame from out of her past is going to step onto the boat and mess up all the efforts that Hachibei, this agent with a capital *A*, has made!' And with that, he set to moving bags and what all back into place.

"Well, Yakumo was distraught. 'It's as you've heard,' she said. 'I thought I had escaped the trials and tribulations of a life in the quarter, but because of Daddy, I've fallen back into this hell.' And she collapsed onto my lap, shedding tears that seeped into my every pore and left me unspeakably sad.

" 'Not to worry,' declared I, this one who had so learned his lesson in matters of sex. 'I myself will gladly pay the 150 *ryō* and you won't ever have to work again,' and there on the boat, as proof of my claim, I pulled from my bag four packets containing fifty *ryō* each and lined them up before them.

"The courtesan was overjoyed. 'Hachibei-san, it's as you've heard. I beg you please to make my apologies to the Senpūs for me.'

"Hachibei eyed the 200 *ryō*, which lit the fire of greed in his heart. 'I am known to be a man who has made his way in this world doing his utmost to oversee the affairs of the courtesans in our employ. Now, in accordance with the accepted custom of the quarter, once the ransom is paid and the parent's consent given, starting that day the woman is officially a Senpū-employed courtesan. Now, if your feelings for her are indeed so very deep and if you intend as you say for her never to return to work, then you should ransom the woman. Now, if we put this to the master, he would no doubt look you over to gauge your wealth and then set a ransom somewhere around 300 *ryō*, but since I have a heart, I'll work out a deal for you to bring this off. Let's say that on top of the original 150 *ryō* we add, say, 50 more and make it 200 in all.'

"A man who renders such dedicated service was not one to miss a trick. He was certainly of a mind to try on for himself a 50-*ryō* golden slipper. So round and round we went until finally we agreed I'd pay him 190 *ryō* in all. When the boat reached Hirakata, after happily letting the boatman know we were getting off there, we begged our leave of Hachibei, and I escorted the courtesan off the boat to a wayside inn where we stayed the night.

"Though overjoyed that she was mine, in my heart of hearts I knew I had no home to go home to, so I took her off into the backcountry where we could hide away far from the eyes of the world and savor as much splendor as the ten *ryō* that remained could buy. But in no time at all, it seems, we were pulled apart, and she was taken from me. I was left with the shirt on my back and not much else. So much for my second chance at honest work! With no place else to go, I turned up here in these hovels—a playboy and buyer of courtesans, the mess you see before you! It's a miracle that I've been able to hold on this long by the singing of pilgrim songs. Oh, a man should forever avoid the lane of lust!"

After listening to this volunteered confession, Sanshichi realized that he, too, was no different. An unfilial son he had been, and feeling a sharp pain in his chest, he suddenly coughed up a mouthful of blood and died.

Amazing, everyone agreed, this sudden manifestation of the transient god of the wind. Carrying the corpse out toward the fields, "Out with him, out with him!" they cried.

TRANSLATED BY CHARLES FOX

PART II

Exploring Japan
Traveling the Freeways on Foot

Fact, Fantasy, and Foibles on the Roads and in the Cities

GUIDEBOOKS AND TRAVEL LITERATURE

Although travel was a key theme in the composition of classical Japanese poetry, no traveler could have expected to find his or her way based on the oblique and allusive poetic references to notable sites and "famous places" threaded throughout the great poetry collections of the late classical period. Indeed, the notion that a travelogue might actually inform the reader about where to go and what to see or that a guidebook should be a useful companion for the traveler when he or she took to the road did not become widely accepted until the Edo period. Over the course of the seventeenth century, as more common people began to travel and relocate, whether for trade, work, pilgrimage, or recreation, the interest in travel guides and descriptive travelogues grew. Edo-period writers and publishers accommodated this interest by producing a varied selection of travel writing, ranging from diaries of journeys taken by notable scholars or literary figures to relatively terse and factual guidebooks of great Japanese cities, such as Edo and Kyoto. Because it was established as the bureaucratic capital by the Tokugawa family only in 1590, the city of Edo in particular became the subject of numerous guidebooks aimed at the hordes of migrants who began pouring into the city in the early seventeenth century.

Translated here are portions of three popular guidebooks published during the late seventeenth and early eighteenth centuries. Each written in a distinctive style, they focus on particular geographic areas—the city of Kyoto, the city of Edo, and the Tōkaidō, the main trunk road linking those two cities. At the same time, these texts describe many of the same places, events, and cultural phenomena, suggesting that a common stock of images and information about places was emerging in printed and published materials in the early Edo period.

DENIZENS OF KYOTO

NAKAGAWA KIUN

N akagawa Kiun (1636?–1705) was born in Tanba Province near Kyoto and, by his own admission, as a youth was "nearly illiterate, and utterly obstinate." However, he eventually developed an interest in both medicine and literature, and he moved to Kyoto to pursue his medical studies. While there Kiun indulged his growing literary ambitions by writing *haikai* poetry and various types of light prose, ultimately making his name as a writer of didactic popular literature, easy reading books, that often took the form of guidebooks to famous places.

Denizens of Kyoto (*Kyō Warabe*, 1658) is an archetypal example: it is a travel guide written with both stylistic flair and heavy-handed moralism. Although the title literally translates as "child of Kyoto," its connotation is closer to the English term "native son"—namely, someone who is born and bred in a given place and knows that place extremely well. This is the sort of authoritative perspective on the city that Kiun strives to replicate in *Denizens of Kyoto*. In the preface to the book, the author explains that he wrote it to serve as a guide to Kyoto and its environs for visitors from the provinces, like he himself once was. In simple prose occasionally ornamented by the author's poems, cautionary tales, and often ribald commentary, Kiun takes the reader on a tour of more than eighty famous places and historical sites in the imperial capital.

Denizens of Kyoto was the first published guide to the city of Kyoto and formed an important model upon which later travel accounts, of Kyoto and elsewhere, were based. Indeed, the reader cannot fail to notice that many of Kiun's descriptive phrases reappear almost verbatim in later travel guides, though transposed onto different locales. In particular, parts of the passage below describing the theater district of the Shijō Riverbank are incorporated into the description of the theater district in Edo in Asai Ryōi's *Famous Places along the Tōkaidō,* which is also partially translated in this section.

In terms of style, the translations given here of Kiun's descriptions of Buddhist priests' predilection for male-male love found at the end of the "Shijō Riverbank" passage and in the "Chion-in" passage do not do justice to the sexual innuendoes, erotic imagery, and puns of the originals. For example, the poem ending the "Chion-in" section puns on the name of the temple, Ōtanidera, read also as "Daikokuji." The latter is homonymous with *daikoku,* referring simultaneously to the deity Daikoku (who, like Ebisu, is one of the Seven Gods of Good Fortune) and to, in a derogatory term, a priest's kept woman. In other places, however, Kiun's descriptions are more staid. Like all classical writers, Kiun was highly sensitive to the natural world, and he often included poems that draw attention to durable themes such as the changing of the seasons. The inclusion of such poems gave an air of refinement that stood in contrast to the coarser passages in the book. This fluid movement between the refined and common dimensions of the capital is written into the account itself, as Kiun guides his reader through the city, beginning at its political, cultural, and symbolic center, the imperial palace. He reflects on the classical past at the grave of the great tenth-century poet Izumi Shikibu and moves on to describe the major temples and shrines in the center of the city. But he soon fixes his attention on the centers of popular culture—the theater district at Shijō and the brothel district nearby.

(MY)

THE IMPERIAL PALACE

The seat of the emperor was moved from the former capital of Nagaoka to Heian, now called Kyoto, in 794 during the reign of the fiftieth emperor, Kanmu. The year 1658 marks 865 years since its move. Counting from the first emperor, Jinmu, to the present sovereign there have been 113 successive generations of emperors.

As for the palace itself, its buildings and gateways glitter with splendor, and their names follow the progression of the four seasons. In the order of blossoming times in the spring, ladies' quarters are named the Plum, the Pear, the Wisteria, and the Peach, as the gate was called. In summer, sitting inside the curtains of the dais, one may fail to hear the cuckoo beyond the clouds. The perfumed breeze wafts across the floating bridge onto the corridor to the Emperor's Residence. Come autumn, in the long shadows birds search for food and make their homes in the Paulownia Quarter, and the Bush Clover Pavilion of the palace is encircled in mist seven, eight, and now nine times.

The imperial palace. (National Diet Library)

The *sake* set to warm creates a misty shroud. In the winter there are parties to celebrate the remaining chrysanthemums, His Majesty's meal of the season's rice cakes, the dances at the imperial party, the *kagura* dances at the Mirror Shrine, exorcism and other nighttime ceremonies, affairs into which much thought and planning had gone. Courtiers walk around the six gates, a most impressive sight! The wise men from the mountains and forests also pay their respects, the wild beasts cavort, while sidestepping the new grasses, and the land flourishes, thanks to the virtue of our Sagely Lord. The skies are vast and the earth bears up and the world is as blessed as the name "good life." Indeed, the Lord's reign will continue ten times longer than the Takasago pine of longevity and will "live on for a thousand, or eight thousand generations." As the "small pebbles" form a band around me, as I walk along, the dangling cord of my cap swings this way and that.

> In the imperial palace
> one sees courtiers' hats, cherry blossoms,
> flower-patterned sleeves

Lady Izumi Shikibu's grave.
(National Diet Library)

IZUMI SHIKIBU

This is the ancient grave of Izumi Shikibu. She was a lady-in-waiting to Jōtōmon-in, the principal consort of Retired Emperor Ichijō. Her father was Ōe no Masamune, her mother the daughter of Yasuhira, the Lord of Etchū, and her husband, Michisada, the Lord of Izumi. This last connection gave her the name "Izumi Shikibu." She, by the way, was the mother of the poet Koshikibu. She was learned and creative in *waka* poetry. Among her many compositions is the twentieth poem in the imperial poetry collection *A Later Collection of* Waka *Poems* (*Shūishū*), which was written in the presence of the priest Shōkō.

> Out of darkness
> down another path of darkness
> must I venture;
> would that the light of the moon
> shine over the top of the mountain

It is no surprise that Fujiwara no Teika (1162–1241) counted this poem as one in his *One Hundred Poems by One Hundred Poets,* compiled at his hut in Ogura. Sympathizing with the poet's distress over the impermanence of this world, we drench our sleeves with tears even today. Legacies are forever, as they say: her name will remain forever while her body has sunk into the earth. Nostalgically, we wonder what she looked like and wish it were possible to meet her just once. "The copious dewdrops on the mound of her tomb are tears of our longing for her."

> Could it be that the *shikimi* tree
> Is the source of the flowers
> Planted in her memory

... THE SHIJŌ RIVERBANK

On the right is the theater's side door, through which a man slips, arching his back like a cat. On the left of the front turret, a servant looks up, his chin as sharp as a spear. Also sightseeing are men and women, young and old, some wearing their straw hats from Ise with upturned brims, some wearing fine silk gauze wraps. There are also some dressed in casual cotton jackets whose stuffing is spilling out.

In the beginning, what is called kabuki was modeled on the ritual dance of a shrine maiden from Izumo. This shrine maiden chanted Buddha's name while beating a gong, and after performing a dance to praise Amida, she dressed as a man and danced and sang while brandishing a sword. This is what came to be called kabuki. In the early days, female entertainers called *shirabyōshi* (dancing girls in white) had entertained by singing popular songs and danced while dressed in white silk robes and the hats of court nobles. In those days they used to call this "men's dancing."

Up until a certain time, even here at the Shijō Riverbank courtesans danced. The men who came to watch them dissipated themselves, sinned wildly, and threw their money away. Some neglected their parents, some ignored their jealous wives. Day after day, and night after night, whether they could come here or not, they left their hearts and minds here—along with all the savings in their money boxes. Although their money was limited, their taste for pleasure was boundless, so that these men enjoyed themselves, hiding from their parents and deceiving their wives. Just as fish that frequent the beach get caught in the fisherman's net, their secret indulgences were soon known by all. This situation was incessantly obstructive to the state and injurious to the people, so the city magistrate banned kabuki performances by courtesans.

Kabuki theater on the dry riverbed at Shijō Street. (National Diet Library)

This prompted the practice of using young men in their place, so that the performances were called youth's kabuki. It wasn't as if men had never dabbled with other men before, but they had never imagined that their spirits could be snatched away to such a degree that they no longer even tasted the food that they ate. The beloved boy's name ends up being carved on their thigh or arm.

Then there were the young women who dreamed of marrying one of these beautiful young men—they never fail to keep Aizen Myō-ō's passion arrow handy. It goes without saying that priests from every temple turned the alms money into theater tickets, and offerings for ancestors into gifts for the seductive boy actors. The proffered saké cup glittered in auspicious light even though it is not autumn, and the paper flowers that adorn the stage are in bloom even when it is not spring. A priest's brocaded stole may turn into a sword bag for the stage, and his robe may be given to the novice drummer. Eventually the monk is dismissed from the temple where he lived, and he embarks upon a strenuous pilgrimage up the Mountain of Eros, carrying only his umbrella as he travels all over Japan. His hunger is sated only with the help of his begging bowl. Doesn't penetrating another's anus sully the pure heart? …

Chion-in Temple.
(National Diet Library)

CHION-IN

This temple was founded by the priest Hōnen. He hailed from Mimasaka Province. He was born into the Uruma clan in Inaoka. His father was called Tokikuni, and his mother was a daughter of the Hata clan. Some time having passed without bearing any children, and feeling quite forlorn, they began to pray to the gods and buddhas to bring them a child. One night, Hōnen's mother dreamed of swallowing a razor, and when she awoke and told her husband Tokikuni about it, he interpreted this to mean that she was finally pregnant. The mother's belly grew steadily heavier, and on the seventh day of the fourth month of the second year of the Chōshō era, the boy who would become Priest Hōnen was born.

The boy's head had dents and bumps, and his eyes were yellowish and glittering. Surely this was no average newborn! During her pregnancy, his mother had refrained from eating fish and fowl as well as using spices. In short, she ate a monk's diet. When the son was fifteen years old, he took the tonsure at Kudoku Temple at the Tendai Buddhist monastery Enryakuji.

Having studied the Tendai teachings, he became a follower of Eikō at Kurodani. He read the monk Genshin's *Essentials of Salvation* and quit his monastic practice to preach the doctrine of the Pure Land. In the fourth year of Shōan he left Kurodani and came here to Chion-in to live. But then Lord Kujō Kanezane turned to him for lessons on the Pure Land, and so Hōnen wrote the *Collection of Passages on the Nembutsu and the Original Vow*. On the twenty-fifth day of the first month of the second year of Kenryaku, while chanting the Buddha's name, he faced to the west and passed away. He was eighty years old.

> Chion-in is also called Daikokuji.
> The priests at this temple
> who vow abstinence
> still get stiff
> Daikokuji, what a name!
> Please forgive me, readers, for this silly pun.

CASTLE-TOPPLERS DISTRICT

What used to be Misuji-machi in the Rokujō district was moved here more than ten years ago. There the courtesans were kept like caged birds, unable to go outside the gate of the walled compound in which they lived. Surely, when they saw the coming of the autumn moon, they dwelled on thoughts of home—seeing this, there is not a person who is not reminded of the poems of Tang poet Yong Tao. Thus, sex-obsessed young men frequented the place day and night, and of course, they weren't averse to encountering the girls. As the saying goes, when traveling to meet one's lover, miles seem like inches.

The idea that women "topple castles and ruin the state" can be traced back to ancient China. Li Yannian's poem said:

> In the far north there was a fine lady
> Who stood alone in her peerless beauty;
> When she glanced back, a castle toppled,
> When she looked twice, a state declined.

She lived alone in a paradise-like world. If a man looked upon her a single time, his castle would be ruined; if he looked twice, his country would be ruined. This is the origin of the phrase "castle-toppling state-destroyer."

In China, the consorts Xi Shi, Yang Guifei in the Tang dynasty, and Wang

Shimabara entertainment district. (National Diet Library)

Zhaojun in the Former Han dynasty were all castle topplers. In Japan, Shima no Senzai and Waka no Mae, who flourished during the time of Retired Emperor Toba, were these castle topplers and were the original *shirabyōshi* dancers. In the olden days in ports like Murozu and Mishima-e, boat travelers would fall in love with these girls, and so they were called "the women of tides." Nowadays, in every corner of every province there are many courtesans; there is no place that lacks a beauty. Rare is the person who has not succumbed to this foolishness. Even if one leaves after death a pile of gold high enough to reach the Big Dipper, it can never compare with the value of a barrel of *sake* while alive, they say. . . .

One can say that the sweet call of lust easily leads people astray. Indeed, wasn't that the case with the courtesan Kamegiku, who caused the Jōkyū Uprising? Surely it is this type of affair that brings down states and ruins great men! It is not enough to say that one should be prudent and make cautious choices at the forks in the road of life.

FAMOUS PLACES ALONG THE TŌKAIDŌ

ASAI RYŌI

B orn sometime in the second decade of the seventeenth century, Asai Ryōi was of the samurai class but became a *ronin*. Settling in Kyoto around 1650, he took vows as a Buddhist monk. Late in life he became a prolific and well-known writer of *kanazōshi*. Ryōi wrote on a diverse range of topics, including Buddhist tracts, primers on women's proper behavior, translations of Chinese and Korean folktales, and guidebooks to "famous places" (*meisho*). The guidebook translated in part here, *Famous Places along the Tōkaidō* (*Tōkaidō Meishoki,* ca. 1659), is one of his best-known works.

Like Ryōi's later guidebooks *Famous Places of Edo* (*Edo Meishoki,* 1662) and *Sparrow of Kyoto* (*Kyō Suzume,* 1665), *Famous Places along the Tōkaidō* is based on the author's own travels and observations, augmented by details and literary flourishes, many of which were not only inspired by but also lifted, almost word for word, from other published guidebooks and travel accounts. *Famous Places along the Tōkaidō* functions as a travel guide in that it gives many factual details about travel along the Tōkaidō, the main trunk road linking the shogunal capital of Edo to the imperial capital of Kyoto. But it is also a fictionalized travel tale about the adventures on the road of a young monk named Raku Amida Butsu (literally, "Amida Buddha of Pleasure"), also known as Raku Ami. Raku Ami is both protagonist and amanuensis for Asai Ryōi. Although Ryōi's work is understood primarily as fiction, its wealth of description of actual places and of local culture and folklore made it an important precedent for later, more factual travel accounts that began to appear in large numbers in the eighteenth century.

In the first section of the translation, the author introduces his travelers and sets up the premise for the journey. In the second section, Raku Ami tours Edo's many entertainment districts, describing the theaters and pleasure quarters there by emulating, or sometimes copying whole phrases verbatim from Nakagawa Kiun's descriptions of the analogous areas of Kyoto. From the perspective of our time, in which plagiarism is condemned and plagiarizers punished and shunned in the scholarly and literary communities, it is tempting to dismiss Ryōi as a mere imitator, trying to pass off the words of others for his own observations. However, Ryōi was only doing what many writers before him and after him also did—that is, alluding to and incorporating previous texts into his own as a matter of course. To borrow the work of another in this way was not to pretend to own it, but to acknowledge and honor it, as generations of poets and writers had always done. Ryōi's love of parody may also have given him an incentive to portray the new capital of Edo as an effective replica of the old capital of Kyoto, a suggestion most Kyotoites, with their disdain for the uncivilized eastern region, would have found appalling.

The excerpts translated below focus on the beginning and the ending of the journey on the Tōkaidō. Deciding to return to Kyoto, Raku Ami heads to the southwestern part of Edo, known as Shiba, to the entrance of the Tōkaidō. There he meets a young man who has been working as a clerk in the Edo branch of an Osaka-based store. The clerk, described as a handsome young man and also an inexperienced traveler, welcomes the companionship of Raku Ami, who is familiar with the ways of the road. The pairing of the young clerk with a monk seems to parody the well-known predilection of both priests and male shop clerks for engaging in same-sex relationships. Together, the two decide to journey back to their respective homes in the Kamigata. The unnamed fellow traveler—referred to throughout the text only as "the man"— serves as a fictive foil, since he becomes the audience for Raku Ami's constant narration of the journey on the Tōkaidō.

The last two sections bring the travelers to Yamashina, on the outskirts of Kyoto. Here their observations of male prisoners in a jail provide the impetus for a discussion of the corruptibility of human nature. The translation then skips to the last excerpt, which describes Kyoto and its entertainment district at the Shijō Riverbank, again borrowing heavily from the text of *Denizens of Kyoto,* where now-familiar characters and events are described in the blend of unembellished description and playful invention that were hallmarks of Ryōi's guidebooks.

(MY)

EXCERPT FROM "BOOK ONE: FROM EDO TO ŌISO"

"Send a treasured child on a journey," the saying goes. To become one who possesses the knowledge of myriad things, there is nothing better than travel. In my extensive and meandering travels on distant back roads I have seen things that have depressed, delighted, angered, and intrigued me, moved, frightened, endangered, and amused me, one experience after another, each different from the last. The minds of the people and their manner of speech are also this way, varying from province to province and place to place. Each person has his own fate; this goes for the cultured and the boorish.

And that's not all—there is the nature of the road itself. Over seas and rivers, mountains and hills, bridges and flatlands, over rocky plains and sandy expanses run narrow roads, bisecting paths, and forks in the road.

There are aids for the traveler: for making one's way in deep snow there

From Odawara to Hakone: Futako Mountain. (National Diet Library)

are sleds. For fording high waters there are rafts; for deep rivers there are
ferries. There are packhorses for rent to carry people and their luggage. For
those who are walking, the horses can also be used to carry the luggage alone.
There are horses for riding without luggage as well as palanquins and other
forms of conveyance. Or if no horses are available, a porter will carry your
luggage. There are people who will guide you on unfamiliar roads or to a
faraway inn. A store might sell rice cakes and dumplings, and tea stops might
offer toasted rice cakes. Depending on the region and the particular shop, local
delicacies, *sake,* and snacks are offered along with steamed or grilled fish.

Having walked all day, as evening approaches, one comes to post towns
where there are various inns. In the old days, these towns were courier stations
designated by the emperor for all twelve official highways so that messages
from the capital to all the provinces and circuits could be carried by postal
horses. All you had to do was say, "Postal horse coming!" and people would
hurry to move to the side of the road. Even today if you say those words, travelers will stand to the side of the road.

Now, there was once a useless fellow, a naive sort who had recently taken
priestly vows, who went by the name of Raku Amida Butsu, a pun on the
popular Buddhist prayer *Namu Amidabutsu.* He traveled from province to
province, not thinking of his next life but enjoying this one to its fullest. He

went on the eighty-eight-station pilgrimage around Shikoku and to Ise and Kumano Shrines. At Kumano Bay he boarded a boat that stopped at various ports, and he visited all sorts of famous places. At one point a tremendous storm struck, and Raku Ami thought, "Ah, it seems as though the boat is going to be torn apart!" and he went cold with fear. As long as he was on the boat, only one thin piece of board separated him from the roaring ocean, which made his heart freeze. "This is scary," he thought, and his balls shrank. This calls to mind the old poem "Seize each passing moment as if it were a family jewel in the sand." Indeed, it's true, people say. When said by this illiterate monk, people laughed their heads off, saying, "What ridiculous things he says!"

As the boat approached Edo, the captain said that because many boats come from the western provinces and southern seas, they must dock first at Teppōzu. Some proceed to Hatchōbori, and others approach Nihonbashi Bridge via Shinbori and Mitsumata. Beyond that some go to Reigan Island, said the boatman. Each boat approached the dock to let the passengers land.

Raku Ami had boarded the boat as a stowaway, so no one bothered to greet him. He was politely told to get off at Teppōzu, but when he did, he had no place to go. Since he was a no-good beggar in the guise of a priest, he was going to play a similar role in collecting for an imaginary temple as a mendicant monk from Kumano, performing for contributions. On the side, he would be able to enjoy some sightseeing.

Raku Ami said: "There will be places here where we won't be able to get horses. Generally, some places on the road have a glut of horses, other places a shortage. Where there is a shortage, it's best to reserve your horses the night before you set out. Now, shallow waters stretch along the road from here to Kawasaki. On the right-hand side, in the mountains, is the shogun's teahouse. If you climb up into these mountains, you can look at the sea stretching out below you. It is a sight worth seeing. Tōkai Temple is well known because of its founder, Takuan Washō, who lived there. Since Washō's death, high-ranking monks from the Murasakino Daitokuji in Kyoto take turns going to Tōkai Temple to serve a one-year term as the head of all Daitokuji-sect temples in the Kantō area. On the right, at some distance from the town is a Lotus-sect temple called Myōkokuji. The gate of this temple used to be the main gate of the residence of the chancellor of Suruga, Tokugawa Tadanaga. From this area they gather round stones and sell them in Edo as decoration. Dried seaweed from Shinagawa is also a famous product. It is small, has a reddish color, and is shaped like a cock's comb. In the inns of Shinagawa there are a lot of prostitutes who rush out, their hands still wet from kitchen work, and gesture for travelers to stop. Seeing this, the man with whom Raku Ami was traveling recited: "Hands beckoning / travelers passing / wet hands craft / the Shinagawa beach." "What an artful poem!" said Raku Ami. "It's the hands that are tricky here either way." Next is Suzunomori, or Bell Forest, where there is a famous rock called Suzunoishi, or Bell Rock, within the premises of the shrine. The line that says, "The Bell Rock evokes the sacred dances of Iyo Province" must refer to this place. The area is said to be unsafe; you must be careful and avoid passing through late at night.

"To the right of the sea road at a distance of not more than two *ri* one can see the place where the Lotus sect was founded. The spring water source is large, as is the five-storied pagoda. You can see both clearly. Rokugō Bridge is 120 *ken* in length. At the end of the bridge on the right side is the road that leads to Ikegami. On the left side of the road half a *ri* away is Haneda village, which is populated by hunters. Trout are found in the river at Rokugō, and from the top of the bridge to the west you can see Ōyama. This mountain is said to be about a day's walk away on this road."…

EXCERPT FROM "BOOK SIX: FROM YAMASHINA TO UJI VIA KYOTO"

In this way, they arrived at Yamashina. Here there is a fork in the road. If one veers left, the road leads to Shirutani Pass, from which you can see Otowa hamlet. You can see Tsuji Slope on the left and mountains on the right, with rivers running through the valleys below. The road ends south of Mount Kiyomizu. You can see Rokuhara Hall and the Great Buddha statue to the left, and then you arrive at the Gojō Bridge.

If you take the right fork, the road will take you to Jūzenji Temple. On the right, you can see the gate of Shinomiya Shrine. Below Hino Hill is a teahouse. From here it is one *ri* to Sanjō Bridge. On the left, there are the execution grounds. In the old days, you would climb the sea road, and it would have been on the right. Passersby would look up to the place from below and considered it a bad omen. Therefore, it has been moved to lower ground on the left. Nowadays, to the left are some shabby-looking settlements.

Everyone automatically thinks that having a son is a good thing, and the new father welcomes the baby with joy. The mother, too, is delighted. The baby, they think, will grow up so that the parents can depend on him. It may be the nature of the child, however, to grow up to admire the great thieves of Ancient China, to commit the sin of adultery for the sake of a one-night stand, to kill someone while compelled by momentary anger, or to be blinded by insignificant profit, violating the law and being chased out of his home and dragged here to have his severed head displayed to the public. Those who become known for their crimes are mostly men. If the son turns out to be human trash, happy are the parents who have no children. Whenever there is an execution, all rush to see the spectacle. Among the crowd, there are bound to be thieves who cut the strings of your purse. These people, indeed, are called "hell's prison guards" as opposed to "temple frequenters."

When Raku Ami's traveling companion looked to the south, he saw numerous small booths across the river from one another, on the east and west sides. He asked, "What is that over there?" One only has to hear the noise to know that it is the Shijō Riverbank. In olden times, kabuki was founded in the capital by a priestess from Izumo Shrine named Okuni. She performed at the east end of Gojō, at the foot of the bridge. She did a dance called "Boy's Dance." After that, a stage was set up to the east of Kitano Shrine, where she danced and sang and shouted praise to the Buddha. She held a painted umbrella and wore a crimson straw rain cape. She wore a bell around her neck and danced to the beat of flute and drums. At that time, there was no shamisen accompaniment. Okuni then took as a husband a comic actor named Sanjūrō and also added another called Densuke to the troupe. On the east side of Sanjō and behind Gion, stages were set up, and they performed on both of these. Sanjūrō acted and Densuke did puppetry, carrying away the entire capital with their shows.

There was a dance troupe from the pleasure quarters in Rokujō called Sadoshima. They set up a stage on the Shijō Riverbank, and numerous courtesans danced. Then a brothel called Wakajōrō set up another stage and performed nō. They did the *waki* and *tsure* parts of the nō, and they also sang regional songs. All of them were courtesans, and they sang in peculiar voices that sounded like the buzz of mosquitoes. Afterward, they had men sing the accompanying regional songs. Excess ensued, and pleasure quarters appeared in Gion, Ryūzen, and Maruyama. There was carousing all night long. The noblemen from great families changed their names and disguised themselves in order to come and go. Women's kabuki was banned. In spite of this the nobles can be found going to Rokujō, night after night. From Misujimachi and Nishi no Tōin to Chūdōji on western Seventh Avenue, combined with the part of Seventh Avenue in Nishi Shushaka was all enclosed and made into the pleasure quarters, and from this area no one could escape to the outside.

After that, young men's kabuki began for obvious reasons. Grown men grew their forelocks long like a boy's. There were Ebisu and Kichirōbē, Yamato and Rokubē, Murayama Matabē. This Sanbyōe banged on a *taikō* along with them. Kokumochi Kantarō made an enormous racket. Matakurō and Shumenosuke were playing old women. These are all comic performances. It is more amusement than a person can possibly bear.

TRANSLATED BY MARCIA YONEMOTO

GLITTERING HIGHLIGHTS OF EDO:
TRACES OF FAMOUS PLACES NEW AND OLD
KIKUOKA SENRYŌ

In contrast to the often entertaining if preachy works of Nakagawa Kiun and Asai Ryōi, many other guidebooks and travelogues presented information in a more straightforward, fact-oriented style familiar to today's reader of any tourist guidebook or website. The following excerpt comes from one such urban guide, entitled *Glittering Highlights of Edo: Traces of Famous Places New and Old* (*Edo Sunago Onko Meisekishi,* 1732). In its preface, the author, Kikuoka Senryō (1680–1747), explains that the title refers to a saying from the Confucian *Analects* that instructs readers to "learn something new from something old." He writes that he has taken this message to heart and has collected the lore of many of Edo's most knowledgeable old-timers, whose ubiquitous presence and constant chatter about the city earned them the nickname "sparrows of Edo" (*Edo suzume*).

In writing a guide to Edo in the early eighteenth century, Senryō was targeting an undeniably important audience: the fairly recent migrants to Edo who made the city, by the 1720s, the world's largest urban agglomeration, with a population of some 1.2 million. A compilation of fact and hearsay (hence the frequent use of "it is said"), *Glittering Highlights* takes its reader on a tour of the major and minor sites of the shogun's capital. Local history, folklore, important cultural developments, architecture, commerce—few details about life in Edo escape Senryō's notice. Like many guidebooks, including the two others excerpted here, *Glittering Highlights* devotes a considerable amount of space to the popular arts, such as the various forms of live theatre that had sprung up in Edo by the turn of the eighteenth century. Theatre in its various forms—kabuki, *jōruri,* nō, and nō's comic counterpart, *kyōgen*—had all achieved great popularity with urban commoners by the time Senryō was writing *Glittering Highlights.* Not far from the theater district, one could find another source of entertainment, the licensed pleasure quarters called Yoshiwara. The capsule histories of kabuki and *jōruri,* as well as the description of Yoshiwara found here, would have given the consumer of popular culture some sense of the development of the arts and entertainments of which he or she was fond, but without the moral messages found in the writings of Nakagawa Kiun and Asai Ryōi.

Glittering Highlights moves outward in ever-enlarging concentric circles like the urban structure of Edo itself, beginning from the shogun's castle, the symbolic center of the city. After describing in very general terms the layout of Edo Castle (maps or diagrams of the castle grounds themselves were not allowed to be published for security reasons), Senryō starts his tour just north of the castle compound at Nihonbashi, the "Bridge of Japan," which was the formal starting point for measuring traveling distances on the five major highways leading out to the provinces. The neighborhood surrounding the bridge was one of the most prosperous and lively commercial districts in the city at the time, home to many of the wealthy merchants who had been designated official purveyors of goods to the shogunal house.

As in all writing of this genre, there is a great deal of wordplay that is difficult to translate here. For example, in the section describing Ikkokubashi, a major bridge near Edo Castle, a medium (a low-class person capable of speaking with the dead) is seen crossing the bridge, a rather odd sight. A medium's method is referred to as "bringing one's mouth" to the dead, which is the source of the playful reference of the possible reason why she might be crossing the bridge. The reader will also see a characteristic pun on the name of the bridge, which invokes units of weight measurement that were used chiefly for grains. There were ten *to* in one *koku*—hence, "*go-to* and *go-to*," or five *to* and five *to*, make one *koku* (*ikkoku*), the name of the bridge. Similarly, readers familiar with contemporary Tokyo will find in Senryō's guide the etymologies of many place-names still in use today.

(MY)

NIHONBASHI BRIDGE

Runs north–south. Length: approximately 28 *ken*. Said to be the center of Edo. The roads going in all directions begin here, and traveling distances are measured from this point. On the northern end of the bridge is First Street of Muromachi; its western side is called Amaya, a property originally granted by the shogunate to Amagasakiya Mataemon, a lacquerware merchant. It has the so-called front store, which is an extension made by added layers of eaves, where packhorse fittings and other smaller lacquerware accessories are displayed. The east side of the bridge is Ōfuna Street. The stores there hold a fish market every day.

IKKOKUBAS HI BRIDGE

A little more than two blocks to the west of Nihonbashi, the Ikkokubashi Bridge, formerly called Ōhashi, crosses the Nihonbashi River running along-

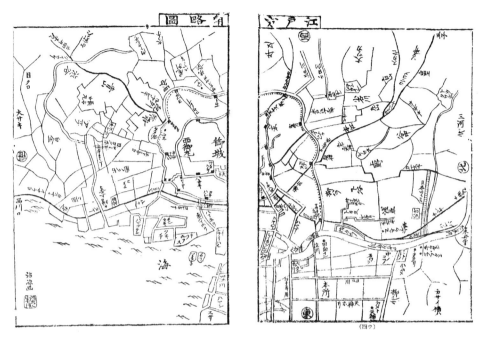

A map of Edo and vicinity. (Keio University Library)

side the moat of Edo Castle. At its northern end is the mansion of the confectioner Ōkubo Mondo. The area is also called Tokiwabashi. It is said that when the shogun went on a boating excursion during the Kan'ei era (1624–1644), he asked about the place and learned that it was Mondo's store. The poet Nakarai Bokuyō, who happened to be among the shogun's party, received a command to compose a poem. He said,

> Even a medium
> Would cross this bridge
> To bring her mouth
> Close to Mondo's cakes.

To the south of this bridge is the clothier Gotō and to the north is the money changer Gotō, and so they have a saying that "Goto and Goto make Ikkoku-bashi." They also call it Eighth Bridge because from this bridge you can see seven other bridges nearby, making this one the eighth. All eight are Nihonbashi, Edobashi, Gofukubashi, Kajibashi, Zenigamebashi, Dōsanbashi, Tokiwabashi, and Ikkokubashi.

EDOBASHI BRIDGE

It is about two blocks to the east of Nihonbashi. At its northern end is Ise-chō.

MUROMACHI

Long ago, outcasts resided in this area, making a menial living in minor labor. That tradition is still alive in the candlewicks sold at the crossroads today.

THE FOURTH STREET OF HONCHŌ

It is said that long ago this area was punishment grounds.

HOURLY CHIMES

This bell, on the new road on the northern end of the Third Street of Kokuchō, is said to have come from inside the precincts of Edo Castle. After several fires, it no longer rang well, so it was recast recently by Shiina Iyo. The bell is said to produce a resonant, reverberating sound in the traditional Hoshiki tune.

JIKKENDANA

This is a boulevard located between Honchō and Kokuchō. Every year merchants sell Girls' Day dolls before the holiday in the third month. Before the Boys' Day holiday in the fifth month they sell figurines dressed in samurai armor. In the twelfth month, they sell bows and arrows as well as wooden paddles for badminton games. It is a very lively place.

TEPPŌCHŌ

This area was called Chiyoda Village in the old days.

THE FIRST STREET OF KOKUCHŌ

Now called Ginmachi, the area used to be called Fukuda Village.

THE EMBANKMENT OF SHIROGANECHŌ

It is said to have been built during the Meireki era (1655–1657) to prevent the spread of fires. It runs seven *chō* east to west. Nowadays, storehouses built

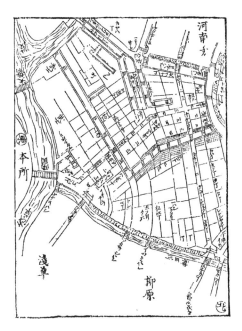

A map of the area north of Nihonbashi Bridge. (Keio University Library)

with rammed-earth walls are seen here and there, leaning against the embankment.

SHIRATA INARI SHRINE

It is on the First Street of Shiroganechō. Its chief priest is Daijuin (belonging to the Sambōin sect).

KODENMACHŌ

In olden times this place was a post station called Roppongi, where a traveler could exchange his tired horse for a fresh one. Today that tradition still exists, for there are inns and horses for rent there.

JAIL

This is on the north side of the First Street of Kodenmachō. When the shogun first moved to Edo, around here there were four or five large nettle trees. In those days they arrested criminals and put them under these trees. The prisoners were entrusted to a person called Head Guard Ishide Tatewaki. He was a man of valor, and eventually this became his official duty.

THE FRONT OF YAKUSHI SHRINE

This refers to the upper part of Kodenmachō. On old Edo maps, it is sometimes called Shirinawachō. In the old days, the Asakusa Tōkōin building was here, and its chief buddha was Yakushi. This is why Yakushi is included in the name of the shrine.

CHIYODA INARI

Suwa Nyōjin resides here. On the upper street of Kodenmachō, there is Betto Kyokōin. In the past, the shrine was in the forest of Shinobuoka. It was moved here later to the property of the Miyagi family. Examples of miraculous efficacy have been reported. Strange stories are still circulating.

HORSE STABLES

These are located on a street running behind the northern end of Bakurōchō. It is the oldest stable in all of Edo. The place is distinguished by the fact that, at the time of the Battle of Sekigahara (1600), this is where the shogun's inspection of horses and troops took place. Two shogunal grooms, called Takagi Genbē and Tomita Hanshichi, managed these stables, so the area became known as Bakurōchō, or "Groom's Street."

THEATERS

Kabuki:

Nakamura Kanzaburō, Sakai-chō
Ichimura Takenojō, Fukiya-chō

Puppet *jōruri:*

Yamamoto Dewa, Sakai-chō
Tatsumatsu Hachirōbei, Fukiya-chō

Long ago, these theaters were located in Shibai-chō. At that time, they were outdoor street-corner shows. Eventually, theaters were built at Nakabashi, where the space was enclosed with straw mats, in the manner of the shrine-style theater buildings we have today. Later, the theaters moved to Negi-chō, and then to the location they occupy now. Also, it is said that there are small theaters at the edge of the castle moat.

Kanzaburō's theater:

In the first year of Kan'ei (1624), Nakamura Kanzaburō put on, with the government's permission, his first performances of kabuki in Nakabashi. The original Kanzaburō was talented at comic scenes and famous for his singing. It is said that in the ninth year of Kan'ei, the shogunal vessel *Atakemaru* returned to the capital from Izu. On this trip, Kanzaburō received the shogun's baton and stood on the bow of the boat, pounding out a log-driving song. In the Keichō era (1596–1614), he had performed at Edo Castle and was rewarded with money as well as gold brocade costumes. These are said to be among the Nakamura troupe's treasured possessions today. The second-generation Nakamura is called Akashi Kanzaburō. When he went to Kyoto after the Meireki Fire, the court nobles, who desired to watch Edo-style comedy, summoned him to perform. Kanzaburō, accompanied by this son who was still in training, performed the comedy. As a measure of their appreciation, the court bestowed upon the son the name "Akashi," and thereafter he was known by this name. The present Kanzaburō is the sixth generation.

Takenojō's theater:

In the tenth year of Kan'ei (1633), Murayama Matasaburō set up a kabuki theater. Coming from Sakai in Izumi Province, Matasaburō became famous for solo performing and singing. The second head of the lineage was named Murayama Kurōemon. Ichimura Uzaemon Hikosaku was the manager and owner of the theater. While they specialized in dance only, in the Kanbun era (1661–1672), someone named Ukon Gonzaemon from Kamigata joined the theater and played the part of a woman in a series of plays. This troupe also performed at Edo Castle several times and received money and clothing in return. The third in the lineage was Takenojō, Ichimura Uzaemon's son. From this point on, each successor was called Takenojō. From the original Matasaburō to the present Takenojō is eight generations. In the past this theater was called the "big show." In addition, there is the Miyako theater, led by Miyako Den'nai.

The origins of kabuki lie with the monk Fujiwara no Michinori, the counselor of Retired Emperor Go-Toba (1180–1239), who was gifted in all the arts. He adapted the courtly all-male dance to teach a woman named Iso no Zenji. Because she danced waving a sword and wearing a courtier's white robe and hat, it was called the "man's dance." Zenji passed on her art to her daughter,

Shizuka. Later they abandoned the swords and became the *shirabyōshi,* who flourished for many generations. In the late sixteenth and early seventeenth centuries, a female dancer from Sado Island named Okuni assembled a group of women and performed on the riverbed at Shijō in Kyoto. Because they were women of pleasure as well as performers, their art came to be called kabuki, or "outrageous acts." After many incidents of chaos and unseemly behavior, women's kabuki was banned, so from that time on, youth's kabuki flourished. This too became disruptive in the same way, however, and eventually kabuki was closed down completely. In Edo this was the time of Ichimura Hikosaku's and Nakamura Kanzaburō's theaters. Theaters petitioned and received permission to perform again by shaving off the young actors' forelocks, thus turning them into mature male actors. These men donned women's wigs and contrived to perform the role of courtesans in plays that depicted erotic pleasures at Shimabara, Kyoto's chief pleasure district. "Kamikiri Shimabara" and "Sakata Shimabara" were the titles of some of these skits, and therefore those plays came to be categorized as "Shimabara." Shimabara came to incorporate classical nō plays, as in "Yashima Shimabara" and "Ataka Shimabara." Shimabara plays no longer exist.

What is known as *jōruri* originated with Lord Oda Nobunaga's serving girl Ono no O-tsū, a gifted writer. After her service with Nobunaga, she served the wife of Grand Minister Hideyoshi. At his behest, she composed a twelve-scene work about the love between Princess Jōruri, the daughter of the head arrowsmith, and the great hero Ushiwakamaru, who was later called Minamoto no Yoshitsune. Her stylistic verve was like that of *The Tales of Ise.* Hideyoshi was moved and said that just as the lute player Shōbutsu had put music to the version of *The Tales of the Heike,* written by Shinano no Zenji Yukinaga, Blind Master Iwafune should put music to O-tsū's ballad. He had her composition read by Yamanaka, the Lord of Yamashiro, and had the music added by Blind Master Iwafune. It became popular in the countryside around Kyoto, and a female performer named Rokuji Namuemon staged it on the riverbanks at Shijō in Kyoto. Later, when people got tired of the twelve-scene ballad, she put music to such pieces as *Yashima* and *Takadachi.* She called these songs *jōruri,* which became a general term for all these chanted narratives.

They also say that Takino and Sawakado, both blind minstrels who were skilled lute players, changed the chanting of *jōruri* by making the tunes more melodious. At that time they did not include the shamisen; it is said that they used the fingernails of the right hand to rap out the rhythm on the ribs of a fan. After this, they created a piece called *Tour of the Capital.* This was written by one of their disciples, a person from Kyoto called Higashi Tōin Menukiya Chōzaburō.

In the early seventeenth century, the emperor requested a performance of this piece. Puppets were added, and after repeated performances, the emperor bestowed on the performers the title of "*jōruri* master." In Edo, theaters were beginning to spring up, established by troupes such as Ōzatsuma and Kozatsuma, and leading actors like Shirō, Yukichi, and others. After this, Aburaya Mohei, Toriya Jirokichi, and Nanboku Kidayū, followed by Toraya Gendayū, Tosadayū, Izumidayū, and Edo Handayū, all opened theaters. As for the origin of the use of puppets, puppeteers from Nishinomiya were first called in to work the puppets.

ALL THREE PIECES TRANSLATED BY MARCIA YONEMOTO

A Journey to Ise

SOME SIBLING SCRIBBLES

MUKAI KYORAI AND CHINE

Most people are not eager to take a road trip with their siblings. In *A Journey to Ise: Some Sibling Scribbles* (*Ise Kikō*, written in 1686), however, a brother and sister decide not only to travel together but also to record for posterity their experiences along the way.

Travel writing was a venerable genre by the autumn when the *haikai* poets Mukai Kyorai (1651–1704) and his younger sister Chine (dates unknown) set out from Kyoto, heading southeast. Their ultimate destination was the Grand Shrines at Ise, one of Japan's most famous sites and, being dedicated to Amaterasu—the Sun Goddess and alleged progenitor of Japan's imperial lineage—the holiest of holy places in Shinto. The hundred-mile-or-so road linking the imperial capital with the shrines was so well traveled over the years as to be virtually littered with well-known spots and literary allusions. Yet this account may please most when providing sketches of relatively unknown but arguably more colorful attractions, such as an old lady who sells wrinkle-free rice cakes (section 4).

More poetic diary in snapshot form than fine-grained travelogue, *A Journey to Ise* spares its readers many details. For one thing, the authors presumed that their contemporaries would already be familiar with the terrain, the literary associations, and the poetic techniques employed. This was certainly the case with Matsuo Bashō, who as one of the first to read the manuscript was charmed enough to contribute the postscript. For another thing, it is the poetry, rather than the straightforward prose, that leaves the greater impression upon the imagination.

Several poetic forms are represented here: haiku, linked verse, the 31-syl-lable *waka*, and Chinese verse. Twenty-eight of the poems are in Japanese; fourteen are attributed to Kyorai and fourteen to Chine. Although no name is attached to the two poems in Chinese (7), most likely it was Kyorai who penned them. Some poems capture the surprise of encountering a new landscape (2 and 9); others address the challenges of their journey (5, 10, 18); still others make observations about the locals they meet (12, 14, 15). The tone tends to be light, even humorous, and this may help explain the absence of any verse to commemorate their stopping to worship the deity of Suzuka (11) or even their culminating visit to the awe-inspiring Grand Shrines themselves (19).

Perhaps the most unusual, if not moving, aspect of the work is its glimpse into the relationship of its brother-and-sister authors. Travel had long been associated with exile, pilgrimage, or romance, not family outings. And the perspective in such writing is almost always that of the lonesome traveler, not bickering siblings. Although the paths, both physical and literary, that Kyorai and Chine followed were hardly new, the authenticity of their repartee feels refreshing—as when Kyorai unconventionally equates Chine's whining with the persistent cry of a deer (8). Chine emerges as the quicker to complain (5 and 7), but from her very first poem she also embodies the excitement and charm of the novice traveler. Chine and Kyorai complement one another and make for lively companions.

It was not only on the road that the two had their differences; their shared poetic talent notwithstanding, in life their paths diverged significantly. Kyorai, for his part, got around famously. Born in Nagasaki, he went to stay with an uncle in Fukuoka, where he lived among samurai and practiced martial arts. He later gave up that life for one of greater leisure and refinement in Kyoto, where his father's connections with the imperial family as a Confucian scholar and physician gave Kyorai access to court circles and aristocratic culture. Kyorai met Bashō through the introduction of the poet Takarai Kikaku (aka Enomoto Kikaku, 1661–1707) and quickly became one of the great master's ten leading disciples. He eventually authored an important treatise on *haikai*, titled *Conversations with Kyorai* (*Kyorai-shō*, ca. 1702), which makes clear his indebtedness to Bashō's teachings. Kyorai also built a small cottage west of Kyoto that served as a favorite gathering spot for Bashō and his school's poets when passing through the imperial capital.

Chine's life, in contrast, remains mostly veiled in mystery. In *A Journey to Ise,* she comes across as the neophyte alongside her more sophisticated brother. This may have been a literary pose or the result of a sheltered life as a young woman, or a combination thereof. Regardless, it is her ingenuity that not only inspires their journey in the first place but also imbues many of the scenes along the way with such vividness. Chine seems to have set the expressive pace, in other words, while Kyorai set down the record on paper. It is a shame that little is known about Chine's life apart from what is recorded in this poetic diary.

Some information on the literary allusions made by the two poets may be of use to the reader. The commentary after Kyorai's poem in section 2 refers to a famous *waka* by Nōin (988–1050?). The reference to autumn wind is taken from Nōin's poem, in which the speaker journeys from the capital to the famous Shirakawa Barrier in the north, leaving the capital in the mists of spring and arriving at the barrier with the autumn winds. "Deer Enclosure," by Wang Wei (699?–761), is suggested by Kyorai's poem in response to Chine in section 8. As in the Chinese poem, the travelers' surroundings only appear to be a forbidding landscape deep in the mountains, as Chine sees it. Kyorai responds by teasing his sister and insisting that the forest is not as deep as she thinks it to be, exaggerating her concerns with literary allusion. As is the case with Kyorai's response here, the siblings occasionally fall into a pattern of creating linked verse. This can also be seen in section 17, in which Chine's two 17-syllable lines link to Kyorai's preceding poem.

The present text existed only in handwritten manuscript copies until it was printed for the first time in 1850 to celebrate the 150th anniversary of Kyorai's death.

(SB)

(1) The days were balmy and the winds refreshing when my sister became obsessed with the idea of a pilgrimage to Ise. We headed out while it was still dark, around the twentieth of the eighth month.

> Take us with you
> on a fine passage to Ise!
>   Oh, morning geese—
>
> —Chine

I added these lines,

> Down toward the southeast
> where the moon shadow lightens.
>
> —Kyorai

(2) We made our way to the Shirakawa Bridge. Little by little the houses appeared humbler—their eaves tattered and their roofs threatened by the passing autumnal gusts.

> At Shirakawa
> they lay rocks on rooftops—
> wind in autumn.
>
> —Kyorai

Everyone knows the famous poem by that priest Nōin. Well, Chine started grumbling about how the harbor guard or whoever it was in that old poem couldn't possibly have made the trip all the way to that barrier because even this nearby Shirakawa is such a distant haul. I tried to tell her it was just an amusing anecdote, like the ones we hear about travelers taking lodging with the celestial Weaver Maiden.

(3) On our way to Ōtsu, horse carts passed by noisily, so we couldn't very well compose any poetry. But at Matsumoto we happily gave ourselves over to the idea of a boat trip across Lake Biwa. Many people were gathered on the beach there.

> In the eighth month
> what may delay those who wish
> to cross to Yabase?
>
> —Chine

She spat that one out and tried another:

> In the mist
> spreading like wings before us—
> Lake Biwa.
>
> —Chine

> Even the autumn wind
> does as it pleases
> on Lake Biwa.
>
> —Kyorai

Delighting in the scenery, we went on like this.

(4) We came to stop for the night at Kusatsu and saw this sign: *Granny Rice Cakes—Once upon a Time Wrinkle Free!* The proprietress of the locale turned around to face us—she certainly was a granny!

"I've just torn off this piece, hot from out of the mortar, so it isn't cold yet!" she shouted. Chine found this all endlessly amusing, and in the madam's stead came up with this:

> I apply my rouge
> without fail and everywhere—
>   so, no matter when you peek,
> wrinkles you'll never see
> on these granny's cakes!
>
> —Chine

(5) We stopped at Isobe while the sun was still high. We rinsed off our feet and grabbed a bite to eat, though it wasn't seven o'clock yet.

> Even autumn evenings
> become familiar shelters
>   sleeping on the road.
>
> —Kyorai

This was really the first time Chine had been away from home. For the most part, things thrilled and impressed her, but now and then she'd feel homesick and distract herself with a poem.

> So weary am I
> even through a long autumn night
>   I could sleepy soundly!
>
> —Chine

(6) What a wintry shock we got crossing Yokota River in the early morning hours! As we passed Minakuchi, we were too sleepy to utter a single word to one another.

(7) The horses could make it over Mount Tsuchi only by scrambling sideways like crabs.

> Crab Hill—we clamber over it once like a crab!

Chine didn't even lay her eyes on the landscape here. She missed home and demanded another line from me.

> Mount Centipede—we crawl around it seven times like a
>   centipede!

(8) We made it up Mount Suzuka, but many others that day didn't. The surrounding pine and oak trees flourished lushly, and the tips of their branches
were a rich green. The clamor of the autumn wind was impressive. Chine
recited this:

> Even the birdies
> cannot make it across—
>   so deep is the mountain!
>
> —Chine

One cannot but respect great poems by the likes of Wang Wei. I came up with
this modest response:

> Mountain so profound!
> We hear the deer repeatedly wail
>   its high-pitched song.
>
> —Kyorai

(9) We didn't see any woodcutters in this area, and the autumn grasses were
growing in wild profusion. Needless to say, it made for quite a wonderful sight.

> From the mountain path
> we emerge, hats heavy with
>   bush clover and eulalia.
>
> —Chine

(10) To the east, the crags rose raggedly one after another. Dew made the way
slippery; it was hard to keep oneself steady.

> Hold on tight
> to that horse's bit—oh how misty
>   this deep valley!
>
> —Kyorai

(11) When we made it through the valley, we went to worship the great
deity of Suzuka. As we paid the head priest our contribution for the torch, he
said, while putting the money away, that the road back would be difficult for
us because it was getting dark. How funny the way he's so good at his trade!

(12) Since it wasn't much farther to the bottom of the slope, we took lodging for the night at the pass there. A group of women—some young, some old— were gathered at the house across from where we stayed. They ground out songs as they worked their mortars. Until it grew dark, we kept the shutters up and listened.

> Night after night
> even the rice-pounding ditties
>   vary at each stop.
>
> —Chine

(13) The rain had finally let up during the night, but a cloudy mist filled the sky. We couldn't even see our bags fastened onto the backs of the horses.

> Such morning mist!
> I must ask the locals
>   if it means rain.
>
> —Kyorai

Finally, as the wind picked up, the sun came out and cleared everything. Everyone got excited, and half of us took off for Musashino. Headed south on horseback, changing rides at each stop: Kusuhara and Mukumoto. Finally, we passed Toyokuni.

> The field grasses
> can't hold onto the dew—
>   no matter how high they grow!
>
> —Chine

(14) At Tsu we stopped for a while and fed our grumbling stomachs before heading out toward the Kumozu riverside. Although many people halted their horses and carriages and clamored for a boat, the ferryman stopped on the other side and didn't even turn to look at us. All this hustle and bustle reminded me of a fine morning in Fukawaga at the home of my old poetry master Bashō.

The autumn wind blew mercilessly, and the ferryman's face was no less cruel!

I spoke up:

Hey, ferryman,
use the autumn winds
to clear out your earwax!

—Kyorai

One way or another we managed to get across, and by nightfall we arrived in Matsuzaka.

(15) The village looked prosperous and the people spirited, but this certainly was the boondocks!

Beaten down
by the echoes of thrashing straw—
the fulling block!

—Kyorai

(16) When we got up this morning ready to set off for our visit to the Grand Shrines at Ise, the last hints of the moon shone in the eastern sky.

At dawn
we follow the way lit by
the crescent moon.

—Chine

When it comes to song
each and every insect
can sing one.

—Kyorai

(17) We walked past Kushida and crossed the river at Inagi. As daylight broke, we stopped for a bit of a rest at the Morning Star Teahouse. Once our legs felt rejuvenated, we headed out across the fields of Yudano.

Now it's over
the season for hunting the wild rose—
eulalia sways.

—Kyorai

Near this village
unfamiliar mushrooms sprout.

—Chine

(18) We passed the village of Obata without help. At Miyagawa, the ferryman wasn't anything like the one we encountered the other day.

> Before too many
> clog the way, let's dip in
> and wash away our sins.
>
> —Kyorai

> My hands, now clean,
> may be dried by
> the autumn breeze.
>
> —Chine

(19) We changed out of our traveling robes, tidied our hair, and humbly presented ourselves at the Grand Shrines. Deeply moved, we shed tears for quite some time. The one hundred and twenty shrines, the Heavenly Plain, and the Gate of the Celestial Rock Cave—leaving nothing out, we paid homage to them all. Of course, we couldn't take our eyes off the divine Mount Kamiji or the Isuzu River. We looked upon every stone and tree in such awe that our hearts hardly appreciated the beauty of the landscape. We wandered around until it grew dark, then returned to the village at Uji.

(20) We passed that evening buying souvenirs and supplies. The next morning Chine was still carping about having not yet seen any of the famous Ise fisherfolk, and so we set out for a look around Futami. Along the shore, where flowering grasses cling tightly to the craggy slope and the briny sea slaps, we found clusters of small huts. The scene made me recall a poem by Kikaku about sleeping on pampas grass during the early summer rains, and even though the time and place were now very different from those of the poem, we found ourselves coming up with some of our own:

> In no time at all
> we see more and more sails swell
> across the misty sea.
>
> —Chine

> Around midday
> an autumn breeze to cure the rain.
>
> —Kyorai

In the fields
the horse hauling rice weed
    gives a howl.

                        —Kyorai

In the cold of the embankment
they seem to be hurrying home.

                        —Chine

And with these we ended our journey.

POSTSCRIPT

Rootless grasses bear neither blossoms nor fruit, and these words are just the playful mutterings of a humble chatterer. Anyway, around the time when Kikaku had been sleeping beneath the skies of the capital for about a year, we came to know this man Kyorai coming from the Mukai family, and quickly fell into friendship. Whether sipping *sake* or talking over tea, splashes of sentiments, sweet and bitter, conveyed the shallows and depths of faint human hearts. Indeed, from just a few drops, we could savor the taste of one hundred streams.

This autumn Kyorai accompanied his sister on a journey to Ise. Setting out with the autumn breezes off the Shirakawa River, they snapped and spread reeds on which to slumber. As a memento of their travels, night after night they recorded all that was moving in a diary, and they have sent it here to me at my grass hut. The first time I read the diary, I did so silently, and my emotions were stirred. The second time, I recited it out loud and lost myself within it. The third time, I found it nothing less than perfect.

Kyorai has mastered the way of poetry.

East and west
all that is moving caught
    in the autumn breeze.

                        —Bashō

TRANSLATED BY STEFANIA BURK

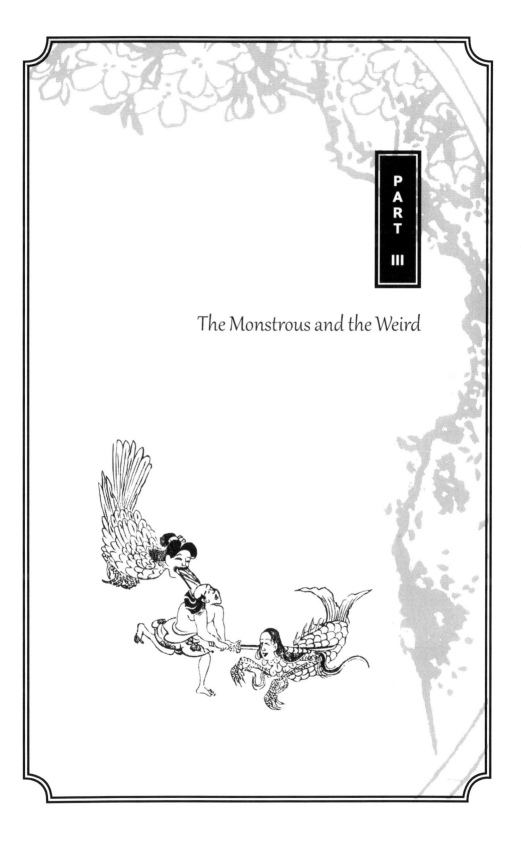

PART III

The Monstrous and the Weird

One Hundred Tales from the Various Provinces

ANONYMOUS

In spite of its seemingly bland title, *One Hundred Tales from the Various Provinces* (*Shokoku Hyakumonogatari,* 1677) is not simply a nondescript assemblage of myriad stories from the countryside of early modern Japan, each installment offering a bit of local color. Rather, to a contemporary reader when the collection was published in Kyoto in 1677, the "hundred tales" indicated a specific story genre and a particular type of social storytelling practice that had already become a popular phenomenon. In this practice of sharing "one hundred tales" (*hyakumonogatari*), sometimes referred to more descriptively as a "gathering for one hundred tales of the strange," thrill-seeking individuals assembled at night to tell stories of encounters with ghosts, the supernatural, and the marvelous creatures now known collectively as monsters (*yōkai*). Often held on a moonless night, the event began with the illumination of one hundred lampwicks. As each raconteur extinguished one of these lights at the conclusion of his or her tale, the ambience grew steadily spookier, preparing participants for an otherworldly experience of their own, once total darkness had descended upon the group—or at least upon those who had dared to remain.

Two collections from 1659 confirm that the "one hundred tales" genre was already well on its way to becoming an established point of reference in the popular consciousness at midcentury. These and other texts attest to slight variations in method; one procedure, for example, required each storyteller to gaze into a mirror at the conclusion of his tale. The practice of telling one hundred ghost stories under these progressively creepy conditions seems to have enjoyed particular favor as a form of entertainment, as well as a means of testing one's bravery, through the late Edo period.

As we see in the following selections, *One Hundred Tales from the Various Provinces* self-referentially invokes the one-hundred-tales practice in the frame narrative of its preface and in its final episode, both of which take the story-telling event itself as the scene of encounters with the unknown. More broadly, the theme of proving one's mettle by undergoing a frightening ordeal resurfaces in other tales from the collection, such as those that feature a samurai making a late-night trip alone to a deserted shrine or spending the night in a haunted temple.

A few of the stories appearing in this collection, especially those contained in the first of its five volumes, overlap closely with those appearing in other works, particularly *Sorori's Tales* (*Sorori Monogatari*), compiled at least a decade earlier. Moreover, the supernatural figures whom the characters encounter include some that are general types well known from much earlier sources, such as the fork-tailed cat (*nekomata*). Traditional lore had long attributed to cats as well as foxes the ability to alter their appearance, often to that of a beautiful woman, and to bewitch human beings. Such linkage of animals, shape-shifting, and sexual desire recurs in two stories herein featuring snakes as common figures of attachment that each story exploits differently. One other animal familiar from everyday experience that was believed to share such powers of deceptive transformation was the raccoon dog (*tanuki*), though as one story suggests, its powers as a trickster were often associated more with comic mischief than erotic allure.

In spite of such intertextual connections, however, one noteworthy feature of this collection was its performance of veracity. As the compiler assures readers in his preface, the stories all derive from firsthand reports of local individuals who either saw directly or heard accounts of the related events. The story below that touches on the persecution of Christians in seventeenth-century Japan, for instance, makes a point of noting the names of the villages where the events took place. One scholar has connected such truth claims to what he argues was a contemporary distinction between unsourced stories (*hanashi*) that tend to involve anonymous individuals, and tales (*monogatari*) that provide richer details about their settings and the names of the individuals involved.

The stories sampled here have been chosen to illustrate both the collection's recurring themes of revenge, obsession, and trickery as well as its tonal range, from broad comedy to unsettling horror.

PREFACE

Where did this sequence of one hundred tales come from, you ask? Well, there was a ronin named Takeda Nobuyuki who dwelled in a place called Suwa in Shinshū Province. One rainy night, he was whiling away the tedium along with three or four young samurai who were his companions on a journey. As they chatted away about any number of topics, Nobuyuki remarked, "It has been said since ancient times that if people sitting round a circle tell a sequence of one hundred tales, then something mysterious will surely transpire at the place where they have gathered. How about it? Let's tell stories tonight and see what happens!"

They seated themselves in a circle, placing one hundred lampwicks at its center and lighting them. They began telling stories, going around the circle in sequence. As each story was told, a single lampwick was extinguished. They proceeded in this way until they had told ninety-nine stories and just one lampwick remained lit. At this thoroughly eerie moment, a terrific noise thundered out, as though a huge rock had dropped onto the room's ceiling. Just then the lamp went out, to everyone's astonishment. Unfazed, Nobuyuki said, "I've got this covered," and he seized something, pinning it down. "I've subdued the monster! It's like the thigh of a giant man! Quick, light a lamp!" As each of the men lit a lamp and brought it close, they realized that Nobuyuki had grabbed ahold of the thigh of one of the samurai who was present in the circle. Everyone erupted in laughter before going their separate ways. We have taken the written text of the stories that a scribe recorded that evening and carved them into printing blocks with the intention of spreading them in the world as an amusement for all, whether young or old, man or woman. While it is true that some illustrated books with the title of *One Hundred Tales* have been published, they are but entertainment intended for children and their sources are dubious. This book, by contrast, gathers together stories that are properly documented: tales that were actually heard or witnessed by people from each of the various provinces. We have assembled these stories into five volumes and given it the title *One Hundred Tales from the Various Provinces.*

A PRACTITIONER OF ASCETIC RITES ENCOUNTERS A DEPARTED SPIRIT IN THE PROVINCE OF SHIMOTSUKE

Long ago, a monk who had never once violated the precepts of the Buddhist priesthood was making his way down to Shimotsuke Province to carry out some ascetic religious training. It became dark while he was still in the midst of his travels, and since it was still a long way to the nearest inn that could offer him lodging, he decided to spend the night in the middle of a field. As he was reciting Buddhist scriptures and intoning the Buddha's name, he heard the faint sound of a flute coming from somewhere, though it was impossible to pinpoint the source. The monk listened and thought to himself, "To hear the sound of a flute in such a remote place is peculiar indeed." Fearful thoughts in his heart, he devoted himself to reciting the holy name with even more zeal.

The sound of the flute drew closer to him bit by bit, and when he looked up, he saw a young man, perhaps just sixteen years of age. The youth's appearance was most elegant and noble; it made one wonder if perhaps Narihira, the dashing lover of ancient times, might have looked something like this. The monk thought this even stranger yet and reasoned that it could only be some kind of apparition that had come to a deserted field such as this one, especially in the dead of night. As the monk began to intone the *shingon* and *dhāraṇī* incantations of esoteric Buddhism, the youth asked, "Honorable monk, for what purpose have you come to this sort of place all by yourself?" The monk responded, "Evening fell in the midst of my travels, and so I am spending the night here. But what about you, sir? What sort of person might you be to have come to a place like this?" His timidity in asking was obvious, and the youth responded, "Honorable monk, it seems as though you believe that I am an apparition. Verily I declare to you that this is not the case. Rather, on nights like tonight when the moon shines clear, I take comfort in playing my flute. Do not be alarmed. I would like to accompany you to my cottage and offer you lodging for the night." Although he remained uncertain and apprehensive, the monk reasoned, "If that youth is in fact an apparition, he is surely not going to leave me in peace here." He departed with the youth, and when they came to a village, there was a large castle standing there. They passed through two or three nested gates and then across a moat. The youth beckoned the priest farther and farther into the castle's interior until they came to a handsomely appointed parlor with tatami-mat flooring. "Please go in here," he said, bringing out some cooked dried rice to serve to the priest. He then offered the priest tea and so forth, saying, "Please relax and stay here. I always sleep on the other side of these sliding paper doors. I am sure you must be tired from your journey." Having offered these polite and attentive remarks, the youth withdrew to the interior. The priest thought this was even more mysterious, and he could not sleep all night. Just as dawn was about to break, many people arrived, jostling each other and saying, "There is a strange priest here! What sort of thing can he be that he was able to steal into the interior of the palace, where the guard is strict? How did he get in? Let's bind and torture him!" The priest was astonished and said, "All of you, please wait a moment," and he told them his whole story from beginning to end. Observing that the people were surprised and shed tears upon hearing his tale, the priest inquired into the details. One responded, "This is what happened. Just twenty days ago, the young lord of this castle perished after having contracted a cold. He was just fifteen years old, and since he was always practicing the flute, we placed a flute made of Chinese bamboo before his memorial tablet on the altar. We placed tea and other offerings of food there too. It must be that the spirit of our deceased young lord revered you, honorable monk, and brought you here to this room. That being the case, please stay for a while to offer mourning rites for the remains of our young lord." So saying, they communicated this intent to the lord of the castle and provided the priest with lodgings, treating him to various delicacies.

ON THE MONSTER CALLED SHUNOBAN FROM SUWA SHRINE IN AIZU

There was a fearsome monster called Shunoban in the Suwa shrine of Aizu in the province of Mutsu. One evening, a young samurai about twenty-five or -six years old passed before the Suwa shrine by himself. He had often heard that there was a monster there, so his heart was filled with terrifying thoughts.

Just then arrived another samurai, aged about twenty-six or -seven. Thinking he would be a good traveling companion, the first samurai continued in the company of the second. As they chatted along the way, the first samurai asked, "It is said that the infamous monster Shunoban dwells here. Have you ever heard of it?" The second samurai replied, "Now, this monster you mention, is it something like this?" No sooner had he said this than his face suddenly transformed: his eyes became as big as saucers, and a horn appeared on his forehead. His face was the color of vermilion dye, and the hair on his head was like wire. His mouth was split all the way to the sides of his ears, and the sound of his rattling teeth was like rolling thunder. The samurai saw this and fell faint. He stopped breathing for about an hour but came to his senses before long. Looking around, he found himself in front of the Suwa shrine. After a while, he began walking again and came to a house. Entering it, he asked for a drink of water. The woman of the house came out and inquired, "What's wrong? Why are you requesting water?" The samurai told her about his encounter with Shunoban. The woman heard this and said, "Well, what a frightful thing to meet! Would this Shunoban you mention be something like this?" And he saw that her face was now transformed to become just like the one he had seen before. The samurai lost consciousness again, but before long he revived. Yet, on the third day thereafter, he breathed his last.

THE AFFAIR OF THE *NEKOMATA* FORK-TAILED CAT IN ECHIGO PROVINCE

In the province of Echigo lived a certain wealthy man. One day a very dignified-looking woman stood lingering beside his gate. She called in to offer her services. Hearing this, the lady of the house said, "How fortunate! I would like to enlist her as an attendant for my daughter," and the woman was taken into the family's employ. From painting pictures to tying knots in the shapes of flowers, not to mention calligraphy and sewing too, there was no womanly art with which the woman was unfamiliar. Husband and wife alike were delighted that they had taken such an accomplished person into their household, and they engaged her services with kindness.

One day the lady of the house happened to notice that a lamp was burning in the woman's quarters and so went to investigate. She saw the woman remove her head and place it atop the mirror stand before her. She applied toothblack to it, put makeup on it, and then attached the head again to her own body, sitting as though nothing unusual had happened. The lady of the house was frightened, and when night had come to an end, she summoned the woman before her. Without saying as much, the lady of the house made it clear that the woman was free to go. Yet upon hearing this, the woman's appearance changed, and she said, "I had intended to offer my services to you forever, and now you suddenly dismiss me like this. What is it that have you seen?" The lady of the house replied, "No, that is not the reason why. In any case, we just want to let you go. When my daughter's marriage has been decided, we shall summon you again and welcome you back." The woman exclaimed, "Oh, what muddled words!," leaping suddenly upon the lady of the house and gnawing right at her throat. Someone overheard the commotion, drew his sword, and struck the woman, slashing away to weaken her. He knocked her over, and when he attacked her again with a sword thrust, the beautiful figure of the woman was suddenly transformed into an old cat. It was a *nekomata,* a fork-tailed cat, with its mouth split to the sides of its ears and a horn atop its head. A cat that had been kept in that house for many years had at some point disappeared to no one knows where and had become a *nekomata.* It is said that the lady of the house was tormented for fifty to sixty days thereafter.

The man's lust for his daughter-in-law turns him into a huge snake, Book 2, Story 12. (Tokyo National Museum)

ON THE ATTACHMENT OF A MAN NAMED HORIKOSHI OF TŌTŌMI PROVINCE TO HIS SON'S BRIDE

In the province of Tōtōmi, there was a man called Horikoshi something-or-other. When he was in his sixteenth year, he fathered a son, and before too long his son had also reached his sixteenth year and welcomed a woman into the home to become his wife. At that time, Horikoshi was thirty years old. The bride had charming features and a lovely appearance; in all respects she was a thoughtful and skillful woman. Yet whenever Horikoshi met her, he would not speak directly to her but would instead sit with his eyes cast downward. Everyone thought this unusual and would ask him, "Don't you care for your son's bride?" "No, as long as relations between the two of them are good, there's nothing for me to be concerned about."

Over the next three years, it seemed that, for some reason or other, he was feeling out of sorts. As his discomfort gradually grew more serious, the young bride said, "I should like to visit and comfort him in his distress," but the man's response was, "There is certainly no need for you to approach the bed of an unpresentable invalid," and he would not let her near. When it was clear that his end might come at any moment, the young bride came to Horikoshi's pillowside. As she looked after him, rubbing his hands and feet, her mother-in-law went into the adjacent room to relax for a bit. After a while, there came from the interior a sound of something rapping up against the folding screens and sliding paper doors. Everyone was perplexed by this, and when they went to have a look, they found that Horikoshi had become transformed into a snake with its coils wrapped around the bride three times. Water gushed out from the ground, and the tatami-mat room turned into a deep pool, the snake and the bride along with it sinking beneath the water.

Until recently, it was said that on clear days the pillars and other parts of the house were visible in Horikoshi's pond. But now that the pool has apparently become smaller and shallower, perhaps the giant snake no longer dwells there.

ON THE GHOST OF A MEMBER OF THE CHRISTIAN SECT

There was a sect of Christians in Tsu, Ise Province. Instructions came down from Edo ordering that these individuals be hanged upside down, executed by decapitation, and then taken to a place called Otobe, where they would be cremated. At dusk two or three days later, a group of several samurai was passing through a place called Furukawa. They saw a beautiful woman, wearing a robe over her head, pass by in the company of a maid who carried a bag for her. Upon encountering her, the samurai thought that such a woman was not like any that they were accustomed to seeing in Ise. They were puzzled and wondered where she had come from. As they gradually began to pursue her, they found that she was headed in the direction of Otobe. She traveled to the side of the pit where the Christians had been incinerated, and there she proceeded to nimbly gather up their bones. Then two or three young female companions emerged out of nowhere and began to gather up bones in just the same way. But after a while they all vanished.

HOW OBSESSIVE ATTACHMENT TRANSFORMED THE DAUGHTER OF ŌMI RESIDENT SHIRAI SUKESABURŌ INTO A GIANT SNAKE

In a place called Ryūge Pass in the village of Tochiu in Kita County, Ōmi Province, lived a wealthy farmer named Takahashi Shingorō. He had a son who was just entering his fifth year. Across from Takahashi lived Shirai Sukesaburō, a farmer who was no less prominent, and he had a daughter who was entering her third year. The parents became such good friends with each other that they had their children become engaged, exchanging cups of *sake* to commemorate the betrothal.

The years and months passed by, and before long the boy had reached his tenth year. But Shingorō came down with a slight malady and eventually perished. Afterward, the house gradually crept toward decline, and Sukesaburō altered his initial agreement, making plans for his daughter to wed a wealthy farmer from the neighboring village when she reached fifteen. When the day of the nuptials came, the daughter thought, "Ever since I was a little girl, I have been engaged to the boy who lives across from us. His family's finances have declined, but it goes against morality for me to now be bonded to another because of that." She entreated a maid to secretly summon the boy who lived across the street, and she said to him, "Now then, from the time that you and I were little children, according to our parents' plan, we agreed to become man and wife. But now I have been promised to another, which gives me no end of regret. The nuptials are scheduled to take place tonight, but I ask that you take me off somewhere and allow me to escape." The boy heard her request and replied, "I am much obliged at these heartfelt words. But since I am one whose position has declined to this extent, I bear you no grudge at all. Please accept the better marriage proposal."

When she heard this, the girl said, "If that's how it is, then I don't have the strength to go on," and she prepared to end her life. Shocked to realize her intent, the boy intervened to stop her and said, "If you feel so strongly, let us be together wherever we shall go," and under cover of night he escaped with the girl. However, having no certain plans for where they might take refuge, when they stopped to rest in a certain place, they found that they were completely at a loss for what to do. The girl declared, "Our wish to be together as husband and wife in this life will not be granted. Let us cast ourselves from this ledge into the waters below so that we may be together for eternity on the same lotus blossom in the next world." The boy replied, "You're right!" The couple took each other hand in hand and joined the drifting weeds in the water below. Yet, by some chance, the boy got hung up on a tree branch and did not sink beneath the water's surface. A traveler who was traversing the area saw him and rescued him by pulling him out of the water. As the boy pondered intently what had happened, he thought, "That I was unexpectedly caught up on the tree branch must be because my allotted span has not yet come. That being the case, I ought to take holy vows and pray for the girl's enlightenment." He thereupon returned to his house.

Out of longing for her betrothed, the deceased young woman returns as a dragon, Book 3, Story 4. (Tokyo National Museum)

Now then, it had been the long-standing wish of the boy's mother to make a pilgrimage to the Kannon at Ishiyama. As she came back from this journey, she spotted a girl of fourteen or fifteen standing beside the Seta Bridge and weeping softly. When the mother approached her and inquired as to what had happened, the girl said, "I am from a village to the north of here, but I have been tormented in various ways by my stepmother. I could stand it no longer, and so I left home and have come here to cast my body into the river." Hearing this, the mother felt pity for her and said, "Fortunately, I have a son. You ought to become his wife." The girl said with delight, "I will gratefully entrust these matters to you." The mother was also pleased to hear this, and thinking that Kannon must surely have brought her and the girl together, she took the girl back home and had her become her son's wife. Her son began to forget his past sadness, and now he and the girl engaged in lovers' talk that deepened their bonds to be like two single-winged birds flying together as one. He fathered a son, and before long the boy had turned three.

One day while her husband had gone off somewhere, the woman entered her room to have a nap. The boy entered his mother's room, took one look at her, cried out, and then fled. Three times he went to look at her only to cry out and leave the room. When her husband returned, he surveyed the scene and thought it strange. Entering her room, he saw that his wife had become a giant snake measuring one *jō*. It lay there sleeping contentedly. The husband was terrified and called out to rouse it, whereupon it returned to the original form of the girl. Facing her husband, she said, "Well, well. Up until now I have been most cautious, but now you have seen my form. I am so ashamed! I am the daughter of Sukesaburō from long ago. The attachment that came from my desire to be together with you was not dispelled even upon my death. Now I have changed my form into a girl's again and have become familiar with you over these several years. But now this too must come to an end. I am so reluctant to part!" So saying, she disappeared.

After that, her son would always inquire about his mother, and so the man, overcome with loneliness, took his son to the edge of the pond and said, "This child longs for you so much; won't you please reveal yourself to him just once?" Immediately the form of a woman appeared in the pond and began to emerge from it. She took the child in her arms and fed him at her breast for a while before bidding him goodbye and returning into the pond. After that, the boy longed for his mother even more keenly, and so the father brought him to the pond a second time, calling out once again. But this time the form of a giant snake appeared from within the pond. Emerging from the water, it flicked its red tongue about, looking as though it might swallow up the boy at any moment, and then it disappeared. From then on, the boy longed for his mother no more. The husband was so saddened by her appearance that, according to the story told by someone who lives there, he later returned to the pond with his son and the two of them cast themselves into the water and died.

HOW THE ATTACHMENTS OF LOVE LETTERS BECAME A DEMON

There are sixty temples in a place called Kūhachi in the province of Iga. Ikkyū had gone out to engage in religious training and having found himself in this place when the sun set, he went around to the temples to ask for lodging, but he found that not a single person was present. Ikkyū thought this strange and went around inspecting each and every one of the temples, eventually finding a beautiful youth in a certain temple. Ikkyū approached and said, "Please put me up for the night." The boy replied, "That is a simple enough request, but night after night, an apparition comes to this temple and takes people away." Ikkyū said, "Since I am a priest who has left the secular world behind, it should be no problem." "In that case, please stay here for the night," said the youth, conducting him to the guest hall and retiring to the next room.

In the middle of the night, several balls of fire appeared from beneath the veranda of the room where the youth lay sleeping and seemed to enter into the youth's chest. No sooner had this happened than he transformed into a demon two *jō* tall and came to the guest hall, searching around and saying, "Where is the visiting monk who is staying in this temple tonight? I'll seize him and gobble him up!" But since Ikkyū had, after all, carried out religious practices, he was undetectable to demons. Before long, dawn came, and it seemed that perhaps the demon had returned to the youth's room, but in fact it had vanished. Ikkyū thought this peculiar and said, "I want to see the area beneath the veranda of the room where the youth slept." When he went to have a look, he learned that beneath the veranda were countless letters with blood on them. Inquiring into the situation, he found that they were secret love letters that had been sent from near and far to the youth, who had thrown them under the veranda without making any reply to them. The attachments of the various authors of these letters had accumulated, coming night after night to the breast of the youth, transforming him into a demon.

Ikkyū retrieved all the letters, put them in a pile, and burned them up while reciting a sutra. It is said that, after this, nothing unusual happened again.

HOW A MAN'S WAGER LED TO HIS SON HAVING HIS HEAD CUT OFF

In a certain village in the province of Kii, five or six samurai got together, and as they told stories into the night, one proposed a wager: "If you go halfway up the road from this village, there is a shrine by the side of the mountain. In front of the shrine is a river. Dead bodies come floating down the river from time to time. If any of you will go tonight to this river, cut off the finger of a corpse, and bring it back, I will give you my sword."

At first no one wanted to go. Among those present, however, was an avaricious coward who stepped up to accept the challenge, saying, "I'll go!" He went back to his house and told his wife, "I made this wager, but I just can't get up the courage to go." His wife replied, "You cannot very well go back on your word now. I shall go and slice off a finger. You stay here and mind the house." She strapped their child of two years on her back and went off to the appointed place. Before the river, there was a forest that extended for one *chō*: a fearsome place to pass by. Arriving at the shrine, she went down underneath the bridge, where she found a woman's corpse. She withdrew the short sword

The greedy and merciless woman receives her just reward, Book 3, Story 20. (Tokyo National Museum)

she had placed in her kimono, cut off two of the woman's fingers, and tucked them into her bosom. Looking back at the forest, she heard a hoarse voice coming from above the trees saying, "Look! Look at your feet!" Scared, she had a look down, discovering something wrapped in a small straw bundle. When she picked it up, it was heavy. It must be my fortune that the gods and buddhas have felt pity for me and provided this, she thought, and taking the object, she headed home.

The man could hardly bear to wait for his wife's return and sat quaking in fear in his nightclothes. Just then, from atop the roof came the sound of twenty or so people's feet trampling. "Why have you not gone to the place you wagered on going?" they called out. The man became even more frightened and sat cowering without even breathing. The wife came back to the house, and he heard the sound of her flinging open the front door; the man thought that this

must be a ghost entering the house, and he screamed out, "Ah!," his eyes
darting around. His wife called to him, saying, "It's me. What's wrong?" When
he heard his wife's words, the man came to his senses and was delighted. Then
the wife withdrew the fingers from her bosom and handed them to the man.
Announcing "And now for the truly happy thing!," she proceeded to open up
the straw bundle she had brought back with her. Inside she found the head of
her own child, which she had been carrying on her back. "How can this be?"
she wailed, and hurriedly took the child down off her back, but it was just a
headless corpse. Though the wife lamented and mourned as she stared at this,
it was no use. But since the man was an avaricious sort, he took the fingers and
apparently traded them for the sword.

HOW HASHII YASABURŌ GAVE A GHOST PASSAGE IN A BOAT

Among the retainers of Lord Nobunaga was one named Hashii Yasaburō, a
samurai skilled in both the literary and military arts. Later when he dwelled
in Kiyosu and served the Lord of Bingo, he became deeply involved in a sexual
relationship with the son of Lord Inuyama. Night after night, he would tra-
verse the three *ri* that stood between them. One night, after he had concluded
his evening responsibilities, he departed for Inuyama. It happened to be a
fierce night: utterly dark and with rain falling constantly. There was a river
crossing along the way. Yasaburō called out to the ferryman, but he was sleeping downstream and no reply came back. As Yasaburō stood still on the bank,
gazing up and down the river, a flame was visible upstream. Observing it carefully as it gradually drew closer, it appeared to be a woman, her hair arranged
to extend the length of her body. She was upside down, moving along in a
headstand as she exhaled fire and smoke from her mouth. Yasaburō saw her
and loosened his sword, saying, "What are you?" In a pained voice, the woman
said, "I was once the wife of the headman of Yamura, the village across the
river. My husband conspired with his concubine to strangle me, and to prevent
me from ever returning, they buried me upside down at a place upstream. I
would like to take my revenge, but being upside down in this way, it is impossible for me to cross the river. It has been my fervent hope that I would encounter a military man who would take me across, but although I have constantly been observing the people who pass by this place, there has never been
one as stouthearted as you, sir. I beseech you to have compassion and take me
across the river." Yasaburō said he understood and called for the ferryman,
telling him, "Take this woman on your boat, and let her cross over to the opposite bank." The ferryman took one look at the woman and dropped his oars
as he fled away. Yasaburō gathered the oars, picked up the woman, and loaded

A brave samurai plays boatman for an upside-down ghost, who takes revenge on her murderer, Book 4, Story 1. (Tokyo National Museum)

her onto the boat. Once they had crossed over to the other bank, the woman leapt out and headed off in the direction of Yamura. Yasaburō followed after her and stood outside the village headman's gate, listening. He heard a female voice scream out, "Ah!" and shortly thereafter, the first woman came out carrying the concubine's head. Facing Yasaburō, she said, "Thanks to you I have been able to easily take down my hateful enemy. I am grateful." Then she disappeared without a trace.

Thereupon, Yasaburō went to Inuyama, coming back at dawn. When he passed through Yamura, he inquired, "Did nothing unusual happen last night in this village?" A villager explained, "The headman of this village recently welcomed a wife, but this evening something plucked off her head and ran away. What could have happened?" Yasaburō found this mysterious, and so he told the story to the Lord of Bingo. When the lord had the area upstream

A man persuades a giant monster to change itself into a pickled plum ready to be swallowed, Book 4, Story 3. (Tokyo National Museum)

excavated, they unearthed the body of a woman who had been buried upside down, just as expected. It was an unprecedented case, and it is said that the village headman was executed.

HOW GHOSTS WERE SUBDUED WITH THE POWER OF *SAKE*

It was said that a monster dwelled in the Great Buddha Hall of Sanjūsangendō, and after around the seventh hour no one would venture there. This matter came to the attention of the emperor, and placards were erected stating that anyone who could subdue the monster would be granted whatever reward he wished. A certain ronin who was fond of drinking came to the imperial palace and announced, "I shall undertake the task." Having accepted the mission, he put *sake* in a gourd and went to Sanjūsangendō. He waited in the corner of the hall, and at around midnight, just as expected, a priest about one *jō* tall, his eyes shining as bright as the sun and moon, extended his rake-like hand and attempted to seize the ronin. The ronin immediately bowed his head to the ground and said, "Might you, sir, perchance be the honorable monster about whom I have heard for so long? Please allow me to offer my humble greetings on this day that I have the pleasure of making your acquaintance." Grinning as he heard this, the monster uttered in a terrifying voice, "Well, well. What a strange man you are! Though I would like to devour you in a single gulp, I'll spare you for the moment. Tell me, what brings you here?" The ronin answered, "I have come with no special purpose, but I have heard, Mr. Monster, that you are able to transform yourself in myriad ways. Might you be so kind as to do me a small favor and show me how you can transform into a beautiful court lady?" The monster replied, "You have fancy tastes, don't you? I will transform myself as you wish, and then I will gobble you up." And so he revealed himself in the form of a giant court lady. The ronin said, "Oh, what fun this is! I wonder if you would be so good as to transform yourself again, only this time into a temple acolyte?" And the monster's form became that of a handsome acolyte. "Oh, how excellent! Will you now transform into a demon?" said the ronin, and the monster revealed himself as a demon measuring one *jō* in height, with horns bulging from its head. "Oh, Mr. Monster, you are a true artiste! You are able to transform into whatever you wish! But how about transforming yourself into something small like a pickled plum? It would be impossible, I suppose."

Hearing this, the monster said, "If I transform into a pickled plum, then it will be time at last for you to be devoured, all right?" "It is unavoidable." "Well, in that case, I will show you," he said, and transformed himself into a tiny little pickled plum that rolled around here and there. "How commendable are your skills at transformation! Why don't you come up into my palm?" said the ronin, extending his hand. As soon as the pickled plum rolled up into the ronin's hand, he popped it straight into his mouth and chomped away fiercely. He downed seven or eight cups of *sake* from his gourd one after another and fled back home while it was still nighttime. When he reported to the throne, "I have subdued the monster," the emperor was more than a little impressed and bestowed upon him a large amount of land. It was all due to the power of the *sake*.

The grateful crab rescues the girl from her forced marriage to a dragon, Book 4, Story 12. (Tokyo National Museum)

HOW HASEGAWA CHŌZAEMON'S DAUGHTER LOVED A CRAB

There was a man named Hasegawa Chōzaemon in Matsuyama, in the province of Iyo. He had a single daughter, beautiful in face and form alike. She had a sweet-natured disposition, and she composed Japanese and Chinese poetry. She was a girl who had a deep sense of compassion and she had even read and understood all the Buddhist scriptures and discussions of Buddhist teachings.

One day she discovered a small crab inside her wash bucket. She picked it up and gave it some food, taking care of it lovingly for a long time. Near her residence was a pool of deep water, and in it dwelt a large snake. Having become fixated upon the girl, the snake transformed itself into a man and said to her father, Chōzaemon, "I am a giant snake that lives in the pool nearby. I have become obsessed with your daughter. Give her to me." Chōzaemon reasoned, "If I say no, the snake will surely take my life and my daughter's too. But if I offer my assent, I would be so sad to see her go," and he began to weep. His daughter overheard this and said, "This is something unavoidable. I shall abandon my life and save yours, father. This must be karma from a previous life. You must give your reply immediately." Hearing this, Chōzaemon tearfully faced the snake and granted permission, saying, "I shall give you my daughter." The snake was overjoyed, and after they fixed a date, he returned. The daughter then turned to her crab and said, "I have loved you for these many years. I shall not live much longer, and now it is time for me to take my leave from you." She then released the crab, and it ran off into some bushes. When the appointed day finally came, a great many snakes large and small crawled into the garden. It was frightening beyond words, but the daughter was unfazed. She fingered a crystal rosary in her right hand and had the fifth book of The Lotus Sutra in her left. She was already in the garden, and perhaps because of the sutra's efficacy, the snake cowered and withdrew. At this moment, giant crabs appeared out of nowhere, gathered together, and set upon the snakes. From the side, they raised their pincers, and the snakes cowered in fear, all of them fleeing. Truly, was it because of the marvelous power of the sutra or because of the depth of her compassionate intent that her endangered life was rescued?

HOW A *TANUKI* WELCOMED THE DESCENT OF TWENTY-FIVE BODHISATTVAS

There is a village in eastern Ōmi called Sakōdō. Deep in its mountains stands the community's temple hall. Whenever the priest of the temple would go into the village, a *tanuki* would come after him and eat the priest's food. One time the priest picked up a rock that looked like a rice cake at the riverbank and returned with it. He cooked it on the stove and waited for the sun to set. Just as expected, the *tanuki* came and looked in the place where there was always food. The priest said, "If you don't steal anymore, I will let you have a gift," and he took out the hot rock with fire tongs and threw it down. When the *tanuki* took it and tried to eat it, he burned himself severely and fled. After this, the principal image on the priest's altar began to shine from time to time. Gazing upon it, he thought himself fortunate and devoted himself to his prayers with even more piety.

One night, Amida Buddha appeared at his pillow and said, "You must quickly leave this world below and take the penance of fire. When you do this, I shall descend and save you, guiding you to the Western Paradise." No sooner

A virtuous priest
sets himself on fire,
expecting to be
saved by a cloud of
merciful buddhas,
Book 5, Story 8.
(Tokyo National
Museum)

had these words been uttered than the priest woke up. He was grateful and
had an announcement circulated in the village that said, "On such-and-such
a day I shall immolate myself and enter the next life. Come and pay your respects." The villagers thought, "What a meritorious act!" and were moved to
tears. Now then, when the appointed day came, people from the nearby villages came to observe and pray. The throngs were tremendous, everyone
waiting to see the descent of the Buddha. In front of the community temple
hall, the priest stacked rocks to make a fence enclosing a square area of one
ken on each side, inside of which he piled up charcoal and firewood. He came
out wearing new priestly garments over his white robes and a cap on his head.
He climbed atop the firewood and began to meditate.

Just as expected, at high noon there appeared from the west the Amida
triad along with other bodhisattvas. As the twenty-five bodhisattvas made

their descent, they emitted light and played music on the *shō* mouth organ and the *hichiriki* flute, as well as other wind and string instruments. The people all looked on thankfully. "Well then, light the fire!" And at once the firewood was ignited, and the priest was incinerated. At that moment all of the buddhas appeared and burst out laughing in unison. The crowd looked upon this with astonishment, and then they saw two to three thousand *tanuki* fleeing into the mountains. It is said that the *tanuki* that had received the scorched rock had gotten his revenge.

HOW MASTER MANKICHI BECAME THE TEACHER OF A MONSTER

There was a variety show actor named Master Mankichi who lived on Kami-dachiuri Street in the capital. He was terrible at nō acting, and so his finances

A nō actor imperson-ates a monster better than the real one, who becomes his disciple, Book 5, Story 12. (Tokyo National Museum)

had declined to the point that he decided to go down to Osaka. He stopped in to have some tea and relax at a teahouse in Hirakata, and while he was there, the sun began to set. He said, "I'd like to get a room and stay here for the night." In reply, the teahouse master explained, "That's a simple matter, but since there is a monster that comes here every night and abducts people, my staff and I won't be spending the night here." Mankichi replied, "That's no problem at all." He lodged there for the night. Just as expected, at around midnight there came the sound of people crossing over from the other side of the river. When he looked, he saw that it was a well-fed priest some seven *shaku* tall. Thereupon, Mankichi called out, "You call that a monstrous transformation?! You're still a novice!" The priest heard this and said, "What sort of person are you to say something like that?" Mankichi replied, "I am a monster from the capital and I heard that there were monsters living here, so I thought I would come meet one and see if he was a good or poor monster. I am staying here because I figured that if I meet one who is good at being a monster, then I can take him as my teacher, but if he is poor at being a monster, then I can make him my disciple." The priest countered, "Well, in that case let me see your feats of monstrous transformation." "All right, then," agreed Mankichi, and he proceeded to take out his nō costumes from his wicker clothes trunk. He made himself into a demon, and the priest was astonished, saying, "Well now, you are good at it! Make yourself into a courtesan." "All right, then," he said, and then became a woman. The priest exclaimed, "How surprisingly good you are! From now on, I shall rely upon you as my teacher. I am a fungus that grows beneath the enoki mushrooms across the river. For many years I have dwelt here and tormented people." Mankichi heard his explanation and asked, "Is there anything you cannot eat?" "For me, broth made from three-year-old miso is a no-no," he said, and then asked, "What about you?" Mankichi replied, "A large sea bream steamed whole is something I must avoid; it is fatal if I eat it." As they talked to one another, it began to get light. The priest bid farewell and left.

When Master Mankichi told his story around Hirakata and Takatsuki, all the people collaborated together and prepared a broth from three-year-old pickling miso that they scattered on the fungus. Instantly it faded to nothing. Afterward no more monsters sprouted up there, or so it is said.

HOW TO BECOME RICH BY TELLING ONE HUNDRED TALES

There was a rice merchant named Hachirōbei who lived around the intersection of Gojō and Horikawa in the capital. He had ten children, the eldest of whom was sixteen, though he had been a widower for some time.

A widower with ten children to feed survives one hundred tales and is rewarded with one hundred *ryō* in gold coins, Book 5, Story 20. (Tokyo National Museum)

One day Hachirōbei had his children mind the house while he went to Ōtsu to buy rice. He told them, "Mind the house well, I'll be back tomorrow," and left. That evening seven or eight of the youngsters in the neighborhood came over to play, and they started telling one hundred tales. After some forty to fifty stories, the youngsters began returning home one by one, and soon only two or three remained. By the time the number of stories reached eighty to ninety, they all got scared and returned home, leaving only the rice merchant's eldest son. He thought to himself, "The whole point of telling one hundred tales is to compare monsters; this is no fun! Under the circumstances, I will complete the sequence of one hundred by myself." When he finished the hundredth tale, he went out the back door to pee. While he was in the garden, a hairy hand grabbed his leg firmly. Startled, the eldest son exclaimed,

"What are you? Show yourself!" At that moment, it became a girl of seventeen or eighteen and said, "I am the former owner of this house. I died in childbirth, but because no one mourned my death, it has been impossible for me to attain Buddhahood. Please engage a priest to read a thousandfold sutra for me." The eldest son then said, "My father is a poor man and so he cannot afford to have a thousandfold sutra read. Please attain Buddhahood with the invocation of the holy name." The woman replied, "In that case, since I have buried money beneath the persimmon tree by the back door, you can use it to have the sutra read," and then she disappeared. When dawn broke, the son's father, Hachirōbei, returned, and his son told him what had happened the previous night. When they dug up the ground beneath the persimmon tree, they found one hundred *ryō* in gold coins. They immediately took it out and prayed for the woman's repose. After that, the rice merchant gradually became more fortunate and eventually became the most successful rice merchant in the lower part of the capital.

TRANSLATED BY MATTHEW FRALEIGH

The Bearded Lady of the Haunted House

TOMIKAWA FUSANOBU

*T*he Bearded Lady of the Haunted House (*Bakemono Hitotsuya no Higeonna,* 1770) is a representative example of the early picture book (*kusazōshi*) subgenres known as the black book (*kurohon*) and the blue book (*aohon*), referring to the color of their respective covers. These illustrated stories were usually twenty to thirty pages in length and drew their inspiration from the puppet theater and kabuki, tales of heroic valor, and, as in the case of the present piece, monster legends. Most black books and blue books were published roughly during the thirty-year period between 1744 and 1774. Because the same work was often printed as both a black book and a blue book, distinctions between the two formats have become blurred. Sandwiched chronologically between the earlier picture books for children known as red books (*akahon,* dating from the late seventeenth century) and the humor-oriented and often satirical yellow books (1775–1806), blue and black ones are considered transitional genres—more than the simple retelling of popular children's stories that characterizes red books but also lacking the sophisticated wit found in yellow books.

There is little information on the illustrator for this piece, Tomikawa

Fusanobu, also known as Tomikawa Ginsetsu. He is said to have studied under Nishimura Shigenaga (?–1756). A prolific artist, he provided illustrations for well over two hundred works between 1761 and 1777. As is the case with many of the early picture books, the author here is unknown, an indication of the importance the illustrations held over the text. Recent scholarship suggests, however, that Fusanobu also wrote the words for these works.

Fusanobu was a master of the monster (*bakemono*) story, producing over twenty works in the genre. His monsters have a distinctly recognizable style. They literally fill the page, towering menacingly over their human adversaries. Although the monsters in the present piece are all meant to be the incarnations of shape-changing foxes, a large part of the visual appeal lies in the depiction of a wide variety of supernatural types. Some of the creatures are drawn from legend and earlier visual representations. For example, the *mikoshi-nyūdō* monster takes the form of a heavyset priest who can extend his neck at will and peer ominously over people's shoulders. The cackling head and the vengeful ghost with its hair standing on end are common forms assumed by female apparitions. In contrast to these traditional monsters, the bearded lady of the title is unique to this work. In some of his other picture books, Fusanobu would devise new monsters based on popular songs or trends, and while it is possible that the bearded lady here has such a history, her origins remain obscure. In any case, she adds a note of humor to an otherwise grisly tale.

The haunted house of the title refers to the *hitotsuya* legend in which a traveler, the sun about to set, seeks lodging at a lonely house in a desolate field. The host, who is usually an old hag or witch, gives the traveler a pillow of rock upon which to sleep; in the middle of the night she kills the traveler with the rock and robs him of his belongings. In one variation, the traveler is charmed by the hag's beautiful daughter. The scene in which Gōsuke is seduced at a lonely inn—really a barren field bewitched by foxes—evokes both this legend and a famous episode from a 1699 puppet play by Chikamatsu Monzaemon. In the play, an itinerant priest, Hōjō Tokiyori, asks the mistress of the house for lodging during a snowstorm. She is hesitant at first because of her impoverished circumstances and because her husband is away. Later, unable to provide firewood for her guest, she burns her husband's prized bonsai trees instead. This scene is, in turn, based on the nō play *Potted Trees* (*Hachi no Ki*).

In most of the early picture books, a stalwart warrior ultimately vanquishes the monsters. This work has the unusual twist of pitting the monsters against a corrupt samurai and adding a vendetta plotline. Stories revolving around the avengement of a murdered family member (usually a child avenging the death of a parent) were prevalent in Edo-period performing arts and literature and became especially prominent in late picture books.

Monster stories are common to yellow books as well. Here the monsters take on a new comical identity as country bumpkins striving to imitate the ways of the Edo sophisticate. The transformation of monsters from scary creatures rooted in legend and fairy tales into objects of contemporary parody mirrors the evolving history of the genre itself.

Illustrations reproduced courtesy of the Tohoku University Library

A certain samurai by the name of Yokokawa Gōsuke had set his sights on Oman, the daughter of Kamesaki Gon-no-shin. Although he wooed her ardently with frequent letters declaring his love, he never received a single reply, and in the end she married a man called Ozu Tomosaburō. Gōsuke's resentment knew no bounds. One night he crept stealthily into Oman's room while she was asleep, sliced off her head, and then escaped silently into the dark.

GŌSUKE
How quickly a slighted love turns sour. Well, I feel much better now. Bekunai, did anybody see me? Keep a sharp watch out.

GŌSUKE'S SERVANT, BEKUNAI Master, this dog was howling so loudly that I had to slit his throat. He won't bother us anymore.

And so Gōsuke hid out in the mountains of Kōshū. It so happened that in the neighboring village there lived a blind woman who made her way by playing the shamisen and singing. Gōsuke, an incorrigible lecher, set out to seduce the woman. Believing him to be sincere, she gave herself to him in the end, and they became husband and wife.

GŌSUKE I don't mean to brag but you'll find few men as kind-hearted as I am.

According to the ancient Chinese encyclopedia, foxes are also known by the name of "purple night." They beat their tails, carry torches in their mouths, and wear human skulls on their heads. In order to perform their transformations, they must balance their skulls adroitly as they pray to the Big Dipper.

Gōsuke abandoned Kōshū, wandering here and there. Now with the sun about to set, he decided to seek lodgings at Mokuisaka. The innkeeper's wife, a woman around thirty, was more than delighted to rent Gōsuke a room.

INNKEEPER'S WIFE Having you stay here while my husband is away reminds me of that scene from the famous puppet play. My husband's visiting the next province, so feel free to stay as long as you like.

GŌSUKE What good luck finding this place. Since I'm traveling at my leisure, I just might take you up on your offer.

The night wore on as the innkeeper's wife persisted with her seduction of Gōsuke. Then, all of a sudden, her face changed into the spitting image of Bekunai, the servant Gōsuke had killed. Oman's severed head appeared out of nowhere. She cackled as she glared at him. And Gōsuke's murdered wife was now a vengeful ghost. Imagine Gōsuke's shock when the inn suddenly turned into a barren field!

BEKUNAI Master, it's been a long time.

Gōsuke ran with all his might, but when he caught his breath and looked up, Bekunai suddenly appeared before him.

After slaying the phantom Bekunai, Gōsuke hurried off down the road until he came to a small temple where he decided to hide out for the night. But when he crept his way inside and peered through a hole in the paper doors, he was greeted by a horde of monsters. No words could describe the horror. Just then Gōsuke's murdered wife appeared riding on a bull, playing the shamisen as she sang.

GŌSUKE'S WIFE ♪ *Will he pay for his sinful ways or not? The world is far too cruel a place.* Strum, strum, strum.

FEMALE MONSTER I curse you for killing me, Gōsuke. Oh, how I long for this world. Now watch me eat you alive!

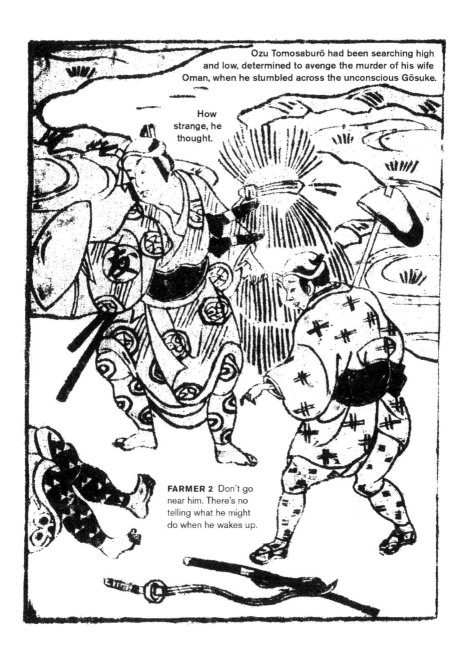

Tomosaburō took charge of Gōsuke, reviving him with some medicine. On hearing Gōsuke's story, he was overjoyed to realize that this was the very man he had been seeking.

GŌSUKE I owe you my life, so why keep anything from you. This all started because I killed a woman named Oman.

TOMOSABURŌ It must have been those monsters that made you faint. But, tell me, why did you kill this Oman?

Not realizing that he was falling into the enemy's trap, Gōsuke gradually revealed to him the entire story.

GŌSUKE I'm telling you all this in the strictest of confidence. A woman's wrath is truly frightening.

TRANSLATED BY ADAM KABAT

Staging the Supernatural
Heroism in Kamigata and Edo Theatre

A Courtesan's Soul within Incense Smoke

"MATABEI THE STUTTERER" EXCERPT FROM BOOK ONE

CHIKAMATSU MONZAEMON

The leading figure in popular theater who wrote both kabuki and *jōruri* plays during the early Edo period was Chikamatsu Monzaemon (1653–1725), born of an old samurai family with a considerable stipend of three hundred *koku*. When he was a young teen, his father, Sugimori Nobuyoshi, lost his position for unknown reasons and moved his family to Kyoto. Showing their strong penchant for popular culture, the family published in 1671 their joint compositions of haiku poems, including one by Chikamatsu. He came to work for the high-level courtier Ichijō Ekan, younger brother of Emperor Go-Mizuno-o, and other aristocrats, among whom puppet plays were a favorite pastime. Having worked as a street storyteller in Sakai and backstage in Kyoto kabuki theaters, he began to write *jōruri* and kabuki plays around 1677, producing works that were well known and resulting in a 1683 staging that would become the first written record of a performance of one of his plays. His experience as a samurai, courtier, and commoner and within the theater classes gave him a unique insight into the society of his time as well as a richness of action and expression in his work. He wrote as many as 140 plays, 30 or so for kabuki and the rest for *jōruri*.

Chikamatsu's writings ranged from historical and political plays—both of which were sometimes based on actual history, other times on Chinese and Japanese legends such as *Battles of Coxinga* (1715) and *Twins at the Sumida River* (1720)—to romantic plays often based on incidents of the time, such as *Love Suicides at Sonezaki* (1703), *Love Suicides at Amijima* (1721) and *Women Killer and the Hell of Oil* (1722). His mature period plays, although set in the past, were conventionally understood to be about contemporary public affairs. As many as fifty of his major works remained in print during the Edo period and were a frequently used source for playwrights and fiction writers. Within the theatrical world he was called "Great Chikamatsu" and even "the god of writers."

"Matabei the Stutterer," presented here, is a part of the first book from Chikamatsu's three-book *jōruri* play *A Courtesan's Soul within Incense Smoke* (*Keisei Hangonkō*, 1708), performed at the Takemoto Theater in Osaka. Chikamatsu highlights two themes: the power of art, and human will. The play, though set in the sixteenth century, mixes characters from different time periods to create a lively drama. One of the two stars of the play is the woman Miya (also known as the courtesan Tōyama and daughter of Tosa Mitsunobu), who falls in love with the painter Kanō Motonobu. Although she dies before marrying Motonobu, the strength of her love keeps her in this world in order to spend seven days with him as his wife. The title of the play comes from her story, that of a spirit appearing within the smoke from burning incense. The other star is the painter Ukiyo Matabei, the hero of the scenes translated below. The first of the two scenes has been performed fairly regularly, but it is the second one that has attracted much contemporary attention.

As is often the case with *jōruri* and kabuki, the play was first performed to coincide with a particular anniversary, in this case the 150th memorial of the death of the real-life painter Kanō Motonobu (1476–1559). Chikamatsu's son is known to have been a painter too, and in his own writings Chikamatsu uses metaphors from the visual arts to describe the art of drama. The timing of the play is also thought to be a memorial to the Edo actor Nakamura Shichisaburō I (1662–1708), a specialist in romantic lead roles who often performed in Kamigata as well as in Edo and whom Chikamatsu would have known personally. Shichisaburō was famous for his depiction of the legendary ronin Nagoya Sanzaburō, often called Sanza, whose dashing and rebellious presence added color to many plays.

The Tosa and Kanō painting schools were the official artists, respectively, of the Kyoto Court and the Tokugawa government (and daimyo lords as well). Kanō Motonobu, featured in this play, is considered the most important artist of the Kanō School. (Chikamatsu's text has "Kano," but "Kanō," with an elongated vowel, is the standard pronunciation today.) The styles were different, the Tosa being the traditional "Japanese" tradition, and the Kanō based also on Chinese painting techniques and motifs. On the more commercialized level, "floating world" art (ukiyo-e) flourished. Ōtsu-e pictures were cartoon-like simple drawings produced traditionally in the area around Ōtsu on Lake Biwa. The elevation of the lowlife figure Ukiyo Matabei to the official painting realm follows Chikamatsu's favorite pattern of raising ordinary people, in this case a handicapped person, to the level of a true hero. It is also interesting that the villains are led by Hasebe Unkoku, which is a clear reference to Hasegawa Tōhaku (1539–1610), founder of the Hasegawa School of art, also active in the time period of the play and a rival to the Kanō and the Tosa. Further, Unkoku Tōgan (1547–1618) was another painter and the founder of the Unkoku School. These schools vied with one another for power and authority throughout the sixteenth and seventeenth centuries.

Several times in the play, characters perform supernatural acts through the power of their will and skill. The first is when Kanō Motonobu paints a tiger with his own blood, bringing it to life to scare off his attackers. The second is when a pupil of the painter Tosa Shōgen Mitsunobu (1434–1525) is able to use his brush to make the tiger disappear. The third incident occurs within the second scene translated below, when the simple small-time painter of Ōtsu-e cartoons Ukiyo Matabei, frustrated at his inability to impress his master, Mitsunobu, that he is worthy of the Tosa name, concentrates as hard as he can—vowing to die if he fails—to paint his portrait onto a water basin made of stone. Miraculously, the image penetrates through the thick stone and appears also on the other side. His master rewards him with the name "Tosa no Matabei Mitsuoki." Later he is able to make his simple paintings come alive to frighten off attackers. This would have been a lively scene with gadgets and puppet tricks. Chikamatsu is clever in depicting the magic of the painter's brush to make things come alive, since he himself, in fact, was conjuring the miraculous actions from words drawn from his own brush.

This drama, now performed in kabuki and *bunraku,* was originally played by puppets with a chanter voicing both the third-person narrative and the dialogue, and a shamisen musician accompanying the voice and actions. *Jōruri* puppet play texts were published with the full notation for voice, because chanting was a popular amateur hobby. Performance is paced on a set of "musical paragraphs," which usually began slowly with narrative and then rhythmically built up in intensity to a peak, before a relaxing cadence marked the transition to the next paragraph. The translation includes only the notation "*cadence*" (in italics) to indicate the conclusion of a musical paragraph. The division into scenes follows current *bunraku* theatre practice.

The painter Tosa Mitsuoki (1617–1691) was a historical figure, the distinguished founder of the Tosa School of painting. In the play, he gives his own name to the painter Iwasa "Ukiyo" Matabei (or Matahei, 1578–1650), whose original name would have been well known to Chikamatsu's audience. Chikamatsu, whose samurai birth and upbringing had been in Echizen (Fukui), most likely had a special affection for Matabei, who from the age of thirty-eight had spent twenty years as a painter for the Echizen daimyo. The character Matabei the Stutterer is portrayed as a simple fellow with a severe handicap who possesses great determination. His wife, with a far more forward personality than Matabei, makes an affectionate companion and partner for him. The scene where he and his wife dance "Daigashira" is in the style of the *kōwaka-mai* ballad dramas, in which two actors chanted. He can speak without a stutter as long as his voice rides a tune. Matabei is a comic figure throughout, but as he strives to overcome his handicap and rise to greatness both as a painter and as a loyal fighter, he grows in stature as a role model for common folk—such as those in Chikamatsu's audience. Finally, as readers will know, the tiger existed in Japan only as a figure in mythology and a subject of the arts. Chikamatsu uses this figure as a sign for power in the new mythology he creates.

(CAG)

Characters

FARMERS *from neighboring villages*

MAN *carrying a lantern*

SAMURAI, *who is identified as* **SURINOSUKE MASAZUMI**, *disciple of* **MITSUNOBU**

KANO NO MITSUNOBU

MITSUNOBU'S WIFE

UKIYO MATABEI SHIGEOKI, *later* **TOSA NO MATABEI MITSUOKI**

MATABEI'S WIFE

UTANOSUKE

ICHŌ NO MAE

LEADER OF NEIGHBORHOOD SECURITY

FUWA NO BANZAEMON

HASEBE NO UNKOKU

SOLDIERS

PHANTOMS

HASEBE NO TŌGAN

INUGAMI DANPACHI

INUGAMI SANPACHI

SCENE ONE

Residence of Tosa no Shōgen Mitsunobu in Yamashina near Kyoto

(*Earlier, the famous painter Kanō no Motonobu escaped death by drawing a tiger, which came alive and saved him.*)

NARRATOR: Truly the tiger is the lord of the animal kingdom. The spirit of this king of beasts has ravaged the countryside, tearing up paddy fields. The angered farmers have come together and call out:

FARMERS: The tiger passed behind Miidera Temple and has gone as far as Fujino-o. It's sure to have fled into the forest in Yamashina. Let's kill it without damaging its hide. Let's go!

NARRATOR: (*cadence*) Yelling out to each other, they agree on a plan.

NARRATOR: From the hut nearby a man runs out holding a small lantern in one hand and a pole in the other.

MAN: You, over there! Who are you and what're you doing, yelling "beat him to death" in front of a person's house?

FARMERS: Forgive us, we're farmers from Yabase and Awazu. A tiger came down from Mount Shigaraki and has been tearing up the fields, so several villages banded together to hunt him down in this forest. Please help us.

NARRATOR: They all beg him to join them, but the samurai laughs aloud.

SAMURAI: What? There's no record of a tiger ever being in Japan. Impossible! This must be a robber's trick to frighten *you*. Do you know whose hut this is? It's the hermitage of the painter Tosa Shōgen Mitsunobu. There was an incident, and he received an imperial order to take refuge.

He is now an old man, but I am his disciple Surinosuke Masazumi. I won't let you get away with disturbing my master like this!

NARRATOR: He yells out, threatening them with the pole. Mitsunobu and his wife open the sliding door.

MITSUNOBU: I've heard all that's been said. It's hard to be absolutely sure that something strange cannot be born into this world. We will join the hunt!

NARRATOR: He takes a spear in one hand and a bamboo rake in the other. They shout a war cry, setting out for the hunt, torches raised. Then in the shadow of a bamboo thicket,

MITSUNOBU: Look, over there, something moved.

NARRATOR: They shine the torches higher, and see the fierce-looking shape of a wild tiger. It seems unafraid of humans, (*cadence*) just curled up resting peacefully.

NARRATOR: Mitsunobu claps his hands in delight.

MITSUNOBU: How strange! The scene is exactly as in Ganhi's painting *Tiger in a Bamboo Grove.* This is no real tiger: it's surely a tiger that's appeared after a master artist imbued his painting with a spirit! Moreover, it's freshly painted. I know of only one painter alive today who could conceive this: the son and heir of Kanō no Masanobu, Shirōjirō Motonobu. No matter, the proof will be if there are no paw prints. Look for prints.

NARRATOR: The farmers search among the grasses but find no prints at all.

FARMERS: Surely this is the workings of a master artist, but what a master to have known all this. He is a genius beyond compare!

NARRATOR: Even the uneducated farmers bow to Mitsunobu, (*cadence*) respecting the knowledge of this old man.

NARRATOR: Surinosuke steps back a bit and bows to his teacher.

SURINOSUKE: How grateful I am to see this tiger! It has opened my eyes to understand the way of painting. As proof, I will use my brush to make the tiger disappear. I beg you to grant me a new name as a painter.

NARRATOR: Mitsunobu is delighted to see this fervent desire.

MITSUNOBU: From today you will be known as Tosa no Mitsuzumi.

NARRATOR: He offers him a brush bearing the seal of approval. Surinosuke accepts the brush and dips it in ink. He aims the brush at the center of the tiger's body, and stroke by stroke he indeed makes the tiger disappear, first the head, the front legs, and finally the body and tail—they all disappear before their very eyes, (*cadence*) like a miracle of the gods!

NARRATOR: The jaw of each farmer drops in amazement.

FARMER ONE: This story will surely pass to our descendants for many generations to come. I'd love to have this master artist paint me a series of ten beauties! I'd be rich.

FARMER TWO: If only I'd met you at the end of last year. You could've erased all my debts! Time to go home.

NARRATOR: They all laugh as they set off.

SCENE TWO

NARRATOR: Ukiyo Matabei Shigeoki, a low-level student of Tosa Mitsunobu, was born with a stutter. Given his trouble talking, he has remained poor, with few possessions, his only garments made of thin hemp, his house a small hovel, the size of a matchbox. He scrapes by, (*cadence*) dividing one meal into two to survive.

NARRATOR: Matabei rents a house in a remote area of Ōtsu. His wife prepares ink and pigments, and Matabei paints, a cheap brush his sole tool. He sells simple pictures for a few copper pieces as souvenirs to travelers going to and from the capital. His life strings along somehow, the coins trickling in. Loyal to his master in exile, each night he and his wife walk half a *ri* to visit his old teacher—(*cadence*) a noble disciple indeed.

NARRATOR: Matabei bows as a greeting, but because of his stutter, his wife speaks for him.

WIFE: Delighted to see that you are still up. It's finally nice and warm, and the days are getting longer. Everyone is enjoying the cherry blossoms or hiking in the hills. Everyone seems so busy! Since you must be weary living as a hermit deep in the mountains, we've brought you some steamed greens and tofu stew. Why don't we bring along this bamboo bottle of *sake* and take a walk to Sekidera Temple, or to Kinshōji Temple to see the Kannon statue, and watch the throngs enjoying spring? It's only an idea we had. At this time of the year, the crowds are terrible and the shops all busy. My laundry piles up, and we'd get no work done and come home exhausted, having to stand all day long. It'd simply be a useless day. If we hurried, then all we'd do would be to go in a big circle; simply put, haste makes waste. Just now we got a Seta eel at the market in Zeze, and a little Ōtsu *sake* made from Nerinuki spring water. May you slither out of your misfortune this springtime like an eel out of his hole and return to favor in the capital! My, my, how I babble on and on. I do all the talking since my husband stammers. I'm such a gabber, and he's silent—quite a nice pair we make. Oh how embarrassing!

NARRATOR: (*cadence*) She laughs good-naturedly. Mitsunobu's wife has listened patiently.

MITSUNOBU'S WIFE: How delightful for you to be so generous in your offerings for our success. Tonight there's been a wondrous event: Surino-suke has been granted the Tosa name and will now be known as Tosa no Mitsuzumi. The good fortune should rub off on you, Matabei.

NARRATOR: Hearing this, Matabei sees his chance and pushes his wife onward, himself bowing deeply, hands to the floor, seemingly ready to make a formal request. His wife understands his intentions and steps forward.

MATABEI'S WIFE: We heard about this happening from farmers on our way here. They said, "Matabei was poor and handicapped. The younger student was granted the Tosa name while the elder one just continues to draw figures of 'courtesans in wisteria kimono,' catfish, and other simple Ōtsu-e pictures for tourists. He just bides his time, lazily getting by with no prospects." Matabei was miserable to hear them talking even though he knew it was true. I couldn't help but cry and pity him. Mistress, we've spoken to you before about this, but it's the first time to speak directly to the master. Even if just a memory from this life, he wants so much to be known on his gravestone as "Tosa no Matabei." Please, could the master have pity on us and grant this one wish?

NARRATOR: She breaks down in tears. Matabei, too, puts his hands together and bows three times to Mitsunobu, crying into the tatami, (*cadence*) frustrated at his inability to speak.

NARRATOR: Short-tempered by nature, Mitsunobu yells at Matabei.

MITSUNOBU: We've been through this time and again! There's no way a stutterer will be a Tosa! I was exiled over a dispute with Oguri, the official Imperial House artist. Had I given in to Oguri, I would have become rich, and my daughter would not have had to sell herself into prostitution! Why do you think I'm living this life where I have to sell a child just to get by? Can't you see how precious the honor of the Tosa name is? Surinosuke just now proved himself through a magnificent deed. What have you done? The arts of the *koto, go,* calligraphy, and painting are necessary in high society. A painter must often attend aristocratic gatherings. How could a stutterer who can't speak do that? It would be rude beyond belief. Know your station, and just draw Ōtsu pictures to make your living. Have some tea and be on your way!

NARRATOR: (*cadence*) His words are scathing and cold.

NARRATOR: Matabei's wife loses all her courage.

MATABEI'S WIFE: You were born with this stammer; you can only hate your parents for doing this to you.

NARRATOR: She loses all hope. Matabei too is desperate and grabs his throat in anger, then puts his hand in his mouth, trying to pinch his tongue. He breaks down into tears, and we can only feel sorry for his desperation (*cadence*) and grief.

NARRATOR: Just then, from the woods outside, a voice is heard. "Mitsunobu, Mitsunobu!" A young man badly wounded crawls up to the veranda and struggles to stand up.

UTANOSUKE: I am Utanosuke, a student of Kanō Motonobu. Do you not remember me?

MITSUNOBU: Yes, I certainly remember you. Hurry, come inside. I've heard that Motonobu was attacked due to Unkoku and Fuwa's treachery. Please tell me all the details. What has happened?

UTANOSUKE: Yes, you've heard correctly. I was with Motonobu and got this wound in battle with Unkoku. Nagoya Sanza, Motonobu's dependable ally, was away in the capital at the time. Motonobu was in grave danger, but I heard that he managed to escape and fled somewhere. I have another crisis. The young princess Ichō no Mae loves Motonobu and ran away from home with the family seal granted by the shogun, but her enemies have stolen it from her and taken her to the west side of Mount Daigo. If we cannot save Ichō no Mae and get back the seal, then our honor as artists will be lost. My wounds rendering me useless, I've secretly come here seeking allies to help us.

NARRATOR: Mitsunobu interrupts him.

MITSUNOBU: No need to say another word! The Kanō and Tosa are as one family, so we will certainly help you. Try to attack them with swords and we will be no match for them. Ichō no Mae, too, might get hurt. We need to find a clever talker who can convince them that he's following the lord's orders, and trick them into allowing her to return. There must be a way to do this. Everyone, let's hear your ideas.

NARRATOR: Each furrows his brow, some rest their cheeks in their hands, and (*cadence*) others cock their heads trying to think.

NARRATOR: Matabei seems to have something to say, tugs at his wife's sleeve, and pokes her in the back with his finger, but she does not respond. Finally, irritated, he pulls her aside, steps forward, and bows to the floor before his teacher. He swallows before speaking.

MATABEI: I-I-I'll be the one to attack the v-villains. Ichō no Mae and the t-treasured s-seal as w-well, I-I-I'll g-get it b-back!

NARRATOR: Mitsunobu glares at him.

MITSUNOBU: What a nuisance, you stuttering fool! You've merely disturbed our concentration. You're only in the way. Stand up and get out of here.

NARRATOR: Severely scolded though he may be, Matabei is undaunted.

MATABEI: When you're at wit's end, even your own knee is worth consulting, as they say. I'm not able to speak well, but neither my heart nor fist fear anyone, anywhere. I'll try my best, and if it doesn't work, then my trusty sword will do the trick! I'll either drive them away or capture them, gambling the pittance of my life in a game of dice. Even if I proclaim my name as Ukiyo Matabei, I've no parents, no children, only myself alone. My life's nothing more than the dust we sweep away, but my name is worth everything, as precious as Buddha's Mount Sumeru. From my youth I've served you, putting my life on the line all for my dream of inheriting my master's name. Please send me to fight the enemy! Please, please, won't you allow me to go? Will I not get permission from you after all my entreaties? It's all because of this stammer! How I-I-I h-hate myself. I-I-I want to tear out my th-throat. Wife, what a heartless teacher I have.

NARRATOR: (*cadence*) He yells out and breaks down in tears.

NARRATOR: But Mitsunobu is all the more determined.

MITSUNOBU: Just like a cripple to cry like a baby! Your whining tears will bring us bad luck. You'd be no good in the fight. Surinosuke, you go there and figure out a plan to get back Ichō no Mae and the seal.

SURINOSUKE: Yes, sir.

NARRATOR: In a flash, he puts his sword in his sash and stands to leave. Matabei holds him back.

MATABEI: W-w-wait, please wait. Even if our teacher is merciless, please, you are a fellow student, aren't you? Take pity on me! Let me go as well. You can be the leader. P-p-please, Mr. S-s-surinosuke.

SURINOSUKE: Now, Matabei, no matter how eager you are, I cannot go against the order of our teacher. Let go of me.

MATABEI: N-n-no, n-n-never let you g-go.

SURINOSUKE: If you don't let me go, I'll draw my sword and strike.

MATABEI: Th-th-then s-strike and k-k-kill me. I-I'll not let g-go.

NARRATOR: Surinosuke is flustered.

SURINOSUKE: Let go of me! Get off.

NARRATOR: (*cadence*) They struggle on. Finally both Mitsunobu and his wife yell out, 'Let go of him,' and try to stop them, but they don't listen. Matabei's wife finally grabs her husband.

MATABEI'S WIFE: Listen, the master has ordered you to stop. Have you gone crazy?

NARRATOR: But Matabei grabs his wife, throws her down, and kicks her angrily.

MATABEI: Even you have turned on me and called me crazy! Does my own wife now despise me? (*highest pitch*) What a fate to be a stutterer!

NARRATOR: He sits down cross-legged, pounding the tatami, wailing uncontrollably. (*cadence*) We can only feel for his grief.

NARRATOR: Mitsunobu speaks again to Matabei.

MITSUNOBU: Listen, and listen well. You can receive the Tosa name only by achievements in the discipline of painting. You must prove yourself. There's no way that someone can be granted an artist's name for feats of martial bravery.

NARRATOR: His words are final. Matabei's wife sits up.

MATABEI'S WIFE: Well, Matabei, prepare yourself. Now is your final chance. See this stone basin as a stone tablet and draw your own portrait, here and now commit suicide, and receive your artist's name posthumously.

NARRATOR: She prepares the inkstone and ink block. Matabei nods and dips his brush. He faces the stone surface.

MATABEI: This will be my farewell painting to this world. Though my body will decay among the moss, my name will remain as spirit within this stone.

NARRATOR: He concentrates and begins to draw his own image with the power of his brush. His force of will is strong, and the ink penetrates the thick stone, thicker than one *shaku*. Somehow the power of his brush penetrates to the opposite side. The ink remains on the surface but the painting appears on both sides of the stone, (*cadence*) as if he were painting on both at the same time.

NARRATOR: Mitsunobu is amazed.

MITSUNOBU: Although overseas in China we know of Wang Yizhi, who painted through stone, and Zhao Ziang, who painted through wood, there are no precedents in Japanese art. You have surpassed your teacher. Your name "Ukiyo Matabei" will be hereby changed to Tosa no Matabei Mitsuoki. Now riding your newfound strength, set off to recover the princess and the precious seal!

NARRATOR: At his words Matabei is overwhelmed and can only babble his thanks. With tears of joy running down his face, he jumps up and hops around. Mitsunobu and his wife are delighted.

MITSUNOBU: Your heart is brave and your will loyal, but how will you be able to negotiate with the enemy?

NARRATOR: Matabei's wife answers immediately.

MATABEI'S WIFE: Matabei loves to perform the Daigashira *kōwaka-mai* ballad dance. I have danced it with him, and I know he never stammers whenever there's a tune!

MITSUNOBU: That's it. Try to sing and dance an auspicious piece for me.

NARRATOR: Matabei stands up and begins to perform in the manner of an old song, but alters the lyrics to suit his new situation. His wife accompanies him on drum.

MATABEI: (*chants*) Long, long ago Lord Yoritomo ordered a group of brave warriors to set off to kill his half-brother Yoshitsune. That was one Tosabō Masatoshi, but here we now have Tosa no Matabei Mitsuoki. He will repay his teacher's kindness by taking on responsibilities far above his ability. In Ōtsu at Oiwake the paints he uses are cheap, but his fame as a Tosa artist will be that of one worth a thousand gold pieces, his brushwork known far and wide.

NARRATOR: His wife keeps time with his song and dance.

MATABEI'S WIFE: (*chants*) Don't linger here, your master may change his mind, who knows? Hurry! Set off on your way.

MATABEI: (*chants*) Yes, you're right. I'm a poor man drawn only with black ink on paper, but I am tough and strong, not inferior to a painting of multicolor covered with the most durable gold leaf.

NARRATOR: His fervor is infectious, inspiring.

MATABEI: Though I say it myself, my brush is powerful and brave. I take strength from the world of Chinese art. Think of me as bolstered by the valor of the warriors Fankuai and Zhangliang. I bid you farewell.

NARRATOR: He stands up proudly, truly a model from old tales. (*scene cadence*) No one could not praise his valor.

SCENE THREE

Matabei's residence, before dawn the next morning

NARRATOR: Near the famous Osaka Barrier east of Kyoto just before dawn a townsman walks his route, shouting in a voice that usually cautions, "Watch out for fire," but this time saying, "Princess Ichō no Mae is missing, whereabouts unknown." All travelers are being checked and properties searched by the barrier guards, and no stone will be left unturned.

Matabei awoke early, planning to depart at the seventh hour, and as usual celebrated his setting off by drinking three cups of warm *sake*. Just then an elegantly attired lady, though barefoot and dirty all over, comes wandering up from the direction of Fushimi.

ICHŌ NO MAE: You over there, tell me the way to the capital, and give me what you call sandals.

NARRATOR: Matabei ignores her, angry at her haughty manner of speaking. His wife runs out of the house.

WIFE: She's no ordinary woman. She has dignity and charm.

NARRATOR: She approaches the lady.

WIFE: Excuse me, but you seem to be the young lady missing from the residence. We are disciples of Tosa no Mitsunobu; my husband is a painter known as Matabei the Stutterer. We have been asked by Kanō Motonobu's disciple Utanosuke to bring you back home. So please don't be afraid to tell us your name.

NARRATOR: She whispers to Ichō no Mae, who is delighted to meet them.

ICHŌ NO MAE: Yes, you are right. I am Ichō no Mae. The henchmen of Dōgen and Unkoku are fast on my trail. Please help me escape.

NARRATOR: At her words Matabei bows to the ground. His face is aglow with delight and fervor, but the more excited he becomes, the more tied his tongue. He speaks with gestures. Folded arms signal his strength and resolve to help. He moves about, showing his readiness to protect her, even mimicking drawing his sword to attack. He wrestles with opponents, throwing them to the ground, holding them in headlocks, and tossing them about. He twists their arms and punches them, showing her his samurai spirit. She takes refuge in Matabei and his wife's humble hut. (*Scene cadence*) She finds the couple kind and dependable.

NARRATOR: A moment later, neighborhood security appointees from Ōtsu arrive, searching for Ichō no Mae, shouting angrily.

LEADER: Ichō no Mae, princess of Lord Rokkaku, has stolen the family seal and fled. The lord's senior minister has ordered an investigation. We will be checking every house, backstreet, and alleyway, particularly the houses of artists. Don't anyone leave, not even a dog or cat!

NARRATOR: Saying that, he and his men slam the doors shut, front and back. Even fearless Matabei is trapped (*cadence*) like a deer in the hunt.

NARRATOR: Fuwa Banzaemon and Hasebe no Unkoku lead an army of one hundred soldiers, attired in chain mail, who arrive and ransack all the houses, searching for Ichō no Mae. Matabei is desperate at this crucial moment as he and his wife hide the princess. From the adjoining house, the soldiers kick through the wall, opening a wide hole. A soldier sticks his head through and Matabei, flat against the wall raises his broadsword like a chunk of ice, ready to chop off, one by one, all the heads that would peek out. Unkoku yells out.

UNKOKU: Well, well, so this is the home of the famous disciple of the Tosa, Matabei the Stutterer! Tear the house apart and search them out!

NARRATOR: The soldiers attack with cries of "I'll be the one to catch them," but they quickly jump back in disarray.

SOLDIERS: How scary, how frightening! I don't know what's going on, but the house is packed with people. Some look like hired punks. Others are actors and girls. What, some aren't even human! They're monkeys, wild boars, eagles, and even crested eagles! With their sharp claws and angry eyes! No way I'm getting near these things. No way! Too scary!

NARRATOR: They all shake with disgust and fear, (*cadence*) mouths open in awe.

UNKOKU: Don't be stupid, you idiots. This broken-down hovel can barely hold three of you. How could it be full of people? You thought the paintings on the wall were real people and animals! Your fright has tricked your eyes. Don't be such pansies. You over there, yank open the latticed shutters! Don't be so timid.

NARRATOR: So ordered, the soldiers use a fire hook to pry open the door to cries of "All together now!" When they look inside, they behold a wondrous sight, just as the soldier described: thugs ready and waiting, not shadows, nor apparitions. In the faint light of dawn, these fierce figures stand ready, armed with spears strung with feathers. The spirit of this Tosa painter has infused his works, which have come alive. The soldiers attack, trying to overwhelm each creature, but they are beaten back every time. Although they strike, the soldiers cannot hold these phantom warriors.

PHANTOMS: We owe our dew-like lives to Matabei and will die to protect him.

NARRATOR: With their rough-looking blue jackets flowing, they fiercely take on all comers (*cadence*) to protect their master.

NARRATOR: One of Unkoku's students, Hasebe no Tōgan, a no-good soldier, yells out while swinging his sword wildly.

TŌGAN: Leave them to me!

NARRATOR: A phantom warrior, his hair loose, twirls around a giant *sake* cup, scattering chili powder, which gets into Tōgan's eyes. Tōgan screams out in pain, his eyes red like the finest damask, (*cadence*) unable to see anything.

NARRATOR: His teacher Unkoku can stand this no more.

UNKOKU: I'll attack them all and show how its done!

NARRATOR: He flies in fearlessly but is met by a brave, gentle, and elegant woman skilled in female martial techniques, her face covered with a scarf. She holds wisteria branches, which coil around his body, beating it. (*cadence*) He thrusts, and she parries.

NARRATOR: Elegant is the young priest who emerges briskly, wearing a hemp robe with his sleeves tied back with a cord. Bold and brave, he rushes into the fray like a wave on the shore. He is so hard to catch, it's like trying to pin down a catfish with a gourd. He pounds the soldiers like a priest pounds out his prayers on a gourd. The soldiers try to strike him, but he slips away from their grasp. The soldiers keep coming (*cadence*) but are unable to advance.

NARRATOR: Fuwa's trusted soldier Inugami Danpachi steps forward.

DANPACHI: Everyone, step aside, out of the way!

NARRATOR: Danpachi enters the fray, only to be met by a blind priest who suddenly appears out of darkness, hobbling on a cane. The priest feebly raises his stick and whirls it blindly around and around, hitting whatever is in its path. Danpachi's younger brother Sanpachi, still only a boy of fifteen, yells out:

SANPACHI: You'll not get away from me!

NARRATOR: He jumps in, doing a conjuring trick with a stack of wooden headrests, tossing them up and juggling them all at once. He spins them about and tries to attack, but the headrests just land in a jumble, crashing like waves on the shore. (*cadence*) All the soldiers retreat in disarray.

NARRATOR: Fuwa no Banzaemon is furious.

BANZAEMON: You're a worthless lot. What on earth are you doing? Let me show you what a true samurai's sword can do!

NARRATOR: He dashes straight forward when suddenly a strange creature appears. What is this? It looks like a priest, but his head has the horns of a demon and he chants demon prayers, his fang-like teeth gleaming and horns shaking, ready to take on all comers, with a great mallet in hand beating a bell, clang, clang, clang, clang, to a deafening roar that shakes the bones! No one able to advance, they all retreat, chased off by a sudden swoop of falcons, vicious hawks, and eagles. The brigade of soldiers is routed, and everybody flees, running off in every direction, pecked and kicked by all kinds of animals, disturbing the dawn with a great storm of feathers. (*scene cadence*) Eagle cries echo through the Osaka Barrier.

NARRATOR: The cocks crow in response to the clamor, and as the dawn's light grows brighter, the animals, demons, and other figures turn back into color on white paper, their spirits having been roused by the power of the painter's brush, (*cadence*) truly a heavenly wonder!

NARRATOR: Matabei eagerly pulls at his wife's sleeve, indicating that he wants to speak; his mind moves forward, but his tongue is tied, so only gibberish comes out.

WIFE: What's wrong with you? In an emergency when the enemy is attacking, no time to worry about your speech. Dance and sing, intone the words like in a ballad drama!

MATABEI: (*sung/chanted*) That's it! How could I forget? We've just witnessed a miracle here! It wasn't because of me—it was because I was granted the Tosa name. It was my master's benevolence that pursued the enemy and destroyed them. We attacked the retreating soldiers, jumping into their ranks, driving them from west to east, from north to south. With spiderlike movements, we wielded our swords deftly in all directions, up and down, crisscrossing and in circles. We gave chase after them, cutting them down. Ousted with such force, they scattered in all directions; (*cadence*) none remain. We did it! Now all we need to do is get away from here as soon as possible and take the princess back to the capital!

NARRATOR: At the Osaka Barrier the cuckoo has yet to cry, like Matabei, whose heart is as firm as stone, but his jaw still as stiff as metal. But what a peerless man, who now crosses the mountain peak at Hinooka on his way to the capital, he and his party passing through rocky fields and grassy moors, wandering along round and round like the st-st-stuttering of M-Matabei's t-tongue!

TRANSLATED BY C. ANDREW GERSTLE

Kagekiyo
ANONYMOUS

Kagekiyo is one of the so-called Eighteen Favorite Plays of the Ichikawa Danjūrō acting line, the most important kabuki acting dynasty in Edo. It shares many characteristics with other plays in the series, particularly in the abrasive and confrontational attitude of its superhuman hero toward authority and the bravura (*aragoto*) style in which the role is always performed. The play is staged less frequently today, but in medieval and Edo Japan, Kagekiyo was regarded as a folk hero, and his deeds inspired works in many genres, including nō, *kōwakamai,* and puppet theatre.

The historical Akushichibyōe Kagekiyo was a Heike warrior involved in the famous struggle for power between the Heike and Genji clans in the late twelfth century. He plays only a minor part in the great literary chronicle of that war, *The Tales of the Heike,* but from the thirteenth century on, a number of apocryphal legends began to grow up around him. These stories tell of Kagekiyo's mastery of disguise in his attempts to assassinate the Genji leaders Yoritomo and Noriyori, his relationship with his wife Akoya, a former courtesan, and his eventual capture and torture. During the eighteenth century the story of Kagekiyo became indelibly associated with the Danjūrō line of kabuki actors. The first holder of the Danjūrō name to attempt the role of Kagekiyo was Ichikawa Danjūrō II (1688–1758) in 1739 at the Ichimura Theater in Edo. So strong was the popular association between Danjūrō and Kagekiyo that a special scene showing the actor in the role was written to celebrate the return of Danjūrō VII (1791–1859) to Edo in 1850 after several years of banishment. The fearsome Heike warrior became so associated with the Danjūrō line that in the end no fewer than five plays out of the Eighteen Favorites feature variations on the Kagekiyo myth.

Why, though, the link between a line of actors and a medieval warrior? The Danjūrō line occupied a special place in the hearts of audiences in their home city of Edo, a focus for their dreams and desires—some would even say a focus of commoner identification and resistance against samurai hegemony. Because the Danjūrō actors were famous for playing self-possessed and physically powerful heroes who stand up to authority, the role of Kagekiyo was thus a natural for them—but also one that they deliberately tweaked to better appeal to their audience. In the language and intonation of his vehement abuse of his samurai tormenters—a kabuki technique known as *akutai*—Kagekiyo sounds less like a twelfth-century warrior and more like an Edo carpenter or boatman in full, enraged flow. The very extremity of Kagekiyo's actions—breaking his prison cell with his bare hands, tearing an enemy limb from limb—could easily be read as a wish fulfillment fantasy for a politically oppressed audience. The physicality of the role too was perfectly suited to the Danjūrō line's bombastic *aragoto* style of acting, replete with dynamic poses and the characteristic vigorous, bounding exit (*roppō*) through the audience that ends the play.

If the central character of the play was a vivid distillation of Edo commoner desires, the trappings with which he is surrounded in the play are more or less conventional. The device of the missing "treasures" was a familiar one in Edo drama and popular literature. Important families did indeed sometimes possess valuable heirlooms (*kahō*) said to be of great antiquity, and these items often came to accrue a symbolic value. Many kabuki plots revolved around the loss and recovery of these items, usually swords, pieces of calligraphy or tea bowls, but here more unusually a magical lute (*biwa*) and flute. The instruments played in the torture scene are a little unusual: the *kokyū* (a stringed Chinese fiddle, held upright and bowed), and the *koto* (a zither-like instrument played with both hands and usually having thirteen strings) were more likely to be played in samurai or aristocratic households than in plebeian ones. The Chinese references in the play, such as Lu Sheng, who fell asleep and in five minutes dreamt of a lifetime of wealth and glory, would have probably flown over the heads of some but would have been familiar to the more educated spectators. Chinese functioned in a similar way in Edo Japan as Greek and Latin did in pre-twentieth-century western Europe—that is, as an emblem of learning.

Kabuki plays were rewritten each time they were performed, so the text used for this translation dates only to 1842. Originally there were no detailed stage directions, and the lines were marked by the names of the actors who spoke them rather than by those of the characters they played. This translation follows the practice of modern editions, which supply stage directions and characters' names.

⌒(AC)⌒

Characters

UNNO NO KOTARŌ YUKIUJI

TAKENOSHITA NO MAGOHACHI SAEMON

CHICHIBU NO SHŌJI SHIGETADA

IWANAGA SAEMON MUNETSURA

NITAN NO SHIRŌ TADATSUNE

KAJIWARA HEIZA KAGETOKI

SOLDIERS

AKOYA, *wife of Kagekiyo*

HITOMARU, *daughter of Kagekiyo*

HASE HACHIRŌ MASAKAGE

HANZAWA ROKURŌ

BANBA NO CHŪTA

RETAINERS TO IWANAGA SAEMON

HŌDŌMARU, *son of Atsumori of the Heike*

AKUSHICHIBYŌE KAGEKIYO

TOKIWAZU MUSICIANS

(*To slow and regular beats on the large drum offstage, the curtain opens to reveal a three-panel backdrop painted with a bamboo grove. A sturdy latticed wooden cage occupies the center stage, its roof weighed down by a boulder and a tree trunk. An elegant pine tree stands at stage left. To stage right, four singers and musicians of the Tokiwazu School sit in a row on a low dais. A formally dressed actor enters and declaims the title and the names of today's actors and musicians. As he exits, a flute melody begins offstage. UNNO NO KOTARŌ YUKIUJI and TAKE-NOSHITA NO MAGOHACHI SAEMON enter along the hanamichi runway, dressed in the long, trailing trousers and bulky formal kimono of Kamakura-period nobles. Both wear tall black lacquered hats and carry a fan and a short sword.*)

MAGOHACHI: Lord Unno, fifty days have passed since we imprisoned Shichibyōe Kagekiyo and still he hasn't revealed the whereabouts of those two precious items we're after. What a blasted, stubborn wretch that man is!

KOTARŌ: What's more, he refuses to accept any favors from the Genji, so not a drop of water or grain of rice has passed his lips. Things have gotten so serious that the big guns have been summoned here today. The shogun Yoritomo has sent his retainer Chichibu no Shigetada, while his brother Lord Noriyori has sent Iwanaga Saemon, and the lords Nitan and Kajiwara are coming to give them support.

MAGOHACHI: Noriyori must have some plot up his sleeve if he's sent Kajiwara and Iwanaga.

KOTARŌ: But you can be sure Shigetada and Nitan have their orders direct from Yoritomo…

MAGOHACHI: So when Kagekiyo submits, he's certain to join Yoritomo's side.

KOTARŌ: Though I'd prefer that he went over to Lord Noriyori.

MAGOHACHI: But come what may, today all will be set to rights.

KOTARŌ: Then let us wait and see what transpires.

(*They nod and move to sit, flanking the cage, on black lacquered stools. Tokiwazu shamisen accompaniment begins, and a stage assistant spreads a red cloth in front of the musicians' dais. A percussion ensemble of three drummers and a flute player take their places.*)

TOKIWAZU CHANT: ♫ Just as Confucius brought peace to Lu / in but three months / the glory of the current reign / leads the world to virtue. / In correct deportment / they await the arrival of the envoys from Kamakura…

(*The large drum beats regularly offstage as SHIGETADA and NITAN enter along the hanamichi accompanied by six SOLDIERS. Each carries two swords and is dressed formally in trousers and a vest with stiffened shoulders. The soldiers bear a lavish array of food on lacquered trays and a long-handled sake kettle. Simultaneously, IWANAGA and KAJIWARA enter along the temporary hanamichi, both dressed formally, carrying two swords and followed by six SOLDIERS. IWANAGA is a red-faced villain, while KAJIWARA wears a white wig. Their soldiers carry a huge abalone shell filled with food, a sake barrel, and a ladder. Both parties stop two-thirds of the way along the hanamichi.*)

SHIGETADA: As Confucius said, when you govern with virtue, you will be like the North Star, fixed in your place while all the other stars array themselves around you. So, having been commanded by our lord, the shogun…

IWANAGA: Lord Noriyori has entrusted us with a grave mission, to turn Akushichibyōe Kagekiyo over to our side.

NITAN: I, Nitan no Shirō Tadatsune, have also been given the strictest of orders.

KAJIWARA: If he will not join us, that will be his ruin. Death is but a word away.

SHIGETADA: Come, it is already past noon…

IWANAGA: And each minute brings the prisoner Kagekiyo closer to his end…

NITAN: Or the time of torture.

TOKIWAZU CHANT: ♪ They cross the white sands of the inquisition courtyard.

(*To slow drumbeats, they enter the stage. SHIGETADA and IWANAGA take up position at stage left with NITAN and KAJIWARA to their right, and the soldiers lined up behind them.*)

KOTARŌ: We thank you in advance, my lords…

BOTH: For your work here today.

IWANAGA (*with relish*): No need to thank me. I've been looking forward to today's torturing.

KAJIWARA: You'd be advised to take careful note of his demonstration.

IWANAGA: Now, Lord Shigetada, if by some miracle Kagekiyo should resist confessing the whereabouts of the Seizan lute and Aoba flute and refuse to join us…

KAJIWARA: Then we shall drag him down to the shore at Yuigahama, strike off his head, and impale it over our camp gates.

BOTH: Such is the command of Lord Noriyori.

TOKIWAZU CHANT: ♫ Shigetada appears not to hear.

SHIGETADA: Come, I well understand that Lord Noriyori is desperate to have Kagekiyo as an ally. But in all the fifty days that have passed since he was captured, in his stubbornness Kagekiyo has let neither water nor any scrap of Genji food pass his lips.

NITAN: If things are left to continue in this manner, he is sure to die. There is no way to draw out the location of the things we seek from the mouth of a dead man. And any hope of his joining our cause will be lost like froth on the water.

SHIGETADA: Rather, let us persuade Kagekiyo to eat and regain his strength.

SHIGETADA & NITAN: This we believe to be the most judicious solution.

IWANAGA (*laughing*): Did you all hear that? Kamakura rumor has it that Lord Shigetada is a wise man gifted with knowledge of the Four States of Existence. But feeding the prisoner? Is that really the best you can come up with?

KAJIWARA: I agree. (*Laughs evilly.*) Fortunately, just the other day we managed to capture Kagekiyo's daughter Hitomaru. We have brought her here today.

SHIGETADA: She will make a valuable prisoner. For my part, Kagekiyo's wife, Akoya, surrendered herself to me voluntarily, and I have brought her here today.

NITAN: Let us bring out both prisoners.

KAJIWARA (*shouting offstage*): Banba no Chūta! Drag Hitomaru out here immediately.

SHIGETADA (*shouting offstage*): Hanzawa Rokurō! Bring out our prisoner, Akoya.

(*The curtains at the far end of the two* hanamichi *open simultaneously.*)

TOKIWAZU CHANT: ♩ No news an occasion for tears, / the scented charm of a love / that will not reveal its true nature. / Bound by parental ties and / dragged out so pitifully, / Akoya and Hitomaru, / flowers so utterly transformed.

(*As the musicians sing these lines, AKOYA appears on the hanamichi, dressed in a patchwork kimono and with a rope tied around her waist. Behind her and holding the rope is HANZAWA ROKURŌ, wearing his long hakama trousers tucked up and carrying a lacquered box. HITOMARU enters along the temporary hanamichi, in a tattered long-sleeved kimono. She too has a rope around her waist and is followed by BANBA NO CHŪTA, who carries a sword. The women mime their distress.*)

SOLDIER: Get down on the ground!

HANZAWA: This prisoner is Akoya, the wife of Kagekiyo, who gave herself up voluntarily.

BANBA: And this is Kagekiyo's daughter Hitomaru, whom we captured on Kobukurozaka.

IWANAGA (*glaring at the prisoners*): Akoya, Hitomaru, so you want to see Kagekiyo?

TOKIWAZU CHANT: ♩ Just hearing her husband's name / Akoya wipes away her tears.

AKOYA: I heard that my husband had been captured, and it was out of desire to see him again that I gave myself up. I think you know the answer to your question.

HITOMARU: Is that voice really that of my own mother? I so missed you.

AKOYA: And that must be my daughter Hitomaru. How I longed to see you!

TOKIWAZU CHANT: ♩ In her desire to embrace her daughter / Akoya strains against the ropes, / bonded by ties of blood.

SOLDIERS: Stay where you are!

TOKIWAZU CHANT: ♩ Parent and child both / are thrown to the ground.

(*They try to move closer, but there is not enough slack in their ropes and they collapse, weeping, on the ground. SHIGETADA stares meaningfully at them.*)

SHIGETADA: Such is the love of parent and child. Dragged together to this place, the joy of their meeting undone in shameful bondage.

NITAN: Just look at their anguish. Imagine how they will react when reunited with Kagekiyo.

SHIGETADA: Indeed, indeed. I have an idea. Unbind them both. And you, Hanzawa and Banba, unlock the door to Kagekiyo's cell.

BOTH: As you command, my lord.

(*Using a huge key, they unlock the cell door.*)

TOKIWAZU CHANT: ♫ The bell of the Gion Shōja tolls / the impermanence of all things. / The color of the sala flowers reveals / the truth that the prosperous must decline. / Since seizing power / the Heike years of glory / were but twenty some years, / a dream awoken from in a sea of earthly desires abandoned. / The moon glimpsed between the waves, / the pure shadow of Kagekiyo / hearing the voices of his wife and child / cannot but be moved.

(*As the musicians sing, KAGEKIYO thrusts his head out of the cell. He wears a bushy wig symbolizing the length of his time in captivity, a primitive hemp kimono with a padded jacket, and shin and forearm guards. His face is painted with bold red stripes. He is bound with a huge rope. As AKOYA and HITOMARU catch sight of him, again they strain against their bonds.*)

KAGEKIYO: Akoya, Hitomaru, I never expected to see you again before being questioned by the shogun. Fortune surely smiles upon us today. My faith and prayers to the bodhisattva have been answered. My thanks, my thanks. But wife, daughter, you have changed so . . .

TOKIWAZU CHANT: ♫ As they gaze at each other / the power of the Lotus Sutra revealed.

AKOYA: Husband, it has been too long. But my joy is tempered by pity at your appearance.

HITOMARU: Though we parted when I was but a child, to see you again when bound by ropes like this is so dreadful.

AKOYA: Mortifying...

BOTH: Beyond measure!

TOKIWAZU CHANT: 🎵 Mother and daughter weep in despair. / Even the sleeves with which they try to conceal their tears / increase the pathos.

(*They cling together, weeping in despair. KAGEKIYO closes his eyes and begins to chant the* Lotus Sutra.)

SHIGETADA: Lord Iwanaga, what say you we have Kagekiyo brought out and begin the torture?

IWANAGA: An excellent suggestion. Guards, bring forth that wretch Kagekiyo.

TOKIWAZU CHANT: 🎵 More than his arm and leg shackles / it is the ropes that bind his wife and daughter / that tear at his heart. / Refusing food has weakened his body / but his heart remains undaunted / within his skeletal frame.

(*Soldiers drag KAGEKIYO out of his cell to center stage.*)

TOKIWAZU CHANT: 🎵 Shigetada sidles up to Kagekiyo / before drawing a prison of mercy on the ground. / He undoes his bonds.

(*With the point of his scabbard, SHIGETADA draws a circle near KAGEKIYO and cuts his ropes. KAGEKIYO is startled.*)

SHIGETADA: You're right to be puzzled. (*He indicates the circle.*)

TOKIWAZU CHANT: 🎵 Though undaunted in the face of power / Kagekiyo recognizes benevolence / and he straightens his posture. / Iwanaga Saemon's voice is ragged with rage.

(*KAGEKIYO enters the circle and sits.*)

IWANAGA: An imprudent move, Lord Shigetada. Kagekiyo's intentions are still unclear. By loosening his bonds, I see that your torture today will be half-hearted.

KAJIWARA: And this circle you have drawn in the dirt into which you have placed him?

SHIGETADA: I can well understand your doubts. In the administration of King Wen of Zhou, it was common to place even serious criminals within a hexagon drawn on the earth. It was referred to as the "benevolent prison of the wise." While even an iron shield can be shattered, this little stratagem of mine will never be broken.

(*The players of the hip drum and shoulder drum begin to punctuate the music with sotto voce calls.*)

TOKIWAZU CHANT: ♫ This benevolent prison hides a measure of compassion. / Kagekiyo is deeply affected by his gesture.

KAGEKIYO: Shigetada, I thank you for your magnanimity. This prison, be it but a line in the earth, shows me your sincerity, and I will do my utmost not to break it. I have but one further request—just permit me a meeting with your lord, Yoritomo, and I will die a happy man. Lord Shigetada, hear my plea.

SHIGETADA: I am inclined to grant your request. Hanzawa, bring out the items I ordered.

(*He brings out a lacquered black hat and a box containing a formal kimono.*)

TOKIWAZU CHANT: ♫ Shigetada takes the hat and robe / and hangs them from a pine branch.

SHIGETADA: Kagekiyo, look upon them. These are the hat and robe of the shogun himself.

(*KAGEKIYO gazes at them.*)

KAGEKIYO: Lord Yoritomo's, you say? (*He glares angrily at them.*)

SHIGETADA: None other, for this special occasion.

NITAN: Feast your eyes upon them!

KAGEKIYO (*half-sung*): How strange. I feel as if I am gazing upon the shogun himself. But even so, Shigetada, still I will not break this circular prison.

SHIGETADA: In that case, perhaps your heart has softened toward Lord Yoritomo...

NITAN: And you will consent to ally yourself to him?

IWANAGA: No, no, Kagekiyo, you must join Lord Noriyori. But before then I must interrogate you about the whereabouts of the Seizan lute and the Aoba flute.

IWANAGA & KAJIWARA: Spit it out—where are they?

KAGEKIYO (VEHEMENTLY): I have no idea. You may tell me that Lord Yoritomo wishes to perform an act of charity, to put on a good face to the world by praying for the souls of the vanquished Heike. Or that he plans to have music performed at a great memorial service for their souls led by thousands of priests and that he needs the Aoba flute and lute for those services. But I know that his real motive is to seize the treasures of the Heike for himself. And even if he really wanted to hold a mass, why on earth would the Heike want to be celebrated by the Genji general? The Heike need no fancy memorials with thousands of priests and melodies of every mode—all they need is the head of Yoritomo presented at their graves. That's the only prayer to lay their souls to rest. And even if I did know the whereabouts of those two treasures, do you really think I would tell you? But I don't know, so there's no way I can tell you. Iwanaga and Kajiwara, you're even less the men than rumor suggested. You call yourselves samurai?

TOKIWAZU CHANT: ♫ At this tirade Iwanaga's mouth gapes open / and his face swells in anger.

IWANAGA: Not only do you refuse to confess, but you insult us too. (*Shouting offstage*) Hase no Hachirō, bring out Hōdōmaru, the son of the Heike prince Atsumori.

(*To hand-drum accompaniment, HACHIRŌ drags out HŌDŌMARU, who is dressed in a child's kimono with wide dangling sleeves, tied with a brocade obi.*)

HACHIRŌ: As you command, here is the prisoner Hōdōmaru.

IWANAGA: Throw that brat into the cell.

HACHIRŌ: Immediately, sir. All right, you sniveling kid, get in there. (*Raises his hand.*)

AKOYA & HITOMARU: Please, don't.

(*HACHIRŌ brushes them aside and shoves HŌDŌMARU into the cell. Without thinking, KAGEKIYO jumps to his feet, glaring around him.*)

ALL: So you're going to break the circle!

(*With visible effort KAGEKIYO restrains himself and sits back down.*)

HACHIRŌ: You all saw, didn't you, the only child of Atsumori of the Heike, dragged here from Tsurugaoka. So, Kagekiyo, you say you won't cough up the whereabouts of those treasures and you won't join us, eh? But how about if we throw Hōdōmaru into that cell and let him starve there? Still not going to confess? If you want to save the kid's life, tell us where those items are now.

KAGEKIYO: Cowards, the lot of you! It disgusts me to look at you. (*He glares so fiercely that HACHIRŌ recoils in fear.*) This can only be the work of Iwanaga and Kajiwara. I knew not whether Hōdōmaru lived or died, so it is with great joy that I see his face today. But to throw an innocent child into a cell is inhuman beyond belief. You are worthless men.

IWANAGA: What did you just say? I'd like to see you say it again while I break your bones.

KAJIWARA: Let's see how you like the water torture.

BOTH: Guards, get ready!

SHIGETADA: Please, restrain yourselves gentlemen. I have brought the only torture implements we will need today.

IWANAGA: What?! Which implements?

SHIGETADA: Rokurō, bring out those things I entrusted to you earlier.

TOKIWAZU CHANT: ♫ He rushes off and brings back the implements, / a most refined-looking *koto* / and a *kokyū,* / which he places before them.

SHIGETADA: Kagekiyo, look upon these instruments. Have you seen this *koto* before?

KAGEKIYO (LOOKS CLOSELY): It is the *koto* owned by Captain Shigehira of the third rank. He gave it the name "Asagiri." How did you come by it?

SHIGETADA: That's a good question, Kagekiyo. We know that the Heike possessed three great treasures. The Seizan lute owned by Tsunemasa, the Aoba flute of Atsumori, and this Asagiri *koto* owned by Captain Shigehira. It is well known that he greatly valued this *koto* while he lived.

NITAN: And now that he is dead, it has become a Kamakura treasure.

SHIGETADA: It was my honor that Lord Yoritomo chose to entrust it to me.

NITAN: And you must have a secret use in mind for this *kokyū* too.

IWANAGA: Come now, Lord Shigetada. You keep talking about torture implements, but all I see here are two musical instruments, instruments of pleasure if anything. (*Laughs.*) Perhaps you want to lighten the mood, eh?

KAJIWARA: If you keep referring to those things as torture implements, I'm likely to split my sides laughing. How do you propose to use a *koto* and a *kokyū* to torture anyone?

SHIGETADA (LAUGHS): Do you not recall the story of Shoshiki, who cried out involuntarily on hearing the *koto* playing of Hakuga no Sanmi? Melodies possess a rare power. Let us have Akoya play the *koto* and her daughter the *kokyū* so that Kagekiyo may be moved to confess.

(*Mother and daughter look meaningfully at one another.*)

AKOYA: This is a shameful form of torture, but I will accept...

HITOMARU: This *koto* is indeed the pangs of conscience...

KAGEKIYO: These past two decades, like Lu Sheng I know not whether they be dream or reality.

SHIGETADA: Come, the *koto* has many modes...

NITAN: When you are unable to bear suffering...

SHIGETADA: It produces the tone of melancholy...

KAGEKIYO: When your heart is filled with malice...

IWANAGA: It sounds bloodthirsty...

AKOYA: When you long for someone...

NITAN: The tone is like mutual love...

HITOMARU: When you are crooked in your morals...

KAJIWARA: It plays out of tune...

SHIGETADA: Play with an honest heart, with a natural and true sound, and the melody itself will become our torture for you, Kagekiyo.

NITAN: To put it another way, even if Akoya changes the words of the song in order to hide the truth, any muddiness in her sound...

SHIGETADA: Will give away the location of those treasures. Akoya, Hitomaru, play for us now.

IWANAGA: Play, play, damn you both!

TOKIWAZU CHANT: ♫ Compelled, they face each other / and unwillingly they begin to strum.

(*AKOYA plays the* koto *and HITOMARU the* kokyū *as a master shamisen player from the onstage instrumental ensemble joins them to make up a trio.*)

TOKIWAZU CHANT: ♫ Green the curtains, red the room, / waning moon and scattered blossoms. / Pillows once twinned / will one day molder and decay, / a dream fled without a trace.

SHIGETADA: Hanzawa, pass me that tray.

IWANAGA: Banba, place the abalone shell in front of Kagekiyo.

(*HANZAWA places the lacquer food tray in front of SHIGETADA, and BANBA places the abalone shell in front of KAGEKIYO.*)

SHIGETADA: Shichibyōe Kagekiyo, you must surely be exhausted. Please take some nourishment and pledge yourself to Lord Yoritomo.

IWANAGA: Lord Shigetada, wait just a moment. We are both after the same dish; you want to bring Kagekiyo to Yoritomo, while Kajiwara and I want him for Noriyori.

KAJIWARA: It is the kindness of us both that saves you from this fifty-day starvation.

IWANAGA: Come, Kagekiyo, bow to us three times in gratitude . . .

KAJIWARA: And eat your fill.

(*Hand drum music as IWANAGA thrusts the abalone shell toward KAGEKIYO.*)

KAGEKIYO: They say that high and low should never mix, but only cats or dogs eat out of a shell. By comparing me, a mighty warrior, to beasts you mock me. Iwanaga, Kajiwara—dare you to compare Kagekiyo to a beast?

IWANAGA: Are we now feeling humiliated and angry . . . ? (*Laughs evilly.*)

HITOMARU: You and Shigetada are seated side by side, my father, but how differently they treat you! Look at the table full of food in front of Shigetada.

AKOYA: Even if you eat, there's no need to ally yourself with the Genji. Make yourself strong in mind and body, husband, so you can achieve your goal.

HITOMARU: For fifty days you have had no food nor even a drop of water. How can you continue to live like this?

AKOYA: Please, we beg you, take something to eat now.

HITOMARU: Father . . .

AKOYA: Husband . . .

KAGEKIYO (*laughing*): You think I need women and children to tell me what to do? I've refused your rice all this time, but now I'm going to change my mind just because my wife is here? My daughter's words may sound sweetly in my ears, but even that will not make me change my mind. (*Laughs.*) You fools! Shichibyōe Kagekiyo puts his faith in the Goddess of Mercy of Kiyomizu Temple. Reading the sutra a thousand times night and morning will keep me safe from illness for a thousand days, ten thousand days. I'd sooner die than ally myself to you. Wife, daughter, be silent.

IWANAGA: Kagekiyo, just come over to Noriyori's side, and all these vessels...

KAJIWARA: Shall be filled with whatever delicacies you desire.

MAGOHACHI: Come, be grateful, and eat...

ALL: Your fill.

KAGEKIYO: Bo Yi and Shu Qi hid themselves on Shouyang Mountain and lived off bracken. The soul of a wise man is like a phoenix, while you turncoat samurai, loyal to the Genji one day, the Heike the next, are nothing but sparrows stealing the nest of a fallen eagle. How could the likes of you ever understand the soul of a phoenix? You urge me to eat, but I've seen through your trap. If I touch one grain of it, I'll be Noriyori's man, taking his ration. Take this filthy food and eat it yourselves, you sniveling wretches! Akushichibyōe Kagekiyo will not touch a single grain of Genji rice, and I will stand my ground until I have revenged myself on the enemies of the Heike. You call yourselves samurai, but for the last twenty years you lived fat off Heike charity. Did we not show you our favor? All you care about is filling your own foul bellies. Kagekiyo will never serve two masters—and still you dare to think you can convert me to your side? If your stinking food is so good for eating, you two get down on your hands and knees and eat it! (*He kicks over the abalone shell.*)

KAJIWARA: Such a vile torrent of abuse. Well, we'll have to change our method of torture then. You think we won't drag the truth about the flute and the *biwa* out of you!

IWANAGA: Now it's my turn to show you how an interrogation should be done. Chūta, bring me that sword. (*He grabs HITOMARU as CHŪTA hands him the sword.*) Look, Kagekiyo. I hold in my hand your very own

Azamaru sword, decorated with the engraving of the poet Hitomaru. And I'm going to skewer your very own darling Hitomaru with it! Tell me where those items are now!

(*He holds the sword at HITOMARU's throat. AKOYA pleads with him.*)

IWANAGA: Will you make Kagekiyo ally himself to Lord Noriyori?

AKOYA: Well, I . . . I . . .

IWANAGA: You want me to slit her throat?

AKOYA: Well, I . . . I . . .

IWANAGA: Do you? Well . . .

BOTH: Well, well, well.

IWANAGA: Well, do you? (*AKOYA is speechless.*) If you don't make him change sides, I'll kill Hitomaru with your husband's own sword. (*He moves to stab HITOMARU, but KAGEKIYO wrenches the sword out of his hand, pulls HITOMARU to his side, and turns the sword on her.*)

KAGEKIYO: I am bound by ties of love to my wife and daughter, but I will never join the Genji. You think killing one or even two of my daughters would do the trick? Fools! Watch as I rid myself of this encumbrance, watch as a father puts his own daughter to the sword. Praise be to Amida Buddha.

AKOYA: Husband, no! Don't kill her.

KAGEKIYO: Her father will take her life with the Azamaru blade. It has been predestined; we must all reap what we have sowed. (*He moves to stab her, but AKOYA holds him back.*)

AKOYA: Stay your hand, I beg you.

KAGEKIYO: You timid woman! You should be begging me to give her a glorious death. Remember the insults the Genji have heaped upon us, and wipe away your tears. Let go of me, I tell you, let go!

SHIGETADA: Kagekiyo, don't be too hasty. Wait! (*He seizes the sword and forces AKOYA and HITOMARU back to their original places.*) You may be parent and child, but you are still my prisoner, and a murder would bring shame upon me. Hitomaru and Akoya, your music has plucked the heartstrings of grief. Where were we?

AKOYA & HITOMARU: You mean ...?

ALL: Play, play!

(*AKOYA and HITOMARU again pick up the instruments and begin to play.*)

TOKIWAZU CHANT: ♫ An evening when voices cry out in panic ...

AKOYA (*sings*): ♫ *Such gorgeous birds.*

TOKIWAZU CHANT: ♫ A mother bird in floods of tears, / a blind bird wanders in darkness, / a nightingale spits blood on its deathbed.

(*The large drum begins to play a muffled beat offstage. Two small clouds of smoke arise from the instruments and snake upward toward the roof of the stage. Smoke also appears amidst the audience and on the hanamichi. Everyone gazes at them, mesmerized.*)

ALL: What on earth ...? (*Hand drum accompaniment begins.*)

KAGEKIYO: An uncanny form. As though drawn by Akoya's playing on the Asagiri *koto,* an auspicious form has appeared and trails through the air. Its color is of blue tinged with yellow, like the ocean waves or river water.

SHIGETADA: Another is the shape of bamboo leaves scattered and buried in the earth.

NITAN: They seem to move with the music as though searching for each other.

KAGEKIYO: It must mean that the flute is sunk in water.

SHIGETADA: And the lute must then be buried in the ground!

KAGEKIYO: Then the instruments were neither lost nor destroyed.

SHIGETADA: Indeed, Kagekiyo and Akoya...

NITAN: Knew nothing—of that there can be no doubt.

KAGEKIYO: A happy omen summoned up by the sound of the *koto*.

SHIGETADA: The flute and the lute...

NITAN: In sympathetic resonance...

KAGEKIYO: The mysteries of silk string and bamboo...

ALL THREE: An auspicious omen, indeed!

TOKIWAZU CHANT: ♫ Shigetada, so elegant in his response, / happy he needn't interrogate.

(*The* koto *song comes to an end, and the tendrils of smoke disappear.*)

IWANAGA: That smug look on your face is tiresome, Lord Shigetada. You've been far too lenient. Hachirō, dispose of these meddling women!

(*HACHIRŌ marches up to AKOYA and holds her down while he tries to grab HITOMARU. They struggle briefly until KAGEKIYO grabs HACHIRŌ and tosses him to the ground. He then rips off his arm and begins to gnaw hungrily on it.*)

HACHIRŌ: My arm, my arm—I needed that! No matter how handsome I am, with only one arm I'll be without a leg to stand on at the Ōiso pleasure quarter. But to have my arm ripped off by the legendary Kagekiyo, I really have to hand it to you!

KAJIWARA: Wait, Kagekiyo. You say you won't touch a grain of Genji rice...

KOTARŌ: But you're happy to eat...

MAGOHACHI: The flesh of a Genji soldier?

IWANAGA: So you've decided to join us after all!

KAGEKIYO: He's no Genji soldier. He was born in my ancestral lands of Kazusa, in the village of Hase. I fed his father and gave him a position. He's no better than a shape-shifting cat, but since he was born and bred on my lands, his flesh is by rights mine. I'll accept no burden of obligation from you Genji for it. With no meat to fill my belly, I had to endure your insults, but now I feel my strength returning. (*Stands and strikes a fearsome pose.*)

(*KAGEKIYO stands up and glares at them.*)

KAGEKIYO: First I'll pay a visit to my mortal foe, the shogun Yoritomo. (*The music changes to a lively drum and flute pattern as KAGEKIYO rips the robe and hat from their branch.*) Learning a lesson from Yu Rang of Jin, I'll pretend that this hat and robe are Yoritomo. (*He takes the Azamaru sword, strikes a pose, and then slashes at the robe.*)

KOTARŌ: Kagekiyo, the circle on the ground...

MAGOHACHI: Before our very eyes you have violated it.

KAGEKIYO: Since I have slashed the robes of the shogun, the benevolence of Lords Shigetada and Nitan is thus ended. And since I've broken out of their prison, I might as well do the same to this cell. Then I'll rescue Hōdōmaru. You overdecorated sword racks, sit there and observe.

IWANAGA: Soldiers, seize him!

(*They approach KAGEKIYO but are tossed to left and right like chaff.*)

KAGEKIYO: That feels better. A million stars in the heavens can never eclipse the light of a single moon. Just try me!

TOKIWAZU CHANT: 🎵 As he speaks these lines... /

(*Rapid flute accompaniment as the soldiers attack, but KAGEKIYO easily throws them aside. He strikes a dramatic pose with his right hand on the cage.*)

TOKIWAZU CHANT: 🎵 His right hand on the lattice / he exerts all his strength / and the cage begins to sway / as he brushes aside his attackers.

(*Bodies go flying as he shakes the cage until it falls apart. KAGEKIYO plucks out HŌDŌMARU from within the wreckage and hands him to AKOYA. He lifts one of the cage's huge beams and uses it to sweep aside his attackers, finally striking a pose with it.*)

TOKIWAZU CHANT: 🎵 He poses with legs spread, / so glorious yet so terrifying.

(*KAGEKIYO scatters his attackers with the beam, and they run offstage. He poses center stage with SHIGETADA, IWANAGA, NITAN, and KAJIWARA to his right and left.*)

SHIGETADA: Kagekiyo, it would be a simple matter to cut you down now. But in his benevolence Lord Yoritomo has ordered me to let you escape. I entrust the life of Hōdōmaru into your hands.

NITAN: Accept that as our parting gift. Now take your wife and child and flee.

IWANAGA: It would be to my lord's honor were I to arrest him.

KAJIWARA: We have caught him once. It's a shame to let him go.

KAGEKIYO: You fool. I only let myself be captured with the hope of meeting your leader face-to-face. Instead, the great generosity of the shogun and the kindness of Shigetada have interfered with my plans. We may part for the moment, but I will see you again, and then I shall take your lord's head with ease, and those of Shigetada and Tadatsune too. I shall guard Hōdōmaru with my life, and one day the red flag of the Heike shall rise again, and the land shall be ours.

SHIGETADA: Your spirit is admirable. I hope we meet again on the battlefield, but then it shall be I who takes your head.

NITAN: We shall meet again on the hills of Kamakura.

KAGEKIYO: Till that day, Shigetada and Tadatsune.

BOTH: Till that day, Kagekiyo.

KAGEKIYO: You cockroaches!

ALL: Farewell.

TOKIWAZU CHANT: 🎵 The farewells ring out / for Kagekiyo, / a warrior without peer; / his glory shall echo / to future generations.

(*AKOYA and HITOMARU lead HŌDŌMARU away at stage right. KAGE-KIYO swaggers toward the hanamichi, where he glares once more at the soldiers, who fall over in fright. IWANAGA and KAJIWARA reach for their swords but are restrained by SHIGETADA and NITAN. The actors strike a tense group pose. The drums play a martial pattern as the curtain is drawn shut, leaving KAGE-KIYO outside on the hanamichi. The rhythm builds in intensity as KAGEKIYO bounds down the hanamichi in a vigorous and defiant roppō.*)

TRANSLATED BY ALAN CUMMINGS

PART V

Landscapes and Seasons

Saikaku's Hundred Linked Verses, Annotated by Himself

IHARA SAIKAKU

The poetic career of Ihara Saikaku has been overshadowed both by the fame of his later works of fiction and by the dominance of the *haikai* style practiced by the revered master Bashō. Though also a restless traveler, Saikaku was quintessentially the poet of his native Osaka. The urban panorama glimpsed in his late seventeenth-century *haikai* has much in common with his stories of the floating world. Even sex and money, then as now obsessive themes in best-selling fiction, have their place in his kaleidoscopic linked verse.

Saikaku's *haikai* sometimes extended to immensely long, improvised oral performances, but even the most extravagant sequences reflect conventions of medieval linked verse. The seventeen-syllable hokku—ancestor of the haiku—is followed by a fourteen-syllable related verse, then by another of seventeen syllables, and so on, in an alternating pattern predicated on constant change. Seasons, topics, moods, and hints of narrative shift with a dreamlike freedom from time, space, and logic, but always by association with the immediately preceding verse.

In 1692, during a burst of creative energy near the end of his life, Saikaku paid an autumn visit to a distant pupil and composed a chain of one hundred verses, to which he later added a commentary in the exuberant style of his prose fiction. These were recorded in his own striking calligraphy along with colorful ukiyo-e illustrations perhaps also by Saikaku, if not in his usual rakish style, in a sixty-foot-long scroll. By then his comic vision had darkened, but startling juxtapositions and flashes of compassionate humor remain the hallmarks of his poetry.

The opening verse of *Saikaku's Hundred Linked Verses, Annotated by Himself* (*Saikaku Dokugin Hyakuin Jichū Emaki,* completed in 1692) evokes both a spacious Japanese mountain scene and the supposedly Chinese origin of the autumn Chrysanthemum Festival: these are joined by a classical verb that can also be taken as marking a businesslike calculation. The distant exile of the legend as well as the longevity promised by the festival are sixfold greater if measured by the Japanese rather than the Chinese term for *li,* often translated as "league." Chrysanthemum wine, prepared by dropping petals into *sake,* is the elixir of life!

Since Japanese hand scrolls run from right to left, the scenes are reversed in order to facilitate an English reading from left to right. To accommodate the change, the poems and Saikaku's commentaries are placed appropriately for reading and not exactly where they appear within the original images. The translator's comments are added at the bottom of the pages.

Illustrations reproduced by permission from Tenri Central Library

Saikaku's Hundred Linked Verses, Annotated by Himself

1   *The long roads of Japan—*   Saikaku begins with auspicious imagery
       if you calculate the mountain path,   appropriate for an autumn visit to a pupil beyond
       chrysanthemums for a thousand ages   the lofty Yoshino mountains.

Our new *haikai* isn't just linked by fancy words in the old style but flows from verse to verse, with a special twist by the third one. As for the *hokku*, I compare our well-known Chinese legend of the youth who became immortal by drinking chrysanthemum dew, after being sent into exile down a long mountain path, with the six times greater distance as measured by the leagues of our ancient realm. The mountain streams along our roads yield an elixir to drink at the Chrysanthemum Festival, when we sing "A Thousand Autumns!"

2 *Even parrots are at home under our moon and begin to mimic us*

The classic Japanese autumn moon shines down on an exotic (and expensive) bird.

An old-fashioned verse would have linked our own woven Chinese brocade to the colorful autumn foliage along that mountain path, but I dislike such close linking. So I imported a foreign bird instead of a Chinese legend, a parrot that's been taught to squawk in our tongue instead of Chinese gibberish. Nothing too startling—just a link in the modern taste.

3 *Actors under their sedge hats—*
stared at endlessly
in the autumn evening

The third verse shifts to show business: actors on their way home from the theater. So now the parrot is in a show booth—for once the billboard doesn't lie! "Don't miss it. Seats going fast!" But people are wary if you tell them a red demon was caught alive in Tamba, or beat the drum about a thunder god that fell to earth on Mt. Shigaraki in Ōmi. These days people soon hear about it if a "novelty" is only a fake. Yet the familiar peacocks and performing badgers— like the old tried and true links of plum blossoms and cuckoos, pines and snow—never seem to lose their appeal.

And as for the flowers of the Osaka theater district—not one of the young actors of the four theaters could fail to charm. Some of them stir up deep pools of love. That fellow crossing the bridge wears a crest of oak leaves and triple commas—there he is! Suzuki Heishichi, renowned for his art, turned out in all his finery. Who could compare with him? Wanton city women set their passions loose, and their spirits leap up his sleeves. Poor priests from temples and monasteries hide their faces with their black robes and forget who they are—"If only I had the Buddha's money!"—and long to share the same pillow with him in a brothel till dawn on each of the Ten Holy Nights! Again, prim-looking pedants with the Ancient Writings engraved in their hearts are smitten; even priests of the Great Shrine at Ise want to present the

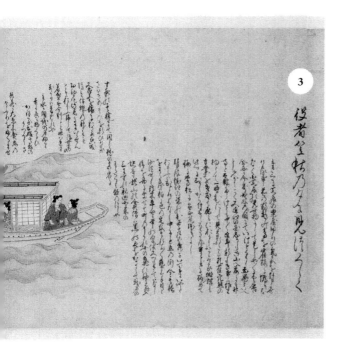

first rice of the season to this handsome youth. How much the more natural for worldly men still in their prime! All dreams!

Then there are the actors who play female roles: Mondo

The sudden turn to a peopled scene inspires Saikaku to a flight of floating-world prose. In the illustration the wide crimson banner of an Osaka theater is balanced by a splash of the crimson under-kimono of an actor leaving across a bridge and by the kimono of several rapt women staring at him from a canal boat.

miming a courtesan . . . Kichisaburō playing a madwoman . . . the beauty of Kaoru's Princess . . . Hyōzō's Ōhara woodseller feeding the fires of love . . . Tatsunosuke's dancing . . . Handayō's pretended weeping . . . Katsuya's flirtatious manner. . . Samanosuke's sad scenes drenching the audience's eyes in tears day after day . . . and especially the actor-managers: Jimbei as Wankyō, Kōzaemon as Head Retainer, Hanshirō's meaningful poses as a samurai, Arashi San'emon's expansive stride as a slippery lad singing "I'll shield you even from rough winds," and taking the girl's hand to begin their love scene . . . The drum beats for the play to begin, but birds remain undisturbed in this peaceful realm.

4	*Folding up their clothes*	Now the wide hats are worn by rustic pilgrims (instead of actors)
	as they wait for the boat	returning from their devotions and their strenuous sightseeing.

Here a group of country folks (in broad-brimmed sedge hats to shade—not hide—their faces) are on their own way home, after a pilgrimage to the Ise Shrines. They have gone around to see the sights in Kyoto, including a pious visit to the Buddha at Honganji, stopped off at Osaka for a quick bow at Sumiyoshi and Tennōji—and then spent day after day entranced by all the plays. Now they cheerfully await a fair wind for the boat back to their province. The link is to a scene at the harborside shop where they finish their packing.

5	*A shell clinging*	The place and mood change from a bustling waterfront to a
	to a bit of driftwood—	lonely beach.
	the travelers ask its name	

As they wait on and on for fine weather they stroll out at evening along the shore, asking their guide about the unfamiliar songs of the region, or perhaps the name of a strange worn shell they find clinging to a piece of seaweed-tangled driftwood floating in an inlet. This is how the verse is linked. In recent years matching contests using shells inscribed with old Japanese and Chinese poems have become popular. Many kinds of shells have been given names, besides those used in the thirty-six and hundred link contests.

6 *The smoke of a secret tradition* | The unknown becomes the secret, perhaps by a deliberate
hangs over a sovereign remedy | mystification.

A strange fellow in a long cloak calls himself "the new Doctor Chikusai," and goes around
spinning out a long spiel to sell charred oyster shells, monkey's-cheek shells, and the like as all
sorts of secret remedies. Yet charred newts do make an aphrodisiac said to have been handed
down by Narihira, and the fact that the lids of the horn shells found off Kamakura can be used
in incense is recorded in Kenkō's Grasses of Idleness.

7 *Instructions* | Smoke leads from medical to military secrets.
for a crucial battle—
leaving nothing to chance

How to make waterproof torches in the Kusunoki house tradition, or the kinds of fires for
smoke signaling, or gunpowder for muskets, to say nothing of the scents used for subtle communication—these are also handed down in secret writings.

8　*To teach a child—*
　　an open window on a snowy night

Military rigor becomes a fine old educational discipline. This completes the eight-verse first section, after which the poet is traditionally free to introduce more disturbing imagery.

A proverb advises sending your beloved child out on a journey. If a person is not toughened up from an early age, it is hard for him to meet emergencies. So this is another kind of instruction: a strict father has his son break through ice to use the washbasin, and wear thin clothing on a frigid winter night.

9   *"Listen to that voice!*
      A goblin's asking
      'Who broke off the plum branch?'"

Here, however, the discipline has a warm comic tone, and spring arrives after a snowy winter.

White plum blossoms in snow (a classic *haikai* link for early spring) are the flowers most valued by connoisseurs of the tea ceremony. Since such a sight is extremely rare, the mistress of the house was distressed to find that a plum branch had been broken off and thrown away by her thoughtless child. Another need for discipline! The mother hit on the idea of having her maid dress up in a frightening costume and ask the question in a strange, scary voice. All on the spur of the moment, the maid's costume was assembled from anything that happened to be lying about: a kimono dyed in a water-wheel pattern, a wooden spoon and pestle for the ghost's two horns, loud clattering lacquered clogs, and a bright red apron. A harmless goblin indeed!

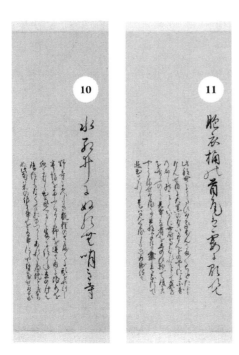

10 *The pond crimson and warm* | A Buddhist theme appears, along with a genuinely
  by the deserted temple | malevolent specter.

A wily old fox or badger haunting the small temple out in the fields transformed himself into various shapes to taunt the abbot. He made the willow fronds hang upside down (like hair standing on end!) and turned the water of the pond to blood. This was too much even for one who had given up the world, so the monk finally moved away. Since then no one has lived in the temple, and the whole area has become deserted. This verse is linked to the previous one (also in the warmth of spring) by shifting the image from a mock-ghost to a real (and really alarming!) one.

11 *The hidden placenta tub* | Even more alarming to an indiscreet monk is the evidence of his
  emerging as the snow melts | sexual misconduct.
  through the spring haze |

Here is another reason for leaving. As the lately popular ditty goes: "Monk, dear monk! / Restrain yourself a little! / Don't you even have / A woman in your temple?" Take the case of a certain worldly monastery where the abbot not only had a taste for fish and fowl but even secretly kept a beautiful woman, who soon bore him a child. When the parishioners heard about it, the monk was expelled, with only the usual umbrella to his name. A most disgraceful incident!

12 *A lady, dreaming of her distant home,*   Saikaku uses ironic classical imagery for a scandal
     head pillowed on her arm   involving the ruling class.

Day and night the daimyo's lady in Edo dwells on affairs back home. As in the verse before, suspicious thoughts arise. Wherever you go, you will find women indulging in foolish jealousies. In this case, however, the lady's husband had in fact plucked a flower from the pleasure quarter of the Capital and taken her back to his domain, where she soon became pregnant. Hardly surprising that his wife should have jealous dreams! If you seek the cause of marital quarrels among the common people, you will find they all start the same—but after she throws a saké kettle at him they have a drink together and make up. . . .

TRANSLATED BY HOWARD HIBBETT

Starving Poets, Courtesans, and Sandal Makers

THREE SEQUENCES FROM BASHŌ AND HIS DISCIPLES

In the late sixteenth century, a revolution in classical Japanese poetic language occurred with the introduction of colloquial speech and expressions deriving from Chinese, alongside a new trend depicting the lives of commoners and peasants. The Teimon and Danrin Schools responded to the demands of the new age, the superficiality of the former and the vulgarity of the latter becoming the fashion. The refined traditional *renga* was challenged by such new practices of *haikai*. In response, Matsuo Bashō called for a renewed seriousness toward poetry. Bashō, a low-ranking samurai from Iga Province, studied with a Teimon School poet while serving his young master. With the latter's untimely death, he left for Kyoto, leading the life of a young man about town, consorting with kabuki actors, and visiting pleasure quarters. In 1672, like many artists and tradesmen, he moved to Edo, where he encountered the Danrin School. However, he could not remain satisfied with poetry concerned mainly with comic and novel effects. He turned to travel as a way of life, producing some five travel journals written between 1684 and 1689 in the style known as *haibun,* or *haikai*-based prose. *The Narrow Road to the Deep North* (*Oku no Hosomichi,* 1689) is the best-known among these. Long before his death in 1694, Bashō's style (Shōfū *haikai*) would displace Danrin as the main current in the Edo poetic milieu.

It was Bashō's discontent with the *haikai* of his time that motivated him to revisit medieval principles of existential loneliness (*sabi*) and material privation (*wabi*). Inspired by these ideals, Bashō identified himself with the wandering monk Saigyō and the *renga* master Sōgi and learned as well from Sōgi's teacher, the monk Shinkei. He aimed at poetry that transmitted, at one and the same time, the paradoxical dual nature of experience: the fleeting, transient quality of the moment but also that moment's vitality and timelessness, when seen through the lens of Zen meditation. Bashō's style also reinstated the classical Japanese attentiveness to the seasons as a vehicle for expressing the temporality of daily life. Moreover, his seasons are made newly palpable through concrete tactile and olfactory sensations. Bashō's efforts reshaped *haikai* into a serious art form. In particular, his way of endowing the low and common with numinosity has seldom been seen in older poetry.

As illustrated in the three *kasen* (thirty-six-verse sequences) presented here, *haikai* resembles a conversation among friends and acquaintances governed, as with any social practice, by implicit rules. Rules of duration dictate the occurrence of the common topics (the seasons, Love, Travel, Buddhism) in the links: Spring and Autumn verses can continue for at least three but not more than five contiguous verses, Summer and Winter for at least one and not more than three, and Love only two. Highly marked images of the moon and flowers should appear at certain places in the thirty-six-verse duration. The *kasen* manuscript consists of two sheets of art paper of a specific size, each folded along the middle to make a front and a back page, thus making four pages in all. The verses are recorded by hand: the first six on page one, the next twelve on page two, another twelve on page three, and the last six on page four. The moon is expected to occur three times in the whole sequence: once each on pages one, two, and three. Flowers should appear only twice: once every eighteen verses. The rules prevent monotony, inspire expectation, and provide guidelines for the progression of the sequence as a whole.

Each participant connects his verse to the preceding one by maintaining or changing the theme, by developing a story, or by providing a response to a certain word according to poetic convention. The essence of *haikai* lies not in a perfectly constructed, predetermined entity but rather in the excitement arising from the very unpredictability of the session's progression. The form generates a variety of interpretive possibilities along the way, despite the general rules mentioned above, which exist only to facilitate the session and enable a minimal coherence in the progression of the whole. As in a game, the rules enable the external structure of the progression, but it is the players and their specific moves that constitute the experience and excitement of the event.

In the following, ripostes in response to base verses are indented. Comments between verses by the translator discuss the link between the preceding and following ones.

 (ER-C)

THE PEDDLER OF POEMS

MATSUO BASHŌ AND ENOMOTO KIKAKU

A 1683 duet sequence between the thirty-nine-year-old Matsuo Bashō and his disciple Enomoto Kikaku, then a rakish young man of twenty-two, "The Peddler of Poems" (Shiakindo) is one of nine sequences in the anthology *Empty Chestnuts* (*Minashiguri*, 1683). Kikaku's preface and Bashō's epilogue constitute in effect a manifesto declaring their aspiration to create a "new" poetics of ineffable depth and stillness (*yūgen kanjaku*). Critical of both the Teitoku and the Danrin Schools of composition, he returned to the Japanese sublime of the medieval poetry of *The New Collection of Poems Old and New,* as well as in *renga* of the Muromachi period. Bashō also acknowledges the spirits of Tang-dynasty Chinese poets Li Bai, Du Fu, and Hanshan, while delving into the ideal merging of austerity (*wabi*) and poeticity (*fūga*) in Saigyō, the medieval wandering poet.

"The Peddler of Poems," however, is not free of Danrin-style levity and occasional vulgarity; moreover, the connections between verses are often loose, indicating the difficulty, at this stage, of achieving the sublime while dealing with quotidian subjects. Ultimately, what Bashō desired to achieve was no less than the overcoming of vulgarity or meanness as such, or the purification of the vulgar without comparing it negatively with the noble and refined. This is a very difficult task. Can one divorce the sublime from its aristocratic history? It is often said that Bashō embarked on his life of travel in the last ten years of his life as a means of spiritual growth, in order to realize by physical deprivation and hardship, and by the discipline of meditation, the essence of what poetry is. Perhaps, indeed, that is what was required to bring his art to its highest realization.

The sequence begins with Kikaku composing the long verse of 5-7-5 syllables, and Bashō the short response-verse of 7-7 syllables. The poets take turns throughout, allowing each to display his versatility in both following and leading. Like all other *haikai* sequences, this one shifts from one social milieu to another, or one region to another, in the course of the participants' conversation, covering an incredible range of topics and moods as various characters make their way across the space of just thirty-six verses and the two poets, with a wit occasionally sardonic, regale us with the passing show of Edo life.

(ER-C)

1

The peddler of poems
waxes maudlin over the ending year,
while his drinking debts mount.
    —Kikaku

2

    Dusk gathers along the winter lake
    as the carp catch is loaded on the horses.
        —Bashō

There is something subliminally lonely about the comparison of a poet's livelihood to that of equally poor fishermen, although their fish, by contrast, are at least edible. The end of the year becomes the end of the day, and the Winter season becomes verbally specified. As for the expression "peddler of poems," it is significant that Bashō would later express a deep distaste for the economic exigencies of a professional poet's position.

> 3
> Gone soft, apt to yield
> even to the dull-speared Ebisu
> the border gates.
> —Bashō

In this link, the fishermen are taken over by samurai relaxing their vigilance by fishing at the lake. Ebisu were the minority who had been driven to the far north. "Dull-speared," a put-down, applies by implication to the samurai themselves in apparently peaceful times.

> 4
> It's the shamisen music, causes
> a man's demon to turn weepy.
> —Kikaku

> 5
> The moon touches his sleeves
> and on his knees a cicada lies
> peacefully asleep.
> —Kikaku

> 6
> It is already deep in the night,
> the snipe's wings are securely tied.
> —Bashō

Autumn, represented by the images of the snipe in verse 6 and miscanthus in 7, is here introduced by the image of the moon in 5. The Love theme suggested in link 5/6 will be verbalized in 10. Here the image of a cicada asleep on a man's knees while he listens to the shamisen music in 4 suggests a raptly intimate scene, as does the following reference to the snipe's wings being "securely tied" as the night deepens.

7
Laughing, is it,
at the priest who knows no shame—
the miscanthus grass.
    —Bashō

The snipe in link 6 has been caught by the "priest who knows no shame."
Catching a snipe to eat violated the prohibition against meat.

    8
    To Yamazaki in the winter rain
    he dances off under an umbrella.
        —Kikaku

By verse 8, Love becomes an unmistakable theme as the same priest figure
turns into one dancing off to a brothel in Yamazaki. This verse evokes the
"Narihira Dance-Song" popular in the age when kabuki was performed by
young male actors admired for their looks and available as companions. The
song describes the perilous pleasures of a visit there.

9
He's dyed it especially
in indigo, the workman's robe
in a bamboo-grass pattern.
    —Bashō

    10
    Gazing in yearning at the young master
    from a concealed spot in the hunting field.
        —Kikaku

11
The eldest daughter,
she was sent to be brought up
by a steward in the country.
    —Bashō

The priest in link 7/8 turns into a stylish workman in link 8/9 but is bound
for the same quarters. Love and social class are in conflict in link 9/10, where
a manservant yearning after his young samurai master in secret is superim-
posed on the workman, and that conflict remains in 10/11, where it is a con-

cubine's unwanted daughter, sent to be brought up in the country, who longs for the young lord.

12

They even pressed her to compose
on the topic "notorious for snoring"!
—Kikaku

13

So now the cuckoo
keeps crying out in her stead:
"I am her wrathful spirit!"
——Bashō

In the country, the frustrated daughter is made to compose poetry on laughable topics—no doubt another self-referential allusion to the comic levity of some provincial poetic milieus. The poor girl leads such a humiliating existence that she sickens and dies, full of unappeased resentment.

14

That apparent Cold Meal Day thinness
is just the fashion in the floating world.
—Kikaku

15

His shoes on the flowers
are shockingly poor, and his hat is
the lid from a grain barrel.
——Bashō

16

Tap it and see if it will fly,
Master Bashō's butterfly!
—Kikaku

The young woman passes from the foreground, which now features a dandy affecting a fashionable thinness, presumably from the pangs of love. The dandy, in turn, is identified as a starving poet, perhaps the very same that opened the sequence. Bashō projects a positive attachment to the Daoist image of the poet as a poverty-stricken, ridiculously unworldly creature flitting among the flowers, to which Kikaku responds by directly mentioning

"Master Bashō's butterfly" by name. This is a near-unprecedented move in these typically impersonal sequences, and a confirmation of the allusion to the Daoist philosopher Zhuangzi and his dream of being a butterfly.

> 17
> On such rotten
> old verses, not even dogs
> would feed!
> —Bashō

The startling vehemence of Bashō's self-deprecating reply seems to manifest his thorough impatience with his lack of progress in demonstrating a new path through the poems themselves. This pair of verses recalls the one at the opening of "The Peddler of Poems" and foretells the final link in this collection.

> 18
> Eyes staring, unblinking,
> sleepless the night, the moon.
> —Kikaku

> 19
> As the wedding day
> approaches, already the first sound
> of the fulling block.
> —Kikaku

The tortured, sleepless poet in 18 is reinterpreted as an anxious bride already anticipating the sorrows of love. Here, however, the bride turns into a wife whose bitter yearning for her husband, gone away to war, is appeased by news of war's end.

> 20
> The battle is over, no arrow-
> root of bitterness remains.
> —Bashō

> 21
> Derisive, the world grumbles:
> he might as well cast her in gold,
> the beauty Komurasaki.
> —Kikaku

Amazingly, in 20/21, that "battle" turns on how much a famous courtesan has cost a client, apparently too much, in the public's eyes.

> 22
> Yes, and dark as the black sea bream,
> are the nipples of a base woman.
> —Bashō

The line "cast in gold" refers to the Chinese story of Xishi, whose beauty caused the destruction of an enemy kingdom and was thought to deserve the honor of a gold sculpture in her likeness. Komurasaki, a famous courtesan who actually existed, is clearly a parody of the virtuous Xishi, and the reference to gold is not to a statue but to the price a man had to pay to buy Komurasaki's services or perhaps her contract with the proprietor. The world thinks Komurasaki's price too steep, but Bashō, in his ironic reply (22), resists the derision and reminds the other, in startlingly graphic terms, that a cheap prostitute is no beauty, but she is certainly more affordable. This link, 21/22, is a very revealing exchange on the commodification of the female body, part of the explosion of ways and means of enjoying the senses in the Edo pleasure quarters with the evolution of a money economy.

> 23
> That bleached seaweed hair
> would coil around and break
> a fist-hard top shell's horn.
> —Kikaku

Connected to the female anatomy in the preceding verse, this one suggestively describes a winding shell with hairlike seaweed around it, recalling the representation of sexual organs in *shunga,* or erotic pictures.

> 24
> Commanding the demons of calamity
> from the promontory of the rough sea.
> —Bashō

The half-naked woman of the preceding link turns into a figure of miraculous powers, such as those mountain ascetics whose arduous religious practices enable them to achieve power over unseen forces of demons.

25
Let appear in the world
a fierce archer warrior
wielding a bow of steel!
　　　　　—Kikaku

26
At morning recalling the tiger that
entered her breast to lodge in her womb.
　　　　　—Bashō

In response, Kikaku prays for a righteous warrior to destroy the evil forces
unleashed by the demons, while Bashō imagines the miraculous birth of such
a fierce, tigerlike savior of the world in his mother's prophetic dream.

27
In the cold mountain
the typhoon blows over the beds
of the four sleepyheads.
　　　　　—Kikaku

28
The glowing embers have died out,
fingers become a burning lamp.
　　　　　—Bashō

The poets' interest shifts to the superhuman, heroic, and strange. The tiger in
the dream turns docile as one of the "four sleepyheads" in Kikaku. The allusion is to Chinese paintings depicting the three Tang-dynasty Zen monks
Fenggan, Hanshan, and Shide, along with the tiger they tamed, sleeping together in the midst of a winter storm. Bashō in 28 references the monks'
mental prowess in the image of a self-immolation practice where lamp oil is
poured into the palm of the hand, and a wick attached to the fingers and set
aflame.

29
The lowborn empress,
hating the mornings,
shuts out the moon.
　　　　　—Kikaku

30
Ridiculous to conceal in brocade
the common watermelon she craves.
                    —Kikaku

A "lowborn empress" may refer either to an empress or a courtesan. Her taste for watermelon, a vulgar fruit, is contrasted with the high-style material in which it is hidden. As here, the subversive aspect of a *haikai* link often involved the ironic or comic juxtaposition of court and entertainment quarter, the high and the low, the sacred and the secular, and so on, in a way that encourages a reading that confuses, inverts, and conflates the two contrasting realms, including class distinctions.

31
Alas, over Miyagino fields,
how the *bota*, being blown about,
must be withering.

                    —Bashō

Bashō picks up on the incongruous association of two incompatible entities in juxtaposing Miyagino with a very rustic-sounding plant, *bota*. Miyagino is a famous *utamakura* (a conventionally famous place in *waka* poetry) that is inevitably linked with the bush clover, both of which represented the young prince in *The Tale of Genji*. The elegance of Miyagino is thus violated by *bota*, vulgar just by its sound, and securely linked to the internal contradiction signaled by Kikaku's *maeku* about fake refinement.

32
The Ezo tribes of the far north can
know nothing of the stone mortar.
                    —Kikaku

Kikaku alludes to shogun Minamoto no Yoritomo's poem in *The New Collection of Poems Old and New:* "In the far north what does not speak and is kept secret one cannot know: yet it is all written out on the stone inscription of Tsubo Village." Kikaku deflates the heroic character of the ancient stone inscription by changing the inscription to a "stone mortar," a rather mundane object. The Ezo tribes cannot know of agriculture, being still a hunter-gatherer people.

33
To warriors fast asleep,
still clad in their armor, they
lend pillows.
                    —Bashō

Bashō connects to the military campaign aspect of the ancient stone inscription and chooses to see the Ezo as offering hospitality to the soldiers, signaling a return to a softer lyric mode as the sequence nears its end.

34
The horses' repeated neighing
announces the snowy dawn.
                    —Kikaku

35
The peddler of poems
waxes maudlin over the flowers,
while his drinking debts mount.
            —Kikaku

Kikaku's verse here returns to the exact wording of the opening link, merely changing "ending year" in verse 1 to "flowers."

36
Dusk gathers on the spring lake as
the wings of poetry, energized, take off.
                    —Bashō

Bashō follows suit, changing "winter lake" to "spring lake" and a mundane transportation, horses, to the ecstatic transport, so to speak, effected by poetry. The sequence thus ends on a positive note, with a pair of verses that quotes, with only slight variations, the first two in the series. The season has moved on to spring, the object of the poet's sorrow is now the falling flowers, and the horses being loaded with the carp catch have become poetry newly inspirited or energized, about to take off.

BENEATH THE TREES

MATSUO BASHŌ, HAMADA CHINSEKI, AND SUGANUMA KYOKUSUI

Some seven years separate "The Peddler of Poems" from "Beneath the Trees" (Ko no Moto ni, 1690), a sequence that is significantly mellower in tone and less given to obscure allusions and sarcastic wit. The notable absence of any allusion to the pleasure quarters excludes the risqué imagery of the earlier work. Hamada Chinseki (d. 1737?), one of Bashō's disciples living on the shores of Lake Biwa, compiled Bashō School anthologies such as *The Gourd* (*Hisago*, 1690), *Fukagawa River Anthology* (*Fukagawashū*, 1692), and *The White Horse* (*Shirauma*, 1699). Kyokusui (1647?–1717) of the Suganuma clan was a local samurai whose poetry was also anthologized in *The Gourd*.

In this session, the seasonal occurrences are fairly regular and are almost wholly confined to Spring and Autumn, with Summer making only two brief appearances, while Winter does not appear at all. The themes of Love and Buddhism are found in several links. Variety is introduced by references to motifs originating from different types of social worlds. Most links are set outdoors, ranging from a picnic to a storm scene. A few references are made to the interior of types of dwelling.

The mellowness characterizing "Beneath the Trees" surfaces through the predictability of the links as well as the freedom from any overwrought efforts to link. A connection is effected, not through the usual contextual or linguistic associations, but through something more subliminal and indefinable, called echo or resonance (*hibiki*) and fragrance (*nioi*). Bashō in verse 4 connects to Kyokusui's traveler by referring to the awkwardness of wearing a sword, a common example of an experiential yoking. Chinseki, on the other hand, places the samurai in a makeshift spatial context that seems to explain his awkwardness with a sword, not in any logical way, but through a kind of metaphorical parallelism. Later, Bashō apparently draws a parallel between the young horse's vitality and speed and the agility of the woodcutter's movements in deftly turning out a threshing mortar. Sometimes the link arises from the sudden discovery of a conceptual similarity between two situations otherwise unrelated, such as different names for the same rain being linked to different shapes and sizes of bodies. Whether the link is plot-like or ineffable, rational or emotional, conventional or innovative, it is not possible to appreciate *haikai* without reading the blank spaces between the verses, for it is not in the verses themselves where the poetry lies but in the charged space that separates and yet invisibly links them.

❦ (ER-C) ❦

1
Beneath the trees,
on seaweed broth, on slices of fish,
everywhere is cherry petals.
                —Bashō

        2
        Serenely shines the western sun,
        we have such blessed fine weather.
                        —Chinseki

    3
    A traveler saunters by
    absently scratching lice—
    springtime is passing.
            —Kyokusui

These three opening verses influence the generally serene and reflective mood governing the whole sequence. Bashō's now famous *hokku* delightfully juxtaposes the people's humble picnic fare with the ethereal beauty of the pink cherry petals alighting everywhere. Chinseki, with his closely assenting joyful response, was especially praised by Bashō for his "lightness" (*karumi*), an aesthetic ideal very much in Bashō's mind at this time. As expected, verse 3 moves away from the first two by introducing the new figure of a traveler even while pushing the Spring season to its close.

        4
        He's had no practice wearing that sword
        in its sheath of wrinkled leather.
                        —Bashō

This verse, nonseasonal, acts as a bridge into the next three verses on Autumn. Bashō links to the absentmindedness of the sauntering figure in 3 by observing the awkwardness in the way he carries his sword, turning the mood of relaxation into a criticism.

    5
    At the makeshift court,
    the roll call of new appointments
    had to await the full moon.
            —Chinseki

6
Ordered to turn out a threshing mortar,
the swift dexterity of the woodcutters' art.
—Kyokusui

7
Autumn comes,
the three-year colt is fitted
with its first saddle.
—Bashō

"Makeshift court," which parallels the samurai's awkwardness, evokes the frequent dislocation of the ruling government during periods of civil war, most famously the one between the Heike and Genji clans, when the court had to move to Suma, along the sea. "Moon," "threshing mortar," and "three-year colt" evoke the rice harvest season.

8
It has different ways of falling
so the rain is called by various names.
—Chinseki

This seems to be a "pass" verse, whose aim is simply to move the sequence out of the preceding passage of three Autumn verses and forward into a new realm.

9
A mixed crowd of bodies
in the steaming hot springs of Suwa
in hazy twilight.
—Kyokusui

Kyokusui is now able to take us to a completely new scene of bodies of mixed age and gender bathing in the mountain hot springs, while securely breathing life into the concept of difference. The conceptual similarity bridges the otherwise wide distance.

10
Emerging tall among them all
the figure of a wild mountain ascetic.
—Bashō

11
When others speak
he always argues them down,
in a one-sided way.
    —Chinseki

In a clearly visible move, Bashō picks out, from the bodies in the public bath
in hazy twilight, the tall figure of a mountain ascetic, now speaking fiercely to
assert his opinion, as befits a strong man who subjects himself to physical
mortification to train his endurance.

12
From the most trivial beginnings
love grows more and more inflamed.
    —Kyokusui

13
A body in the throes
of longing, repeatedly urged to
"eat something"!
    —Bashō

The intensifying tenor of the argument suddenly becomes the similar movement in the course of a passionate infatuation, and the theme here shifts to Love
and its symptoms. The subject has shifted from the monk to a lovesick woman.

14
Face uplifted to the moon,
sleeves heavy with dew.
    —Chinseki

15
In the boat buffeted by
the autumn wind, she is terrified
of the sound of the waves.
    —Kyokusui

16
Are those wild geese flying off
to Shiroko? Wakamatsu?
    —Bashō

Verses 14–16 return to Autumn by the appearance of the moon. The Love theme is still present in 14, but the woman's tears in 14 turn out to be coming from her fear in 15. Verse 16 suggests a woman from the capital longing for her home.

17
A thousand sutra readings
at the height of the flowers' splendor,
on Isshinden.
                    —Chinseki

                18
                Gossamers flit across the road where
                they perished on the pilgrimage circuit.
                                    —Kyokusui

19
But most moving of all is
what is the manifest reality
for the butterfly.
                    —Bashō

The season shifts to Spring through the agency of flowers and wild geese, known to leave Japan for the north in spring. The place-names "Shiroko" and "Wakamatsu" situate the link to Ise, while Senjuji Temple, originally opened by the priest Shinran, is suggested in the reference to a thousand sutras. At this Jōdo Shinshū temple, in the third month of spring annually, sutras are recited a thousand times by one hundred monks taking turns. In 18, death has untimely taken the lives of the pious undergoing the rigors of pilgrimage, set against the splendor of cherry trees in bloom. Verse 19 refers to Zhuangzi's famous question regarding reality and dream, resonating with the images of death and fleeting beauty in 17 and 18.

                20
                Lacking the strength even
                to take up the brush for a letter.
                                    —Chinseki

Here, the attention shifts to the fragile butterfly's inability to express itself, lacking a language. Implied as the "most moving question" is the similar inability in human beings to know ultimate reality, whether dreaming or awake.

21
A thinly veiled figure
shunning the sun, she feels the days
not worth living.
                    —Kyokusui

From here, the sequence returns to a storylike progression. It has been suggested that the sorrowful highborn figure in 21, too weak to write a letter in
20, is the widow of Taira no Koremori, eldest heir of the defeated Heike.

22
Her eyes filled with tears in her
great longing to worship at Kumano.
                    —Bashō

The widow does not discover until autumn that her husband committed
suicide during a pilgrimage to Kumano in the previous spring. Hence the
direct link between 21/22, where Bashō imagines the widow's longing to visit
the scene of her husband's end.

23
Hand gripping the bow,
the border guard at Kii Province
is so obstinate.
                    —Chinseki

24
Doubtless that bald pate
is from indulging in *sake*.
                    —Kyokusui

25
It's so late in the day,
he has to squint to make out
the *sugoroku* board.
                    —Bashō

Kii Province, being the location of the Kumano shrines and temples, harks
back to the link 22 and 23. The Heike, being hunted down, would have found
it difficult to travel freely across territorial borders. Kyokusui in 24 makes a

humorous dig at the unfriendly guard's bald pate and excessive indulgence in *sake,* while Bashō takes the man's ungainliness further by giving him a squint as he struggles to win at the board game *sugoroku,* unaware of the darkening day. From 23 down, the social milieu has moved to the lower classes.

> 26
> Reciting the Buddha invocation, facing
> his portable icon on a makeshift altar.
>   —Chinseki

> 27
> Well, surprise, surprise,
> when I sat on the earthen floor
> there was no sign of fleas.
>   —Kyokusui

> 28
> I am known as the village fool,
> butt of everyone's jokes.
>   —Bashō

> 29
> Despised, he yet
> scrambles to give unwanted help
> at the Obon dances.
>   —Chinseki

Unlike the previous link, in 26 the pious man observes evening prayers on his journey. The third-person voice turns to first person in 27/28, and the voice returns to third person in 29.

> 30
> One moonlit night after another
> till the moon crosses over into dawn.
>   —Kyokusui

The unspoken subject is the annual Obon festival dance held nightly under the moon.

31
The flowering miscanthus
beckoning once too often
wilts from the tip.
                —Bashō

This verse captures the aspect of time passing through the repetitive waving of miscanthus ears until they wither at season's end.

                32
                The dew in the grass hermitage
                barely nine-foot square.
                                —Chinseki

The passage from 30 to 32 evokes an autumnal landscape scroll, with a recluse's hermitage hidden in the corner, barely punctuating the scene, in 32.

33
Disliking complications
he returns the gift of money,
a thousand *monme*.
                —Kyokusui

                34
                As for the doctor's medicine,
                he is resolute in refusing it.
                                —Bashō

35
Yet when the flowers bloom,
there he is again wandering about
in the hills of Yoshino.
                —Kyokusui

                36
                Bitten by these pesky gadflies
                in the mountains of springtime.
                                —Chinseki

Verse 33 evokes the character of the recluse who lives in the hermitage of 32, valuing a free spirit above money and even above the mundane desire for longevity in 34. There is surely a self-referential aspect in this closing passage about reclusion and the devotion to nature, beauty, and poetry, even despite the "pesky gadflies," definitely a humorous, *haikai*-like element, bringing the sequence back to the droll image of pickled fish and broth among the cherry flowers in the opening passage.

THROUGHOUT THE TOWN

MATSUO BASHŌ, NOZAWA BONCHŌ, AND MUKAI KYORAI

The sequence "Through the Town" (Ichinaka wa) was composed in the late summer of 1690, a year after Bashō's return from his memorialized journey to the north. Bashō rested his travel-worn body in his hermitage in Ishiyama. He visited Kyoto in order to plan, with his leading disciples Nozawa Bonchō (d. 1714) and Mukai Kyorai (1651–1704), a new *haikai* anthology, *The Monkey's Straw Raincoat* (*Sarumino*). It was during this visit that master and disciples produced "Throughout the Town," finally a model of fully mature Bashō School linked poetry.

This sequence moves from the Summer season, when it was actually composed, to Spring and Autumn and back to Spring. It also includes other topics such as Lament, Love, and Travel. A contrast between nature scenes and human life corresponds to that of stillness against action. The spatial setting moves from town to country and includes temples, mansions, and cottages, while some story elements are introduced through characters such as a city tough guy, a courtly lover, a traveler, and a craftsman. The lower classes, whether represented by street performer, craftsman, or servant, acquire a certain dignity through the poet's attention to their humble lives, housing conditions, and other material objects. Rather than presuming the poor's aspiration for an upper-class life, the links take from medieval philosophical aesthetics of *wabi,* the spiritual value and dignity of an austere, materially deprived lifestyle.

The diction here is marked by an exact economy: every sound and every word achieves its purpose within the verse itself as an autonomous utterance, while also shaping the verse's relationship to the preceding verse, or *maeku*. Seen in this way, it must be said that the new sublime that Bashō was seeking in "The Peddler of Poems" required a renewed attention to time, the seasons, and their philosophical and religious weight. A subtle and symbolic link based on the qualities of "resonance" or "fragrance" of classical *waka* and medieval *renga* is favored over conventional storytelling or traditionally paired notions. The order of the poets' turns in this sequence remains the same from beginning to end. Bashō's place between Bonchō and Kyorai is ideal for mediating between the two disciples and directing the poetic traffic into new directions when necessary.

☞(ER-C)☜

1
Throughout the town
a redolence of things—
the summer moon.
　　　　—Bonchō

2
My, it's hot, my, it's hot,
voices cry at every door.
　　　　—Bashō

3
The second weeding's
barely done, and already
rice stalks are in ear.
　　　　—Kyorai

4
Thump, thump, the ashes fall—
a slat of dried sardine.
　　　　—Bonchō

The first three verses are linked through the Summer season, while variation is effected spatially. The town scene in verses 1 and 2 shifts to the countryside in 3, transferring the heat to ears of rice. In verse 4, the movement stops on the image of a dried sardine charbroiled for lunch for the farmers, who whack away the ashes from the fish. This kind of smooth progression, complicated here and there by the montage-like effect of contrastive juxtaposition from one verse to the next, is upheld throughout the sequence, showing how *haikai*, like music, shapes itself while in motion.

5
These parts have
never even heard of coins—
how inconvenient!
　　　　—Bashō

6
See him try to swagger
with that enormous sword!
　　　—Kyorai

7
By clump of grass,
he freezes as a frog leaps
in the evening dark.
　　　—Bonchō

The attention now shifts to specific inflections of speech and character. In verse 5, a city boy complains about his inability to buy what he needs while traveling in the countryside, while, in 6, a villager sardonically notes the townsman's apparent unfamiliarity with the sword he is wearing. The implicit censure turns even sharper with the revelation of the man's fear of a tiny frog in the dark.

8
On the way to pick butterbur shoots,
her shaking lantern goes out.
　　　—Bashō

9
When shriveled is
the flower, that's the time
piety's awakened.
　　　—Kyorai

The subject changes from a city boy to a young woman; it is she who is startled by a frog in the dark. The absence of explicit markers of gender in Japanese poetic language—this is determined implicitly, by comprehending the context—works perfectly for linked poetry that depends for its interest on constant change and variation. The woman in 8 then turns into a nun whose faith has been awakened by the shriveling of a flower, implying the transience of beauty.

10
Miserable to live through
the winters at Nanao in Noto.
　　　—Bonchō

11
Toothless gums
sucking fish bones—
I have aged.
                    —Bashō

12
Fumbling with the side-gate lock,
he let in the long-awaited lover.
                    —Kyorai

In 10, the nun transforms into the ascetic Kenbutsu, known for the priest Saigyō's visiting him in the cave along the rough Japan Sea coast of Noto where he meditated: Saigyō wept to imagine the harsh winter conditions Kenbutsu endured. Verse 11 further shifts to a depiction of a toothless old man, who, in 12, turns into a doddering guard at some castle, struggling to open the gate to a clandestine lover. The change also contrasts the first-person voice of lament in 10/11 with the return to the third-person narrative voice in 12.

13
Straining to look,
they knock down the screen—
servant girls.
                    —Bonchō

14
Bareness of the bamboo boards
on the bathhouse floor.
                    —Bashō

In 12, Kyorai makes an allusion to Genji's visit to the "red-nosed princess," who lives alone with aging servants and ladies-in-waiting in a decaying old mansion. In 13, Bonchō animates the comedic aspect of Genji's involvement with the princess but relocates the tryst to the contemporary lower-class pleasure quarters, where the maids are overtaken by a voyeuristic curiosity and inadvertently knock down the painting screen shielding the lovers. And then comes Bashō in 14, who throws cold water, so to speak, on all this sensual fantasy by contemplating the bareness of the wood floor in a rustic bathhouse. The link from 13 to 14 is subliminal but not tenuous; it is as if the knocking down of the protective barrier in 13 suddenly reveals the true unaccommo-dated condition of human existence; there is both *wabi* and *sabi* in this image. But we must pause and note also Bashō's subtle technique of drawing the pro-gression into this new realm, developed below.

15
Shaking down the seeds
on the fennel stalks—
the evening storm.
    —Kyorai

16
In the gathering cold, a monk
hurrying back to the temple?
    —Bonchō

17
Street artist with monkey
together passing through the world—
the autumn moon.
    —Bashō

18
Each year a meager sack of rice
carefully measured out in tax.
    —Kyorai

The *wabi-sabi* mode in 14 carries over into the three Autumn verses present-ing a parallel between the monk and the street artist, different in the way they are "passing through the world," but both exposed to the elements, valuing freedom, recognizing no permanent home, and enduring their own depriva-tion or abnegation, as the case may be. Verse 18 shifts to the life of a com-moner, which is no easier than the monk's or the artist's.

19
Five or six
raw-cut logs thrown across
the boggy ground.
    —Bonchō

20
White socks all splattered
trudging the black dirt road.
　　　　　—Bashō

21
Overtaken by
his master's swift charger,
the sword-bearer.
　　　　—Kyorai

22
All spilled the bucket of water
borne on the lad's shoulder.
　　　　　—Bonchō

The still-life scene in 19 suddenly springs into action in 20 through someone trudging the path. In link 20/21, the splattering of mud turns out to be from a samurai's horse as the samurai gallops past his sword-bearer, who is on foot. In turn, in 21/22, a passing lad spills, from the force of the same horse's passage, the bucket of water he is carrying along the road: a very engaging, and humorous, passage of dynamic motion.

23
Doors, screens gone,
boarded up in straw matting—
a mansion for sale.
　　　　—Bashō

24
When did the pepper pods
become tinged with color?
　　　　　—Kyorai

25
With a quiet rustling,
he plaits straw into sandals
in the rays of moonlight.
　　　　—Bonchō

26
To brush off the fleas, she woke
with a start: autumn has come.
                    —Bashō

27
The mousetrap
lies fallen on its side,
vacantly.
            —Kyorai

Wabi-sabi returns in 23 after the slightly slapstick succession of actions in 20–22, with the image of a deserted mansion. The image evokes a fall in fortune as well as the passing of time, which 24 foregrounds with the ripening of chili pepper pods in autumn. In verse 25, Bonchō highlights the important image of the moon as it shines over the humble maker of straw sandals working in the quiet of the night. In 26, Bashō breaks the stillness with a picture of the wife suddenly awakened by fleas and noticing the chill in the night air, announcing the coming of autumn. Then Kyorai in 27 securely punctuates this passage, 23–26, with an image that is almost like a genre painting, a still life symbolic of the poverty of peasant life and labor, but here dignified by the poets' philosophical apprehension of it.

28
Warped, the lid no longer
fits over the clothes chest.
                    —Bonchō

29
In the hermitage,
staying put for a while, but to
break out again.
            —Bashō

30
Old age has yet its joys—
this news of an anthology.
                    —Kyorai

31
Of various forms
and shapes he's tasted
love's full array.
   —Bonchō

32
But all wine and song ends
in *la belle* Komachi's hag.
    —Bashō

Bonchō in 28 maintains the still-life style and detail of 27 with the picture of the warped lid that does not securely fit anymore over the clothes chest, an admirable parallel to the useless mousetrap. Then Bashō in 29 performs a remarkable revision of the workman's cottage as a poet's hermitage. He reinterprets the lid that won't fit, symbolically, as a free spirit that cannot abide within the confines of its abode but must break out of it. From here, the sequence turns self-referential with evocations of the poets' activity and attitudes. "Anthology" in Kyorai's verse 30 raises the concept of variety in 31, since the poems (in a Japanese anthology) are divided according to themes and topics such as the four seasons, Love, and so on. "Forms and shapes" (*shina*) in 31 alludes to the famous *Tale of Genji* section of chapter 2 that features a lengthy debate among the courtiers about the varieties of love and women, making the implicit subject of this verse Genji himself. It is fitting then that Bashō responds in 32 by matching Genji with another Heian-period icon, the court lady and so-called passionate poetess Ono no Komachi (fl. ca. 850), often depicted in later popular culture as an old beggar woman bereft of her former beauty and loves.

33
Why the hint
of tears, even as he sits
sipping gruel?
   —Kyorai

The image of Komachi as a beggar evokes the scene of someone of formerly of high station being offered a bowl of soup, tearfully recalling his lost past.

34
In the master's absence
looms wide the wooden floor.
   - -Bonchō

Bonchō reenvisions the tearful man as the retainer of a samurai lord who is absent from the castle, having perhaps incurred the wrath of the shogun and been condemned to exile, or worse. The yawning absence in the man's life is effectively brought out by the wide empty space of the wooden floor.

35
Letting lice crawl
on the palm of his hand,
beneath the flowers.
            —Bashō

36
Motionless the spring haze
in the drowsy noon hour.
            —Kyorai

So close to the end of the sequence, Bashō in 35 neutralizes the emotion in link 33/34 by reinterpreting absence, not as deprivation or sorrow, but as a mental spaciousness. The empty wide floor of 34 comes to connote a Zen emptiness, the freedom to let things be what they are—the lice to crawl, the flowers to bloom. The result is the image of perfect serenity in the concluding verse by Kyorai.

ALL THREE PIECES TRANSLATED BY ESPERANZA RAMIREZ-CHRISTENSEN

PART
VI

Nature and Sentiments

Two-Needle Pine

EDITED BY TACHIBANA FUKAKU (SHŌGETSUDŌ)

Although haiku has long been Japan's preeminent poetic genre abroad, it has not always been the major form of *haikai* poetry. In fact, toward the end of the seventeenth century, a closely related form called verse capping (*maekuzuke*) began capturing the imagination of the Japanese population. A kind of poetic game, verse capping was, above all else, fun. Moreover, it particularly appealed to urban commoners by virtue of how it captured something of their everyday world. Verse capping therefore gained a wide following in spite of how "serious" poets—like Matsuo Bashō—condemned it as blurring the lines between art and entertainment.

Much of the appeal of verse capping resided in its being a competitive game, with a point system and even awards. This game spread, through a commercial network of judges and intermediary agencies acting as clearinghouses for prizes and winning verses, from the urban centers of Kyoto, Edo, and Osaka to provincial castle towns and villages. In this sense, verse capping helped transform *haikai* poetry itself from a semi-elite practice of urban literati in the seventeenth century into something of a countrywide pastime during the eighteenth century at all levels of society. The popularity of verse capping thus made Japan a veritable nation of poets.

So what, exactly, is verse capping? Simply put, it is the linking of one verse to another. In practice, a judge (*tenja*) would issue a challenge verse (*maeku*), in either fourteen (7-7) or seventeen (5-7-5) syllables, as a kind of challenge to the participating poets. These poets, who might number in the hundreds or even thousands, then would compose their response (*tsukeku*), in either seventeen or fourteen syllables, respectively, which linked to—or "capped"— the challenge verse. The translations herein endeavor to match the short or long lines of the original poems, not the exact number of syllables.

In linked verse in general, emphasis was placed on the linking of response to challenge verse rather than on any individual verse as a single poetic statement. It was the space between two verses where images mingled, resulting in a hybrid greater than the sum of the parts. In verse capping, by contrast, poets aimed for a strong distinctive response that would stand out and hopefully win the competition against multiple rivals. Consequently, much verse capping tended to the witty, comic, or parodic, especially when composed in an urban context. Increasingly, however, commoner poets began to fashion styles that attempted to capture a slice of life in a more straightforward manner.

Verse capping, like all *haikai* poetry, was a "cool medium," as the Internet generation might say, that thrived on ambiguity. Oftentimes the challenge verse was less a complete poetic thought than a fill-in-the-blank prompt. At times the challenge verse amounted only to a pithy saying or a snappy jingle, a verbal fragment lifted more or less "as is" from popular discourse. Since the challenge verse was meant to be distributed to a large number of poets, its cultural reference needed to be broadly rooted in contemporary culture, rather than, say, high tradition, so as to be sufficiently recognizable by a primarily commoner audience. Both of these trends paralleled the development of the independent haiku verse and are thought to have led to the emergence of the comic haiku (*senryū*) that persists to this day, as seen in many Japanese newspapers.

The following verses were selected from an early Genroku-era collection entitled *Two-Needle Pine* (*Futaba no Matsu*, 1690). Its editor, Tachibana Fukaku, was a native son of Edo. Said to possess enviable social skills and a shrewd business sense, Fukaku eventually established a thriving poetic practice that, by one account, attracted more than a thousand followers. Little if anything is known about most of the poets who contributed to his collection.

Except in one case, in which Fukaku as judge recognized only a single response to his challenge verse as worthy of inclusion, between two and five responses per challenge verse are included below, in order to indicate something of the competitive spirit of the game that was verse capping.

To draw a distinction between the challenge verse and the responses, the latter are indented. Comments by the translator between verses discuss each link.

⌒ (DC) ⌒

SELECTIONS FROM TWO-NEEDLE PINE

> In this world, stumbling seven times
> and still getting up the eighth.

Embedded in this challenge verse is a Japanese proverb, popular to this day: "Fall down seven times, get up eight times," the English equivalent being "If at first you don't succeed, try, try again."

> Defeated warlord,
> sword drawn for suicide,
> stopped by a priest.

This dramatic link suggests a daimyo in his fallen castle or perhaps in his clan's temple. As he prepares to commit suicide in order to preserve his honor, a priest grabs his sword to stop him. Is the priest urging the daimyo to abdicate his position to take the tonsure and begin a new life? Even a defeated daimyo has a second chance.

> Fragrant winter plum blossoms—
> my spirits revive
> bidding welcome to the New Year.

"Plum blossom" is a seasonal word that, along with "bush warbler" and so forth, traditionally intimated the coming of spring. Here the promise of springtime renewal echoes the proverb that the eighth time might be the charm.

> His life changed,
> but untouched on his skin
> linger two characters for "warrior."

It was not uncommon for samurai to lose or intentionally renounce their status for political or economic reasons. In this verse, the *haikai* lens, always scanning the everyday surface for topical grist, zooms in on the unblemished tattoo of a former samurai. The tattoo, a seemingly random detail, suggests the former samurai's pride and lingering identification with his erstwhile class. Or it may be a branded sign of rebellion, since samurai were forbidden tattoos. In either case, it is ironic that the two characters are kept clean, since this suggests his ambition to rise once again in the world.

Dozing off to sleep
while reading a book.

The book here is a text written in Chinese, perhaps a Confucian classic, which would have been dry reading indeed.

"Who are my original parents?"
intones a monk,
keeling over in exhaustion.

The first line is a variant of the popular Zen koan that asks the meditator to imagine the face of his or her parents prior to his birth. The "book" is transformed here into a Buddhist meditational text. Is the monk weary from fervent practice or mere boredom?

"Eat this, you mosquitoes!"
setting out a melon rind
for a decoy.

The link embellishes the book-reading figure above by adding pesky "mosquitoes" and a "melon rind," both seasonal words suggesting a hot summer evening. The Japanese for "decoy" (*migawari*) literally means "in place of my body."

Countless fireflies
shining at the window's edge,
a young woman spellbound.

The firefly is a seasonal image, suggesting a lazy summer evening. The Japanese word translated as "spellbound" (*you*) literally means "to become drunk" and is taken here to connote sensual enchantment. The commonplace that scholars study deep into the night by the light of fireflies is turned on its head, for the fireflies become a distraction while diverting a young lady's attention toward wistful fantasy.

Thinking of this and that,
the years slip by.

This verse evokes a state of mind. Is it a sudden realization ("How old I've become!"), a moment of regret (neglected friendship or failed marriage prospects), or bewilderment (passed up for promotion)? It is a sliver of a verse—just enough for the hundreds of poets composing a link to hang almost anything on.

It knows nothing of the next world,
this body:
five feet of coiled rope.

Five feet was the standard height of a Japanese person at the time. In the Buddhist world view, our thoughts and actions accumulate karma that affect the disposition of our lives in the next stage of existence. The clear perception of the karmic process—often called enlightenment—is exceedingly difficult and probably beyond the grasp of most human beings, who consequently become enmeshed in karma as the years slip by unnoticed. The image thus enacts the Buddhist metaphor of the body as a prison for the soul.

All these young girls
who can't sew a stitch:
off with them to Bare-Naked Island!

Whiling away their time in frivolous pursuits, young women nowadays are hardly ready to get married in the real world. This response turns on the idea of the young women receiving their just deserts by being carted off to a legendary land where the inhabitants supposedly lived au naturel.

Heaven and earth
are a mirror without rust.

Since mirrors in East Asia had traditionally been made out of some metal without glass, they needed to be polished frequently to maintain their reflection. The image of a rusted or occluded mirror was thus widely used as a metaphor for a certain opacity of mind, reality, or even historical events. "Heaven and earth" is probably synonymous with "Way of Heaven," a term current in seventeenth-century intellectual circles that referred to the order of the cosmos and society.

Wanting something
to hide his sins—
ah, a straw rain cloak.

The line refers to an extraordinary garb said to belong to demons and goblins, which was thought to cause the wearer to become invisible. The Japanese word for "sins" can also be rendered as "crimes."

> Even when doodling,
> the samurai lord's name
> had better be spaced.

To show respect when writing the name of one's lord—and to uphold the hierarchy between superior and inferior—one typically inserted blank spaces between the characters. In the end, nothing escapes the gaze of heaven and earth—or one's samurai lord—not even a scrap of paper upon which is scribbled his name.

> A shot of Zhuzi
> sedates the senses:
> state of sobriety.

Neo-Confucianism espoused a dualism of metaphysical principle (*ri*) and the active principle of the senses (*ki*), which was thought to infuse the cosmos, along with a rigorous moralism in practice. The straightforward version of the verse suggests that adopting the Neo-Confucian outlook helps the mind become clear like a mirror that reflects all things in heaven and earth. The poet reverses the normal priority order of *ri* over *ki* to a comic extreme by recasting *ki* as a reference to the floating world. Thus, the verse caricatures the view that Neo-Confucianism serves as an antidote to the Genroku lifestyle of pleasure and the senses.

> For withered tree and blossom
> there is no difference:
> sound of the wind.

The wind that scatters autumn leaves and cherry blossoms alike is no respecter of the seasons. Like heaven and earth, the wind is impartial. This sense of impartiality was also an ideal that the Tokugawa shogunate strove to project in its attempts to establish public authority throughout the realm.

> Living one's life
> doted upon.

The verse suggests a life of ease and contentment. The absence of a stated subject opens up all kinds of possibilities: the spoiled child of a wealthy merchant, a daimyo's mansion, a kept mistress, even the carefree existence of an animal or a flower.

> Unaware of its imminent slaughter,
> a cow battens in the field,
> being readied for sacrifice.

In traditional Japan, cattle were mostly either employed for farmwork such as pulling carts or, as is the case here, offered as ritual sacrifice. The focus of interest in this link is the way "unaware" and "battens" refigure "doted upon": the glazed-over blank stare of the personified cow suggests both her pampered life and an ignorance of her impending doom.

> Eyes filled with moon and flowers,
> ears ringing with nightingale song.

Bashō once quipped that a person is no different from a barbarian until acquiring a taste for the "moon and flowers." This is shorthand for an aesthetic sensibility made possible only by a life of ease and privilege—a life unavailable, and perhaps even laughable, to most commoners, even as it was a source of social aspiration for others with the means to imitate their social betters.

> When he ties up the horse,
> the wicket gate wobbles.

These lines recall a rustic landscape with a modest hut, perhaps belonging to a religious hermit. There is a sense of anticipation in the implied visitor whose unknown identity opens up potential links for the other poets.

> In some humble shack
> he takes up lodging by force,
> a wounded samurai.

By this time, no actual warfare had been waged in the realm for many decades, but the warrior ethos and the great deeds of the past still infused the social imagination. Contemporary writers tended either to lionize the samurai past or to contrast it with the enervated samurai present. Here, an injured samurai, arriving on horseback, must accommodate himself to the crude lodging. Or perhaps the horse belongs to the dweller of the shack, a former samurai similarly defeated or fallen on hard times.

> A winter shower in a mountain village—
> folded up in the rain
> a Chinese sun parasol.

A cold rain beats down on a hut deep in a mountain village. Such parasols typically had a thin bamboo spine, patterned paper, and bright colors, contrasting with the monochrome winter rains and mountain hut. It also suggests the high class of the visitor. Who is it, and what is he or she doing in a dilapidated hut in the mountains? A courtier on a tryst, a samurai bureaucrat making his administrative rounds through the provinces, or a lord hit by a sudden rainstorm while on the hunt?

> Heard nonstop,
> the sound of a pestle.

Pestles were often foot-operated and used for grinding meal. Here location is the enticing unknown: from where is the sound of the pestle coming?

> Sedge-woven hats—
> commanders' helmets of
> a prosperous world.

The scene might be a teahouse where guests, having entered the pleasure quarters wearing broad-brimmed hats to hide their identity, await their courtesan hosts for the evening. In the background the sound of a pestle can be heard nearby, as a sign of prosperity. The commander's helmet was worn by military officers during the warring years. This double vision (*mitate*) links the two historical periods as well as classes.

> At mealtime
> even the emperor
> takes notice.

Is the sound of the pestle supposed to remind the emperor of the dependence of even his exalted station on the work of the lower orders of society? Or, hemmed in Kyoto by shogunate strictures and surrounded by the hustle and bustle of merchant activity, is the emperor imagined to take due notice of the growing confidence of the commoner class?

> Has it gotten so late at night?
> A knock at the door.

The kind of riddle in this verse was a major feature of verse capping that, while attracting many commoners, at the same time repelled other poets of higher standing or literary pretensions.

> Nearest thing to hand
> a *go* box and two lovers,
> a pillow to share for the first time.

The knock heard at the door is here interpreted as an unexpected visit from a love interest that leads to a moment of spontaneous passion. *Go,* a game of strategy, makes an unlikely go-between in a passionate tryst, but it is suggestive of more than just comical incongruity. The wooden box, here used as a pillow, simultaneously suggests both calculation—for love is a game of strategy full of maneuvers and positions—and spontaneity.

> My pulse pounding,
> and in his hands
> are life and death.

The knock at the door is refigured here in the pounding pulse. Who could it be? A physician, a thief, or someone with a vendetta, none of whom were necessarily reassuring presences?

> Just as I fall asleep
> the smell of fish appetizer.

The smell of fish appetizer, served in a deep dish that typically accompanied *sake* at a brothel, distracts someone from an evening snooze. Food, not a part of courtly poetry, occupied a large part of the commoner's cultural universe, evidenced in the large number of eatery guides available to urban dwellers and travelers on the road alike.

> Left unread,
> an open page
> bookmarked by a fallen blossom.

A spring verse. The book has been abandoned beneath a blossoming cherry tree. The evening doze is refigured here in the soporific book reading, a leisurely activity that is all the more aestheticized by the fallen blossom. As the poet begins to doze off, the fragrance and maybe the sound of a nearby *sake* party awaken him to his senses. The wry humor of the link turns on the contrast between the elegant, cerebral activity of reading a book and the visceral, even vulgar, stimulus of the fish appetizer.

> So ebullient and prosperous—
> the sounds of laughter overheard.

Who is laughing, and who is overhearing the laughter? Where is this happening? And how will the ensuing linking verses handle the festive occasion implied in this challenge verse?

> An array of servants
> setting out an imperial banquet
> beneath the orange blossoms.

Peals of laughter are overheard from the precincts of the palace where the imperial meal is being prepared. The link depicts the happy scene of servants laughing among themselves. Nearby, the silhouette of a passerby—probably a commoner—is faintly suggested in the challenge verse's "overheard." What emerges is a double vision of inner and outer circles, perhaps an adjacent courtyard or an alleyway just beyond the palace grounds.

> While the guests caroused on,
> the girl with the smile
> sold *sake* hand over fist.

The ebullient laughter of the challenge verse may be linked to the carousing customers (possibly at a roadside inn). But here the laughter also serves to explain the success of the waitress selling the most *sake,* thanks to her bubbly repartee with customers.

> "A first grandson,
> in the first half of the year no less!"—
> fawned over with great hopes.

The radiant laughter now comes from people celebrating the birth of a first grandson in the lucky first half of the year. The grandson is regarded as a child of promise.

> Both husband and wife
> cut similar figures,
> their flesh full and ample.

The link connects the sound of prosperity in the challenge verse to the fleshy bodies of the couple. Moreover, the similarity of their figures and their merry laughter suggest a deep degree of marital bliss.

TRANSLATED BY DAVID CANNELL

The Jeweled Water Grass Anthology

EDITED BY YOSA BUSON

*T*he *Jeweled Water Grass Anthology* (*Tamamoshū*, 1774) is a collection of *haikai* by Yosa Buson (1716–1783), the eighteenth century's most celebrated *haikai* poet. It is exceptional in that all of its verses were written by women, even though the vast majority of *haikai* poets of the time were men. However, as the example of *Tamamoshū* shows, some women did manage to gain recognition for their poetry.

In most world literary traditions, few women were able to achieve renown as writers before the modern period. This was not true in Japan; women writers are at the center of the literary canon of the classical period (710–1183). Women were especially prominent as writers of *waka,* the thirty-one-syllable verse form of the aristocrats. However, the culture surrounding the *haikai* form of the early modern period was initially not very welcoming to women. Why this was so is not easy to explain, but part of the reason lies in the literary conventions of *haikai,* and part of it lies in the social aspects of its composition.

The humor of *haikai* ranged from bawdy double entendres to sophisticated wordplay that required extensive knowledge of the classical literary tradition to appreciate. It was not uncommon for women to have adequate knowledge of the classical literary tradition; if they were literate at all, a substantial part of their education would have been related to the composition of *waka,* and in any case poetic dictionaries and other reference materials to help aspiring *haikai* poets were readily available. However, social conventions would not have encouraged women to express themselves in ribald verse, and while all *haikai* is by no means racy, even the most highbrow exponents of the genre, such as Matsuo Bashō, did not flinch from earthiness in their *haikai.*

Another social aspect of *haikai* was its collaborative nature. While the seventeen-syllable *hokku* could be composed alone, until the middle of the eighteenth century *haikai* most commonly took the form of linked verse, poetic sequences composed in groups, where members took turns improvising verses consecutively, like links in a chain. In situations like these, it was often difficult for women to participate.

The *Tamamoshū* poets came from a wide spectrum of stations in life. Most were the wives, daughters, or sisters of male *haikai* poets. Given *haikai*'s highly social nature, aspiring poets needed to be welcomed into schools or gatherings where it was practiced. Since many *haikai* gatherings took place in people's homes, sometimes female members of the family also participated, gaining skill from practicing with their male relatives. Some women even became professional poets, but this was rare; those who did tended to have unconventional lifestyles and were either single (such as Kaga no Chiyojo [1703–1775]) or widowed (such as Shiba Sonome [1664–1726]). Many courtesans also included *haikai* among the numerous accomplishments like dance, singing, and musical performance with which they entertained their clients. Some of *Tamamoshū*'s most spirited verses are by courtesans.

Tamamoshū contains 449 verses by 119 women. Its verses offer keen observations of the pathos and joy of everyday existence. Some of them use imagery derived from experiences particular to women's' lives, but most are indistinguishable from men's *haikai*. The verses below were among those whose comic sensibility is apparent even in translation. It is important to note, however, that the humor of *Tamamoshū* is subtle; it originates in the *haikai* poets' delight in incongruous juxtapositions, unexpected happenings, and gentle ironies that reveal human frailty—especially one's own. Some of it is sweet, even cute, but here and there a verse stands out for the pointedness of its insight.

The anthology opens with a very brief preface by Chiyojo, the most famous female *haikai* poet both of her day and of ours. It is short, but so great was her reputation at the time that her participation in this project—small though it may have been—was very much desired. Chiyojo's self-deprecation here is conventional—almost all writers of prefaces to *haikai* anthologies disparage themselves one way or another. Her reference to illness as a reason for its brevity—another common feature of such prefaces—may not have been feigned: she died a year after *Tamamoshū* was published. The "person of poetic sensibility" she mentions is probably Buson himself.

FROM THE "SPRING" SECTION

Chiyojo's Preface

A person of poetic sensibility who is well acquainted both with the blossoms of the flowery capital and with the moon collected the beautiful verses of famous women of old and, giving it the name *The Jeweled Watergrass Anthology,* planned to have it carved into cherrywood for printing. Whereupon I found it difficult to decline the suggestion that I write the preface to it, and putting aside the pillow of my sickbed of the past three years and creeping with humility, when I stained my brush with ink, it was the beginning of the Third Month.

1
At Tsurayuki's plum tree

Scent of the plum blossoms:
inappropriate though it may be
I'm tired from the journey
   —Sonome

The speaker has traveled to a site famous for its association with Ki no Tsurayuki (ca. 868–945), one of Japan's most famous poets. Unlike Tsurayuki, who
was inspired by the delicate fragrance of the plum tree, this poetess can only
think of how tired she is.

2
Picking violets
onto my sleeve:
a jumping frog
   —Fuji

There is humor in the combination of the elegance of violet picking and the
abrupt action of the little creature.

3
On the occasion of heading to Yamato for sightseeing:

For a while
I'm leaving it with you swallows—
travelers' rest
   —Sonome

The speaker has to leave for Yamato but promises the swallows that she will
return. *Tamamoshū* credits Sonome with this verse, but it was written by
Ichiyū, her husband, as one of a pair with verse 4.

4
Having said that, I too am still sorry to leave:

I promise you to come back
You will play with the swallows:
cat in the garden
   —Sonome

Seeing a cat in the garden of the inn mentioned in verse 3, the speaker imagines that it would amuse the swallows in her absence.

5
When the cat got stolen

Cat wife:
who is the lover
that took his heart?
                —Wife of Ransetsu

The noisy abandon with which cats meet in amorous trysts in spring made "cats' love" a popular topic with *haikai* poets. Hattori Ransetsu (1654–1707), the poet's husband, was among Matsuo Bashō's most prominent disciples.

6
A dashing man
who never tires of flowers:
how annoying!
                —Senshi, sister of Kyorai

At cherry blossom viewing parties, women must vie with flowers to gain the attention of men; a man who tires of cherry blossoms is no enemy of the ladies. The poet's brother was Mukai Kyorai, another of Bashō's important disciples.

7
Too ashamed to show my face
in front of these beautiful blossoms:
travel cloak
                —Sonome

As in verse 1, also by Sonome, the speaker has arrived at her destination after a long journey, only to be overcome with chagrin: the scene is so splendid that she feels shabby and hides her face behind her travel cloak.

8
Having received a letter
saying "they've all fallen":
still hunting for blossoms
                —Sonome

The speaker appreciates the absurdity of the situation she has gotten into because of her passion for beauty: having just received a letter reporting that the cherry blossoms are gone, she cannot resist going out to search for the few that might still remain.

9
They don't seem to notice
how old I've gotten:
blossoms in full bloom
　　　　　—Chigetsu

The beauty of cherry blossoms is ageless; the speaker wishes she could say the same about herself.

10
How annoying my friend is!
"Tomorrow," she said:
blossoms in the rain
　　　　　—Mine

It is better not to delay a cherry blossom outing: rain causes the fragile petals to fall.

11
Why are you teasing me?
is it because I am a woman?
blossom-scattering breeze
　　　　　—Shin

Both cherry blossoms and elegantly dressed women suffer in a strong wind. Here the speaker feels singled out for the wind's playful treatment as she walks out to enjoy the blossoms.

12
When we set up the Hina dolls
will she turn into a lady-in-waiting?
little girl
　　　　　—Rin

For the Girls' Festival on the third day of the Third Month, families display dolls dressed in the costumes of the imperial court. Looking at the exquisite dolls, the speaker's granddaughter is transported into a magical world.

13
No matter how old they get
it never changes:
Hina dolls' hair
                    —Shōkin

The return of the Girls' Festival reminds the speaker of how old she is getting.

FROM THE "SUMMER" SECTION

14
At Taima Temple, on the first day of the Fourth Month

Changing to summer clothes:
having done no weaving myself
I feel a deep sense of sin
                    —Sonome

The first day of the Fourth Month marked the beginning of summer, and the day to start wearing light summer clothing. The speaker has traveled to Taima Temple, home of the Taima Mandala, which was associated with a famous medieval legend. After becoming a nun, the pious young noblewoman Chūjō-hime was visited by a mysterious nun who wove ten bundles of lotus stems into a magnificent mandala overnight. In Sonome's poem, the speaker feels guilty when putting on new clothes—none of which she wove herself.

15
Cuckoo
I take down the wind chime tonight
to wait
                    —Mother of Shōhaku

Hearing the first cuckoo call of the summer was a common theme in *waka* poetry. Instead of writing about the thrill of hearing the first cuckoo call, the poetess here describes waiting for it.

16
Without a man
waking up scares me:
mosquito net
                    —Hanazaki

Mosquito nets were made big enough to cover two people sleeping side by side. As a courtesan, Hanazaki was not accustomed to sleeping alone.

17
When I looked this morning
the cat had trampled them down:
irises
                    —Karei

As in verse 2 by Fuji, the combination of beautiful flowers of the season and an animal's unexpected antics gives the verse its appeal.

18
Startled
by its reflection in the water:
firefly
                    —Wife of Shinkyū

At dusk, skimming the surface of a stream in search of a mate, the firefly surprises itself with its own light.

19
Evening showers
sometimes I adore them
sometimes I detest them
                    —Shizuka

Evening showers, an almost daily occurrence, characterize the summer season. For a courtesan, which Shizuka was, evening showers that fell after a client had already arrived were obviously welcome, while rain at other times would keep the best of their clients at home.

20
I thought I'd try
drawing some eyebrows on a melon:
out on the veranda
                    —Sonome

One of the summer's pleasures was to sit on the veranda and eat a melon that had been nicely cooled in well water. The writer practices the latest makeup styles on this melon.

21
Beckoned
by moonflowers:
it's so hot!
　　　　　—Ukō

The white faces of the moonflowers look cool and inviting. However, when the speaker actually goes out to enjoy them in the summer night, she is disappointed to find that the heat still feels oppressive.

FROM THE "AUTUMN" SECTION

22
Bald mountains:
autumn sticks
to none of them
　　　　　—Sonome

This poem recalls a completely bald man on whose head no fly can stay. Though the most obvious sign of autumn is colored foliage, treeless mountains offer no place for such a display as autumn slips past.

23
Full moon
miscanthus grass in the meadow
tugging at my bathrobe
　　　　　—Ume

Miscanthus (sometimes called pampas grass or eulalia) is a tall ornamental grass. Its delicate plumes become soft and silvery right around the time the harvest moon appears. The speaker is so captivated by the brilliance of the moon that she rushes out to see it better, then is nonplussed to find the long leaves and stalks of the grasses pulling at her hem.

24
I let it drop
my *sake* cup
tonight's full moon
　　　　　—Tsune

Intoxicated by *sake,* the poet is dumbfounded by the beauty of the moon.

25
Round moon:
surely it would fill even Izumi Shikibu
with regret
                    —Shūshiki

Izumi Shikibu, a celebrated woman poet of the Heian period, was also known for her many love affairs. The speaker here imagines that a full moon would be inconvenient for her nocturnal rendezvous.

26
Were there two of them,
would anyone argue?
tonight's full moon
                    —Chigetsu

Tonight's moon is perfectly beautiful, so nothing could compare with it except another exactly like it. The verse poses a rhetorical question: if there were, would anyone regret it? Or, perhaps, how could anyone choose between them?

27
Feeling angry—
the sound of the fuller's mallet
out of rhythm
                    —Tadajo

The distant, rhythmic beat of cloth being fulled on a still autumn night is usually melancholic. Tonight, however, it is obvious even to this distant listener that the fuller is out of sorts.

28
Hōryūji Temple

It approaches
even the Heavenly Kings:
kudzu lush with growth
                    —Sonome

The Heavenly Kings, a pair of statues representing gods who protect the ancient Hōryūji Temple, have an extremely intimidating appearance. The speaker is impressed by the strength of the kudzu vine that embraces such

large figures. The weed and its delicate purple flowers make a humorous contrast against the frightening look of the deities.

> 29
> Growing older
> the voice fades:
> katydid
> > —Chigetsu

The call of the katydid is strong in the early part of autumn; as time passes,
though, it gets weaker. Listening to it, the speaker is reminded that she is not
as young as she used to be, either.

> 30
> Sowing millet:
> these tracks were made
> by a flock of sparrows
> > —Kanan

Awa (millet) is a season word associated with autumn. As the farmer stamps
down the seeds he has scattered, a flock of sparrows also seems to do the same.
The poet Kanan was the wife of Kyorai, the Bashō disciple mentioned in the
comment to verse 6.

FROM THE "WINTER" SECTION

> 31
> Must have exhausted
> all possible pleasures:
> a paper robe
> > —Sonome

Kamiko (paper robes) were made of several sheets of paper pasted together
to form a durable material that could withstand rain and repeated washing.
Attire fit for spendthrifts in the pleasure quarters who ended up bankrupt,
kamiko came to be glorified on the kabuki stage as the costume for a tragic
playboy.

TRANSLATED BY CHERYL CROWLEY

Love and Eros

The Tale of Zeraku

ANONYMOUS

Published shortly after 1655 in Kyoto, *The Tale of Zeraku* (*Zeraku Mono-gatari*, three volumes) is a prototypical easy reading book (*kanazōshi*) that jumbles together contemporary topics and old styles. This book describes the escapades of a modern shopkeeper in a mixture of classical and modern styles, borrowing liberally from the ancient and medieval forms of romance, cautionary story, folktale, verse tale, *waka* poetry, and *kyōgen* but spiced up with contemporary forms of *jōruri, kōdan* (oratory as entertainment), and, particularly, travelogue.

The anonymous author probably wrote the book in a playful tribute to a well-known Shijō Street merchant by the family name of Yamamoto, who successfully bought an acclaimed courtesan out of a brothel, an act that cost anyone a fortune. The time of the auspicious event is given as "the first year of Meireki (1655)" while also disguised as an unspecified period according to the conventions of courtly romance. The real-life persons involved in the incident were likely known to the public by their real names and pseudonyms. The name "Tomona," by which the main character is called, means "friendly name" and could well have been Yamamoto's pseudonym hiding his identity at the brothel district. The eponymous Zeraku, a former male prostitute turned professional freeloader, serves as Tomona's constant companion and accomplice in midlife crisis. Befitting his role in the story, his name means "it's all fun" and may have referred to an existing *hōkan,* a freelance entertainer skilled in poetry, song, and storytelling. "Kisa," a fairly common name for a woman, may represent the actual name of the rescued and ransomed courtesan after she becomes To-mona's kept mistress. It is the felicitous change of status on her part that allows her to recover her native name to lead a life in the real world. The story's villain, Kyūsuke, also has a commonplace name, not a pseudonym, and may refer to an actual servant employed in the brothel. The only other named characters, Nakasato Shōbei and Shirakawa Yaemon, may recall the real names of the men who negotiated for the courtesan's ransoming. The tale celebrates them as To-mona's respectable and sensible friends who chide him for his reckless pursuit yet intercede on his behalf with the villain Kyūsuke. All other characters remain nameless, perhaps reinforcing the idea that they belong to Tomona's real life and not the world of his pleasure.

The immediate inspiration for the narrative framework came from Tomi-yama Dōya's immensely popular easy reading book, *Chikusai* (ca. 1621–1623) and its sequels and imitations. Featuring a wayfaring duo that became a main-stay of travel literature, these narratives offered straightforward commentary on the landscape, customs, and amenities of the road, all routinely spiked with absurd madcap verse. Following this format, *The Tale of Zeraku* spotlights a pair of male travelers journeying the short distance between Kyoto and Arima Hot Springs (in present-day Kobe), visiting Buddhist temples, Shinto shrines, and other famous spots in line with the new genre's conventions.

Layered on top of this guidebook strand is a romance. Tomona, for his part, regrets that he has lived fifty years having experienced little if any actual gratification: the story depicts him turning over a new leaf, so to speak, es-chewing the claimed abstemiousness of his previous life and pursuing the philosophy of *ukiyo,* the Japanese equivalent of carpe diem. He is ready to be the hero of his own great romance, and his travel partner, Zeraku, is ready to help him. Zeraku, like all successful *hōkan,* is well versed in the ways of the world but can also hold his own when referencing history, religion, and the arts. His retelling of classics, and his discussion of famous places along the way frequently bubbles over into long-winded *kōdan* narratives. One such episode draws from a ballad by Bai Juyi (772–846), "Song of Everlasting Sorrow" (Chang-hen-ge, 807), which depicts the tragic love affair between Emperor Xuanzong and his concubine Yang Guifei. Zeraku's justification for telling this lengthy, supposedly heartrending narrative in the middle of a conversation among the bathers at Arima is that the two classical Chinese lovers, too, had bathed together in the poem.

The Tale's interweaving of genres and allusions serve to construct the classical edifice Tomona needs for his dream-world narrative featuring himself as a romantic hero. A comic tone updates and spoofs old courtly romances, exaggerating classical tropes. The tongue-in-cheek presentation of natural imagery, replete with hyperbolic embellishment, accompanies a burlesque of recognizable episodes, particularly from *The Tale of Genji*. The presence of the river Akutagawa from *The Tales of Ise* foreshadows the violent fate of Kisa toward the end of *The Tale of Zeraku*. The narrator's use of honorifics and poetic language even transforms the merchant Tomona (who comes to be called Lord Tomona by the slip of the author's brush, as it were) and his kept mistress, Kisa (something like a window prostitute as the illustration here reveals), into veritable aristocratic paramours. Similarly, the description of the brothel district that the two travelers come upon reads like that of an upper-class residential neighborhood betrayed only by occasional hints such as "overdecorated."

The moral tale aspect of this work turns the three male characters into contrasting pairs in terms of class as well as virtue. Tomona, at once an admired merchant and a tragic lover, embodies the highest qualities in both the real and the fictional worlds. Zeraku, who follows Tomona as Koremitsu follows Prince Genji, is an adviser to his master in practical life as well as a facilitator of his romantic pursuits, belonging to his master's dual worlds. Female characters are similarly paired and contrasted. Zeraku's wife—referred to by her husband as the "Mountain Hag," one of those monsters feared in medieval folklore for their cannibalistic tendencies—represents a status-less position as well as questionable morality. Kyūsuke's wife, a scheming servant in Tomona's household, embodies the oppressed classes whose frustrations burst forth in the form of a vengeful "living spirit" in the romantic world created by the two men. Kyūsuke's manipulative calculations may illustrate all evildoings in the real world, while his wife's monstrous fury seems to belong to hell or some such dark universe imagined in Buddhistic folklore. The commendable types are Tomona's wife, who suppresses anger against her husband's wayward behavior while maintaining her dignity within the family and authority over her servants, and Kisa, the object of the great romantic love who turns into the pariah of the entire household; the duo represent the two separate worlds of reality and imagination.

The two travelers—one a member of the nouveau riche and the other making a living at the edge of that class—constitute a segment of a newly risen bourgeoisie. The differences among the three families—merchant Tomona's, entertainer Zeraku's, and servant Kyūsuke's—map the yawning gaps in newly formed social strata among commoners. Ultimately, *The Tale of Zeraku* verges on a modern parable of class relations, reinforcing the social norms of marriage, family, commerce, and society. Its rhetoric is mercantile; characters repeatedly haggle with each other over the legalistic side of Tomona's love affair, and the same characters are downright commonsensical, invoking expressions such as "stands to reason" and "makes sense"—in other words, the values and ideals of the emerging bourgeoisie. The folk Buddhist ending is incongruous with the worldly love-and-revenge story, but the bodhisattva's blessing affirms merchant-class values, restoring the pleasure and prosperity of the "floating world."

The following translation comprises the opening of the first volume and the entirety of the third, skipping the part about Arima Hot Springs, which is largely occupied by Zeraku's expounding.

I-1. HOW TOMONA MET A GREAT BEAUTY IN HIS DREAM

> So deep and vast
> Anyone venturing in
> Will surely be lost:
> Love, as they say,
> Is a bewildering forest!

On the Shijō Street of Kyoto, probably during the first year of Meireki (it matters not in which reign), there was, among many revered gentlemen of commerce, a certain Yamamoto So-and-So Tomona. He began as a *sake* maker, selling his wares within the city to accumulate enough fortune after his retirement to run a pawn shop. Among those who often hung around Tomona's splendorous mansion was a certain Somebody-or-Other Zeraku, who came from a long line of eccentrics. Zeraku was as poor as Mount Fuji is high.

Now, much to the dismay of Tomona's wife, this Zeraku was Tomona's bosom companion in his secret affairs about town. Her husband's behavior was, in her view, inappropriate for somebody halfway to one hundred. Although she hardly welcomed Zeraku to their mansion, no social event of significance could be held there without his presence and worldly know-how. His wife's objections were of no concern to Tomona, however. After all, he conducted himself according to the realization that people live no longer than seventy years, so having already spent fifty in toil and labor himself, he might as well spend the rest of his allotted time in the dreamy world of pleasure, just as tasted by Kantan in the nō play.

Spring passed, and the sound of cuckoos echoed through the mountainsides, announcing summer. Irises withered on fences while mandarin orange blossoms spread their fragrance. The heat of the afternoon being unbearable, the noble Tomona lay down for a rest. As he dozed off, he caught a whiff of a

Surrounded by Chinese classics, our hero dreams of an angelic beauty, Volume 1, Episode 1. (Department of Japanese Linguistics, the University of Tokyo)

luxurious fragrance and looked up to see a gently curved beauty of about sixteen years appear before him. In the dream, the two seemed to have known each other for many years. Just as Tomona and the woman of his dreams were in the midst of engaging in an intimate conversation, however, he awoke with a start. Sadness would naturally overwhelm anyone ripped away from such a sweet dream; pearls of tears are inevitable even when the lover knows he will open his eyes to his real-life darling. Such is the way of love. Imagine, then, Tomona's anguish at knowing he might never again behold this heavenly maiden!

The king of Chu once dreamed of a magical night spent with an angel who turned from a morning cloud into an evening rain. In the same manner, that fleeting moment with his dream girl set Tomona afloat upon a torrent of tears and then a cloud of obsession. Longing day and night for his angel, he wandered in and out of another world; his inability to confide his situation to anyone left him preoccupied and distracted. Deep in thought, he could neither sleep nor rise. He finally took to bed, looking thin and wan, seeming as though his very life would vanish into an abyss of grief.

I-2. HOW TOMONA'S PARENTS CONSULTED VARIOUS PHYSICIANS

The new moon, over two thousand *ri* away, sheds no light, leaving the world pitch dark. In the same way, the bottomless pit of filial affection and anxiety envelops parents. Hearing about the state of affairs, Tomona's parents not only spared no cost in hiring physicians specializing in the healing arts of moxibustion, acupuncture, and herbal medicine but also appealed to the gods of each and every religion for their son's recovery, banging furiously on gongs and drums for good measure. But there was no sign of recovery—either the deities declined to listen or else the timing was all wrong. Worried relatives gathered at the mansion day and night, and, as usual, Zeraku had to be called in for a consultation.

Zeraku sat reverentially before Tomona's relatives and spoke: "There is no improvement in the master's condition because ordinary medicine cannot cure his illness. This may be forward of me to say, but please listen carefully as I offer my frank opinion.

"In the Way of Medicine, there are four types of doctors: godly, holy, technical, and masterful. A godly doctor has the ability to detect illness afflicting the inner organs merely by glancing at his patient. The holy doctor can spot all diseases merely by listening to the sounds emanating from his patient's mouth. These two types of doctors no longer exist in our world today. At a lower level, the technical doctor makes a diagnosis upon hearing the patient describe the symptoms, and the masterful doctor does the same but also takes the patient's pulse. Even then, it's difficult to differentiate the four hundred and four symptoms while also taking into account the twenty-four types of pulse. Preparing medication is fraught with errors, and many folks have departed this world as a result of misdiagnosis. As the ancient sage put it, 'Past remedies do not fit current illnesses; medicines may just as easily kill as cure.' The common cold is called the king of all one hundred diseases, but true illness emanates from one's heart. For this reason, the seven human sentiments disturb a person far more drastically than the six changes of weather."

Zeraku continued, "Judging from what I observe, pouring medicine down the master's throat is no answer. In my view," he added cheerily, "instead of relying on doctors to treat his illness, he needs to convalesce by getting away from everything and visiting the country! Not languishing at home for a night or two will do him good. Let him behave according to his wishes." All the relatives and especially Tomona's parents agreed, saying, "After all, life is the most important thing! Let's entrust Tomona to Zeraku's care."

Zeraku hastened to Tomona's side to recount the gist of the consultation. Unlike his physicians and relatives who put Tomona ill at ease, Zeraku was familiar and trustworthy, so Tomona bared his soul about the cause of his suf-

The lovesick hero takes to bed and consults a distinguished doctor, as Zeraku looks on from the edge of the room, Volume 1, Episode 2. (Department of Japanese Linguistics, the University of Tokyo)

fering: the tryst that had seemed to entwine dream with reality. Zeraku listened intently and said, "It may be audacious of me to correlate an example from China's history with a mere romance, but Sima Qian once wrote a detailed account of the sage king Gaozong, who lived during the Yin dynasty. Gaozong learned in a dream that heaven was to grant him a virtuous vassal, so he had a portrait made and scoured the country to find its human likeness. Now, there was a highway repairman in Fu Yan named Fu Yue who so resembled the portrait that he was brought back to the city to manage the affairs of state.

"If you are so disturbed by this tryst of yours, by all means have an artist paint a portrait of the young lady. Though I myself am getting old, as long as I have legs, I'd go anywhere for you to find someone who matches the portrait!" Inclined by nature toward an interest in amorous adventures of all sorts, Zeraku embroidered his rhetoric in order to persuade Tomona, who, by and by, regained his appetite and arose from bed. Encouraged, Zeraku obligingly continued to inquire about the symptoms of Tomona's discomfort. When Tomona would say, "My feet are unbearably cold," Zeraku would reply, "Then first visit Arima Hot Springs to shake off your gloom! There are a lot of interesting things along the way." One day Tomona at last came around, saying, "Perhaps you're right," and Zeraku answered, "I'll leave you tonight, but I'll visit again in the morning." He then made sure to emphasize his usefulness to the family by turning to Tomona's attendants to declare, "It goes without saying that you must guard against fire. Be sure to please your master in any way you can." He thus fussed over Tomona, presenting some insignificant gifts to him before returning to his own home.

I-3. HOW ZERAKU GOT SCOLDED BY THE MOUNTAIN HAG

On his way home, Zeraku reckoned that there would be no unforeseen complications. After all, aside from the authority of Tomona's parents, his plan was all up to him and Tomona. Still, he thought it diplomatic to relate the upshot of the events to his wife, whom he referred to as the Mountain Hag. After only two words, though, the Mountain Hag interrupted him vehemently, roaring: "This isn't the first time you've tried to pull this kind of trick on me! You claim it's the master's orders, but that's no reason to take such a long trip, leaving me alone! I'm no fool: you're using the master as your excuse! Don't think I'm not onto you! Once again you're scheming to sponge off your loaded patron!" As she finished this harangue, her face seemed transformed, her red-ringed eyes suddenly making her look like Yaksa, the most frightening demon in the woods. Zeraku was flabbergasted, and his eyes popped wide open. So this was the true face of the woman to whom he had been married all these years! The hairs on the back of his neck stood on end at this revelation. Had an unsuspecting stranger come upon the two of them, the shock would have been enough to drive any lifelong illness out of his body. The longer Zeraku stood before his wife, the steeper his troubles, so he hid, cowering in a closet corner, spending the night there without even loosening his sash.

At the break of dawn, he felt nothing like the despair that wracks lovers as the dawn birds twitter the end to a night of lovemaking. On the contrary, he greeted the morning with eagerness, intoning a line from a seemingly classical poem, "Hearing birds at dawn ain't nothing to me!" Now was the time to sneak off from his house and visit his master's bedroom to discuss plans for their hot springs getaway. Still, Zeraku knew he would eventually need to sweet-talk the Mountain Hag into granting him permission to sally forth. Otherwise, how else could he expect to ward off storms and other misfortunes along the way? And so he would return home to appeal to her: "Please listen to me just this once! I've been to my patron's mansion this morning, and it is by his command that I implore you to allow me to accompany him on his convalescence journey!"

Zeraku tells the Mountain
Hag of his plan, but she
isn't having any of it,
Volume 1, Episode 2.
(Department of Japanese
Linguistics, the University
of Tokyo)

He tried all possible rhetorical modes to soften her will, yet she remained hard-hearted. As a last resort, he made a promise: "I vow never to engage in anything like this again—ever! I know I'm asking you to compromise your principles, but won't you just please close your eyes and agree this one time?" With her grudging consent, off he flew to visit his patron. One more minute might have changed her mind, and that was a danger he could hardly risk.

I-4. HOW ZERAKU BADE FAREWELL TO HIS MISTRESS

The itinerary set and all preparations made, Zeraku wished to let his mistress of many years know about his trip and share with her tender moments of parting. Promenading around on the carriage of his own feet, he arrived at the lady's quarters. The whispered recollection of the two lovers about the beauty and sadness of things was soon punctuated by the repeated intrusions of messengers from the Mountain Hag, demanding Zeraku return home immediately. How could she have learned of his tryst so quickly? Zeraku was dumbfounded by the Mountain Hag's all-seeing surveillance! But since bewilderment bears

Zeraku tells his mistress of his plan and shares a tender goodbye, Volume 1, Episode 4. (Department of Japanese Linguistics, the University of Tokyo)

no benefit, there was nothing else for him to do but leave for home. Luckily for him, the Mountain Hag had gone next door on some errand, so he snuck off yet again, reuniting with his patron and readying their travel gear for the road.

The very next day, the eleventh of the eighth month, which happened to be the autumnal equinox, the master and servant set off on their journey.

III-1. HOW TOMONA FELL IN LOVE ON HIS WAY BACK FROM ARIMA HOT SPRINGS

After a pleasant stay at the hot springs, at the break of dawn on the sixth day of the ninth month the travelers left the inn. Although only a temporary lodging, the place had become so familiar that they found it hard to leave. They passed Segawa and Kōriyama, crossed the Akutagawa River, and traversed various hills, including Yamazaki. As they approached Mukō in the foothills on the western side of the mountain, the skyline of the capital came into view, and their hearts leaped for joy. They punted up the Katsura River, cutting a pictur-

Our Genji knockoff, Tomona, sees a great beauty who just happens to be in the window, Volume 3, Episode 1. (Tobacco and Salt Museum)

esque silhouette against the moonlight. As they were about to enter the metropolis by way of Tōji Temple, they caught sight of a village to the northwest. The houses were conspicuously ornate for the countryside, and the lily-white plaster walls of the storehouses suggested a district abuzz with men, all attracted by the seasonless bloom of beautiful, fragrant flowers not found on any tree.

They reached Seventh Avenue just as the sun was finally descending westward. There, lost in longing behind a curtained door, a woman sat blushing even to look at the men who walked to and fro before her house. Glimpsing her as he passed, Tomona was struck by her resemblance to the woman of his dreams! All this traveling and bathing to cleanse her image from his mind, only to refresh the very source of his old agony upon his return to the city! Tomona was about to blurt out, "What sort of lady lives here?" but such an inquiry might tarnish his reputation. Feigning indifference, he instead addressed Zeraku: "What's this street called?" Thanks to many years of experience in romantic matters, Zeraku quickly guessed what Tomona had in mind, replying to him with the same affected indifference.

On behalf of his master, Zeraku meets with the lady's mother to negotiate the financial side of the deal, Volume 3, Episode 2. (Tobacco and Salt Museum)

The day after Tomona returned home, the family held a seasonal celebration for Chrysanthemum Day. A stream of visitors kept Tomona's mind off his desire to know more about the lady he had spotted on Seventh Avenue. A few days later, unable to contain his interest any longer, he summoned Zeraku. "I have a good friend who lives on that street, so I'll ask him about the lady," Zeraku offered accommodatingly. "What luck!" exclaimed Tomona. "Do ask him as soon as you can." Repeated urgings by Tomona compelled Zeraku to take immediate action. That very day, a certain neighbor came by Zeraku's house to say: "The lady's the daughter of a masterless samurai. Although a very distinguished family, they've suffered misfortunes, as is often the case in this ever-changing world, so now the lady leads a desolate life." To Zeraku's queries, "Does she live with someone? Is she spoken for?" the response was, "Well, she's not engaged. Many men have made proposals, but she hesitates even to respond because she won't abandon her aging mother. Still, she can't live alone all her life…" Thinking to himself, "Master will want to hear this right away!" Zeraku swiftly returned to Tomona with his report. All the more in love, Tomona was inspired to write the lady about the history of his yearning and asked Zeraku to deliver the letter.

Zeraku, prefacing his request with endearing stories, persuaded the most influential resident of his street to deliver the letter. The lady felt it was the natural course of things for hidden longings to emerge this way, and the gentleman's writing did show far greater emotion than that of the run-of-the-mill love letter. And yet, from the start, she had resolved to remain in this place so long as her aging mother was alive. She thus replied curtly. The lady's delicately halting handwriting had Tomona exclaim to himself, "Such feminine writing!" as he fell even deeper in love, as though his heart were fluttering away.

Tomona continued to send love letters, but the response was always unfailingly the same: her duty to care for her mother prevented her from replying favorably. In the meantime, Zeraku managed to befriend the lady's mother! After hearing of Tomona's courtship, the mother spoke: "As you realize, I'm over sixty now, an old lady well past her prime. Even by the most optimistic reckoning, I can hope to see no more than twenty springs and autumns. Besides, concern for my daughter's fate is the one hold this world has on me— my only prayer, day and night, is that she'll have a good life. If what your master proposes is suitable for her, I'll leave her to his kindness. I ask that he from this moment give her all the advantages he would give a daughter or niece." Zeraku, delighted by the mother's cordial wish, assured her that all would go well for her daughter. With that, he returned home straightaway, but it was already the middle of the night.

III-2. HOW TOMONA AND THE WOMAN OF HIS DREAMS SHARED A PILLOW FOR THE FIRST TIME

Evening is the time when lovers long for each other "o'er the clouds," as they say, and bells toll at sunset and again at sunrise. In the meantime, unable to sleep, Tomona lamented that if only the bells would toll while he awaited his lover, at least he'd have something to look forward to. As that wasn't the case during that night, however, he shed endless tears, sinking into inconsolable grief. As if on cue, though, Zeraku returned to report what the mother had said. Exhilarated by the news, Tomona suddenly returned to a more youthful, even cheerful man. Impatient for dawn to break, he spilled his heart out in yet another love letter. As usual, Zeraku delivered it to the lady, who agreed to grant Tomona's wishes, knowing it would please her mother. This was an extraordinarily felicitous turn of events.

Out of all the days in the year, this was the finest: man and woman finally untying their under-sashes to lay together—an elegant scene, indeed! As they spoke about longings and sadness now past, they exchanged enough romantic talk in one night to fill one thousand. Even then, their emotions exceeded words. "Those noisy crows are detestable!" "Why is the sixth-hour bell being

Tomona and his beloved are happily "wedded," Volume 3, Episode 3. (Tobacco and Salt Museum)

rung already?" Still, endless sweet nothings are useless against the arrival of dawn. The woman's mother had been waiting outside for this moment. Her compassionate maternal sentiment was evident in her prayers for their ever-lasting love and prosperity. At breakfast, the lovers ate with zeal. How much more fulfilling to eat in a humble abode, famished from intense lovemaking, than to be treated to a full-course meal at some formal occasion at one's own mansion! Tomona, recalling the proverb, said: "Only those who have eaten both duck and pigeon know which is tastier!"

As another saying goes: "Even a cracked pot may find its lid." Recalling with embarrassment the burning passion of his earlier affairs, Tomona was elated to have at long last found his true love. Naturally, parting was hard the morning after sharing a pillow for the first time, especially since the two lovers had pined for each other for so long. Tomona turned again and again to gaze upon his ladylove, while she gazed upon him until his back disappeared from sight. "Why is it he's so in love with me after only a single night?" the woman wondered, drawn completely into Tomona's romantic notions. Tomona could hardly stop mumbling to himself about their night together, but his walk home was too brief to enjoy more than a fleeting reminiscence, and once home, he wandered about in a daze as if having stayed up all night in observation of some religious ceremony.

III-3. HOW KYŪSUKE BECAME GREEDY

The nature of women is to be suspicious of every little thing, and Tomona's wife was no exception. She felt agitated because, even after such a long absence, her husband continued to spend his days and nights away from home. Being a refined lady, she refrained from speaking of this matter directly, and so now it was her turn to "spend days lost in thought and nights sleeplessly," as the poem goes. One evening, the Mountain Hag called on Tomona's wife and, cloaked in the pretext of neighborhood gossip, dared to inquire of her, "Madam, why is it that you look so troubled?" As the madam spoke of Tomona's nightly outings, the Mountain Hag said, "That good-for-nothing of mine is to blame! Please tell your husband nothing. I'll use my resources and get to the bottom of this matter! And when I do, I'll speak to your father-in-law and make sure everything is to your liking. Leave it to me!" Returning home, she interrogated her husband, Zeraku, who, being at least a semblance of a man, did not easily yield to her leading questions. At this point, it seemed that the Mountain Hag had been foiled.

Still having her wits about her, though, she kept Zeraku under surveillance. Following her suggestion, Tomona's wife appointed spies to follow her husband too. Never suspecting a thing, Tomona carried on as usual, even scheming to move his paramour closer to home. The distance to Seventh Avenue being an inconvenience, he now wanted to look in on his lover even while out on short errands. Tomona and Zeraku met to discuss the relocation, using the pretense of a temple visit to get out of the house. "A servant called Kyūsuke, whose family has worked for us for generations, should be able to keep my sweetheart at his place," Tomona proposed. Zeraku, again acting as go-between, convinced Kyūsuke readily. Now Tomona would be able to visit his lady as often as he liked.

How is it conceivable that this Kyūsuke and his wife would, while serving their master this way, take advantage of the situation? Disgraceful, indeed! Convinced that nobody on earth could be more faithful to Tomona than they, the couple began to make all sorts of demands. The woman of his dreams in their hands, Tomona yielded, no matter how unreasonable their wishes were. Consequently, the couple became more emboldened, insisting on even greater rewards. When Tomona finally began to resist, Kyūsuke and his wife resolved to make trouble for him. To do so after having received the favor of the master's family for generations was truly shameful!

Tomona's servant Kyūsuke is as cunning as Iago, with the lady Kisa as his live-in Desdemona, Volume 3, Episode 4. (Tobacco and Salt Museum)

The lady in question, by the way, the woman of Tomona's dreams, was named Kisa. The first step of their scheme was for Kyūsuke and his wife to accuse Kisa of stealing silk cloth from them in order to sell it to someone else. Hearing their complaints, Tomona responded: "Such an accusation would distress my lady. If there's any chance it's true, she'll be so ashamed that there's no knowing what she'd do!" Being so hopelessly in love, he dared not mention this matter to her. His inaction angered the conniving couple even more. Determined to come between the two lovers, Kyūsuke reproached his master, Tomona: "Not only do you care for a woman who steals, but you're also practically calling us liars! We have no choice but to report this matter to your wife and your entire clan!" What an impudent statement coming from a servant! Tomona tried to appease them both by saying, "If you feel that way, I'm willing to give up my beloved lady so that there will be no further trouble." But Kyūsuke replied: "In that case, please put it in writing that you'll never so much as exchange words with that woman again in this life or the next!" Realizing he could mollify Kyūsuke and his wife only by breaking with Kisa, Tomona rationalized that the day would eventually come when he would see his love again. Still, he gave it one last shot by stressing the importance of loyalty between master and servant. Kyūsuke, however, having abandoned such lofty ideals, once more threatened to expose Tomona's affair to his wife and relatives, insisting he would not withdraw his demand for that promise in writing. His heart sinking, Tomona found himself forced to choose between ruining his reputation and parting from his dear Kisa forever.

Meanwhile, two of Tomona's old friends, Nakasato Shōbei and Shirakawa Yaemon, hearing about his troubles, visited Kyūsuke in order to look into the situation. After listening to the details, one of them said, "It's not like you, Kyūsuke, to behave this way!" Kyūsuke snapped back: "My wife and I are acting reasonably! We don't care if we're ruining our reputation and causing Lord Tomona a great deal of trouble, or if we all end up in hell. Go talk about right and wrong with somebody else!" Kyūsuke's doggedness appalled Tomona's friends, who gave up on the idea of reasoning with the man. They informed Tomona, "Given the predicament with your family, we advise you never to mention this to any of your relatives."

III-4. HOW THE LADY ATTEMPTED TO TAKE THE TONSURE

Saddest of all was the lady at the center of this imbroglio. As she listened to Kyūsuke's increasingly ludicrous accusations, her heart plummeted. Kyūsuke even declared, "If you break up with Tomona, we'll be happy to introduce you to someone far more affluent!"

"How can he say such a thing," it occurred to her, "when he's calling me a thief?" Yet, because she was in his custody, she could hardly talk back to him with such blunt words.

If she chose to end her relationship with Tomona for the sake of some other man, it would of course mean betraying his devotion. Either choice could only lead to tears! She would have to endure slander for as long as she remained among people of this secular world. Entering the apartments that Tomona had newly built for her, Kisa was seized by the desire to shave off her hair, becoming a nun. Grief had lately prevented her from coiffing up her hair properly anyway. Now she decided to dress up as she used to for Lord Tomona, adorning herself opulently, one last time in this life. Gazing upon herself in the mirror, she muttered, "How gaunt I've become! How cruel life's been to me!" Tearfully she smoothed out her hair, took it in one hand, and was about to shear it off . . . when suddenly a woman from next door who happened to be passing by stayed Kisa's hand, saying: "It's the way of the world that people rise and fall many times, and you're the kind of person who'll rise again and get what you want! So what's the use in such a pointless act? Young people are so rash!" As the neighbor woman scolded and consoled her, Kisa listened,

In the face of the false accusation, the lady attempts to take tonsure as many courtly women in *The Tale of Genji* do, Volume 3, Episode 5. (Tobacco and Salt Museum)

eventually abandoning the idea of becoming a nun. Nonetheless, she spent the following days in tears.

III-5. HOW KYŪSUKE'S WIFE EAVESDROPPED

Nakasato Shōbei and Shirakawa Yaemon advised Tomona: "What's happening here is outrageous. But Kyūsuke is unreasonable. A poor man's bitterness provokes his misbehavior, so be prepared to pay him off! If you don't, your liaison will be exposed to everyone in the world." Tomona agreed. The whole affair was hardly doing anything positive for his reputation to begin with. The two friends thereupon visited Kyūsuke, having decided along the way not to divulge the sum of money Tomona was willing to pay. Kyūsuke demanded, "If you'd like us to tolerate this situation, have Tomona pay us twenty *ryō* for our trouble." They managed to conclude the negotiation peaceably by paying only ten *ryō* and adding some nice-looking gifts to the money.

Just to please his friends, Tomona consented to give up his lover. This was a woman with whom he could live for a thousand years, yet his friends would have him part with her after less than six months! Tomona became so desperate that he summoned Zeraku and consulted him in private. Zeraku, eyes welled up with tears, observed: "Both Confucius and Buddha spoke strongly against straying deep into the Way of Love. But when we think in terms of human feeling, is there any creature—from birds soaring in the sky to animals running on the earth—who can go without love? Nevertheless, this advice coming from your two trusty old friends, you ought to cut off ties with the lady, at least for the time being. If you think it's unbearable to let her go far away, you could send her to serve a highborn nun in a temple for a year or two. I don't think something like that can be arranged right away, but in the meantime, just for several days, she could stay with someone we can trust." As Tomona learned later on, that someone they could trust meant Zeraku's own mistress. Since Zeraku had been taking care of all of Tomona's amorous affairs, Tomona felt he might as well enlist him to relocate his lady. Under the cover of night, they moved Kisa to the home of Zeraku's mistress. Before long, Tomona began visiting Kisa there, at the new hiding place, picking up once again exactly where he had left off.

One night, as darkness deepened and the insects stopped chirping in the gardens of Tomona's house, his wife suddenly heard footsteps along the fence. Thinking it strange, she followed the sound and found Kyūsuke's wife lurking about. Various noises during the day had enabled the intruder to hide, but night's stillness revealed her presence. Even though Kyūsuke had already plucked a great deal of money from his master's pocket, he still wanted to thwart Tomona's love affair, so he had sent his own wife to spy on Tomona's wife as well as his beloved. The conjugal love between Kyūsuke and his wife was so deep that their warped hearts beat in unison, and together they burned with envy as they dreamed up even more wicked schemes.

News of evil travels a thousand *ri,* as they say. Hearing about the scheming of Kyūsuke and his wife, Tomona's wife summoned the Mountain Hag to discuss the situation. The Mountain Hag, furious, threatened to expose the fact that her own husband's mistress was harboring his master's mistress, but the servants restrained her. Kyūsuke's malicious wife, however, took advantage of the wife's alarm, reporting what had happened and embellishing what had not. She expected to be rewarded handsomely, of course, for surely such a report would put her in the good graces of Tomona's wife. Instead, Tomona's wife rebuked both Kyūsuke and his wife: "You're most faithful servants. But if what you say has really happened, you should've informed me immediately! Instead, you sided with Master Tomona and have even provided lodging for his floozy. And now you report as if this was something new. You make it seem as though you act out of loyalty, but you're only trying to avenge yourselves on Tomona! Faithful servants would've let me know everything before I heard

Hearing about the latest developments from the master's wife, the Mountain Hag is about to dash off in fury, Volume 3, Episode 6. (Tobacco and Salt Museum)

about it elsewhere. Such a disloyal pair of servants shall never again be allowed to enter our house!"

Furious, Kyūsuke and his wife replied: "Well, then, to please you, we'll remove ourselves from your sight for good!" Thereupon, they returned home and locked the gate tightly. How shameful! Never admitting that they had deserved such treatment, they only loathed Tomona's mistress, Kisa, all the more. Hatred working deep within them, the couple were well on their way to becoming transmogrified into vengeful spirits bent on cursing the lady. How dark their hearts!

III-6. HOW THE LADY TORMENTED BY KYŪSUKE'S WIFE WAS DRIVEN TO DROWN HERSELF

Tomona's wife felt that her husband's surreptitious nightly visits to his mistress adversely affected their children. Being a clever woman, she came up with a plan. She surrounded herself with screens and pretended that the recent incident had seized her with a paroxysm of distress, rendering her unable to eat or drink. Tomona's parents and servants all lamented the family's sad fate.

Tomona had been ill the year before and, in addition to all the misfortunes that had befallen the family this year, his legitimate wife had now also taken ill. No amount of prayers offered to the gods and buddhas could produce any lucky signs.

Suspecting that Tomona's nocturnal outings had given rise to his wife's indisposition, Tomona's aunt encouraged her niece-in-law to speak without restraint. The ailing lady said, "I'm embarrassed to address such matters, but how can I keep anything from someone so concerned for me?" Listening to her story, the aunt replied: "Everything you say makes sense to me. I'll definitely admonish Tomona about this!" The wife, unconvinced, said, "It's a ridiculous infatuation, but Tomona cares for the woman above all else. If you talk with him, he'll pretend to break up with her only to appease you, but she'll remain in the depths of his heart, so he's bound to go back to her sooner or later." "How, then," asked the aunt, "can we calm your anger and clear your suspicions?" The wife answered: "If it's not too much trouble, please have him sign a note promising that he'll never lay eyes on that woman again."

No part of his lawful wife's request going against common sense, the aunt spoke to Tomona about the matter. Although Tomona was convinced that, rationally speaking, the request made perfect sense, he could still not bear to part with his beloved lady. He appealed to his aunt to be spared from such a dreadful punishment, but she refused unequivocally. "I may have to refrain from sharing a bed with her," he thought to himself, "but the chance should arise for me to see her one way or another." Tomona pleaded for the right to have only a glimpse of his love occasionally, but his aunt found such bargaining tedious. "Of course, what you say is true enough," conceded Tomona. "But were I to sign a pledge never to see her again, I'd have to fear divine punishment even when laying eyes on her on the street unintentionally." His aunt replied, "In that case, we can amend the pledge so that you'll never lay *hands* on her!" Tomona countered, "That's exactly what I'm driving at! When walking in the dark of night, how can I be sure that my hand might not accidentally brush against hers?"

Finally, after many other groundless excuses, Tomona consented that he would never let "a drop of bodily fluid" pass between him and his mistress. Now, it has been known since time immemorial that merchants are wont to haggle over prices. But here was a merchant driving a hard bargain over a written pledge. What an extraordinary love affair! Tomona continued to rendezvous with the lady, of course, but from that moment on, he merely sat gazing at her. It was like visiting a mountain heap of treasure only to go home empty-handed.

In the meantime, with fierce anger and vindictive supplications, Kyūsuke's wife invoked every deity in town—cursing Tomona's beloved lady. Although

The living spirit of Kyūsuke's wife, like Lady Rokujō's in *The Tale of Genji*, is exorcised to reveal her monstrous self, Volume 3, Episode 7. (Tobacco and Salt Museum)

the gods themselves never grant malicious wishes, there are lesser demons in their families who do. How could such demons miss a chance to cast evil spells on someone? Old romances are brimming with people doomed by magic, and Kisa suddenly began to tremble and speak deliriously, as though subject to some cruel curse—no doubt brought on by the living spirit of Kyūsuke's wife. Tomona called upon distinguished and noble exorcists; he made offerings at holy temples and shrines. Perhaps on account of the sincere prayers of the exorcists did the vengeful spirit appear on the altar, though it promptly left after screeching incomprehensibly.

Overjoyed by the result, Tomona once again visited all the holy places to offer his gratitude. Once the news of the mysterious illness and miraculous cure had reached her, Kyūsuke's wife mumbled to herself, "I could've taken that woman's life! What a shame!" With bared teeth and bulging eyes, she faced the rising sun and prayed to the demons in all directions, beseeching, "Even if you toss me into a most unthinkable fate in the future, let me accomplish my heartfelt wish today!" Biting on a ceremonial jinxing wand, she drove nails into the sacred tree on the grounds of Nanatsuno Shrine and scattered the shrine's holy sand to seal her curse. As Kyūsuke's wife relentlessly attacked, heedless of her own eternal damnation, a sense of life's insignificance overwhelmed Kisa, who decided to throw herself into the nearest river.

What a pitiful woman! Once she had made the decision, she stealthily inquired about the depth of various waters. One person said, "There's a bottomless spot near the Seta Bridge." Vowing to herself to find that spot one way or another, Kisa asked, "Please, where's this Seta Bridge you mention?" The reply: "It's on the way to Ise." Having received directions, Kisa snuck out of the house at dawn and turned toward Seta. Merely hearing this would move anyone to tears. She gazed one last time at the face of the moon, which had been a familiar sight for her and Tomona. She thought, "What a sad world it is!" and tears drenched not only her sleeves but also her collar and the front of her kimono all the way down to her toes! Crossing the Kamo River where ducks quack mournfully, she thought of the uncertainty of the life to come.

She passed Awata and Hinooka and was filled with loneliness while traversing the heartrending landscape of Oguruma and windblown Yokogi. Any hope of seeing her beloved vanished as she crossed the Osaka Barrier and walked toward Seta along wind-rippled Lake Biwa. Resting under a tree, she picked up stones to weigh down her sleeves. Approaching the deep water near the bridge, she knelt, then bowed to the ten directions, offering her prayers. She had heard this was the place where the Dragon King's seven-year-old daughter had been reborn into the Pure Land, thanks to the sutras offered by the bodhisattva Monju. People said that this exact spot marked the gate of the Dragon King's palace. "What deep karma enmeshes me!" she thought as she plunged into the water while chanting *The Lotus Sutra*. Her chanting voice reached the depths of the water far below.

Seeing her plunge in, a passerby enlisted others to help save her. It goes without saying that it is almost impossible to find a body in a stream running as swift as an arrow shot from the bow of a great archer. It therefore took some time before they brought Kisa to shore. By then, she was no longer of this world. People shed tears, thinking of old tales like the tragic death of a man falling from a bridge in Sano on his way to visit his lover. The stories of her death that witnesses told to their families and other loved ones were so profuse that they can hardly be related here.

Just then, a certain physician named Genteki—an old friend of Tomona—happened to be passing by on his way home from visiting the Grand Shrines at Ise. Seeing a crowd gathered on the road, he stopped. The dead woman and her clothes seemed so familiar to him that he inspected the corpse more closely. In the pocket of her kimono he found a poem, which he recognized as an old *waka* that Tomona had included with a gift of clothing sent to the lady during their separation.

"Never to meet again..."
I long at least to whisper
Into your own ear
And spare you that message,
Delivered by a strange hand.

In the old days, the poet Fujiwara no Michimasa secretly visited a lover. Because spies and guards were ordered to follow him, he was unable to see the lady as he wished. Given the close watch of his every movement, he composed this poem to explain that there was no way for him to see her. Although he would have to give her up, he longed to tell her as much himself, rather than through some messenger. Sadness overflows from the words he composed.

Now, because Genteki was a physician, he attempted to revive Tomona's lady, using all the possible techniques of medical science, but his attempts were futile. Being a virtuous man, he was saddened even by the death of a stranger, so his grief was beyond imagining as he beheld this woman beloved by his dear friend. He entrusted her body to an inconspicuous little temple nearby and rushed back to Kyoto without stopping to catch his breath.

Kisa's drowned body is found by the Seta Bridge. Unlike Ukifune in *The Tale of Genji*, she cannot be revived, Volume 3, Episode 8. (Tobacco and Salt Museum)

Tomona had sent people to search for the lady, but upon hearing Genteki's account, he had his men bring her corpse back to Kyoto, where he offered the most ceremonious memorial in her honor. The woman's mother could hardly hear the story to the end before she went blind with tears of grief.

It is said that the dead are forgotten a little more with each passing day. And yet Tomona's sorrow only increased as time passed by. His attempts to observe adequate funeral rites were frustrated because the affair had to remain secret. In a daze, he spent the seven days after her death in mourning and would dine only with his closest friends.

III-7. HOW THE LADY WENT TO NIRVANA, THANKS TO THE HOLY EFFECTS OF THE SUTRA

Life is like the step of a sheep: uncertain, slow-moving, but incessant. The forty-ninth-day memorial held after the lady's death passed quickly, and now it was the one-hundredth-day service. The holy priest from a famous temple was invited to continuously chant the eight volumes of *The Lotus Sutra,* which had been much cherished by the deceased. In addition, the priest later made

Kisa, now the buddha of their dreams, descends with other gods on seven-colored clouds to bless Tomona, Zeraku, and all, Volume 3, Episode 9. (Tobacco and Salt Museum)

offerings to other priests and beggars in her honor. Indeed, *The Lotus Sutra* is the king of all sutras. By its virtue, which is higher than any mountain and deeper than any ocean, the deceased immediately turned into a man, a required path for enlightenment in the Buddhist tradition. This deity then appeared as an enlightened buddha within the dreams of twenty-two people, including Tomona, his wife, Zeraku, his Mountain Hag, and many others among their servants and acquaintances who had something to do with the whole affair. Even in this heartless world, they say, the sutra's holy words have an everlasting effect. All who witnessed this transformation came to follow *The Lotus Sutra,* and each and every one of them achieved enlightenment. As they had given a heartfelt burial to the deceased, she appeared in their dreams as her old self and promised to become a guardian deity for them all. Indeed, Tomona's lover guarded his fortune, and it is said that his family flourished for generations.

Such is an example of something mysterious and holy that can indeed happen in this world.

TRANSLATED BY SUMIE JONES

Puppets of Passion

EARLY EDO SONGS

Like *gidayū,* the other genre of *jōruri* are, first and foremost, vocal music. That's not to say that they are a cappella or exclusively vocal music; rather, they are music in which voice and texts play a vital part. In that way, *jōruri* belongs to a large family of Japanese musical traditions. Its individual genres of *itchū-bushi, katō-bushi, bungo-bushi, tokiwazu, kiyomoto, shinnai,* and so on are varieties of music in which a chanter tells a story, taking the roles of each of his characters as well as that of a narrator. I use the male pronoun here, not unconsciously, but in the awareness that most professional *tayū,* or chanters, in both contemporary and traditional Japan are male.

Gidayū is one of the oldest of the *jōruri* genres mentioned so far, and it commands a historical as well as a modern prominence. There are many masterpieces in the genre, but the fact that it is performed most characteristically in connection with the puppet theater, today called *bunraku,* has also given it a fame that overshadows its *jōruri* cousins.

Most of the other genres of *jōruri* have had roles in kabuki performance, but their vitality was traditionally assured by having a broader performative context—in private recitals or party performances—and by spreading to sig-nificant amateur practitioners.

Although most of these genres are little known today except to people with a particular interest in traditional Japanese music, in their heyday they were perfectly familiar to the public. There seems to have been something of a star phenomenon with many of them, and the genres themselves generally take their names from specific individuals who found fame or notoriety in performance of the eponymous genres.

Miyako Itchū (1650–1724), who worked for some time with the most celebrated of all *jōruri* writers, Chikamatsu, was himself successful in Kyoto and Osaka in the early eighteenth century. Satsuma Geki I (d. 1672), one of the early *jōruri* chanters in Edo, invented *ōsatsuma-bushi,* which was incorpo-rated into the Edo-style *nagauta,* and had his moment in the limelight in the late seventeenth to early eighteenth century. Once he was gone, his genre faded away too. In other cases, however, the genres created by these ephemeral stars established themselves and continue to be performed to the present day.

Bungo-bushi is named after Miyakoji Bungonojō (1660–1740) and became so popular that his long black coat and high topknot were imitated by men and women in town. This encouraged the appearance of women chant-ers who turned into the so-called geisha performers. Miyakoji Bungonojō provides an example of an individual *jōruri* star whose genre of performance died with him, even as he must also be counted as one of the most successful progenitors of *jōruri* as a whole. Although his own performances were pro-scribed by the shogunate in 1737, his legacy was inherited by a tremendously talented group of his disciples who each went on to sow the seeds of important genres of *jōruri,* most of which survive into the twenty-first century. When Bungonojō left Kamigata for Nagoya and eventually Edo, he left behind a dis-ciple named Miyakoji Sonohachi I (dates unknown), who founded *miyasono-bushi,* or *sonohachi-bushi.* Another disciple, Tokiwazu Mojidayū I (1709–1781), was the founder of *tokiwazu-bushi,* and yet another disciple, Tomimoto Buzen no Jō I (1716–1764), created *tomimoto-bushi* (which in turn gave birth to *kiyomoto-bushi*). Finally, Tsuruga Shinnai (1714–1774), another of his dis-ciples, in partnership with a superbly talented vocalist, created the genre *shinnai.* In late-Edo fiction and theater, *shinnai,* which was spread by door-to-door performers, was often associated with the fate of attempted suicides and disowned children.

It's difficult to keep all these genres of *jōruri* straight today, and some, like *tomimoto,* have for the most part given over their identity to other genres, but even in the eighteenth century there was apparently confusion, as well as a concomitant interest in making distinctions between genres. A comic verse of the time reads:

Dress pants for *geki-bushi*
and long ones for *gidayū,*
for *han-dayū,* it's an overcoat,
and for *katō-bushi,* a two-piece suit.
Bungo-bushi's buck naked,
now, ain't that cute!

༄ (**TH**) ༄

LOVEBIRDS' FIRST JOURNEY

KON HACHIRŌEMON

"Lovebirds' First Journey" (Hiyoku no Hatsutabi) is a ballad that was popular as *bungo-bushi* that turned into *shinnai*. The performers claim that the piece, which remains in their repertory, is the closest we can get to the work of Bungonojō. For that reason, it is the first piece translated here.

The story, which led to versions in other genres of *jōruri* as well, concerns the ill-fated couple Shinbei and Kojorō in the Mikuni pleasure district in Echizen. As is frequently the case in the stories of *jōruri,* money plays a central role in this story. Shinbei has been unable to settle his debts with a brothel, where he was accustomed to meeting Kojorō. So, according to the district's custom, he has been imprisoned in an upturned wooden bathtub, a capsule-hotel version of debtor's prison outside the establishment. Most of the piece takes place with him locked away in the tub, with access to the world only through a small window cut in its side. Outside the window, his lover, Kojorō, shares with him the misery of his situation. The pathetic tone of her lines as well as her hopelessness in not being able to save him make this song one of the most tear-jerking pieces in the genre.

That Shinbei is a well-known merchant in town makes this song atypical of a *shinnai,* in which the chief characters are downtrodden nobodies. Instead, it echoes the theme in Saikaku's and other prose fiction, in which the sons of the rich ruin the family fortune by frequenting brothels. Unlike Shinbei's historical existence, Kojorō's is questionable at best, and she may be a product of the imagination representing a beautiful and passionate courtesan who might have inhabited a nostalgically old district such as this one.

The *kuruwa,* or entertainment district, of Mikuni was said to be the greatest of pleasure quarters in northern Japan. Mikuni, however, was a local setting, unlike Shimabara and Shinmachi, the two well-known districts in Kyoto and Osaka the song refers to. In comparison, Mikuni is far from the highly developed districts in larger cities, making the impossible embarrassment of Shinbei plausible and Kojorō's grief more heart-wrenching. The reconciliation suggested at the end of the song is not as happy or as tragic as a story taking place in an urban district.

(TH)

Love eddies and splashes like the swell of the sea, on payday here in Passion's Port—why, the capital itself doesn't have anything more on offer than this: Mikuni, that special part of town, with girls galore, the best in all the North Country!

Give yourself over to a lady's love on a houseboat—there's hardly a visitor who hasn't dropped his anchor there, and among them all, it's Shinbei of the Tamaya Stores who catches the eye.

Just as the vespers' bell begins to sound, he comes in, anxious in his thoughts, for time is the enemy of the floating world, they say, and time after time he's been asked to settle his accounts, but all his plans have brought him down, now this:

"Farewell to all that savoir faire; it's into confinement in an upturned wooden bathtub. What agony!"

Tears well up in Shinbei's eyes. "How could I have done this! I've been well known to the town here as Shinbei of the Tamaya Stores, but, out of passion, all my worth frittered away to nothing more than a worm or a snail, confined here in a wooden tub; the darkness of passion shuts out the very light of day." Yet to be in this very part of town where she lives, the one fine lady of the night that he so wants to meet or even just to see, and not to be able to look for her out of fear of the Madam and her minions—he bobbed his head in and out of a hole cut in the tub, like a bobble-headed doll on the end of a novelty writing brush. "I wonder if I can't get a look at her, maybe today." He sticks his head out of the hole, weeping with yearning, no end in sight to the downpour of tears.

Just then, from deep inside one of the houses, three of the most prominent girls in the Quarter, Kikukawa, Wakamurasaki, and Kojorō, top-notch girls all, step outside for a breather. They send the master back inside, and Kojorō, her love as deep as a river, plummets in her thoughts out of anxiety for her man and can't face the shame of meeting people on the street; she's so drenched with tears and dank with desperation that she calls to mind a weeping bush clover covered in dewdrops and withered in the wind—

A barrel becomes a debtor's prison for a brothel patron: cover of "Lovebirds' First Journey."
(Reproduction anonymously provided by a publisher)

The Madam has a good sense of things, and Kojorō's companions can read her mood: "There's nobody to entertain just now, so take a little break while you can."

Happy to sneak away, she heads out back with a show of thanks, then turns away.

There's the upturned tub. She draws near, "Shin, it's me, Kojorō. I had a chance to get away, so I've come to see you.

> "This law of the *kuruwa* is so cruel.
> When I heard that they were going to lock you into a bathtub
> I nearly gagged, imagine how I felt:
> What shame, what mortification!
> How sad, oh how sorry I feel for you.
> What a disgrace, what suffering!
> That Shinbei of the renowned Tamaya,
> somebody with a reputation,
> should be put in such a situation
> here, in the hustle and bustle of the Quarter,
> just for a shortage of cash—
> What mortification, oh, what shame!

> "In Shimabara in the capital or Shinmachi in Osaka,
> a top-notch *tayū* would set her pride aside
> and beg for a loan from one of her customers—

there'd be some way to get through this,
but me, I'm in the same profession
and I have a pretty good reputation,
but with your troubles in business
and our relation known to one and all,
the locals don't seem to want to patronize me anymore,
so there's no one I can even ask for money.

"My nerves are all strung out,
No matter how I struggle for a way out,
My mind is just threadbare.
You say it's your fault, but I'm oh so downhearted and sad.
In parents' eyes, a woman like me is just there to seduce their sons,
other people's kids, and pull them into bad ways,
and disgrace the young and lead them into grief
without the slightest excuse.
Your own mother must be feeling just this way,
I bet she's got nothing but contempt for me,
she must just hate me, she must want to shred me limb from limb,
I bet she hates me just that much."

"That more than anything else makes me so sad," said she, and grabbed hold of the
tub in a deluge of misery, whereupon Shinbei poked his tearstained face out,
blinking repeatedly as if he'd just come up out of the bathwater—and spoke under
his breath,

"You saw through to the depths of my heart,
that's how we fell in love, so to have come to this,
and to die imprisoned in the bathtub here—
if that will set you free
and you will pray for my repose after death,
that's the best I could ever hope for," he sobbed.

"Oh, it hurts to hear you talk like that.
How ever could I go on living
being who I am,
and having brought you to this misery,
having so defamed you in the Quarter,...
but what good would it do you for me to die!
I would sell my very body piece by piece
if somehow I could save you from these trials."

She cast about for some kind of a plan
and threw herself upon the mercy of the Madam:

> "I don't care if it means heading east to Karatsu, Sotonohama, or up to the
>   castle town of Matsumae
> where the aborigines abound,
> or off to Maruyama in Nagasaki out west,
> where you have to service the Chinamen—what a dreary fate!—or even south
>   to Awajishima.
> Even if I rot from the waist on down,
> if I can just get the money we need,
> then I won't resist a posting to Akita up north
> or the mines of Sado, even as a street whore."

She made the force of her intent clear to the mistress,
who replied,

> "Don't worry. I've taken your position into good account
> and found a way to come to a settlement here."

By that night she had an agreement with the house and now had no idea where
she would end up, so she came for a last goodbye.

> "I've got to see your face once more," she said,
> and clung to the side of the tub, weeping all the while,
> but how cruel, even as she tried to hold him close,
> the bathtub stood between them and there was nothing to do but bring face
>   to face, cheek to cheek in a rain of tears, and you couldn't help but feel
>   their pain, just to see the sight.

TRANSLATED BY TOM HARE

EVENING MIST OVER MOUNT ASAMA

HARA BUDAYŪ

The *itchū-bushi* song "Evening Mist over Mount Asama" (Yūgasumi Asa-magatake) draws from a scene in the kabuki play *The Courtesan and Mount Asama* (*Keisei Asamagatake*), first performed onstage in 1698 in Kyoto, featuring the star actor Nakamura Shichisaburō I (1662–1708). The production drew a sizable crowd because it claimed a connection to the famous Asama festival in Kyoto by including the name of the mountain in the title. The play was about the suicides of samurai Ozasa Tomoenojō and his courtesan lover Ōshū, woven into a typical revenge drama surrounding a missing family treasure. According to the traditional belief, the burning of love pledges exchanged between the lovers conjures up the living ghost of Ōshū from within the smoke. This scene inspired many songs and dance plays that came to be called "Asama pieces."

The festivity and the theatrical production not only enhanced the appeal of the story but, at the same time, fueled the song itself. In 1734, when the play was presented in Edo, it featured Segawa Kikunojō I (1693–1749) as Ōshū and Sawamura Sōjurō I (1675–1734) as her lover, with music composed by Hara Budayū (1697–1776?), chanted by Miyako Hidetayū Senchū (d. 1765) accompanied on the shamisen by Takagi Joyū (dates unknown). The *itchū-bushi* version presented here, "Evening Mist over Mount Asama," proved such a phenomenal hit in Edo that crowds of amateurs rushed to take lessons in performing *itchū-bushi*. "In all Edo," the saying went, "there's not a single house without mouse droppings and a copy of this song." Thereafter, "Asama pieces" appeared not only in *itchū-bushi* but also in *katō-bushi, tokiwazu, tomimoto,* and *kiyomoto,* the last of which was based on the *tomimoto* version.

Ozasa Tomoenojō could also be called Kyō no Jirō, and Ōshū was named Togire no Koman, depending on the version. In the one translated here, these alternate names are used. Although I have unified the male role under the name "Kyō no Jirō," I have retained the change from "Togire no Koman" to "Ōshū," because the change of names marks the boundary between Jirō's longing and his hallucinatory vision of his dead lover.

The voices articulated in the song are kaleidoscopic. Jirō doesn't know his own mind, so he argues with himself, and then, when the vision of Ōshū takes center stage, a new set of voices appears, Ōshū's own, in the dramatic present, with her recollection of their past history, using direct quotations. Add to this an impersonal narrative voice, and the result is a remarkably sophisticated and complex reimagining of the Asamagatake ghost vision. The text is richly allusive and, among other things, quotes the celebrated nō play *Eguchi* at its most philosophical: "For as long as we live, at times we're dyed by passion, / And it's no shallow hold that wanting takes on our intent."

(TH)

Oh, how sharp the yearning when the past is brought to mind!
As months give way to years, checkpoints mark the passing time,
Even before the barrier guard knows it, blossoms give way to the gale

And then to white snow, night after night.
But it melts away in the madder light of the rising sun,
Just as lovers' bickering through the night stiffens into silence;
The couple goes estranged like lovebirds separated by a mountain crag.

Jirō Sukeshige from Kyoto takes his brush in hand sorrowfully
To sketch the figure of a woman, with tears welling up like rain clouds blanketing
    the sky:
And he gives his thoughts over to Togire no Koman,
The very one, says Jirō to himself,
She who met a sad and unexpected fate, like a dewdrop in a tempest over an
    ocean reef.
My own fault, thought he. The fire of his passionate regret arose
Like the undying smoke from Mount Fuji.

The moment he throws her pledges of love into the fire,
Out of the trail of smoke that rises from an incense pot nearby,
Her spirit takes form, just as she looked in the old days of the pleasure quarter,
Wearing her robes one on top of the other, the very image of Ōshū:

> [ŌSHŪ:] "Love and resentment alike linger on. I suspected all along you were
>   unfaithful,
> But now your love for me is all gone—so cruel,
> What a bitter blow, the tears stream down.
> How could you have soiled my name with such unmerited rumor
> And given me over to the smoke!"

Resent her though he did, he longed for her still, and there:
The exact image of her flickered before him, from long ago,
When they were so in love, the way she held up the hem of her robe
As they walked out together, and the old Quarter, so familiar, came back to him.
That was the last day he saw her sweet unchanging smile.

The streams of a river cleave like the branches of a tree
And run on and on but never go back to their source.
Yet a blotch of ink dropped into the water
Can be beautiful when transposed to paper:
Charming faces mirrored in full flower, such a pair!
But the pair doesn't last.

[ŌSHŪ:] "You see this hair of mine, fallen in a tangle after our quarrel?
Like tittering plovers flapping their wings—"

[JIRŌ:] "And you hiding my jacket to hold me back and make me feel bad!
With that pipe in your hands and the moon glowing above,
As the memento of that final night of our love."

[ŌSHŪ:] "The dawn came as you pleaded, forgive me, please, forgive me!
I knew it all along, but all the same, we piled the covers over ourselves.
I would show you how I cried, and you'd try to peek in,
Or try to cheer me up by singing
And plucking your shamisen on the upstroke…
If I could only get you to listen to one of every ten things I said,
That pine tree on the mountains, far away, would grow a deeper green,
To rival the evening mist, thick on the heights of Asama Mountain.

[ŌSHŪ:] "The clock in my heart ticks round and round
And already it's the sixth hour at dawn.
Of a thousand or two or even three, there'd just be one man for me!
That was my pledge and my pleasure,
Springing up like the fresh green of the season when our names were linked
        the first time,
But fated to be with you, what pain, what sadness, what a shame!
And what's to become of the one who was deceived?
Give that a thought! For if it seems so real you can't forget it,
It's still just the empty folly of a picture."

[JIRŌ:] "Indeed, for as long as we live, at times we're dyed by passion,
And it's no shallow hold that wanting takes on our intent.
Deep in a secluded room from the second floor,
    the sound of her heavy hem flopping stair by stair as down she runs:
"I won't let you go," she says and pulls me back by the sleeve,
I shake her off and down cascades her hair, like a cluster of kerria roses
Scattering forth, and whose pale blue clothes would those be?
No reply to that, the gardenia guards her confidence,
And goes as deaf to my questions as the Peak of Old Earless.
After all the trouble we went to, pledging our love to gods,
With sacred wands and blessings—I've heard all that before!
I reached out to touch her back, but the sound was hollow,
Like the night wind clapping at the bedroom door, as it is inclined to do.

> I shudder at the shimmer of her willowy hair; the comb running through it
> Should be in its box, and though I can't see her shape, there's a single voice
> *Coocooroo,* off goes the little warbler, and I'm wet with tears."

Azaleas, crimson red right here,
And over there, bright white baubles,
Camellias falling off the bushes, scattered on the ground,
Dewdrops raining off the leaves down low,
But hardly so much as a whiff of her now,
And the harder you look, the fainter the shadow grows…
As under a misty moon, she vanishes
Like a puff of pollen showering off a butterfly wing,
As it flutters into the grass to disappear.
No matter how I stretch and reach,
Away she goes. She's gone.

TRANSLATED BY TOM HARE

TO TORIBE MOUNTAIN

ANONYMOUS

"To Toribe Mountain" (Toribeyama, 1706) is the most frequently recorded piece in the repertory of *sonohachi-bushi,* originated by Sonohachi, one of Bungonojō's progeny from Kyoto. The genre is also known as *miyasono-bushi,* reflecting the sociopolitical tensions attendant on its early years. Miyakoji Sonohachi was Miyakoji Bungonojō's disciple, and he established himself securely in the world of Kyoto performance after Bungonojō had left for Nagoya and eventually Edo.

Once Bungonojō's fortunes declined and his performances were banned in 1739 for sparking real-life imitators, his disciples in Edo struck out on their own, with new names like "Tokiwazu" and "Tomimoto," which didn't bear the taint of their master's. Sonohachi, in Kansai, maintained his claim on his lineage, as Miyakoji Sonohachi, but his successor took a new tack as Miyasono Ranpōken. The genre has had its ups and downs historically. Ranpōken's early successes in Edo failed to secure him an immediate following, but the genre reappeared and continues to the present, its artistic line recently maintained, uncharacteristically, by female *iemoto* (school heads).

"To Toribe Mountain" is far and away the most famous piece in all the

Sonohachi repertory. Accounts of the history of the piece vary, but it seems to begin with the real-life love suicide of a samurai and a prostitute from Gion in Kyoto in 1626. A song focused on the two lovers setting off to their deaths became popular and was expanded into a longer song by none other than Chikamatsu Monzaemon, of *gidayū* fame, with music by Koide Kinshirō in 1688. The song was incorporated in 1706 into a kabuki play. It seems to have taken its present form, more or less, by 1766.

Toribe Mountain (also known as Toribe Moor, or Toribeno), in southeastern Kyoto near the celebrated Kiyomizu Temple, had been known as a cremation site for many centuries. Even though it isn't described in the piece, the place-name itself would have created an immediate sense of sadness and foreboding in all listeners. *The Love Suicides at Kasane Izutsu Brothel* (*Shinjū Kasane Izutsu*), mentioned near the end of the piece, is a 1707 play by Chikamatsu.

Coming first as one,
then two together, setting off for the World of Bliss, the Pure Land,
as the bell from Kiyomizu sounds:
Evening's done,
The bell tolls ten;
By midnight
Under black unfigured skies,
hearts go dark in the shadows of Love's Path.
Nuinosuke stitched into a fateful link to Ukihashi,
first in faint infatuation, somehow it suddenly turned to love.
The two of them imagined they could marry and be a proper man and wife,
but thinking didn't make it so,
So in exasperation and despair, the pair gave up on the fickle world:
On, then, to Toribe Moor.
Against her pale skin, an under-robe of pristine white,
and over that a purple gown with wisteria crests,
Wrapped 'round in a black satin obi
lined with crimson plain weave on a figured twill:
She, at seventeen, in this first blossoming of youth,
was thirsty like a flower for the rain.
And for his part, her lover wore, next to his skin,
a short-sleeved white kimono,
then a figured black satin robe lined with pale blue,
eager he, at twenty-one, at the height of his vigor,
to cast his life adrift in a scuttled skiff

called love, with no isle in sight
where the two might come to harbor.

Ukihashi recalled her parents,
whose every question had once chafed and nagged at her,
But now she thought how hard it would be for them, once she was gone,
and she felt she wanted to turn back from this pass.
She fell down weeping into her sleeves,
And through her tears called out, "O Father, Mother Dear…"
And then she said to Nuinosuke:

> "It must be just the same for you,
> Who made us into these unfilial miscreants,
> Ready to subject our parents to such agony?

> "It must have been the go-between called passion,
> or maybe it was the pillow we shared that's to blame.
> Love falls outside all your expectations.
> That's just how the Madam put it, or something like that, last night
> when she gave me a piece of her mind:
> 'It's only because true love exists
> that we put up with the nasty work we have to do,
> just for the sake of the special customer whom we love.
> If your love is really fast and true,
> you should be satisfied with three rendezvous
> instead of five, or one instead of two.
> Then the proprietor wouldn't get upset;
> there'd be no breaking yourself down for 'love,'
> no more double suicides,
> no more slander on the family name for money or misbehavior,
> with money or a name for misbehavior—
> no more dying for love.
> Passion is the first step toward obsession,
> and when it's at its height, anything that gets in the way
> is as hateful as a palanquin coming to rouse you in the morning.
> Bittersweet, the exchange of poems on parting
> by the morning glories,
> but what frustration when being apart drags on
> until the moonflowers open at nightfall!
> It's all bitter suffering then,
> nothing the way you want.

How sad it is, how crushing,
even with life and death staring you in the face,
But you have to hold back the ardor of youth
and stop being rash."

On she went like that, with a better sermon than the one in *Kasane Izutsu,*
but for all her savoir faire,

"I was too far gone,
lost in my thoughts about you, so I just sat there amused by it.
I've made a mess of things,
sabotaged your responsibility
to your parents and the world out there. Forgive me!"

And with that she clung to him and wept.
And when he held her tight and she felt him next to her
and told him all that was over now and couldn't be undone—

[*Taking turns:*] "Forget all that. Don't cry."
"No, I won't cry, but what about your parents?"
"No, what about yours?"
"No, yours…"

They gazed into each other's eyes,
And burst into tears, step by step inching closer to the end.
Like a spring snow melting away over the moor;
the temple bell's already fallen still,
the night descended, white, on Toribe Moor
as their road comes to its end there.

TRANSLATED BY TOM HARE

A PUPPET MASTER OF THE FLOATING WORLD
SATSUMANOJŌ GEKI

There are several different songs among the various genres of *jōruri* about puppeteers plying their trades in the streets, with portable stages in which they hang marionettes and act out stories for passersby. The oldest datable example was apparently created in the 1670s or 1680s by one Satsumanojō I,

Geki. His *geki-bushi* recitations were popular in the late seventeenth century in Edo but died out in the 1720s and 1730s. Before that, though, his school made an impression on other forms of *jōruri* and *nagauta,* and its characteristic melodic styles can still be heard in those genres.

"A Puppet Master of the Floating World" (Ukiyo Kairaishi, 1718) began as a *geki-bushi* piece but was transmitted by Satsumanojō Geki to Masumi Katō in the 1670s or 1680s and then transposed according to the conventions of *katō-bushi* to become a central piece in the repertory of the latter, as well as a representative piece of Edo-style *jōruri.*

The piece is a briefly sketched picture of an itinerant puppeteer who carries on his back the tools of his livelihood, a box of puppets that can serve as dressing room and stage for them, and makes his living as a street performer. The description of his performance here gives us a picture of Edo street life but also contains a couple of extra touches in an allusion to a haiku by Takarai Kikaku (1661–1707) and a conventional expression of celebration and gratitude for the regime in its last lines. The haiku reads:

> Gentle spring rains.
> A puppeteer carries
> his green room on his back.

⌢ (TH) ⌢

Our wearying occupations in this floating world
point off to the Western Sea,
And so the puppet master ranges far and wide,
beyond his home near the tidal shrine of Ebisu,
to ply his vocation in provinces both near and far.
Today he wanders off from his companions and,
under a gentle spring shower,
walks along with his dressing room on his head.
From a window in a garden wall,
a voice calls out, catching his attention,
and when he stops there
he finds a pretty servant girl with a request:
"Play us a piece, Mr. Puppet Master."
And before she can even finish asking, he begins to sing,
with a gravelly voice to a rhythm beaten out
upon the puppet case:
one by one the puppets make their entrances,
each with a little ditty to sing, what fun!

西宮傀儡師。余社領今日神と狙ふひと漢名維お城を窺ふ飾陳盃と敷へのごと笑人を作る乞を飲將單十君を躬ふおし傀儡のこゝろなり

A puppet master entertains a crowd of children. From Shimokawabe Ikei, *Famous Places of Settsu*, 1796. (National Diet Library)

"On the fields of Okura stands a clump of plume grass,
when its flower blooms,
it's the flora of love, eventually shedding its mourning dew,
which would wilt and wither it away.
The wildcat in the foot-dragging mountains
has a long, long tail,
but oh, how could I sleep alone for the long, long night?
A wife, last night I took a wife!
Her scythe cuts well, and before its blade all grasses fall,
she'll make me a good old wife
and I don't mean to brag,
but she sews so nicely and
weaves as well, right well, indeed.
Twill damask and multicolored weave and
figured satin with gold,

and from our sweet interludes together,
three sons, the treasures of our family:
the eldest son and heir
he's a big-hearted one,
hands in his pockets,
speak to him and won't reply.
The second boy is tall.
The third is full of mischief,
And, but six or seven, at his worst,
but he's a full-blooded kid, and too cute to resist.
Piggyback, we tour the sites of the capital,
here and there, a pinwheel in his hand,
a papier-mâché toy, a pretty little drum,
a rattle on a stick,
there, you take it and have fun!
If it's blossoms you want, then off to Yoshino,
put a blossom-covered sunshade on your head,
Aren't we slim and smart!
This servant's got a bamboo *sake* flask,
wrapped up in his sleeve,
and he's draining it to the last drop.
Now the sky's clear and blue,
so off to find some cherry boughs
before dark falls."

With that, the puppet master
packs up his box and heads off,
ending with a word of praise for the regime:

"How fortunate for all of us to live
under a reign that gathers in fine silks and
brocades in tribute to its benevolence."

TRANSLATED BY TOM HARE

Passions among Men

Mongrel Essays in Idleness

KONOE NOBUHIRO

*M*ongrel Essays in Idleness (*Inu Tsurezure*), written in 1619, is a work ex-tolling the love of youths from the perspective of an adult samurai who was once, in his own youth, the object of the amorous attentions of older men. The narrator conveys with wit and enthusiasm his opinions and prejudices about this "Way of Love," recounting gossipy tidbits from the past and offer-ing advice to young men, from the hindsight of his mature years, about how they ought to behave and comport themselves in response to the men who would love them. At times the essays read as bittersweet memoir, at other times as instructional primers on letter writing and other practical issues; in other passages still, the work waxes philosophical, drawing indiscriminately on Buddhist and Confucian ideas to argue its points.

In all this, *Mongrel Essays in Idleness* reflects a conscious imitation and reworking of Yoshida Kenkō's *Essays in Idleness* (*Tsurezuregusa,* ca. 1331), a popular work of opinion and recollection written in the essayistic mode (*zui-hitsu*) by a man of the court who idealized courtliness in the tumultuous early years of the fourteenth century, when samurai warriors held sway over the land. The celebrated opening line of *Essays in Idleness* reads: "In my tedium, I spent the day facing my inkstone, writing down aimless thoughts as they came to me, and what a strange feeling of sadness it brought." In a close parody, the opening line of *Mongrel* reads: "In my tedium I shut myself in my room and, facing my inkstone, wrote down whatever nonsense came to mind; such silliness had me splitting my sides with laughter." Clearly, the *Mongrel*'s author is bent on humor and entertainment in this and other reiterations of revered lines and themes throughout Kenkō's text.

The "mongrel" (*inu*, literally "dog") of the title reflects a debt to comic linked verse (*haikai no renga*), in particular to the founding text of that poetic tradition, *Mongrel Tsukuba Collection* (*Inu Tsukubashū*), compiled between 1524 and 1539 by Yamazaki Sōkan (1460–1553). In contrast to the formal and somewhat restrictive court tradition of *waka* composition that traces its beginnings to the first imperial anthology, *Poems Old and New* (*Kokin Wakashū*, ca. 920), comic linked verse flourished in the fifteenth century because it permitted a variety of themes and poetic diction that could only be described as "comical" in the liberties it took with *waka* convention. Certainly, the author of the *Mongrel* passages that are translated here wanted to exploit all the connotations of irreverence and unconventionality inherent in the *haikai* tradition when he titled his text *Mongrel Essays in Idleness.*

Scholarly speculation as to the identity of the author of *Mongrel* has settled on Konoe Nobuhiro (1599–1649), a member of a distinguished noble family, or possibly a close attendant to him. If Nobuhiro was indeed the author, he would have been only twenty-one years old at the time he finished writing it in 1619. In that case, the apparent wisdom of the adult narrator of the text represents a pose for the young Nobuhiro, who would probably have only attained adulthood a year or two earlier when he was in his late teens, according to the custom of the day. In any case, his lively account of the mores of male love in the early years of the seventeenth century found an avid audience with the book's publication in 1653, four years after his death. The text's popularity appears never to have waned among the cognoscenti of the eighteenth, nineteenth, and early twentieth centuries, as attested by the surviving copies of the woodblock edition of *Mongrel* that can be traced to the personal libraries of such literary luminaries as Ryūtei Tanehiko, Ōta Nanpo, Edogawa Ranpo, and others.

Mongrel Essays in Idleness survives in two forms: as a fifty-two-section manuscript, dated 1619, and in a revised and illustrated sixty-two-section book first published from woodblocks in 1653. One of the illustrations depicts the opening lines of the preface with the samurai author seated at his desk and engaged in writing the text we are reading, and the second depicts some of the corrupting behaviors the author (in section 6) warns youths to avoid—namely, gambling with dice and arm wrestling.

〜(PGS)〜

PREFACE

In my tedium I shut myself in my room and, facing my inkstone, wrote down whatever nonsense came to mind; such silliness had me splitting my sides with laughter.

Alas, from the moment a man is born into this world he must work without respite, for time is precious and there are many tasks to be accomplished. If he fails to govern well in all matters, what then? He may fall recklessly in love with a young man, dissipate his energies in his prime, and expend quantities of paper and ink for no benefit at all, utterly wasting his allotted life span of one hundred years, or he may break the law of the land and forget his duty to honor his parents, living each day without a thought of tomorrow. It is in his youth that a man brings ruin upon himself.

Even so, there is nothing in this world that can compare with the allure of a handsome youth, dressed well but without appearing overly fussy, whose robes exude a long-lasting fragrance. A few stray locks of hair frame his face. He greets you with a smile when you pass and winks with a knowing look, as if perceiving your thoughts. He speaks only when spoken to, and then shyly and in a low voice. He chooses his words hesitantly and avoids countrified speech. His movements are slow and deliberate; he is friendly and anxious to please. He serves *sake* in an unrushed manner that makes a man feel completely at ease. Such a youth is impossible to resist.

(1) A gem, unless it is properly cut and polished, is no better than a lump of stone or a roof tile, for its brilliance will not show. Stones and roof tiles have many practical uses, but a gem that shows no brilliance is of no use whatsoever. To be truly human, a person must train himself to behave properly. Even if endowed by nature with great physical beauty, a person with an unrefined heart is no better than a gem in the rough.

(2) A man may be instantly attracted to a youth, but unless he goes ahead and strikes up an acquaintance with him, their love will never grow. For that reason, if a man is even slightly interested in a youth, he ought not hesitate to inquire from the youth's close friends what he is truly like and then take the first opportunity to speak to him directly.

(3) Since the human heart is not straightforward, people are not always without deceit. But has there ever been a man who was dishonest about love? Once a man has sworn his love before the gods, a youth ought not question his sincerity further. Spend a night or two in lovemaking and it will become clear if this is true love or just a passing fancy.

(4) Kenkō was absolutely right when he wrote, "What is to be gained by living a long life and allowing the ugliness of old age to overtake us?" In his youth, a young man's beauty is such that he is inclined to feel that all eyes are on him and that he is the sole object of men's desire. He is fearless in his contempt for those he considers beneath himself and speaks his mind without restraint. But the days of his youth are like the span of a dream—their reality is fleeting. His beauty gradually begins to fade and, ashamed to show himself in public, he thinks only of avoiding people. All that remains is the bitter memory of his own cruel-heartedness.

(5) There are many ways to fall in love with a youth. Some men fall in love with the heart, others are attracted by beauty, and for others still it is neither heart nor beauty but something unidentifiable that inspires them to fall in love without knowing why. Each case is different. For that reason, it is not right to scrutinize a youth who is loved by a man and make judgments about that man's choice.

(6) No youth ought to appear to be overly skilled in the arts or he risks losing his appeal. Even if he is highly accomplished, it is better to keep his mastery to himself. Likewise, when he speaks, he ought to do so quietly. It is unseemly to speak too loudly or too much. He also ought to avoid becoming addicted to board games. If he does so, it will lead to nothing but violent behavior and quarrelsome words. It is only a vulgar man who enjoys wagering, and such behavior is highly uncouth. Such people eventually lose all sense of decorum and start singing and dancing wildly. In the end they test their strength in arm wrestling, which always leads to resentment and anger. Is this not what the text of the *Analects* warns against when it says, "Superhuman strength brings chaos to the heart"?

(7) Should the reply to a man's love letter be written in a poor hand and the details be difficult to decipher, it still brings him more pleasure to struggle through lines written from the heart than to read effortlessly through a shallow letter written in a fine hand.

(8) Feelings of various kinds figure in all paths of human endeavor, but nowhere do feelings run more deeply than in the Way of the Youth. A single night of lovemaking, though its pleasures last but an instant, will remain in a man's memory until the day he dies. No text has adequately conveyed the depths of this Way, nor are there poems that do it justice. There is no mention of the Way of the Youth in the age of *The Ten Thousand Leaves*, when the emperors reigned in Nara; likewise, there are many

love poems in the imperial anthologies that have appeared each generation since the time of Emperor Daigo, beginning with *Poems Old and New,* but not one is addressed to a youth. Only in the poetry collection known as *The New Collection of Poems Old and New* and compiled in a certain reign by Fujiwara no Teika was I able to discover a single love poem written by a certain priest—his name escapes me—and addressed to "a beloved boy." All courtiers practiced poetic composition; could it be that they knew nothing of this Way of Love, or did they simply prefer to ignore it? Yet a legend tells us that it was Kūkai of Mount Kōya who first transmitted the love of youths to this land. There are even reports that when Ariwara no Narihira was still a lad going by the name of Mandara, Kūkai bestowed his love on him as his disciple. This Way of Love survived over time, so that when Kumagai met Atsumori in battle at Ichinotani, a single glimpse of the youth's beauty moved him to renounce the world. Likewise, Musashibō Benkei served his master, Minamoto no Kurō Yoshitsune, and in the end gave his life for him at Koromogawa; and when Taira no Tsunemasa fled the capital, an acolyte at Ninna Temple who grieved that they must part wrote him a sorrowful poem of farewell. Such examples prove that the men of old did not ignore this Way of Love completely. It seems to me, on further reflection, that those fellows in ancient times were simply ignorant of its pleasures and that is why they failed to write about it in their poems.

No man sends a love letter unless he is seriously in love and can no longer bear to keep his feelings to himself. Even if a youth has difficulty getting permission to meet the man, he at least ought to write a long and detailed reply. Until his messenger returns, the man will be waiting impatiently, unable to put his mind to anything else.

(9) There is nothing as exquisite as a youth's deeply scented bedcovers, even compared with the everyday fragrance of his scented robes. But if a man arrives for a visit, rushing to scent the bedclothes with incense is worse than not receiving him. In such a case, just leave them as they are. A certain man once told me that there is no real benefit to perfuming one's hair and robes; far better to keep oneself clean at all times so as not to exude any odor at all. Another man once told me that identical advice appears in a text by the name of *Book of Beauties,* if I remember correctly.

(10) A book called *White Jewels* defines a youth as between the ages of seven and twenty-five. Most of us would probably prefer to place him between the ages of fifteen and thirty.

(11) They say that people, especially young men, are apt to judge a potential
suitor based on his wealth. Not just young men, but people in general,
seem to be influenced by such factors when they fall in love. For example,
a youth of average looks will be swamped with proposals if he comes
from a wealthy family, whereas a truly handsome youth may have no
suitors at all simply because he happens to serve as a low-ranking attendant or has no silk jacket and walks around in soiled robes. Most men,
being hopelessly shallow, observe the status of such youths and reject
them. On the other hand, there are instances of older men who pay attention to the youth's person instead of appearance. For that reason, a
youth will sometimes show love to a recluse such as myself. When I
reflect on this fact, I realize anew what a rare and precious thing is the
heart of a youth.

(12) No matter how beautiful the face of a youth might be, if he comes from
the merchant or artisan classes, it is questionable for a samurai to fall in
love with him. Of course, there are bound to be some youths of those
classes who possess an upright nature, so perhaps it is unfair to make
such a categorical statement. It may be no more than a shameful sign of
my own personal prejudices.

(13) The temple precinct of Mount Kōya is strictly forbidden to women.
Perhaps for that reason it is said that no female trees or bamboo stalks
grow there and that all birds and beasts there are male. The dogs on Mount
Kōya can be observed to pursue young male dogs. A man who knows the
situation firsthand told me that when a dog is in love, he leaves a portion
of the food that people give him for the other dog to eat. What a strange
and very charming story. The compassion of dogs puts men to shame.

(14) The world is full of mysteries that defy my comprehension. For example,
I will never understand what lies in the heart of a man that drives him to
his ruin over a youth. He avoids the company of women, whom the
Buddha provided to bring pleasure to mankind, and instead prefers this
Way of Love—truly incomprehensible! This form of affection was first
practiced by priests, and today laymen have usurped it. As a result, this
Way of Love has lost favor with priests lately.

  First of all, it brings suffering to the Buddha's body. Next, it gives
satisfaction only to oneself, while bringing grief to the heart of the other
person. For that reason, it breaks one of the six commandments—
namely, the one against inflicting pain on others. Both of these show
disregard for the Buddha's orders.

Moreover, a youth of great beauty will attract not only one's own love but the love of other men as well. This easily leads to resentment and anger, and one man will end up plotting to kill another. Murdering a man breaks one of the most important commandments of all.

A man walks stealthily to avoid detection and slips through gaps in a wall or fence just to find out more about a youth, or sends someone else to do so. Sometimes he himself stands behind a youth's house and listens in secret to what is going on inside. Such behavior is no better than thievery.

Moreover, a man in love invariably develops a taste for drink. Drink becomes a broom that he needs every day to sweep away his gloom, but it is impossible to escape its terrible consequences: drunkenness leads to nothing but constant lies, boasting, and two-tongued duplicity. Such a man is angry one moment and happy the next, like blossoms at the mercy of a storm or like a bird flitting from branch to branch. In the morning he might feel nothing but resentment for the youth and refuse to speak to him, but by evening a single word makes him forgive it all. Is this not evidence of an unenlightened heart? Not only has he lost self-control, but he commits a sin that the Buddha admonished against—namely, the sin of lust. Such a man refuses to listen to the admonishment of his parents, turns his back on the Buddha's teachings, and ends up committing the ten evils and five recompenses. His sin is deep indeed.

(15) It is also interesting that Tetsumon, Chief Priest of Nanzen Temple, once said that the words "I love you" no longer have any meaning.

(16) One morning after a lovely snowfall, a friend sent a poem asking me how I was enjoying the first snow of the year. At the time I thought nothing of it, but now he is dead, and whenever it snows, I recall the incident with pangs of emotion. It made an unforgettable impression on me.

(17) At quiet times, I think wistfully of a past that is gone forever. One night, when everyone else had gone to bed, I whiled away the hours sorting through old correspondences, determined to dispose of all my letters. Among them were several love letters I had received from a certain man in my youth, and reading them made me feel as if I were young again. Thinking of my present ugly state, I wanted to weep with shame. I must have been quite a beauty in my youth, for the man wrote over and over again in sincere hopes of meeting me. Despite his sincerity, I refused him. In retrospect, I must have done so because I thought my youthful good

looks would last forever. Even if my regret were as great as a mountain, I could not rectify the mistake.

Years do not confront us face on but creep up on us from behind. After the age of twenty, the speed with which the years go by is as swift as a three-feathered arrow. The accomplishments of youth become fond memories in old age. I wish I could convey this truth to young men nowadays, but they always reject it as the foolish words of an old man. They shall learn soon enough.

(18) It is said that a gentleman loves a man of wisdom, while a petty man loves a man of wealth. These words can be applied to all things. Perhaps because the world has become a more enlightened place today, youths with enlightened minds are attracted to men of sophistication, but, as always, the vulgar hearts of unenlightened youths still respond to the words of rich men. That is how it seems to me, at any rate.

(19) It is written in a certain book whose title I have forgotten: "They say that the Way of the Youth neither despises poverty nor considers a lack of money to be stylish. And yet it is no pleasure to take a youth to bed with you under a torn paper robe. Since poverty is an obstacle to the pursuit of any of the various Ways, if a man is poor, he ought to refrain from this Way of Love." I find this most amusing.

(20) It is disgraceful for a youth of tender years to drink *sake*. His behavior when he is drunk is sad to watch, even for a man who has no interest in him, so it is easy to imagine how painful it must be for the man who loves him. Therefore, he must never allow himself to lose control. Nevertheless, it is uncouth to refuse a cup of *sake* that is offered or to sternly reject a cup from another who says, "You haven't had much; do drink just a little more." It is best not to abstain completely from drink. A youth who can hold his *sake* is full of interesting surprises. There are times when he may reveal himself in ways you've never seen, or unexpectedly shower you with the deepest affection.

(21) A youth ought to be ignorant of women. He ought not even mention them in ordinary conversation. Even if others talk about them, it is best if he acts as though he knows nothing about the subject.

(22) Ikkyū of Daitokuji Temple wrote Chinese verses about all manner of things that can be seen and touched. Of all these things, it was this Way of Love that he appreciated the most.

Monju Shiri first opened the way,
Kōbō of Kongō followed it anew,
It has neither yin nor yang,
But is like a circle without end.
People who enter therein exclaim,
"What pleasure!"

Since this Way of Love was transmitted by Kōbō, the men of this land ought to remember it in their hearts.

(23) Any man worthy of being called a samurai studies the dual path of the pen and the sword and keeps always in mind the virtues of courage, wisdom, righteousness, trust, and loyalty. This goes without saying. In addition, no man should ever forget the heart of the Way of the Youth, even in his old age. If a man does forget, then proper conduct of the heart, friendly social relations, and gentleness of speech shall elude him completely.

(24) I once read a book of poems composed in response to debates on a wide variety of subjects. One of them addressed the question of whether it is happier to dream that you met a lover or to get a letter from him.

A brief glimpse
of a lover's letter;
how can seeing him
in a dream
compare?

This judgment makes perfect sense. Nothing compares to the happy feeling of receiving an unexpected letter.

(25) There is no one around today who has survived to the age of eighty thousand years; that is why they say that life is as fleeting as a dream, finished in an instant. Nonetheless, when I look back on my life and count all the changes I have seen, I am struck by how long the past seems. Although pleasant memories have grown dim, I still vividly recall each and every disgrace I suffered. This is why the past seems easily forgotten and yet regrets seem to deepen over time.

(26) There was a man who was plagued with strong feelings for a youth. Many years went by, during which time he showed him plenty of outward

kindness but failed to consummate his true feelings. Before long, the blossom of his heartache scattered and his longing grew faint, resembling a person in thin robes who, contemplating the moon, is pierced by autumn gusts; and in the end the resentment that once showed white like the windblown leaves of the arrowroot vine became a field of shallow hemp. The leaves of words spoken in secret dried up completely. He felt annoyed whenever he encountered the youth, as if he were being pelted by hailstones, and his flesh would crawl in disgust.

(27) It is possible to fall in love with someone within a dream. I have wondered for a long time how this works. What happens is that your feelings for someone are still hidden deep inside and you cannot tell him how you feel. Then he appears clearly within a dream, and in the morning when you awaken, your desire for him is so unbearable that you feel you must send him a letter. Am I the only one who has felt this way?

(28) There are three types of men that a youth finds irresistible: the first is a daimyo; the second is a handsome man of approximately his own age; the third is a man who is generous with gifts. There are five he despises: paupers, men with big tools, old men, men who criticize, and men who are slow in their affection.

(29) You sometimes hear of a youth a bit past his prime who gives in to a man's overtures. From the viewpoint of an outsider, this may appear odd and even a bit humorous, but if you put yourself in the youth's position, perhaps he had no choice but to accept because the man was so persuasive. Particularly if the man is a lord or another important personage whom the youth serves, the youth can hardly refuse, since the man has approached him mindful of what others might think. On the other hand, intervening to put a stop to the relationship would only make them both look bad. In any case, it appears that even a youth of advanced years can be the object of passionate love. I'm embarrassed to say so, but it is very funny.

(30) It is best if a youth's handwriting is somewhat indistinct. If the shape of every letter is written clearly and boldly in black ink, it holds little interest. Even if the youth is a fine calligrapher, in this Way of Love it is important for a youth to write hesitantly when responding to a love letter. Not to write at all, however, would be too cruel and does not inspire deep love.

(31) In our country it is called the Way of the Youth, in Great Tang it was given the name of "the Mistaken Way," and today in China they refer to it as "gargoyle roof tiles." When lying on top of each other, two men really do look like demon roof tiles interlocked!

(32) Sometimes a man will confess his love for a youth and get no response at all. After the matter has been forgotten, the man might find himself once again attracted to the youth, but no matter how longingly he may look at him, it is never with the same intense emotions he felt the first time around. He cannot believe that he once felt so strongly for the youth and recalls with awkward embarrassment the things he must have said to him earlier. A man does not fully appreciate the pleasure of having been loved in his youth until he has passed the age of thirty.

(33) Master Banri wrote about this Way of Love in a text from the Ōnin and Bunshō eras [1466–1468]. In that book, he states: "Young men speak of self-cultivation, but they do not question if a man's feelings are sincere or insincere. Their main concern is whether he is rich or whether they may derive fame or fortune by loving him. They choose high-ranking men to be their lovers and shun those of the lower ranks." So things were the same in those days.

(34) There is nothing more humiliating for a highborn youth than having a man of low birth and insignificant rank fall in love with him. Such a man rarely has an opportunity to bathe, so his skin will be as rough as driftwood. His hair is dirty and tangled like matted grass. He owns only a single robe, so in winter he is as cold as the snow and ice. He cannot make a stealthy rendezvous by carriage, because he does not own one. Instead, he walks through muddy streets and must rinse his feet before boldly entering the youth's house. He has hardly wrapped his cotton undergarment about his hips and gotten settled at the youth's side when he starts to berate him. At other times, he arrives drunk and teary-eyed. There is nothing worse than the smell of his drunken breath. Determined to show that he is in love, he pulls the youth against his bare skin with a strong grip, now and then wiping his runny nose. Just to imagine such a scene is humiliating. He complains about his petty problems, making sure all the while that the youth knows he is not asleep, so that he can engage him in lengthy conversation. He sticks out his rough tongue to lick him from his fingertips to his heels, saying, "Give me your ass." They both feel the urge, though the man enjoys it when the youth offers a little

resistance. "Let's sleep," he says, and as they lie side by side afterwards, he strokes the youth's body with his long, dirty fingernails. Lest the youth abandon him forever, such a man had better watch out. He leaves before dawn and the next morning struggles to pen a poem using old words looked up for the occasion. Rather than have his silly letter be read with all of its clumsy phrases, he would be better off sending nothing at all, letting bygones be bygones, forgetting all about the youth if possible.

(35) They say that the flower of love in the human heart withers easily when buffeted by the wind. On the other hand, there is an old adage: "Love that is from the beginning attentive to the possibility of its ending never fails." This should stand as a universal truth.

(36) When close friends have gathered to enjoy themselves and the *sake* cups have gone the rounds, nothing is more beautiful than a handsome young man softly raising his voice in song. Such a sound is superior to all other pleasures in life. The mournful sound of a bamboo flute or the frost-brittle cries of insects are ugly in comparison and painful to the ears.

(37) It is not necessary to be overly fastidious about hiding letters that are not about love, but these days young men deliberately flaunt letters from their admirers in order to get noticed. Such behavior is disgraceful. A letter may have been written to look as inconspicuous as possible, and even if it elicited only a single sentence in reply, it was surely written from the depths of the heart, higher than the highest mountain and deeper than the deepest sea. Anyone capable of feeling ought to be able to recognize the writer's sincerity at a glance. How cruel it would be to let others know the letter's contents. No love letter should ever be read lightly and discarded in such a way. It is much preferable to secure the letter where no one else will find it.

(38) A man who seeks rebirth in paradise must practice the three teachings and strive to achieve enlightenment. If he practices these and becomes enlightened to this Way of Love, he will without fail attain the rare pleasures of the Way of the Youth. Single-hearted devotion makes this Way like enlightenment in the three teachings. No other path can match the Way of the Youth for teaching a man how to focus wholeheartedly on a single cause; through it, he separates himself from personal desires as well as from two-heartedness based on calculations. There is no path more beautiful for a man's soul. For that reason, those who would prefer this wonderful teaching were welcomed with joy by the great teacher of

Shingon Buddhism of this land, who told them that he would lead them into the very center of paradise.

TRANSLATED BY PAUL GORDON SCHALOW

Male Colors Pickled with Pepperleaf Shoots
URUSHIYA ENSAI

Ihara Saikaku, author of *The Great Mirror of Male Love* (*Nanshoku Ōkagami*, 1687), was certainly not the first to write stories on the theme of *nanshoku*, or "male colors," referring to male homoeroticism. He, however, was a trendsetter in the sense that he explored realism in the genre of floating-world fiction. This bestseller was followed by a number of short-story collections that dealt exclusively, or in significant part, with the theme of male-male eros. Regrettably, most remain to be translated into English.

Such collections of short narratives helped consolidate the various contemporary popular ideals and norms that surrounded the pursuit of "male colors," a term that often appeared as the first word in many of their titles. Those stories provided contemporary models of behavior in male love by depicting normative conventions, but in a humorous light. On the one hand, such stories articulated homoerotic desire according to the period's hierarchical representation of classes, but it also claimed the universality of such desire among all social and occupational classes. *Nanshoku* was conventionally contrasted with *nyoshoku* (female colors) referring to love of women at the pleasure quarters. Such writers as Nishizawa Ippū (1665–1731) and Ejima Kiseki (1666–1735) highlighted the competing attractions that were available to male connoisseurs of the "floating world" of erotic pleasures. They deliberately interspersed, and implicitly contrasted, accounts of male-male and male-female interaction, sometimes alternating one after the other in a contrapuntal fashion.

The fundamental assumption of such works was that "male colors" and "female colors" were competitive, yet not necessarily mutually exclusive, avenues of pleasure and refinement for the adult male. These erotic debates both emulated and parodied traditional debates, religious and philosophical. They offered ample room to each to preach the merits of his preferred mode of diversion (always constructed as a chosen pastime rather than an innate orientation) and to raise questions as to the taste (rather than the morality) of his rivals. *Nanshoku* writings developed a misogynistic component in their disgust with traits of women, such as sloppiness, selfishness, and cowardice, which offset the virtues of young men, such as cleanliness, selflessness, and courage.

"How a Pledge of Undying Love Was Reborn" (Nisei to Chikaishi Sairai no En), translated here, derives from one such anthology, *Male Colors Pickled with Pepperleaf Shoots* (*Nanshoku Kinomezuke*), which was published by the Osaka bookseller Nakamura Zenshichirō in 1702. About its author, Urushiya Ensai (pen name "Jinenbō," dates unknown), little is known except what meager clues the collection's preface provides. In it, Urushiya claims to have been born in the vicinity of Otokoyama—an origin that is poetically appropriate, given its literal meaning of "Male Mountain." The family name suggests an artisanal background. The supratitle (*tsunogaki*) that precedes the main title of *Male Colors Pickled with Pepperleaf Shoots*—"Warriors, Peasants, Artisans, Merchants" (Shi-nō-kō-shō)—explicitly invokes the four official classes of the Edo-period status hierarchy. Thus foregrounding the diverse social origins of the stories' characters, Urushiya stresses the universality of male-male eroticism (likewise a theme of Saikaku's *Great Mirror of Male Love*) while appealing to a similarly broad audience. Urushiya's book also shares with *nanshoku* fiction more generally a taste for extraordinary tales that entertain readers through novelty and comic exaggeration—conversely helping to define the norms of social practice—and a religious frame that authorizes male-male erotic desire in spiritual (typically Buddhist) terms.

Readers today may be interested in this story because it furnishes a vivid contrast with modern narratives of (male) "homosexuality," in which male-male erotic desire is often stigmatized and concealed. The erotic union of two males that stands at the center of "Undying Love" is far from being an object of (self-)revulsion and censure. In fact, it is depicted as being carried out quite openly and even receives varying degrees of encouragement from the other figures in the narrative. The latter characters personify several forms of conventional authority, ranging from the warrior bureaucracy (the district magistrate) to the Buddhist clergy (the master of the temple) to ordinary parents—the key institutions, as it were, of patriarchy.

This lack of evident social stigma contrasts even more with modern sensibilities if one takes into account the ages of the fictional characters involved. The proper object of adult male longing was not another man but instead a preadult male belonging to the category of "youth," or *wakashu,* the equivalent of today's teenagers. In "Undying Love," the adult monk's love object is a mere fourteen years or so of age. Yet far from being cast as the sacrilegious and illegal corruption of a minor, the bond between them is portrayed as a pedagogical boon, blessed with both parental and spiritual approval. Nevertheless, even by Edo-period standards, the second part of the tale is unconventional. Here, the issue of age, so critical to *nanshoku* ethics and aesthetics, manifests itself in an extreme form, and the tone of the narrative blends pious awe with irreverent absurdity.

The story contrasts in interesting ways with earlier forms of narrative as well. Of particular relevance is the genre known to literary historians as *chigo monogatari*, or acolyte tales, which flourished from the fourteenth to the sixteenth century. Narratives of this type centered around love affairs between adult monks and *chigo*, who were preadult males commonly sent by their lay (often samurai) families to spend time in a Buddhist temple so as to receive an education. In most cases, the tale eventually revealed the young love interest to be a manifestation of a bodhisattva, who had in effect "staged" a tragic romance with the monk in order to awaken him to the ultimate futility of earthly desires. "Undying Love," while similarly laden with religious motifs, remains to the end focused on distinctly this-worldly preoccupations, a tendency shared by floating-world fiction in general.

(GMP)

HOW A PLEDGE OF UNDYING LOVE WAS REBORN

A BUDDHIST IMAGE CERTIFIES THE RETURN OF THE BELOVED, AND A LOVER'S FINGER PROVES MEDICINE FOR A BABY

"This feeling of longing, how can I ever forget," a certain poet has written. This persistent love seeker would never lament thus over a woman.

Great metaphors like "the mountain of swords" and "the sea of rough beaches" are possible only in male love. Nearby, in the town of Nanao, stands Jōkōin Temple of the Pure Land sect. Here resided a student monk by the name of Shunchi, who was deeply versed in Buddhist learning. He was a man of humble means. There were many nights when he would borrow the lamp from the altar of the temple in order to pore over Buddhist texts. And when the clergy took leave of the temple during the summer, Shunchi continued his studies in the countryside, taking with him all the books and manuscripts that he had managed to accumulate, packed assiduously in a few wooden boxes.

In the neighboring village of Yamura lived a district magistrate by the name of Ichinomiya Jūnojō. Naminosuke, his son, had been coming to the temple since the spring of his fourteenth year in order to receive an education, and he became Shunchi's pupil. Shunchi instructed the youth in reading and writing, teaching him such works as *The Imagawa Precepts for Children*. Among the lessons he imparted was that a youth was to be valued not on account of his beauty but because of his feelings for his older lover, and that the youth should be devoted to his older lover not because the latter gives him gifts but because he shows the depth of his affection. Innocent jests soon bloomed into a serious attachment. Naminosuke took the monk as his lover, while Shunchi looked after Naminosuke no less dotingly than if he were his younger brother. In time, Naminosuke's parents and Shunchi's master at the temple came to know of the relationship. Recognizing the strength of the couple's devotion, however, they raised no objections.

His disciple having met favor with Jūnojō and his wife, the master found his temple designated an official resting place for the daimyo's business. Over a mile's distance separated the temple and the magistrate's home. Yet rarely did Shunchi send Naminosuke on his way alone. If the sun had set, Naminosuke would remain and sleep in Shunchi's quarters, or if the youth needed to return to his family, Shunchi would accompany him and spend the night there. Each yearned for the company of the other, and hardly a day went by without a visit. So things went until the end of the autumn of the youth's sixteenth year.

For some reason, Naminosuke did not show his face at the temple for two or three days. One evening, well after the seventh hour, he finally appeared. Shunchi was nowhere to be seen in the main reception area of the temple but had shut himself up in his own quarters, looking forlornly out a small window with a sliding paper screen. The monk gazed at the fields behind the temple, where the buckwheat already bore white flowers and the leaves on the eggplant branches had begun to turn yellow. The cry of insects busily issued from the fronds of pampas grass, their voices laden with sadness. Shunchi's thoughts turned to Naminosuke as he reflected on the impermanence of life.

Naminosuke did not enter the monastery but instead stood outside the window, silently observing his friend. "It's been a while," said the monk. "Aren't you coming inside? It's been lonely around here." The youth responded, "I wasn't feeling very well, which is why I haven't been able to visit for some time. Are things all right with you? I don't really have time to talk tonight. I must go to Kōmyōji Temple early tomorrow to participate in a ritual ceremony. I came because there was something I wanted to ask of you. That little amulet that you own, with the holy inscription by Hōnen, could you please lend it to me for two or three days? In exchange I've brought you this." Naminosuke handed Shunchi an image of the bodhisattva Amida made by the sculptor Eshin. The figure was wrapped in a silken cloth, instead of being enclosed in the usual small chest.

"I'd be happy to lend the amulet to you," said Shunchi, "but this is all very sudden. Won't you please come inside?"

"No, I'd rather that you came out here. If I go inside, then I'll feel like spending the night. I shouldn't want to do anything impure before the ritual."

"I see," said Shunchi. "In that case, at least make sure to stop by after the ceremony tomorrow." Naminosuke remained with his face cast downward, uttering something vague.

Taking the amulet from the bookcase where he kept it, Shunchi unfastened the crimson drawstring with which it was bound. He related the object's provenance, as he had done many times before. "While Hōnen was in residence at Ōhara, he made this amulet for the mother of Kumagai Kojirō. It has great magical powers." Naminosuke accepted the amulet from Shunchi, expressing his thanks. He bade farewell and took his leave, not by way of the gate, but rather through a row of cedars in the direction of the cemetery.

Shunchi thought it all very strange. "Wait," he cried, "I'll see you home." Grabbing his robe from the pole where it hung, he rushed out the door. It took him a few minutes to find his clogs, which had gone astray. By the time Shunchi left the temple, Naminosuke was nowhere to be seen. Shunchi hurried to the residence of Ichinomiya Jūnojō. It was nearly the fifth hour when he arrived.

Shunchi entered Naminosuke's room by the garden path, as he always did. But things seemed somehow out of the ordinary. Perplexed, Shunchi went out into the sitting room, then peered into the kitchen. There he found Jūnojō and his wife, beside themselves with grief. "We've just sent someone to find you," they exclaimed.

"What has happened?" inquired the bewildered Shunchi.

"Earlier today, well past the seventh hour, Naminosuke suddenly took a turn for the worse. He's no longer with us!" The parents wailed.

Things simply didn't make sense. Shunchi shared with Jūnojō and his wife the details of what had happened to him in the previous hours. Taking out the figure of Amida, he showed it to them. "That is indeed the protective image that Naminosuke cherished ever since he was a little boy," they confirmed. "He always hated to let go of it." When they opened the little chest that usually held the image, the shelf was empty.

It was clearly a case of a departing soul fulfilling one last wish before continuing on its way. They surmised that the amulet inscribed by Hōnen must surely be inside the coffin where Naminosuke's body lay. This latter-day miracle proved true when later they opened the lid of the coffin and looked inside. Everything seemed normal, except that the corpse was holding something in the palm of its left hand. The barest edge of a strip of paper could be seen.

The strangeness of the incident moved all.

Naminosuke's body was interred at Kōmyōji, and soon the funeral rites ended. Shunchi realized that all was transient in this floating world and abandoned his desire for priestly success. Nothing could induce him to stay at the temple. He preferred instead to let his feet take him where they might. Tear-

The farmer's family threshing grains (*right*). The traveling monk meets a baby in whose hand he discovers the holy amulet that he had lent to his dying young lover (*left*). (National Diet Library)

fully leaving notes of parting for various people, Shunchi headed to the Deep North. Led by fate, he ended up in Yūtsūji, a temple that belonged to his sect in the castle town of Wakamatsu, where he stayed for three years.

A long time had passed since Shunchi had visited home. He decided to pay a call on his old master in order to inquire after his health and express his gratitude for the many favors he had received. Traveling by way of Murakami in Echigo, he crossed from Echizen into Kaga, reaching a village at the foot of Mount Arichi one day around dusk. The road ahead was difficult to see, and Shunchi decided to ask for lodging at a wealthy farmhouse nearby. Outside, two or three maidservants were threshing rice. Dismissing him, they said, "This isn't an inn. You'll have to look for a place to stay farther along the road."

Just then, a woman of about thirty, evidently the mistress, appeared from inside the house. She summoned the monk. "You're most welcome to spend the night here," the woman insisted. Delighted by her kindness, Shunchi entered the dwelling, removed his traveling sandals, and relaxed with his hosts by the hearth. The master and mistress of the house plied their guest with all sorts of food.

"It's strange," said the mistress. "Ever since our son was born, in the fifth month, he has never stopped crying. Even when I suckle him at my breast, he won't let up. Yet when your worthiness entered the gate, the bawling ceased. Why, it's past the fifth hour, and he's perfectly quiet."

Her husband, too, had noticed the change. "It's curious indeed. Go and fetch the baby to show to our guest."

"There's another thing that's just as strange," the man continued. "From the very day of his birth, our son has been clenching his left hand in a tight fist, and there is no way to pry it open. My wife thinks he must be some sort of cripple and is ashamed of the offenses he must surely have committed in a previous life to have been reborn with such a handicap."

The child was brought into the room. Upon being shown to Shunchi, the boy suddenly began dancing with glee, his face beaming. He tried to clamber onto the monk, desperately seeking to be hugged. Shunchi thought it a bit unusual, but he took the child in his arms. When he prodded the boy's clenched fist with one finger, the palm opened with ease.

Lo and behold, inside was the inscribed amulet that Shunchi had given to Naminosuke three years earlier. Amazed by this sight, Shunchi was unable to hold back his tears. Hesitantly at first, he told the boy's parents all that had happened, step by step. The parents, too, were moved to tears.

"Given the circumstances," proposed the father, "you must stay here and look after our son as he grows up. Eventually, you can dedicate yourself to saying prayers for our souls' repose. I don't suppose you want to have a temple of your own, since you say you have cast aside your priestly ambitions. But if you change your mind, we'll make sure to provide you with everything you need. Fortunately, there's a small building on the hill behind the house where we have the prayer services performed for my late father. It is dedicated to the bodhisattva Yakushi. We can contribute some fields for its upkeep, so there should be enough income to support two or three people with ease." The couple begged Shunchi not to leave.

Feeling that it was hard to escape one's karma from a previous life, Shunchi replied, "Then for a while at least, here I shall remain."

ALL HAIL TO THE BODHISATTVA AMIDA!

TRANSLATED BY GREGORY M. PFLUGFELDER

The Back Side of Nō Chant

The cultural influence of the nō theater was more widespread during the early Edo period than ever before. Samurai patronage had continued from medieval times, but now it was not uncommon for daimyo to support nō practitioners or to follow the precedent of the early Tokugawa shoguns by themselves learning to perform entire plays. And although full-scale productions were usually off limits to the general populace, other venues for enjoying the art became increasingly accessible to commoners. One was libretto chanting (*utai*). With advances in print technology that helped make nō chant books broadly available, the practice of chanting had become a popular hobby among the masses. An added motivation was that such chanting was considered foundational to the education of a cultured person. Selected highlights of librettos even appeared routinely in primers used in temple schools (*terakoya*) and other less formal establishments where commoner children were educated.

Nothing attests more to the familiarity of nō librettos than spoofs on them, such as the two pieces translated below (alongside the texts they parody). The spoofs are excerpted from chant books formatted to resemble the original texts and to preserve their rhythmic structure and prosody, though they also undermine the serious tone and decorum of the originals. The parodists make homophonic substitutions and playfully resituate the action in erotic or sometimes ribald contexts, such as pleasure-quarter bordellos. Collections of humorous nō chanting were sometimes referred to as "dressed-down chants" (*yatsushi utai*) or "chants to get a chuckle" (*warai utai*). Like the original chant books, these served as aids to solo performances at banquets, drinking parties, or other festive gatherings.

The first of the two translated pieces treats the parable of the warrior Taira no Morihisa, whose clan was defeated in the Genji-Heike War (1180–1185). While on a regular pilgrimage to Kiyomizu Temple in Kyoto, Morihisa is arrested by agents of the Kamakura shogun Minamoto no Yoritomo, who whisk him to Kamakura to be sentenced to death. At the last minute, the light emitted by the scroll of *The Kannon Sutra* that Morihisa holds in his hand blinds the executioner, whose sword drops and breaks. Summoned before Yoritomo, Morihisa relates his dream of the previous night in which an elderly priest—an avatar of the god of mercy, Kannon, worshiped at Kiyomizu Temple—appeared and promised to spare Morihisa's life as a reward for his years of pious prayer. Yoritomo, awed that he himself had the same dream, pardons Morihisa.

In the nō play, Morihisa's salient attribute is his single-minded devotion to Kannon. This is brought into relief in the narrative by the retelling of

Morihisa's dream about the god's miraculous apparition in the guise of the elderly priest. In the parody *Bad Boy Morihisa* (*Akushō Morihisa*), however, Morihisa's single-minded devotion is to a house of assignation in Kyoto's Shimabara pleasure quarter. During an all-night party, an elderly townsman appears, mercifully offering to redeem the contract for the courtesan of Morihisa's choice. The identity of the old man is unclear, but he is perhaps a merchant representing the Shimizuya shop. Thus is the piety of the nō play's Morihisa turned on its head, an inversion reflected in the parody's titular "bad boy," a character type in popular prose and drama who risks the family fortune for his love of a courtesan.

The second translated piece, *The Male Players' "Takasago"* (*Yarō Takasago*), pokes fun at the nō play *Takasago,* which enjoys canonical stature as an icon of the very art itself. *Takasago* celebrates the Japanese poetic tradition and honors happiness in marriage—auspicious themes embodied by the main characters, the spirits of two ancient pine trees. Although supposedly rooted on opposite sides of Osaka Bay, in Sumiyoshi and Takasago, these pines have miraculously traveled back and forth to visit one another. In the first act, they appear as an elderly couple. In the second, the man appears alone, assuming the identity of the young male deity of Sumiyoshi Shrine, a patron god of Japanese poetry.

The translated excerpt is from an extended passage of narrative (*kuse*) that condenses some of the play's major themes and thus was excerpted in chant books. It is devoted to praising the virtues of the pine, a symbol of longevity. The text also alludes to the sentiment, immortalized in the preface to the first imperial anthology of Japanese poetry, that all sentient beings express themselves in poetic song. The parody, by contrast, indulges another universal desire—the urge to express oneself sexually.

This passage is inspired by the beautiful and erotic young men—actors, apprentices, or prostitutes—associated with the kabuki theater district in Kyoto. Mention is made of Ishigake, an area known for its male brothels. The reference to the nearby Zen temple Kenninji and its famous bell is intended as a spoof of the celebrated allusion in the nō play to a poem describing a bell that sounds on the Takasago shore. The scene suggested is that of a party, perhaps set at a house of assignation in the theater district, just north of Ishigake.

The two spoof texts originally appeared in separate but connected compilations. *Bad Boy Morihisa* was included in a chant book collection titled *Virtuoso Vocal Pieces: Beating Rhythm with a Fan* (*Rangyoku Ōgibyōshi*), published in Osaka late in 1706. *The Male Players' "Takasago"* was included in the collection *Virtuoso Vocal Pieces: A Stacked Pair of Sake Cups* (*Rangyoku Kumisakazuki*), issued by the same publisher in 1707. The preface explains that the

title reflects its relation to the previous collection: as two *sake* cups designed
to be nestled together.

KUSE SECTION OF THE NŌ PLAY *MORIHISA*	*BAD BOY MORIHISA*
SASHI (RECITATIVE)	**SASHI (RECITATIVE)**
Shite	**Shite**
Thus have I believed in his merciful light,	Thus have I passed this time,
Chorus	**Chorus**
day and night, dawn and dusk, never flagging. I have recited that holy scripture, and especially at this time, reminded how close I am to death, I lapse not an instant.	day and night, dawn and dusk, never flagging. I have frequented that Shimabara, and especially these days, devoting myself wholly to courtesans, I lapse not an instant.
Shite	**Shite**
From last evening till before dawn,	From last evening till the break of dawn,
Chorus	**Chorus**
I thus stayed quietly seated.	I stuck it out in the parlor of assignation—
KUSE	**KUSE**
Before light had dawned at the six windows, one patch of sky grew ethereally bright, and, all of a sudden, an old priest who looked to be past eighty,	the party even now in midstream. While a lively tune plays, all of a sudden an old gentleman, who looks to be past eighty,

attired in a *kasaya* stole, clove
    yellow in hue, fingering his
    rosary beads of crystal,

and leaning on a cane, the handle
    in the shape of a dove, says in
    an exquisite voice,
"I have come all the way from
    Kiyomizu Temple
in the Higashiyama district in the
    capital,
on your behalf.
Kannon's original vow of bound-
    less benevolence and
    compassion—
how could it ever be in vain?
Even if calling out my name but
    once,
when done with genuine faith in
    me,
will spare you even a king's
    persecution.

Shite
All the more for you who these
    many years,

Chorus
stand out for your painstaking
    earnestness,
and awakening, exceeding that of
    others.
You may put your mind at ease.
I will sacrifice myself
to spare your life," [the old priest]
    said,
whereupon the dream ended.
Morihisa thought what an
    awesome thing is this,
and the joyful reverence in his
    heart knew no bounds.

attired in a modest padded
    kimono in blue,
fingering his one hundred and
    eight rosary beads,
and leaning on a cane with a
    hammer-shaped handle,
says in properly frugal voice,
"I have come all the way from
    Kyoto,
the area of the [Kiyomizu]-ya
    establishment,
to keep you company.
Your most precious possessions—
    your gold and silver—

why ever did you use them?
Even if only a one-*ryō* coin,

when you are in the prime of
    youth,
you should save it with great care.

Shite
All the more for you who these
    many years,

Chorus
stand out for your dissolute ways

and for licentiousness, exceeding
    that of others.
You may put your mind at ease.
I will adhere to your every whim
about purchasing a courtesan's
    contract," [the old man] said,
whereupon the money flowed.
Our big spender thought, "What
    an awesome thing is this,"
and the buyout celebration knew
    no bounds.

KUSE SECTION OF THE NŌ PLAY *TAKASAGO*	THE MALE PLAYERS' *"TAKASAGO"*
Chorus	**Chorus**
Thus was it also	Thus was it also
stated in the words of the poet Chōnō	stated in the words of the elders
that no voice, sentient or insentient,	that no male entertainer, adult or adolescent,
is lacking in poetic song.	misses a chance for sex.
Grass, trees, earth, and sand,	Fees, gratuities—
the voice of the wind, the sound of the water,	dust before the wind,
all things are imbued with poetic feeling.	for all people are imbued with erotic feeling.
The forests in spring	On a balmy spring day,
swaying in the eastern winds, the autumn insects	stepping out in trendy fashions, or in autumn,
crying out in the northern dews,	disporting through the long night,
does not each of these embody the shape of a poem?	does not each of these entail loving intercourse?
And among them this pine	And among these, this sexiness
surpasses all other trees,	stirs the spirits of the people,
the verdure of the pine tree	the elegant attire of a radiant youth
for a thousand years,	for a thousand years,
is constant, past and present,	a vivid image, past and present,
a tree so worthy that the Qin First Emperor	eros so worthy that wine is served to pledge
bestowed rank upon it in his court.	to this "path of love for young males."
In foreign lands	In foreign lands
and in our realm alike	and in our realm alike
all the people praise it.	all the people praise it.
Shite	**Shite**
At Takasago	In Ishigake
there upon the hill above	from Kenninji Temple
the bell sounds.	the Dharani Bell sounds.

Chorus	Chorus
As day approaches,	As day approaches,
though frost has settled in, the pine needles	though others are rising, our slumbering faces
are the same deep green color.	are drunken in hue.
In the shade of the pine, morning and night,	In the dawning light, morning *sake* is served.
sweep as we might, the fallen needles are never exhausted—	Drink as we might, the spring is never exhausted—
it is true. The needles of the pine	it is true. The male entertainers
do not fall completely, their hue deepening	do not disperse completely. Their charms increase
as the laurel vine grows long, a metaphor	as their lavender caps entice us
for this long reign. Among evergreens,	to ribaldry. Among buffoons,
it is the Takasago pine whose name	it is Ishigake district whose revelries
hereafter too will be singled out	hereafter too will be singled out,
for auspiciousness as the Wedded Pine.	for nothing brings such delight as playing the ass.

TRANSLATED BY SHELLEY FENNO QUINN

PART
IX

Gossip, Reportage, and Advertising

Newfangled Spiels

JŌKANBŌ KŌA

Tracing the mighty river of comic popular fiction known as *gesaku* back to its tributaries, one finds a trickle of humorous short stories collectively referred to as *dangibon*. Ranging from the timelessly universal to what today comes across as inscrutably topical, the best works in this mode were hailed as sidesplittingly—or, in the contemporary idiom, navel-dislocatingly—funny.

Such is not necessarily evident from the word *dangibon* itself. Literally meaning "sermon book," this designation less describes the content of individual works than indicates the genre's roots in soapbox oratory. As preachers of popular forms of Buddhism, like Pure Land and Nichiren, began venturing out from their temple precincts into the public marketplace in search of ever-broader audiences, they spiked their sermons with a dash of vernacular language and earthy humor. Some listeners no doubt preferred the medium over the message. Neo-Confucian types, especially of the Sorai persuasion, appropriated the accessible rhetorical style to expound their particular solemnities. Assorted street performers adopted it as a vehicle of mass entertainment, often rendering bawdy material in a pious tone to absurdly contrastive effect. When routines in this latter vein were set to print, the sardonically named sermon book was born.

Accordingly, *dangibon* stories avoid fire-and-brimstone jeremiads. What few religion-flavored morals are to be had, if any, are tongue-in-cheek. *Biographies of Limp Dicks in Seclusion* (*Naemara In'itsuden,* 1768) or the inimitable *On Farting* (*Hōhiron,* 1774), for instance, can hardly be considered moralistic, at least not in the conventional Neo-Confucian or Buddhist sense. The *dangibon* therefore might best be thought of as a form of mock sermon, a collection of witty yarns that, when occasionally parodying authentic homily, do so mainly in the service of fun.

Although the *dangibon* had its prototype as far back perhaps as Issai Chozan's *Country Zhuangzi* (*Inaka Sōji,* 1727), the genre culminated in popularity during the mid-eighteenth century, when the center of literary and cultural activity was swinging from the Kyoto-Osaka region toward Edo. No wonder the typical *dangibon* paid close attention to the colloquial dialogue of the townsmen of the up-and-coming shogun's capital. To the extent that the book of manners (*sharebon*), the yellow book (*kibyōshi*), the funny book (*kokkeibon*), and other stripes of comic popular fiction were indebted to this chirpy idiom, then, the *dangibon* exerted no small influence upon the course of *gesaku* well into the nineteenth century.

The great exemplar of the *dangibon* is widely considered to be Jōkanbō Kōa's *Newfangled Spiels* (*Imayō Heta Dangi,* 1752). This was, after all, a breakthrough work, attracting imitators, though also lending the genre its form—three to five volumes, lightly illustrated—as well as one of its titular words.

"The Funeral Director's Blowout-Sale Circular" (Sōshichi Yasuuri no Hikifuda Seshi Koto), one of several pieces within *Newfangled Spiels,* describes in darkly comic strokes a bungled attempt at an advertising blitz on the part of a funeral home director, Sōshichi. Then again, one of the fictional readers within the story who present conflicting reactions to Sōshichi's flyer interprets it as a tour de force of satire. Be that as it may, travestying more than the deadly dull drone of contractual jargon, or the preternaturally animated tone of commercial lingo—let alone the all-too-common subordination of human compassion to mercantile greed—the piece nevertheless exhumes the socially constructed nature of funerary practice. In so doing, it raises the specter of a world in which people care less about the death of a loved one than about impressing each other with flashy public display.

(ALK)

THE FUNERAL DIRECTOR'S BLOWOUT-SALE CIRCULAR

"Allow me to commend you, in the form of a written announcement, on keeping yourself remarkably hale and hearty even though that chilly time of year is once again upon us..."

Thus begins the clothier's leaflet blanketing Edo, even down to the back-street hovels of impoverished palanquin coolies. So formidable is the business savvy of this bigwig merchant that he has his leaflet constantly strewn about every nook and cranny of the metropolis the year round, regardless of the social standing of its recipients—and in such quantities as to easily plaster over holy Mount Shumi with papier mâché.

Likewise, loaner umbrellas bearing a registration number along with their shop name in bold lettering—"2760," say, of "The Echigo-ya" or "The Izukura"—pop open in the sudden downpour and proliferate throughout the boulevards. Word has it that from high above the clouds of the evening squall the sight rattles the God of Thunder and flashes in the eyes of the God of Lightning, making them hide their own belly buttons for fear.

Hence the ubiquitous leaflets of smalltime businessmen, envious for a piece of the action, announcing their own bargain sales at guaranteed deep discounts, without having been artificially jacked up beforehand.

In a world where back-alley obstetricians are not held liable for malpractice, what use is there in knocking oneself out over one's progeny with all the annual rituals—the ceremonial hair-growing, the pleated-skirt donning, the first temple visit? Or in making offerings? Or in saying prayers?! For even the deity Ubusuna, that patron saint of children, has been slacking off, his gross negligence in recent years incurring the most horrendous smallpox epidemic ever, the result being that parents mourning their dearly departed raise the water level of the Sumida River with their torrential tears. And when ferrymen at Asakusa hike their fares a couple of coppers in response, even homeless street peddlers with no offspring of their own find themselves every bit as grief-stricken.

Beneath the funerary bunting that perpetually shrouds Temple Row, owing to this cheerless state of affairs, the funeral home director Sōshichi enthused to himself: "Yahoo! *These* are the days!"

Drawing up a price list for his goods and services, this crafty little monkey devised a scheme to have circulars of his own distributed widely. At first he tried to hire some help, but since most people in this world are not completely unfeeling, nobody would be recruited. Plumb out of options, Sōshichi donned one of the floor-sample funeral hats, tugging it as far down as it would go on his bulldog neck, chugged a congratulatory shot of saké the size of a rice bowl

The funeral director, face hidden beneath a sedge hat, passes out fliers brazenly advertising his goods and services. (Waseda University Library)

so as to wish himself the best of luck in his venture, and, bidding bon voyage, hoicked up his pant legs before scurrying off to scatter flyers throughout the city single-handedly.

All sorts of people, curious to know what kind of sale was taking place, took a look-see:

"Please excuse the written notice. And above all, permit us to express our deep appreciation to the heads of the prayer groups and sutra study clubs, without whose patronage our funeral parlor would not have been blessed with such a terrific volume of business! For this we are wholeheartedly grateful.

"Now, owing to this year's universal dearth of kiddy caskets, prices have soared, intensifying the sorrow of the bereaved. What's worse, rush orders for hastily thrown-together crates to offset the shortage too often result in slap-dash craftsmanship, making the procession to the graveyard that much more nerve-wracking.

"Anticipating such misfortune, we stocked up last winter on sturdily constructed coffins to meet any and all needs of you, our customer. This is why the sticker prices on our goods and services are so easy on the eyes. If not fully satisfied with your purchase, simply return the merchandise for an exchange of equal value at any time in perpetuity.

"Our terms are as follows:

"1. Insomuch as the formal attire of pale-blue linen, ceremonial robes, braided sun hat, and so forth are worn only during funerals, these are not in high demand among samurai and consequently are not the most expensive articles in the world. However, one is hardly likely to purchase these in advance of the fact or to make them part of one's everyday wardrobe, after all. So we will provide these items to you on a rental basis. We are pleased to be of service as circumstances dictate.

"2. If feeling morose because you happen to be short on relatives or the proper ride for the escort maids, please let us know right away. We are glad to hop to, dispatching a phalanx of mourners' palanquins crammed with women weeping inconsolably to serve as proxies. We will even throw in their obligatory white padded garments or, depending on your preference, some solid colors, free of charge. Moreover, we train our women, upon reaching your deceased's graveside at the family temple, to break into loud sobs just as the cymbals crash. Should any of these women fail to bawl on cue, however, we guarantee not to charge you for her salary.

"3. Coming soon, we plan a new service renting out the white padded garments, sashes, cotton-veiled hats, summer attire, and the like for the chambermaids, be they your own or those of your relatives. That said, if on the off chance your girls, in the course of shedding tears at your residence, happen to stain the sleeves of our rentals, we reserve the right to tack on an additional service charge for the cleaning—in proportion to the extent of the damage, of course—remittable immediately upon completion of the funeral. We have this proviso because, particularly among families who actually treat their employees kindly, this sort of thing occurs every once in a rare while.

"4. Townsmen funerals have become so increasingly extravagant in recent years that should you get caught without pallbearers, your procession will appear unduly meager. We are therefore always delighted to supply as many dozens of extras as your heart desires. Our estimate (provided separately) will of course take the distance to your temple into account. We reserve the right to raise our rates a bit if, in the absolute worst-case scenario, it rains on your funeral parade. Naturally, we arrange for an impudent, thick-skinned fellow as the expert guide to head up the procession to the temple. This man is instructed to swagger about town, a rosary dangling from around his ear, with an air of utter pomposity. Depending on how hard he works, please consider letting him pocket some of the sweet buns and red-bean rice cakes provided to your funeral party guests.

"5. If you happen to live in some back alleyway or makeshift lane and therefore worry that your loved one's funeral will go unnoticed without Buddhist groups chanting sutras to the throngs, that's where we come in! We will immediately dispatch some strapping young men—paying close attention to every last detail from the half coats tossed suavely over their shoulders, down to the leggings, pipes, and tissue-paper pouches tucked in at their waists—and have them run around as though flying, turning a cold shoulder even to you their patron, and making lewd comments to the ladies along the way. Upon arriving at the temple, our boys will clap their hands and shout boisterously before having their smoke. Depending on the package deal, we also organize religious types to chant an authentic Buddhist invocation in unison. Again, we will customize the arrangements to your liking.

"6. According to recent townsmen practice, neighbors take care to close their doors and hang the customary bamboo blinds even before the deceased-to-be has breathed his last. Since orchestrating such things yourself amid your time of turmoil is always a hassle, upon your request we shall at once have the words 'In Mourning' written in the accomplished hand of the Terazawa School of calligraphy and impressed onto printing blocks so that blinds of new bamboo will be ready to go in a heartbeat. Although the rental fee is contingent upon the length of mourning, our production method is so efficient that we are happy to pass the savings on to you. We eagerly await your order.

"7. We employ a masterless samurai thoroughly versed in burial service procedure to record your big day at the temple cemetery. Rest assured that his calligraphy will be executed without the least trace of vitality. Please allow us to accommodate your needs.

"In addition to the aforementioned, we carry a complete line of funeral goods, everything from tablets bearing the names of the Seven Buddhas, to a rich assortment of graveside chalices, planters, implements for river atonement rituals, and burial shrouds, to wooden memorial plaques. Our prices are guaranteed to be cheaper than the going rate. For the memorial plaques in particular, we use only premium knotless hardwood under warranty to weather even the heaviest of gusts, so that the most unscrupulous priests will be overjoyed when they eventually recycle the plaques on the lowdown to build their temple fences.

"Furthermore, we will see to it that the required sixpence of paper offertory slips gets put into the coffin for the voyage to the Hereafter. Let us serve your needs as they arise. Our sale begins on Friday the 13th. Our shop—located 13 storefronts down from the corner of 13 Tombsbury—is the one with 'Deceased' emblazoned on a white funerary sheet draped over the entryway. You can't miss it!

"Remember: The world is full of funeral parlors. But when the death bell tolls, come on down to Sōshichi's!"

Reactions to Sōshichi's leaflet varied.

"Bloody hell, I've been contaminated!" exclaimed a hypochondriac, even before he had finished reading. How ridiculous that, perhaps already doomed to die by nightfall, he should now sequester himself prophylactically!

"Sheer nonsense!" another fellow muttered, using the leaflet to wipe his pipe.

Someone else was slightly more upbeat: "This is one of the most useful flyers I've come across lately! Unlike other ones advertising antifungal ointments or whatnot that most people can do without, each one of us, rich or poor, will need this stuff sooner or later." So saying, he smoothed out the crumples in the paper, posted it on his wall, and began biding his time until it would come in handy. And in this unpredictable world of ours, who is to say that this was not a shrewd move indeed?

There was yet another fellow, though, who went overboard in his adulation: "This flyer is the work of an extraordinary individual! Not only is he incensed by the fact that in recent years townsmen have stepped way out of line in terms of their funerals, which are even more lavish than those of high and mighty nobles, but he is being ironical in order to condemn such decadence!

"The ostentation of the past few decades has truly been outrageous. It's bad enough that townsmen own rental properties and that their apparel and accessories exhaust any list of the finest luxuries. What's worse is the conspicuousness of their funeral processions, the greatest extravagance of which being the dozens upon dozens of pallbearers.

"Back in the day, the most prominent of townsmen might keep a slipper valet and a porter; slightly lesser townsmen, perhaps a single servant; and the majority, none at all. Among samurai, only those with annual stipends of a thousand bushels or more would employ pallbearers, or so it is said. At present, the funeral procession for even one lowly townsman includes pallbearers, in full linen regalia, stretching out several city blocks in length—and in double columns, no less, just because he's dead! Aren't they ashamed of what people think? Such townsmen show no sign of respect—not even toward the processions of important samurai!—but carry on with smug faces.

"Then again, what does one expect of townsmen, after all, if not superficiality? One observes many such men who, in summer, mistaking reverse-twill robes as formal attire, favor linen garb and who, in winter, would parade their lined reverse-crest jackets and pleated trousers, turning their noses upward snootily as though to say, 'I possess the perfect wardrobe for each and every season!'

"Some five or six years back, a notorious Edo gambler died. People were astonished that the spectacle of his procession outdid even that of a great daimyo. The very next day, another funeral was to be held, at Seiganji Temple in Asakusa, for a tycoon renowned throughout Japan, a Mr. So-and-So of the money exchange district. Having heard this news, spectators began lining up at the crack of dawn, reasoning that if the high roller's funeral had been so grand, the one for the tycoon would be more spectacular still.

"Contrary to expectations, however, the deceased was carried in a solitary palanquin, attended to by a paltry thirty assistants, from carriage handlers on down, without so much as one single escort maid, let alone any in pale-blue garb, woven hats, or the like. Those who witnessed the scene, encountering true unpretentiousness for the first time, realized that a person of quality never indulges in garish display.

"Many people, resting on their riches, have been punished for their outlandish extravagance. The smuggler Hakata Kozaemon is a case in point, as is the monopoly merchant Ishikawa Rokubei.

"The principal charge brought against the latter, according to what people said a while back, was that he dared to call his residence at Asakusayama his 'Secondary Estate.' Even among senior officials, as I understand it, the only ones upon whom such secondary estates are bestowed are those appointed to key cabinet posts. For some overnight billionaire upstart like Rokubei to have used this term so cavalierly is nothing if not the height of stupidity as well as audacity!

"Anyone who is anyone knows that even rental properties also contain items that are illegal for townsmen to have in their possession. Those who manage to spend their entire lives without getting censured owe it not to purity of heart but to dumb luck.

"How I wish that instead of procuring tailored pale-blue outfits for a funeral, people would donate a comparable amount in silver to beggars and wear whatever they have on hand—provided it is not honorary attire bestowed by a samurai lord—even if it does not perfectly suit the occasion, for what really matters is being filled with grief.

"In the event of something like losing a parent, whether you should heed people disparaging you for, say, a warped back pad in your pleated trousers, depends on your social status as well as the circumstances. Standing on ceremony in such instances makes your grief seem like affectation, in which case nobody will sing your praises.

"When burning incense at the time of the funeral, some people actually bow politely to the priests before picking up the incense pellets! As a scholar of old instructed in *The Book of Myriad Good Manners,* 'Not one school of etiquette sanctions such behavior.'

"Indeed, people universally detest anyone who at such times acts too punctiliously. Someone whose eyes are welled up with tears and whose nose is runny with snivel comes across as genuinely pathetic and, therefore, compellingly admirable. Whereas someone who fusses with his appearance, smoothing out the seat of his pants even as he trails behind the coffin of his own parent, comes across as putting on airs, playing the role of bereaved son.

"Emphasizing appearance too much and sincerity not enough—this, broadly speaking, is the fashion of our times! The humble tea-whisk hairstyle and the mournful pale-blue garb are merely bad imitations of hara-kiri scenes from the kabuki stage. And wrapping the hilt of the short sword with paper was probably meant to preserve it as a matter of frugality on the part of the stage manager. Townsmen have no way of knowing that, in point of fact, this is not standard samurai practice. In spite of this, such customs have somehow become entrenched.

"It is when we people are most terribly flustered during a life-and-death crisis that the usual handymen and tenement-house hags rush to our homes, falling over themselves eagerly to prove how helpful they can be. They break the legs and bend the knees of the stiff to cram it into the coffin—even before the poor soul has completely stopped breathing! Or else they cause a hullabaloo by rushing things along that need not be rushed along. Or, upon slicing the toe straps, throw the straw sandals worn at the funeral out with the trash.

"If such practices were really proper protocol, then one would find them among the samurai, so the fact that one does not is evidence to the contrary!

"Disrespect toward the deceased notwithstanding, at the very least folks ought to refrain from the ritual toe-strap slicing and instead leave intact straw sandals out at the gate for some old street lady to make off with.

"So you see, it is truly impressive that, without any thought to the cost of printing, this flyer satirizes such misguided behavior!"

Thus did Sōshichi's blowout-sale circular, being spread out beside tobacco trays far and wide, create a sensation, with people proffering diverse opinions on it, chattering away into the same autumn dusk that comes to us all.

TRANSLATED BY ADAM L. KERN

Stirrups of Musashi

AN ACCOUNT OF THE MEIREKI FIRE OF 1657

ASAI RYŌI

Stirrups of Musashi (1661) is a stirring, often disturbing account of the Meireki Fire of 1657, which consumed much of the city of Edo over the course of two days in late winter, killing tens of thousands of the city's residents and destroying countless buildings. In describing an urban disaster that, in loss of life, was unprecedented in Japanese history, the author Asai Ryōi strives to enrich a straightforward factual description of the fire by establishing the persona of a storyteller who interjects his own personal experiences. Although awkward by modern standards, Ryōi's experiment illuminates the effort in seventeenth-century Japan to accommodate the legacy of medieval tales with the growing demand for what would come to be known only many years later as "news" or "information." He went so far as to insert lists of daimyo mansions and Buddhist temples destroyed, as well as a short history of past disasters in China and Japan; these have been abbreviated in this translation, but it is easy to imagine how they would have enhanced the sense of authority of the work.

Modern scholarship has taught us far more about Asai Ryōi than was publicly known in his own era. He was probably born in Osaka, the son of a Jōdo Shinshū sect priest. After a family transgression forced his father to resign from his post, Ryōi was left to pursue a broad education in hopes of reviving the family temple. From the late 1650s, he became a prolific writer of the popular "easy reading books," which were aimed at a general audience and covered a wide variety of topics. Ryōi is considered the prototypical author in this genre, writing some thirty books that ranged from realistic disaster chronicles like *Stirrups of Musashi*, to travel guides for Edo and the Tōkaidō highway, to ghost stories and humorous parodies of classical works.

While he was developing as a writer, Ryōi also worked assiduously to restore his father's temple of Honshōji, a goal that he accomplished first by moving to Kyoto in the 1640s to become the chief priest of Seiganji Temple and finally in 1675 being given permission to use "Honshōji" (with one character changed) as part of his own name as a writer. His first known published work appeared in 1659, two years after the Meireki Fire. Ryōi probably traveled to Edo for the first time in the summer of 1660, more than three years after the great fire, an expedition that would have provided him with the material not only for *Stirrups of Musashi* (first published in Kyoto in the third month of 1661) but also for his travel accounts *Famous Places along the Tōkaidō* (*Tōkaidō Meishoki,* written in 1659) and *Famous Places of Edo* (*Edo Meishoki,* 1662). While in Edo, he surely spoke with survivors of the Meireki Fire and copied official accounts of the fire that were circulating in manuscript.

This descriptive data of the fire is enriched by literary allusions. The title "*Stirrups of Musashi*" is taken from a common phrase that referred to equestrian gear produced in the Musashi region—that is, Edo and the vicinity. The phrase also alludes to *The Tales of Ise,* a classical poetic narrative from the tenth century. In its thirteenth section, a man from Kyoto now living in Musashi sends a cryptic poem to his former lover in the capital, implying that he has taken up with someone else in his new home. The man labels the poem as "Stirrups of Musashi" to indicate that it comes from that region, punning on *fumi* (text) and *bumi,* part of the word "stirrup" (*abumi*). The former lover responds with an emotionally charged poem, repeating the man's use of stirrups and adding equestrian puns of her own. In the tenth-century text, then, "stirrups of Musashi" connotes a fraught relationship between Kyoto, the imperial capital, and Musashi, a rustic backwater at the time. In Ryōi's seventeenth-century text, the title evokes an image of the Kyoto-based author observing shocking events in the new capital, which Kyoto people still regarded as being less sophisticated.

Stirrups of Musashi is loosely constructed around the fictional narrator Rakusaibō, a survivor of the Meireki Fire who in the opening lines encounters an acquaintance in Kyoto and offers to relate his own experiences of the fire, as a form of penance for past sins as defined by Buddhism. This framework quickly fades, however, as the author shifts to providing detailed information about the neighborhoods that the fire destroyed, the buildings that burned, and the places where the most people perished. For the sake of readability, the longest lists of daimyo mansions, some of which continue for several pages, have been omitted from this translation. Ryōi's methodical narration of the fire's progress provides a synthetic overview of the conflagration that would never have been recounted by an actual survivor of the fire. At the same time, he interjects vignettes that provide poignant moments and comic relief, and in key passages Rakusaibō is revived as a personal narrator to detail his own entertaining (if not particularly plausible) experiences.

In Ryōi's descriptions of the fire, for all his chronicling of the buildings lost by the city's ruling elite, he seems to have been most concerned with telling the story of the fire from the perspective of the ordinary city dwellers, whose trials and tribulations he recounts in passage after passage of moving prose. In his representation of the process of mourning and commemoration that followed the fire, and in his comparison of the fire to the worst disasters from Chinese and Japanese history, such as the allusion in Book Two to the Han destruction in 206 BCE of the Qin emperor's capital at Xianyang, he insistently praises the Tokugawa shogunate for its benevolent rule. At the same time, his account shows a deep compassion and respect for the resilience of all the city's residents, reflecting a spirit of tolerance and sympathy that is surely rooted in his fundamentally Buddhist worldview. In later life, Ryōi moved away from the writing of easy reading books to concentrate primarily on popular Buddhist tracts of explication and exhortation.

The eighteen pages of illustrations that accompanied the text of *Stirrups of Musashi* must have greatly enhanced the popularity of the book, which was reprinted in two later editions in Edo in 1676 and 1772, with revised illustrations. Those from the 1676 edition, of which two are included here, are unsigned but may be the work of the pioneer of Edo ukiyo-e, Hishikawa Moronobu.

(HDS II & SW)

BOOK ONE

He did not reject the world, but the world rejected him. With nothing left to do, he shaved his head and dyed his robes black. Calling himself Rakusaibō, he let his feet carry him where they would, following his heart toward the capital of Kyoto. After worshipping here and there, he paid a visit to the celebrated shrine at Kitano. He prostrated himself before the shrine, its deity Tenjin the same as that of the shrine in Yushima, his own neighborhood in Edo. Looking around the shrine, he chanced to meet an acquaintance, a peddler of sundries who had been traveling between Edo and the capital for many years. The peddler was shocked to see him and asked, "Why in the world are you dressed like that?"

Rakusaibō replied, "I fell into disgrace and have no place to lay my head."

"What could be so disgraceful? I can't imagine."

"It is the kind of shame that will only grow more painful if I talk about it. Surely you must have heard of the terrible fire that broke out in Edo in the first month of Meireki 3?"

"News of that fire has spread far and wide. Even here in the capital, many young people had gone to work in Edo and perished in the flames, leaving behind many relatives to grieve. We have heard the most terrible stories. Why don't you tell me all about it and relieve yourself of the burden of those bitter memories?"

"Pain and sadness—I feel as if they are pressing in on me, all alone in this world. As in the poem from *The Tales of Ise* about 'stirrups of Musashi,' such things are 'painful not to ask about, yet anguish to inquire,' so I never thought

Rakusaibō narrates the
Meireki Fire to a peddler at
Kitano Tenjin shrine, Book
1. (Harold B. Lee Library,
Brigham Young University)

I would tell others what I have seen. But please take this as a kind of confession, as I provide a general account of what took place."

At the hour of the dragon on the morning of the eighteenth day of the first month of 1657, the wind began to blow from the northwest. It soon grew fierce, blowing up dust that rose into the sky and drifted like a cloud—or maybe swirls of smoke, or mists trailing through the spring sky, it was hard to say. All through Edo, rich and poor alike could not open their doors, and though dawn had broken, it was as dark as night. Not a soul walked the streets.

All of a sudden, at the turning of the hour of the sheep, a fire broke out at the Nichiren temple of Honmyōji, at the western end of the fourth block of Hongō. Black smoke darkened the sky, and just as the entire temple began to burn, a wicked wind leapt forth and blew this way and that, spreading the fire in no time east to Yushima. Then the fire leapt from Hatago-chō south across the Kanda River to numerous daimyo mansions in the Surugadai area, including those of Lord Nagai of Shinano, Lord Toda of Uneme, Lord Naitō of Hida, Lord Matsudaira of Shimōsa, Lord Tsugaru of Etchū, and several others. In the nearby row of daimyo mansions at Takajō-machi farther west, several hundred structures were instantly reduced to ashes. From this point, the fire extended southeast through the commoner districts, on to Kamakura Quay next to Kandabashi Bridge.

And so things continued until the hour of the cock, when the wind shifted to the west, still blowing fiercely. The fire passed over Kandabashi Bridge and jumped six or seven blocks to Saya-chō near Ikkokubashi Bridge, consuming the mansions of Lord Makino of Sado, Lord Torii of Takatō, and Junior Assistant Obama of the Ministry of Popular Affairs. Meanwhile, fire spread east to the police barracks at Hatchōbori and destroyed the *bakufu* boathouses on the Sumida River. Great mansions that stood in rows, including that of Lord Matsudaira of Echizen, were enveloped in the smoke that followed the wind and were consumed by fire. The flames were so great that it seemed as though they might ascend into the clouds where the Four Heavenly Kings and Indra dwell.

Tens of thousands of men and women fled in the direction of the wind to escape the smoke, but reaching a dead end, they poured into Reiganji Temple near the water's edge at the mouth of the Sumida. The graveyard there was spacious, so people thought it a good place of refuge. Just as they gathered there, however, the main hall of the temple caught fire, and the flames quickly spread through the temple grounds. The whole place went up in flames, black smoke scorched the heavens, and flames as big as cartwheels spun around. Fanned by the wind, fire fell like rain on the people who had gathered there, burning the hair on their heads and setting their sleeves on fire. It was so unbearable that they panicked with terror. Trying to escape the fire, people scrambled over one another, running to reach the bank of the Sumida and dive into the mud. But they were cold and weak from hunger, and soaked with water, they were unable to move. They might have managed to escape the flames, but they had used up all their energy, and many froze to death. Even worse, those who could not flee to the river were enveloped in the flames, and all burned to death. The sound of their moans and screams was heartrending. Between trials of water and trials of fire, more than 9,600 people perished. All the way up to the edge of the river, everything was reduced to ash. On the island of Tsukudajima as well, four to five hundred yards in the bay, the mansion of Lord Ishikawa of Ōsumi and the surrounding homes were burned to the ground.

By nightfall, the west wind grew stronger still, and the sea became rough with waves. Because no rain had fallen since the start of winter, everything was parched. What were the chances that the fire would ever stop? Scattered by the winds, the flames jumped dozens of blocks and destroyed the shrine of Kanda Myōjin, the temple of Kaizenji, and the mansions of Lord Tanba of

Hori and Lord Ōta of Bitchū, continuing on to Muramatsu-chō and Zaimoku-chō. Many homes were totally destroyed. The fire also moved from Yanagihara across Izumidonobashi Bridge, burning everything along the way.

Meanwhile, the fire at Surugadai had moved on to Suda-chō to the east, making a beeline for the commoners' residences there. When another trail of fire came whipping out from Seiganji temple in Suda-chō, young and old alike could not believe what they were witnessing. Everyone scrambled to escape with their belongings, screaming and shouting all the while. When they stopped to rest in front of the gate of Nishi-Honganji Temple, a fierce whirl-wind appeared, and starting with the main hall, the temple quickly went up in smoke. The fire spread to the mountains of household goods that lay piled around, and those who had gathered there began to shriek and panic. Trying to save their own lives, some jumped into the well, others into ditches. Those on the bottom drowned, those in the middle were crushed by their friends, and those on top were burned by the flames. More than 450 people died there.

The fire continued north to Tenma-chō, where tens of thousands of residents, having witnessed the tragedy at Nishi-Honganji and realizing the difficulty of escape, ran in the direction of Asakusa, countless numbers pulling their wheeled chests behind them. The sounds of their cries, mingling with the creaking of wheels and the roar of burning buildings, seemed as loud as a thousand thunderbolts crashing at once. No words can describe how terrible it was. Parents lost track of their children, children fell behind their parents, and while everyone was pushing and jostling, some were trampled to death, others were run over by carts. Who could have counted the numbers of those who were screaming and moaning, injured and half-dead?

In the midst of such a fire, there were thieves as well. Of all those who ran off with wheeled chests that had been abandoned by their owners, the oddest story is of the thief who stole a chest left behind by a certain maker of mortuary tablets for home altars. The craftsman had thrown tablets of all sizes into his wheeled chest, some lacquered and others gilded, thinking, "This is all I have in the world!" But when the fire got too close, he ran off without it. The thief found the chest and took it to a graveyard in Asakusa. He pried off the lock and opened the lid, only to realize that the chest was full of useless tablets!

Among the thieves who saw the fire as an opportunity to loot and steal, one ran off with a worthless bag of rice bran, thinking it was full of rice. Another took a leather box that he thought contained silk robes but was actually full of cheap straw sandals. And then there was the invalid on the brink of death whose relatives had no choice but to load him into a chest and pull him along. They abandoned him at a crossroads, and he went missing when a stranger ran off with the chest. Some parents who had lost track of their children mistook another's child for their own, grabbed the child's hand and ran off into the distance.

The people crowding Reiganji Temple run from the flames, some crushed by carts (*left*). Bandits attack (*right, foreground*) while others run along the rooftops or carry the infirm on their backs, Book 1. (Harold B. Lee Library, Brigham Young University)

Some fled with their aged parents, young children, or frail wives draped over their shoulders and clinging to their backs, crying all the while.

At this time, the warden of the jail at Kodenma-chō was Ishide Tatewaki. When the raging inferno drew near the jail, he told the prisoners, "There is no doubt that you are all about to be burned to death—a pitiful situation. Since it

would be cruel for you to die here, I will grant you a temporary pardon and release you. Follow your feet and escape wherever you may. If you somehow manage to save yourselves, after the fire settles down, each one of you must come to Renkeiji Temple in Shitaya, without exception. If you honor this obligation and report to the temple, I will testify that your lives should be saved,

Victims drown (*foreground*) or fall under carts and horses at Honganji Temple, Book 1. (Harold B. Lee Library, Brigham Young University)

even if my own life should be imperiled. As for those of you who break your promise and fail to return, I will search for you even to the clouds in the sky, and there will be no hope for you. I will go so far as to punish your entire family."

So saying, he opened the door to the jail and let out several hundred prisoners. The prisoners clasped their hands and shed tears of gratitude for such benevolence. Each ran off in his own direction, but after the fire had died down, they all gathered in Shitaya as they had promised. Rejoicing, Tatewaki exclaimed, "You are all righteous indeed. Even if you have committed a serious crime, why should we kill those who preserve righteousness?" He testified to the shogun's chief counselors to this effect, and they pardoned the prisoners. This is proof of an age in accord with the proper way. Because of the correct decision based on honest governance, many prisoners preserved righteousness and their lives were saved, for which everyone was most grateful. Those who heard this story all remarked that the warden had compassion, the prisoners manifested righteousness, and the elders had spared the prisoners' lives out of benevolence. As a result, the proper way of government was made manifest.

One prisoner, and a particularly bad one at that, took advantage of the opportunity and fled far away. He returned to his hometown, but the villag-

Thieves discover they
have stolen worthless
sandals, rice bran, and
tablets, Book 1.
(Harold B. Lee Library,
Brigham Young
University)

ers, knowing that he was a criminal who stood no chance of being pardoned, were suspicious that he had returned home. When they took him back to Edo, the magistrates felt great hatred for him and sentenced him to death.

In the meantime, countless tens of thousands of people—high and low, rich and poor—had set their sights on the Asakusa gate to make their escape north across Asakusabashi Bridge. As large as the crowd was, a wide embankment lay just beyond the gate, on the other side of the bridge along the Kanda River, if they could only pass through the square enclosure of the gate without being pressed too tight to move. As if the work of some demon, a rumor spread that the prisoners at the jail had broken out and escaped. Hearing this, the gatekeepers thought, "Don't let them escape! Let's stop them!" and they slammed the gate shut. Not realizing this, no one in the crowd understood the situation, as they poured into the area in front of the gate with their wheeled chests. After a while, the road from Kodenma-chō all the way to the Asakusa gate, and all the neighborhoods in all directions in between, were jammed tight with people and chests. There was no room, not a single open space. The gate was shut, and tens of thousands of people pushed in from behind and were themselves then pushed forward, everyone crushed together. Those near

Warden Ishide Tatewaki mercifully releases his prisoners at Kodenma-chō jail, Book 1. (Harold B. Lee Library, Brigham Young University)

the gate tried everything they could to release the bolt, but so much furniture and debris was piled up that they were blocked, and the gate could not be pried open. If you tried to move forward, the gate would not open, and if you tried to turn back, the crowds coming from behind would trample you. As it became impossible to advance or withdraw, people wrung their hands with growing desperation. Just then, fire broke out where it had once died out at Yanagihara along the river west of the Asakusa gate and made its way west to the area of daimyo mansions across from Seiganji Temple—those of Lord Tachibana of Yanagawa, Lord Matsura of Hizen, Lord Hosokawa of Tango, Lord Niwa of Iwamura, Lord Endō of Tajima, Lord Katō of Dewa, Lord Katō of Tōtōmi, Master of Ceremony Yamana Zenkō, Assistant Isshiki Naofusa of the Imperial Household, and others—where a total of thirty-five mansions were burned, and 120 temples as well, including Nichirinji Temple, Honsenji Temple, Chisokuin, Kongōin, and others.

This fire joined with another coming from Kodenma-chō to the south and began to burn more intensely. Flames filled the sky and jumped from one place to another, driven by the wind. It blew from three directions onto the people piled on top of each other near the Asakusa gate, pushing and writhing. It was everyone for himself as the panic mounted. Unable to bear it any more, some climbed over others' shoulders and fled, while others climbed onto rooftops to make their escape. One can only fumble for words to describe it. Some people leapt into the Kanda River from the top of the stone wall thirty yards over the water, thinking that at least their lives might be saved, but they smashed their heads against the rocks or broke their arms as they fell. Those who landed by the river at the base of the wall injured their backs and piled on top of each other, making it impossible to stand up. Crushed to death, trampled to death, pushed to their deaths—they filled the river channel below the Asakusa gate with their dead bodies, more than twenty-three thousand of them. People piled in from neighborhoods in all directions, and the channel became leveled with all the corpses.

Those who jumped later were able to step on top of the corpses of the people before them, so they were not injured at all, and many saved themselves by climbing up to the riverbank on the other side. Meanwhile, the raging fire spread to the watchtowers of the Asakusa gate, which disintegrated and came crashing down on top of the dead bodies. Those who came later still, trying to escape but blocked by people and carts, tried to make their way forward, but the fire was already swirling front and back, with sparks showering down like rain. The crowd began reciting prayers to Amida, their voices raised together in a tumultuous chorus that was deeply moving. As the fire surrounded them from front and back, they chanted in unison. It seemed that their voices could be heard as far as the highest heaven and all the way to the very bottom of the earth. It was enough to make the hair on the back of one's neck stand up. The next day, the dead bodies were lying facedown on top of each other in the quarters of Bakurō-chō and Yokoyama-chō. One could not gaze upon the sight directly.

That night, at the hour of the boar, with the fierce wind still unabated, the fire began spreading toward the bay, destroying the outer residences of the daimyo that lay along the shore, and nineteen buildings in the area caught fire. At this time, there were more than 730 people hiding behind the shogunal rice storehouses along the Sumida at Kuramae. When the storehouses caught fire and it spread to the heaped bags of rice, those nearby died, suffocated by the smoke and falling into the river. From the rice storehouses, the fire jumped seven to eight hundred yards across the Sumida River to Ushijima on the eastern bank. Everything there burned down, including the homes of commoners. The fire finally died down after reaching this point, early in the morning of the nineteenth, at the hour of the tiger.

When morning broke at last, those who were scattered in all directions— parents looking for children, husbands who had lost wives—raised their voices

Rumors of escaped prisoners led to the closing of Asakusa gate, shutting off the only escape route for more than twenty-three thousand who died in the flames or threw themselves into the frigid Kanda River, Book 1. (Harold B. Lee Library, Brigham Young University)

Panic ensues as flames billow out of buildings, igniting carts and clothing, Book 1. (Harold B. Lee Library, Brigham Young University)

through the tears, crying out for so-and-so from such-and-such in a cacophony of voices. Some finally found the one they were seeking and rejoiced, while others had lost their loved ones forever and would not see them again. Many grieved, drained of all energy, deaf to reason. Some picked their way through piles of charred corpses, looking for the bodies of parents, children, siblings, or a spouse. The hair on the heads of the corpses had been burned off, and they looked like nuns who had burned, blackened, and shriveled. The clothes that the victims wore had burned off completely, and the bodies were scorched, the skin split open in all directions like a grilled fish. Many people were at a loss, mistaking this person for that one as they searched among the bodies. Thieves insinuated themselves into the turmoil, making off with the gold and silver that the dead had carried, taking away this scorched metal to sell. So many people gathered around to buy up the precious metal that it was like a busy market. Many became suddenly wealthy by taking away and selling household possessions abandoned at crossroads and in alleys throughout the city.

Servants remove the corpse that Rakusaibō mistook for his mother in the confusion, Book 2 (Harold B. Lee Library, Brigham Young University)

Rakusaibō went on to tell another story, this time about his own experience.

"Since my mother had disappeared, we figured that she probably died in the fire, but when morning came, we went looking for her hither and yon. We found a charred body that resembled her, lying facedown. We thought, 'This must be her! Let's take her back and hold the proper funeral rites.' We placed the body on top of a door and carried it home. When we returned home, the grandchildren, children, and siblings all gathered round and mourned her.

"But just then, my real mother came back home. Seeing her, one of the family exclaimed, 'How can this be? You have already become a ghost! What use are all these sutras we chant daily? You ought to wake up from your worldly illusions and be reborn in the highest level of the Pure Land. And now here you are, still attached to this world of suffering. This is terrible! Go back right away! After you are gone, we will carefully perform all the mourning rituals and visit your grave. You must not waver at the crossroads of the Six Realms!' Mother was shocked when she heard this and replied, 'I made my escape to Shibaguchi, and my life was saved. I've come home alive, but you are not rejoicing—what sort of thing is that to say?'

"Hearing this, we said, 'But your corpse is right here. How can we believe you when you say you have not died?' So we took a closer look at the body that we had brought back on the door and realized that it was that of one who meant nothing to us. To mistake one person for another happens all the time, but in the midst of these awful experiences, this was too much! But we were finally so happy that she had returned safely that we immediately disposed of the other body in secret. Oh, how loathsome that was! Then the whole family decided to celebrate her safe return, so we went out to buy food and drink. We celebrated with several courses, and our joy was without limits."

BOOK TWO

When morning broke on the nineteenth, all of Edo was teeming with people, some joyful and others grieving. What a commotion! Survivors from all walks of life were scrambling this way and that, gathering at the burned-out ruins, unable to abandon their close relatives who had met with the spreading flames. Some brought porridge they had prepared, while others handed out food and drink.

Then at about the hour of the snake, fire broke out at the police lodgings in Shin-Takajō-machi, below the main gate of Denzūin Temple. Seeing the smoke from a distance, some thought it a dust storm churned up by a sudden whirlwind, and others said it was smoke from ruined lots still smoldering from the day before. No one could be sure that it was another fire. But the wind from the north had grown stronger than the night before, and the fire spread in an instant to the academy, lodgings, and subtemples of Kichijōji Temple to the southwest. Flames as big as wheels were flying about in the black smoke, and the fire spread on to ten to twenty neighborhoods beyond. In no time, the fire overtook the outer mansion of the lord of Mito, which caught fire in a swirl of flame and smoke. Crossing the Kanda River, the fire spread to the wooded area below Hon-Takajō-machi and Iida-machi. Dozens of mansions that had been built up in stately rows over the years, great polished structures that were the last word in the good and the beautiful, with tens of thousands of rooms over an area of fifteen blocks—all went up in flames. Black smoke scorched the sky, flames singed the clouds, and the roar of the tiled roofs falling to the ground was beyond words. Heaven and earth were out of balance, while mountains and rivers seemed turned upside down. People were terrified and anxious, bereft of spirit. The whole world became an inferno. It was as if the Three Calamities of fire, water, and wind had all visited at once and the whole country would be consumed in a great holocaust.

From the hour of the monkey, the wind shifted from north to west, becoming fiercer still and forcing the flames in a new direction. The West En-

Victims drown (*foreground*) as warrior fire squads march by with their gear, Book 2. (Harold B. Lee Library, Brigham Young University)

ceinte of Edo Castle, residence of the shogunal heir, and the adjacent Momi-jiyama with its Tōshōgū Shrine were in all the more danger for having withstood the assault until now. The fire ran up against the embankment protecting the shogunal riding grounds and jumped across to Yaesu Quay in the daimyo district east of the castle, from there spreading to some twenty neighborhoods north and south, burning through the commoner districts. The merchants of Nakabashi and Kyōbashi wondered how another great fire could break out while yesterday's fires were still smoldering. The end of the world is at hand, they thought, falling into panicked commotion. Some headed north across Nakabashi Bridge, thinking to escape to the area that burned the day before, while others ran south across Kyōbashi Bridge, hoping to get downwind of the flames. Men, women, households, whole neighborhoods, were thrown into chaos. Those living in Kaji-machi and Nagasaki-machi tried to flee in so many directions at once that no one could move.

Not a drop of rain had fallen on the city for eighty days, ever since the eleventh month of the previous year, so the houses were as dry as tinder while the sparks rained down on them. Fanned by the fierce wind, fire rushed through the city like cartwheels. People pulled their wheeled chests out into

Flames engulf Kyōbashi Bridge, the "Hell of Searing Heat" where twenty-six thousand died, Book 2. (Harold B. Lee Library, Brigham Young University)

the middle of the street but abandoned them as the flames pressed in. Now the chests were bunched together at crossings and in alleys, making it impossible to pass. People pushed and shoved one another, and as they milled about, the fire spread everywhere. Right before their eyes, all the bridges in the area from Kyōbashi to Nakabashi burned and crashed into the canals. Cut off and surrounded by fire, the crowd moved as one to the south, then back to the north, struggling both to east and to west, their voices joined in a chorus of shouts and cries. It became unbearable as the fire finally drew near and began to consume them, everyone trying to use each other as shield from the flames. Some choked on the whirling smoke and lay writhing on the ground, while others went up in flames and fell to the ground in agony. As they pushed and shoved, choking and burning, they toppled like dominoes. Flames fell over them and the smoke swirled around. The screams of sinners burning in the Hell of Searing Heat or the sorrowful cries of those in the Hell of Wailing must sound like this. About twenty-six thousand people burned to death here, with not an inch of space among the bodies. Household furnishings, gold and silver, rice and money—there is no way to count what was left in the streets and went up in flames. Words fails to describe the atrocity of it all.

Warrior fire squads fight to save Tokugawa Ieyasu's shrine inside Edo Castle, Book 2. (Harold B. Lee Library, Brigham Young University)

From this point, the fire burned south to Shinbashi and Kobiki-chō, and east to Mizutani-chō and Zaimoku-chō. Sixteen daimyo storehouses, two blocks' worth, were completely reduced to dust and ash, from those of the great Tokugawa domains of Owari and Kii on to that of Lord Okudaira of Utsunomiya. Eventually the fire blew on to Teppōzu and died out at the edge of the bay at the hour of the cock. From the upper reaches of the Sumida, on to Fukagawa and down to this point, countless tens of thousands of boats were burned in docks stretching for fifteen miles.

At the hour of the monkey, when it seemed that the fire had finally ended, a separate fire broke out in a commoner house on the fifth block of Kōji-machi, west of Edo Castle. The mansions of the three Matsudaira lords of Matsue, Takada, and Ōno, together with Hirakawa Shrine and the grandly beautiful shrine of Hie Sannō, all went up in smoke as swiftly as Xianyang. The west wind grew fiercer still, and flames were blown onto Tōshōgū Shrine in the Momijiyama precinct of Edo Castle, but just when they seemed most in peril, the wind suddenly turned to the north and blew off in a new direction, surely thanks to the protective powers of Tōshō Gongen, the spirit of Tokugawa Ieyasu. Mercifully, the West Enceinte remained unharmed, but the fire then spread to the daimyo districts south of the castle, inside Onaribashi gate, outside the West Enceinte, and at the foot of Mount Atago.

On the grounds of Zōjōji, the shogunal memorial temple in Shiba to the south, the major structures had remained unharmed, including the shrine to Tōshō Gongen, the mausolea of Taitokuin (Tokugawa Hidetada) and his consort, as well as the main hall, the sutra hall, the bell tower, the pagoda, the three main gates, and the back gate to the north. But that night at the hour of the ox, many of the buildings in the temple complex burned to the ground, including countless dormitories, the main sanctuary of Shiba Myōjin outside the east gate, Kagura Hall, and Goma Hall. Numerous small shrines also went up in flames. Since the wind at that time was calm and blowing gently, it would have been a simple matter to put the fire out. But people panicked, running off this way and that to save their own lives. Not a soul remained, and even with no wind, the fire spread freely, extending south from Zōjōji for eleven blocks and finally burning itself out when it reached the shore at the third block of Shibaguchi.

From Hongō, where it began the day before, the fire had already traveled over four miles. For more than twenty miles in all directions, the city had become an endless open plain. Losses totaled over five hundred blocks each of commoner and daimyo land, including more than five hundred daimyo mansions and six hundred residences of lesser samurai. So many homes of the common people were destroyed that one could never count them all. Gone was the great Main Tower of Edo Castle, the watchtowers at the east entrance of the castle, and over thirty of the fortified outer gates from Akasaka Mitsuke to Kanda. Sixty bridges were destroyed throughout Edo, with only Asakusabashi Bridge and the store of the silk merchant Gotō Genzaemon at the foot of Ikkokubashi Bridge still standing as reminders of the old Edo. Of the nine thousand storehouses in Edo, only one-tenth survived. Innumerable family records and household treasures from generations past must have been lost. Numerous shrines and more than three hundred temples were also destroyed.

The great fire had lasted three days, beginning at midday on the eighteenth, reviving from daybreak on the nineteenth, and continuing until the hour of the dragon on the twentieth. During its course, fierce whirlwinds arose to whip up the flames. As the fire jumped distances of ten and twenty blocks, burning ever stronger, people panicked as they tried to escape, not knowing which way was forward, which back, and were scorched by the fire and choked by the smoke.

In the mansions of the samurai lords were countless horses that had been kept as prize possessions for years, and when their mansions caught fire, nothing could be done but to cut the ropes and set the animals free. Terrified by the people and the fire, the horses ran off wildly into the large crowds and could go no further. With humans and horses pushing and shoving, people were knocked down and trampled to death.

Burned by the fire and choked by the smoke, hundreds of people died at a time, falling into ditches and moats, which quickly filled with corpses. After the fire died down and all the victims were recorded, over 102,000 names were on the list. Those with missing family members went searching in temples, but in most cases it was impossible to identify the bodies for sure. It was eventually ordered that all the unidentified bodies should be buried in a common grave by the river. The chosen site was in the district of Ushijima on the far side of the Sumida, on the border of the two provinces of Musashi and Shimōsa, where the bodies were ferried by boat and buried in a hundred-yard-square ditch. They covered the grave with a mound of fresh earth and asked the priests of Zōjōji Temple to establish a new temple there. It was named Shoshūzan Muenji Ekōin ("prayer temple for lost souls of all sects"), and from the fifty-seventh day on, monks from all the temples gathered there to chant a thousand sutras. How thankful we should be that it has become a place for the ceaseless invocation of the grace of Amida. May the people of Edo, young and old, men and women alike, line up to pay their respects and raise their voices to recite the prayer (*nenbutsu*) and pray for the salvation of the deceased.

Elderly men and women survived but lost grandchildren who were in the prime of their lives. Women survived who were separated from their children and husbands. In a single household, three or five or even ten perished, leaving only one or two surviving in this harsh world. They grieved but could not give up their own lives, left only to weep bitter tears. All houses had burned, and Edo was a barren plain. With no bamboo for pillars and not even sedge mats to serve as walls, they squatted on the scorched earth. By day, they were startled by the slightest noise, and at night they grew depressed. As they mulled over what had happened, the sadness and pain were hard to put into words. Out of the overwhelming grief for outliving parents, seeing wives killed, being cut off from husbands, and losing children, they bought grave tablets and delivered them to Ekōin to be placed above the great mound for the unknown victims of the fire.

One man who lost ten relatives went to purchase ten tablets, but he told the merchant to add one more. Cautioning the man that one should not buy more grave tablets than needed, the merchant inquired about the extra one. The man replied that one of his relatives was suffering from burns, and he planned to set up the tablet for her in the event that she died. This reminds us of the comic tale about a person who bargained for an extra tablet, a story that was once the source of much laughter. It is amazing now to think that people could have laughed at that! Since so many unidentified bodies were buried in

Unidentified victims are interred under a massive burial mound (*left*) at the newly consecrated Ekōin Temple, where monks gather to chant a thousand sutras and survivors mourn the dead, Book 2. (Harold B. Lee Library, Brigham Young University)

one place, no one could be sure whether their relatives were interred there. But from a surfeit of grief, they lined up grave tablets on top of the mound, performed funeral services for the immediate enlightenment of the souls of the dead, put flowers in vases with water, came to mourn, and tearfully invoked the name of Amida. To see or hear of these rituals was deeply moving.

A prolonged drought had continued since the eleventh month of the previous year. The sky continued clear and blue as the wells dried up and not a drop of rain fell. But on the twentieth of the first month, the day after the great fire died down, a blizzard struck the city, with violent winds and bitter cold as the snow piled high. By this time, there was scarcely a grain of rice left in all of

Edo, and famine set in for three days. With no wood or bamboo left, the survivors could not build shelters and were all exposed to the snow and frost, so that many men and women of all ages froze or starved to death. Death must have been the karmic lot of the whole city, since those who escaped the fire then either drowned, starved, or froze. Whichever way, their lives were forfeit. What a cruel fate!

Meanwhile, in the Yamanote area west of the castle, the few remaining daimyo and *hatamoto* set up shelters in central locations like Nihonbashi and Kyōbashi, sending their men to cook rice porridge and give aid to the starving. From within Edo Castle as well, daimyo magistrates like Lord Naitō Tatewaki of Iwaki, Lord Matsura of Hizen, and Lord Iwaki of Iyo distributed relief, and people from all over Edo gathered there. With no proper utensils for the porridge, they ate off of shards of charred rice bowls and pieces of roof tile. Some were so cold, hungry, and miserable that they did not even bother with such things but simply slurped the porridge directly from their cupped hands. Some had lost their hair or suffered burns over half their face, while others had suffered burns to the body as they struggled to extinguish their clothes ablaze. Some were weeping from loss of wives, children, or grandchildren. Many young

Shogunate officials watch benevolently as survivors receive gifts of porridge, Book 2. (Harold B. Lee Library, Brigham Young University)

women gathered there who were once rich and proud, in the flower of their youth, but who now had lost everything, escaping only with their lives. Forgetting all shame in the freezing cold, they received their porridge on broken pieces of pottery, shedding tears as they ate. It was a terrible sight.

In the middle of the second month, about a month later, people here and there around the city began to set up little huts to conduct trade. Those who were driven from the city by fire came crowding back in again, drawn by various connections. People high and low moved in and out of the city in numbers, and it seemed to be bustling once again. Around the third month, people pulled their wits together to tie brushwood into huts just to shield themselves against rain and wind. It was a paltry sight in contrast to the neighborhood that had burned. The shogun pacifies the realm, comforts the people, and rules with righteousness, so he graciously bestowed upon commoners a gift of forty tons of silver coin, ordering that the money be used to rebuild homes and businesses. The two city magistrates, Lord Kan'o of Bizen and Secretary Ishigae of the Left Palace Guard, received the money, summoned the property owners from four hundred neighborhoods within the city and over one hundred neighborhoods on the outskirts, and distributed the money to them.

A bustling scene by the foot of a bridge suggests a rapid return to prosperity. Two women are seen sobbing, possibly at the spot where they lost their loved ones, Book 2. (Harold B. Lee Library, Brigham Young University)

Elite samurai in formal attire receive bundles of gold from the shogunate, Book 2. (Harold B. Lee Library, Brigham Young University)

By the ninth and tenth months of that year, the reconstruction was completed and the commoner area had sixty thousand new structures with eaves all neatly aligned. The previous thirty-six-*shaku* width of the main roads was too narrow for the traffic, so they were widened to sixty feet. As a result, carts and horses do not jam the roads, and people can come and go without obstruction. From Shirogane-chō in Kanda extending east to Yanagihara on the Kanda River, one row of houses was removed to construct a stone-paved embankment fourteen feet high and some one thousand yards long, while southeast of Nihonbashi Bridge, from Yorozu-chō to Yokkaichi-machi, houses were torn down to build another embankment along the edge of the Nihonbashi River facing north, twenty-four feet high and extending three hundred yards west to east. In addition, houses were demolished in three locations between Nihonbashi and Kyōbashi to create 180-*shaku*-square clearings in the middle of blocks. Houses in this area had been packed too close together, creating dense crowds of people, so that if fires broke out, they could create great harm to life and property. With the embankments, no matter what happened, people would always be able to escape. To compensate those whose houses were torn down in these five locations, the *bakufu* gave each owner seventy gold *ryō,* as well as an alternative plot of land. By the end of that year, each of the daimyo and *bakufu* retainers who had lost their residences also received gifts of gold from the government. Thanks to the shogun's all-encompassing generosity toward everyone from the daimyo above to the common people below, Edo soon returned to its earlier peaceful prosperity. The nobility was rewarded with generous stipends, and the commoners had their fill of profit. With each day, the prosperity of the city increased a hundredfold.

Rakusaibō said, "Now then, peddler, please listen. As I said before, it was because of the fire that I met with great dishonor. I might as well have you listen to my tale.

"Everyone in my household escaped unharmed from the fire on the eighteenth, and I was so grateful that I went out to buy food and drink. We had a celebration on the morning of the nineteenth, and I got drunk after several cups of *sake*. I was in such a stupor that when word came that another fire had broken out, my wife and children, unsure what to do with me, put me inside a wheeled chest, locked it shut, and dragged the chest out to Shibaguchi on the main highway into Edo, where they left me. I was awakened by the sound of thieves prying the lock to break open the chest. Groping around, I could feel wooden boards on all sides, as well as my sword and robe. I thought that I had died, been placed in a coffin, and carried off to the cemetery. Surely it was the demons of hell that were trying to break open the coffin in order to begin their torture. I thought at least I should try to fight them off, so I drew my sword and leapt out of the chest. The thieves took fright, and all ran off.

"I stood up and looked around. All around me was pitch dark. Far off to the east a fire was raging, and I could hear the sounds of people screaming. That must be the Hell of Incessant Suffering over in the distance, I imagined, with sinners burning in the roaring fires, screaming from the tortures of the demons. How terrifying! All I wanted was to find the path to paradise. As I walked off, a stampede of horses that had been set free came galloping by, and I thought I must have been in the Realm of Beasts. Going a little farther, I saw women, children, and old people fleeing the fire, carried on the shoulders of others, and I thought they were recently deceased sinners being led off from this world by the demons of hell.

"Bewildered, I continued in the dark, and heading north from Shibaguchi, I came across the Hall of the Ten Kings of Hell. A lamp was burning, and I could see Lord Enma, the judge at the gates of hell, and the two spirits who report to him on the past good and evil deeds of the dead. I told Lord Enma that, while alive in the world, I never thought ill of others and never stole anything, taking care to recite the *nenbutsu* from time to time. 'I am certain that my sins must be light,' I pleaded, 'so please send me along the path to paradise.' But of course, since he was nothing but a wooden image, Lord Enma made not the slightest response.

"Terrified, I fled the hall, and all around me I could hear the sound of bells and people invoking the name of Amida. Convinced that I had reached the highest level of the Western Paradise, I started knocking on a gate nearby. 'Who's there?' asked someone inside, and I replied, 'I am one who has been delivered into paradise from the world of suffering. Please open the gate, Lords Kannon and Seishi! I want to mount quickly to the lotus pedestal bedecked with the hundred treasures.' From inside I could hear loud laughter, and a voice saying, 'It's some nut who's gone berserk because of the fire!'

"Dispirited, I left and walked on, as the morning sky began to turn light. Then I saw the burnt-out ruins of a daimyo mansion where porridge was being doled out. People gathered with their hands outstretched, and the sight of them consuming porridge from their hands was so sad and pitiable I thought I was in the Realm of Hungry Demons. Looking around, I saw thieves making off with things they had stolen. As people gave chase and struck them down, I was sure I was now in the Realm of Ashura.

"I recited the *nenbutsu* to Amida and sat down to rest. Then some friends appeared and asked what I was doing there. At this point, I awoke from my dream and was deeply ashamed. Since I had lost my whole family and all of my possessions, I took this to mean that I should take Buddhist vows. I shaved my head, dyed my robes black, and became the wandering monk you see before you. I understood that I had wandered through the Six Realms of Hell while still alive. In comparison with the sadness of living in the ordinary world, I have become like a living Buddha. Following my heart and going where I please, I am enjoying the little bit of life that I have left. Buddha enlightened me and provided me with an opportunity to follow him. It is a great sorrow to have lost everything and everyone in the fire, but since it led to my enlightenment, is it not an opportunity for virtue?"

The peddler replied, "Indeed, there are very few precedents for such a disaster. When something unexpected happens, people are certain to be thrown into a panic, and it is not uncommon to do ridiculous things. You have no reason to be so ashamed."

Rakusaibō continued, "I wonder when it was that the song 'Pebbles turn into a boulder, and a sprig of pine into a tree…' became so popular, sung by high and low alike. Who could have started it? And now, there's a popular song and dance called Shibagaki-bushi, which seems to have begun as a rice-hulling song in the North Country. Even at parties of the aristocracy, it is now the main attraction. A rough disheveled man of ferocious appearance bares his chest to reveal dark, dirty skin and assumes a strange expression. He peers out with his eyes and contorts his mouth, beats his shoulders, and strikes his chest. He looks like a madman as he grabs at his body, twisting left and right. Now he falls down on his back, now he rolls to lie on his stomach as the audience cheers him on. It is disgusting just to watch the audience clapping their hands and amusing themselves. How ridiculous! Eventually, the Shibagaki-bushi came to be sung and danced everywhere, and some people felt they could no longer live in their neighborhood because of the ruckus.

"During the fire, when people were burning with no place to flee, they would quietly expire by a brushwood fence and there reenact the song, furrowing their brows, crinkling their noses, and muttering to themselves. It just goes to show that a time will come for everything, and there is nothing to be surprised about. Faced with a desperate situation, people's hearts were thrown into confusion. But because the shogun was so wise in dispensing charity, all of Edo has once again become prosperous, the country is wealthy, and the people are submissive to authority. The realm is pacified as before, and I borrow the words of a song to describe it:

> From the pine, a small pine sprouts and grows,
> Its branches rich with green anew;
> Worthy of awe, may the lord's reign last forever!

"That is all I have to say. I bid you farewell."
So saying, Rakusaibō passed through the shrine gate and headed south.

TRANSLATED BY HENRY D. SMITH II AND STEVEN WILLS

A Garden of Words from the Boudoir

EDITED BY NISHIDA (SHOJI) MATAZAEMON KATSUTOMI

A Garden of Words from the Boudoir (*Dōbō Goen*, hand-copied distribution, 1720; first printed edition, 1738) is an anthology of light prose interspersed with poetry in Chinese and Japanese and was written by residents and frequent guests of Edo's officially sanctioned pleasure district. The editor of this anthology was a townsman named Nishida Katsutomi, himself a town administrator (*sōnanushi*) and brothel owner in Yoshiwara. Nishida, an adoptive descendant of Shōji Jin'emon (1575–1644), the founding father of the district, was well positioned to gather and publish literary gleanings from the early eighteenth-century world of Edo brothels. Both parts of *A Garden of*

Words from the Boudoir—the first part comprising three volumes, and the second part consisting of one volume—spread as handwritten copies before being later published as a codified printed text. *Sequel to A Garden of Words from the Boudoir* (*Ihon Dōbō Goen*, 1733), which included pieces omitted in the first collection and chiefly featuring the history and customs of Yoshiwara, also circulated in handwritten form, breeding variations between copies. The range of versions may bespeak the popularity of this publication as well as the ease with which commoners' writings could turn into books.

By the time *A Garden of Words from the Boudoir* was in print, Nishida had already edited and submitted, by direction of the shogun's Edo magistrate, records to delineate the history of and, thereby, claim legitimacy for his district, published as *Heritage of the New Yoshiwara Quarters* (*Shin Yoshiwara-chō Yuishogaki*, 1725). He was also known among contemporaries for having "a modicum of literary skills." Nishida had quite a reputation as leader of the Yoshiwara community. Not only did he represent the family of Jinzaemon, who gained the shogunate sanction for Yoshiwara, but he himself also maintained the community of brothels and shops in good order. It is remarkable that he studied and composed haiku and, in addition, edited a great variety of writings from his community.

"Rounding Out the Snowman" (Yuki Korogashi no Ge), which appeared in *A Garden of Words from the Boudoir,* is an allegory of a snowman, shaped as Japanese custom would have it into one large orb and nestled into a clump of early-winter grass. The story was composed by the Yoshiwara brothel owner and *haikai* poet Tenmanya Nizaemon III (1680–1759) under the pen name "Iwamoto Kenjū." He studied *haikai* with Iwamoto Shiei (d. 1712) and Mizuma Sentoku (1662–1726). Like many *haikai* lovers among common citizens, he actively participated in various Edo *haikai* competitions and collections and was listed as the chief of the group after his master's death. Kenjū's verses do appear in a few Edo *haikai* group collections, but he did not enjoy the fame of, say, Bashō's disciples. Kenjū's brothel Tenmanya appears to have been in business for thirty-some years, until around 1718. This date corresponds with Kenjū's debut in the Edo-za salon of *haikai* poets, which often gathered in Yoshiwara and tended over decades to incorporate and subsume the quarter's rich network of cultural patronage.

"Rounding Out the Snowman" reflects contemporary literary interest in allegorical modes of tale-telling rooted in Laozi, Zhuangzi, and commentaries written into those canonical Daoist texts. A lingering snowman by the side of the road is mistaken for a full moon "rising from the grasses and into tall grasses set." This quotes a famous twelfth-century *waka* poem by Kujō Yoshitsune (1169–1206) celebrating the nocturnal landscape of the Musashi moors, which centuries later would develop into the megalopolis of Edo.

The snowman is personified to show two essential traits: an ability to roll past obstacles in life, and a willingness to change shape according to one's environment. Both aspects lend the man the cachet of a Daoist antihero, who would slip by rather than engage frontally with society, in order to avoid the corrosive stress accompanying daily life. Resilience of compacted snow to the elements is occasionally used as a metaphor for the strong-willed life, as we can see in the "Rolling the Snow" scene of *The Treasury of Loyal Ronin* (*Chūshingura*), first staged in 1748. Yuranosuke, leader of forty-seven ronin who spends his days partying at Yoshiwara while secretly plotting to exact revenge for his deceased lord, teaches Rikiya, his son, the importance of loyalty and endurance as represented by the light snow that would scatter in the wind but can become hard as a rock when rounded out. Kenjū's affable snowman is resilient to hard edges and dangerous curves, less destructive than the hard mass Yuranosuke describes, but similar in its ability to persevere. We may assume the narrator of "Rounding Out the Snowman" reflects Kenjū's circumstances at the time he wrote his short poetic fantasy. Advanced in age, he has exchanged the noisy buzz of brothel life for the meticulous, time-consuming toils of the full-time *haikai* poet. His envy for the "old monk wrapped in powder white" is stereotypically expressed but tailored for a particular readership, within or close by the walls of Edo's Yoshiwara cultural complex.

(SJ)

ROUNDING OUT THE SNOWMAN

IWAMOTO KENJŪ

By the edge of a road in Asakusa on the moors of Musashi stands one clump of silver pampas, not totally withered. Yesterday's snows cling to its underbrush, and branches that once shimmered like beckoning sleeves wave in and out, blocking sight of the weeds' true colors. Deep within that venerable clump, and totally out of sync with day and with month, one perfect full moon shines. But wait—another glance shows no moon, just a lunar look-alike, one outsize snowball rolled up and left behind in the bush. A rude jolt to the distant gazer, who'd visioned that old poem about "rising from the grasses and into tall grasses set." What to make then of such an Honorable Snowman, whose rotundity ravishes and stirs in us pangs of envy?

To start with, his heart has no craggy corners for things to get snared on or clutter his way. Folks never tire of him, and he fears no broom will swoop down and brush him aside. He's managed to roll himself up into a tight, white, neat little ball; since he steers clear of avenues where glory meets disgrace, he'll never bite the dust under some blind stud's hoof.

Should he miss the throb of the city, he can roll off with the storm at daybreak and, beckoned by low breezes at dusk, tumble and rumble his way at will. Humming Wu Yuangeng's verse on "Xia Liang Station, midway down our path; half my hair has long gone white," he's likely to bump into a rock and, with a thump, stumble off like a drunk. Or he could pass the night at Maple Bridge Landing. Posed in meditation, just what would he see?

This floating world is so like a dream. Aside the pine root pillow of a napping wayfarer, he takes the shape of a lady, to teach the softness of conjugal life; and when he's mistaken for the tariffs of a rich rice harvest, even the fiercest warrior's heart melts in greed. But you'll never catch this snowman cringing on the mighty, like some straw-hat comic begging for his daily bread, or bruising his knees, swift as cloud wisps, hopping among the manors of the rich. He's packed with good stories to pass the night, and never lacks a friend. As absorbing as the early winter rains, and as sprightly as hail, he's always on cue to ring out the three hundred odes. Even stuck on a stick, dragged in tow by some naive tot, he'll serve gladly as the drum for a sumo wrestling bout. Pulled along by rope, he's a dead ringer for the woodcutter's ox trudging back to its mountain.

But as the saying goes, "Unfold your mind but give it no home." So, though he spends long hours on his sacred labors, he's only a holy roller, so to speak, and by this hour he's half-covered in mud. His dappled physique resembles a drunken tiger, coiled as if to leap, terrifying to passersby. Should he tumble ashore on some wave-scrubbed isle, a foot soldier might wonder which general was passing through in puffy white mantle.

Shaped like a Daruma or carved into a Buddha, you inspire us to awe and lead us to devotion. Well shaped, you lack a mouth, that darkest gate to sure demise; and without two ears, no mortal insult can breach your blessed peace. An inanimate snowlump, stony in silence, awaiting your fate: oozy meltdown under the gentle rays of spring.

Just the sight of you, old Snowman, puts me to shame. The top of my head is hoary like the driven snow, but not my heart—that's a darker shade entirely. I've shriveled up idly, at home, hoarding the fees from marking others' poems. Not a day's rest from these toils—I've never even peeked past the city's gates at Shinagawa. But that doesn't stop me from scribbling over sheathes of ditties on famous places. As they say, the poet sees much without budging an inch: "his art is like silent poetry, his poetry, like a painting read aloud." Paintings are make-believe anyhow: on canvas you find the Great Buddha two inches from Kiyomizu Temple! And so it goes for the Four Points, Four Paths, and

Six Realms of Life. I don't know the answer any better than the next fellow, and wouldn't were I a sage.

> Whatever the question
> He'll snow you in a minute
> That old monk wrapped in powder white

TRANSLATED BY ROBERT CAMPBELL

Laughing at Everyday Life

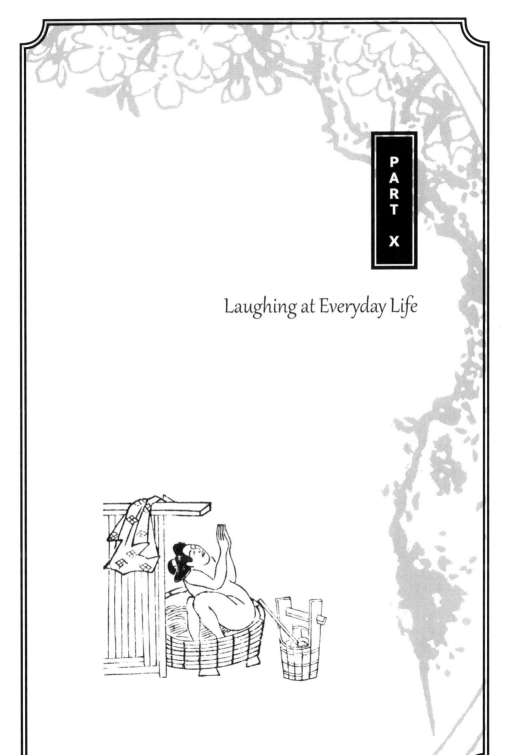

A Sackful of Wisecracks

STORIES BY ENTERTAINERS

The stories gathered here come from eleven classic collections of humorous stories (*hanashibon*) published between the seventeenth and early eighteenth centuries. As a whole, they offer a compelling view of what people in early modern Japan found funny, and of how common tropes like the scatological, the sexual, and the absurd were deployed in situational comedy and critiques of class privilege.

Comic storytelling has a long history in Japan, dating back at least to the thirteenth century, when Buddhist priests in Kyoto began to service themselves out as advisers to warrior-class bureaucrats of the Kamakura shogunate. Their duties extended well beyond cultural chaperoning to include religious sermons, appraisal of imported artifacts, practical political advice, and even gossip about members of the court. These practices eventually converged with existing traditions of storytelling to produce a body of orally transmitted colloquial literature known as bedtime stories (*otogizōshi*), which encompassed courtly romance, military tales, tales of the supernatural, sermons, and folklore. Some stories in books of tales are didactic, but in keeping with the official role of these priests as preachers, most appear to have been composed with the intent to entertain and amuse.

These traditions continued well into the seventeenth century, when Anrakuan Sakuden (dates unknown), a priest at Seiganji Temple in Kyoto, regaled Itakura Shigemune (1586–1657), the Tokugawa shōgun's chief magistrate in Kyoto between 1620 and 1654, with hundreds of humorous tales about members of the court and powerful warlords like Oda Nobunaga. Itakura became so enthralled with Anrakuan's gift for comic storytelling that he commissioned him to commit his stories to paper. Anrakuan's collection of stories, *Awakened with Laughter* (*Seisuishō,* 1623), set a new standard in written compendia of comic tales, insofar as it categorized stories according to theme and gave singular voice to the author as comedian. Many other cleric storytellers followed suit, capitalizing on the rise of secular, commercial publishing in the city of Kyoto to expand their audience.

Early *hanashibon* were written in an idiom inaccessible to many early modern readers, with references to figures in the inner realms of court and shogunate bureaucracy. In contrast, the three decades from the Enpō (1673–1681) to the Genroku (1688–1703) period saw the rise of a new genre of joke books—the "light-mouthed books" (*karukuchibon*)—that were essentially transcriptions of performances by professional storytellers in colloquial language about situations that commoners could more readily identify with. Many collections from this period, and most of the stories collected here, were transcribed from routines given by the three most popular professional storytellers in Japan's principal cities—Tsuyu no Gorobē (1643–1703) in Kyoto, Yonezawa Hikohachi (d. 1714) in Osaka, and Shikano Buzaemon (1649–1699) in Edo.

Tsuyu no Gorobē was a Nichiren-sect Buddhist priest who pioneered a form of street performance called back-alley talks (*tsuji-banashi*), featuring comic sermons and imitations of kabuki actors. A hallmark of his stories is their focus on flawed characters who get their comeuppance, be it because of lustful opportunism, as with the main character in "Taking Care of Smallpox," or cowardice, as in "Fickle Lovers Plot a Double Suicide." While his stories are not satirical in the strictest sense of the term, Tsuyu made no qualms about poking fun at people in positions of authority and privilege—even fellow clergymen, as we can see in "A Tightwad Priest Crazy about a Boy."

In Osaka, Yonezawa Hikohachi expanded upon the form of "back-alley talks" by presenting over-the-top comic impressions, skits with recurring characters, and anecdotes whose funniest moment came in the final line—thus pioneering the use of the punch line (*ochi*) in comic routines. Like Tsuyu, Yonezawa did not shy away from making samurai or Buddhist priests the subjects of his jokes—as we can see in the stories "A Certain Style of Face" and "An Impromptu Performance," respectively. At the same time, the tone of his humor tends to run a bit darker than Tsuyu's, with jokes about the destitute ("Piss-Poor in Arima") and even the deceased ("A Bather Kicks the Bucket").

In Edo, Osaka-born Shikano Buzaemon brought his rendition of Kamigata-style humor to urban bathhouses, street-side stalls, and impromptu stages in the shogunal capital. A trademark of his style was the use of comic gestures and miming of actions—elements of performance that can still be seen in *rakugo* today. But even as he succeeded in expanding the market for comic storytelling, Shikano became a cautionary tale to other storytellers about the dangers of running afoul of the authorities. Accused of misleading his audience about the curative properties of pickled plums and *nanten* berries against cholera, Shikano was arrested and exiled to Oshima Island off Ise Peninsula for six years, eventually dying a few months after his return to Edo. Such was the plight of an early modern comic.

Despite such highly publicized crackdowns, however, comic storytelling became a staple of entertainment in brothels, bathhouses, temples—indeed, anywhere a comic could command an audience. But the rise of print also made it possible for people to enjoy this material in book form, in a private setting without reprisal for laughing out loud at socially inappropriate jokes. The sheer scope of printed books in this genre gives a sense of the early modern demand for comic stories. Whereas the entire corpus of books of tales, dating between the Muromachi and early Edo periods, is estimated to be around 360 stories extant, more than 1,200 *hanashibon* collections were published during the Edo period alone, containing an estimated 50,000 to 60,000 stories. This veritable storehouse of comic material, in turn, became a source for many Kamigata comic fiction writers, including Ihara Saikaku and Ejima Kiseki, as well as for later Edo writers working in genres like "funny books" (*kokkeibon*).

The enduring popularity of these stories owes to the accessibility of their humor, even though the scenarios on which their jokes turn require some understanding of the period and the culture. Suicide might seem like a grim subject for a joke, but the romanticizing of lover's suicides (*shinjū*) in contemporary dramas made it a motif ripe for parody. In "Fickle Lovers Plot a Double Suicide," we find the perfect antithesis of Chikamatsu's tragic hero, a man who ditches his lover when he realizes that he isn't so sanguine about her at all and would rather keep on living. Meeting her again one day at Nihonbashi, the man fixes a triangular piece of paper to his forehead, pretending to be a spirit of the dead. In "Happy Being a Beggar," the bustle of New Year's Eve—traditionally a time for lenders and creditors to set debts—becomes the backdrop for a brilliant joke about the merits of wealth. A homeless man living under a bridge observes the commotion with smug self-assurance, convinced that money is more trouble than it's worth. The joke takes an ironic turn when his father reminds him by that poverty isn't all it's cracked up to be, either. In "A Pickpocket Delivers a Bundle of Joy," we find another pair of characters living on the fringes of society—a pickpocket in the throes of labor and her unborn baby, prenatally wise to the dangers of getting caught by the authorities. Only when word comes down that the lord of the domain has pardoned all prisoners, a customary expression of noblesse oblige, does the baby dare to leave the womb.

(DM)

TODAY'S TALES OF YESTERDAY

ANONYMOUS

A Fare Outcome

A man decided one day that he was tired of having the same old wife year after year. Hoping to get rid of her, he did what he could to start a fight, but she would never oppose him in anything. Finally, he told her outright, "I hate to say this, but the sight of you makes me sick. I hope you'll see it my way and leave."

"I guess it can't be helped," she said. "If that's how you feel, I'll go back to my parents."

Taking out the robes she wore as a new bride, she put them on, oiled her hair, blackened her teeth, and made ready to go.

The man was deeply moved to see her looking like the girl he married, and he wondered how he could keep her from leaving, but having said his piece, he could hardly stop her now.

As it happened, her route home crossed a river, so the man accompanied her to the bank, put her in his boat, and ferried her to the other side. When they reached the far shore, the wife stepped out of the boat and started to leave. "Goodbye," she said, "goodbye."

Hearing this, the man demanded, "Fare, please."

"Surely between us there is no need of a fare," said the wife.

"Well, that was when we were married," he said. "Now that we're divorced, we're strangers. If you can't pay your fare, I can't let you go. You'd better come back with me."

He took her home, and together they lived happily ever after.

TRANSLATED BY JAY RUBIN

TODAY'S BOOK OF JOKES

ANONYMOUS

Supplicant and Cutpurse

There was an old man who placed his hopes on the life to come. One day he went to the dry riverbed in Kyoto to see a puppet performance, when what should happen but that his purse was cut off by someone in the crowd. He spotted the man, however, and shouted, "Stop, thief!" The cutpurse had no choice but to draw his short sword and attack. "Villain!" the old man shouted, instantly drawing his own sword, and the two men went after each other. In the course of their fight, each man had an arm cut off. The cutpurse knew he was finished and ran off to parts unknown.

Meanwhile, the old man, having lost an arm, could only stand there weeping. People approached him from the crowd and said, "You poor fellow! It's bad enough he took your purse, but look at this wound he gave you! What a shame!"

One of those who approached him, a surgeon, said, "This is not so bad. Let's put the arm back on before the blood drains out." They searched the area, found the arm and attached it.

When the old man went home, he called a famous physician, and thanks to this doctor's many treatments, the arm was soon as good as ever. Because they had attached it in haste, however, they had accidentally given the old man the arm of the cutpurse, which soon began to act in accordance with its evil nature. When the old man tried to hold a rosary in prayer, for example, the arm would cast it aside. Or if it saw someone wearing a nice silken tissue pouch or purse, it would creep toward the person's waist. Or so the report goes.

TRANSLATED BY JAY RUBIN

THIS YEAR'S JOKES

EDITED BY SHOEN BUSHI

Death Poem

A thief was about to be executed for his crimes when he said, "Wait a minute. I want to recite a death poem."

"That is highly commendable. Go right ahead."

The man intoned:

"At such a time
I might have clung
To this life of mine
Had I not learned so long ago
That I do not exist"

"Hey, that's Ōta Dōkan's death poem, not yours!"
"Well, sure," said the thief. "What better way to end a life of crime?"

TRANSLATED BY JAY RUBIN

HAND-ROLLED FOR LAUGHTER

ANONYMOUS

A Young Man Learns Country Manners

Once a young man married into a family living in the countryside, but he was lacking in manners. His father-in-law sat him down and said, "Look here, when

A Young Man Learns
Country Manners.
Hand-Rolled for Laughter,
Volume 4, Story 4. (Tokyo
Metropolitan Chuo Library)

you go out into the village, you've got to bow to people. You've got to greet people who are out working in the fields."

"I see your meaning," the young man replied.

One day the young man caught sight of someone at the far end of a field, up in a large tree, chopping off a bough. He waved the man over.

"What is it?" the man said, scrambling down the tree and running over to him. "Can't you see I've got no time for chitchat?"

"Nothing important, really," the young man replied. "I just wanted to say what a fine job you're doing."

TRANSLATED BY DYLAN MCGEE

A Pickpocket Delivers a Bundle of Joy

There's this story someone tells about a woman pickpocket who gave birth to a baby. It goes like this: The woman was having a difficult delivery; the baby's hands popped out first, but the rest of him didn't seem to want to come out. The midwife tried one trick after the next but just couldn't seem to get her hands in there to pull the baby out. Just as she was racking her brains about what to do next, a man came over and said, "I know something we can do."

He placed a stone mortar in front of the place where the woman was about to give birth and scraped the mortar with a pair of long, metal pokers. Sure enough, like mother, like baby, the little nipper mistook the sound of the pokers for the staff of a night watchman and instinctively slipped his hands back inside the womb.

Sensing they were all set now for the final push, the man called out in a loud voice, "Pardon all the prisoners!"

Wouldn't you know it, the baby slipped right out!

TRANSLATED BY DYLAN MCGEE

A Shabby Dresser Gets Hung Out to Dry

Once there was a shabbily dressed fellow who wanted to get his robe clean, but he didn't have anything to change into while it was being washed. He thought long and hard about what to do.

"How about this?" his wife suggested. "You climb up onto my back, and I'll drape my kimono over the both of us while I scrub your robe in the basin."

"That sounds like a plan," he said, mounting his wife from behind.

A Shabby Dresser Gets Hung Out to Dry. *Hand-Rolled for Laughter*, Volume 4, Story 6. (Tokyo Metropolitan Chuo Library)

Just then, a neighbor happened to stumble in on the scene.

"This is bad form," the man said, "but please pardon me for speaking down to you like this!"

TRANSLATED BY DYLAN MCGEE

How to Love a Servant Girl

Once there was a samurai who had fallen on hard times and was reduced to living in a commoner's townhouse.

One day, he took his servant girl over to a spot near the veranda, and proceeded to make love to her in broad daylight.

Along came a bumbling fellow, who threw open the door with a clatter and called out, "I'm here to see you!"

The samurai was startled but managed to keep his composure. "Look at me," he said. "I've fallen so far in the world that now if I want to get pussy, I've got to do it myself!"

The man replied, "Then pass her along to me. I'd be happy to do the work for you."

TRANSLATED BY DYLAN MCGEE

STORIES TOLD BY BUZAEMON

SHIKANO BUZAEMON

The God of Fortune

Once a man made an idol of Ebisu, the God of Fortune, from some boiled wild yams and displayed it on a tray. When the man's neighbor, who was fervently religious, came over one day for a visit, he asked if he could have it.

"You're welcome to it," the man replied, and gave it to him.

So the neighbor brought the little Ebisu home and placed it alongside his kitchen hearth for good luck. His happiness knew no bounds.

The God of Fortune. From Shikano Buzaemon, *Stories Told by Buzaemon*, Book 2, Story 11. (Department of Japanese Linguistics, the University of Tokyo)

Two or three days went by, and the man had a look at his little idol. The eyes had begun to droop, and the mouth was bending into a frown. He looked like he was crying. It was because the man had placed it alongside the hot hearth, you see, that the Ebisu had shriveled up and his face had become contorted. The man called in a mountain priest.

"See there? It's just like I told you," the man said as he pointed out the problem to the priest.

The mountain priest, seeing that it was simply dried out, slapped some water on it. Just like that, the idol returned to its former shape, beaming with a jolly grin.

From that day forward, it was said that the household grew wealthier by the day, all of the family's prayers were answered, and they prospered beyond expectation. In this case, faith truly did bring great fortune, as the saying goes.

TRANSLATED BY DYLAN MCGEE

JOKES TOLD BY TSUYU

TSUYU NO GORŌ

A Son Whose Labels Cut the Mustard

Around summertime, some guests came calling upon an old man, and he served them a meal of chilled wheat noodles. Yet when they asked him for some mustard powder to flavor the broth, the old man had to go to his wit's end trying to find it, because none of the sacks of spices were marked. At long last, he came up with the requested seasoning.

Evening fell, and the old man's son came home.

"Listen here," he said, "you've got to label all those paper sacks with the names of what's inside. What good is a bunch of blank sacks when you're in a hurry to find something?"

His son took this reprimand to heart, so much so that when the old man went to sleep that night, he wrote in big, bold letters across the paper curtain that surrounded his bed, "Contents: My Old Man."

TRANSLATED BY DYLAN MCGEE

A Son Whose Labels Cut the Mustard. From *Stories from Tsuyu*, Volume 1, Story 3. (Department of Japanese Literature, the University of Tokyo)

A Confession, Guessed Wrong

In a certain house, there was a servant named Kyūshichi. He was a hardworking fellow by nature who earned his master's favor through diligent service. Once, when the master was away, Kyūshichi said to the lady of the house, "This is terribly embarrassing, my lady, but there's something I've been keeping to myself, something I want to tell you."

The woman's face turned red. "My, you are a funny one. What is it you need to say?"

"Once I tell you this, there is no turning back, even if your answer is no."

"Well, if you need to think that much about it, then you can always say it at another time."

"Right now there is no one else around to hear. It seems as good an opportunity as any, so I think I will just come out with it."

Kyūshichi came close to her and whispered into her ear. "Starting tomorrow, would you kindly dole out larger portions of rice for me at mealtimes?"

TRANSLATED BY DYLAN McGEE

Taking Care of Smallpox

A thirty-year-old man was passing through the affluent Shinzaike neighborhood at the southwest corner of the imperial palace grounds when a somewhat older waiting woman from one of the aristocratic households to the west happened along with her maid. As soon as she spotted him, she broke into an alluring smile and said, "Please forgive me for being so bold, sir, but I'd very much like to take you to my place."

By no means indifferent to matters of a sensual nature, the man instantly accompanied the woman to her home, which turned out to be an impressive mansion. She opened a side door, led him into a large room partitioned with several fine folding screens, and served him many delicacies.

"I am the wet nurse who raised the young miss of this household," she finally explained. "She is sixteen now and inundated with proposals of marriage, but I would love to have her see you. I hate to impose on you, but please be so kind as to honor my request and meet her."

She took him by the hand and led him to an inner room. Scarcely sure if he was awake or dreaming, the man trembled as he approached a folding screen.

The wet nurse knelt at the girl's pillow and said, "I told you not to scratch, didn't I? If you want proof, look at this man. The minute you start scratching, your face will be covered with pockmarks just like his."

TRANSLATED BY JAY RUBIN

A Tightwad Priest Crazy about a Boy

Once there was a stingy old priest who became anguished with love for a young man and sought to woo him with countless letters filled with rambling professions. The young man himself was something of a player, and so one night he went to stay at the priest's temple.

At dawn, the priest awoke to the sound of falling rain. "Heaven, help me!" he thought to himself. "I shouldn't have let that boy stay the night. Now I've got to fix him breakfast! Wait! On second thought, why don't I just pretend to be asleep and not notice him when he gets up and leaves?"

As the priest was thinking to himself, the young man woke up and quietly stole outside.

"He must have exited the gate by now," the priest thought. Anxious, he got up and went to have a look. Still tarrying there at the gate was the young man. Exposed, the priest shut his eyes and started snoring loudly, pretending to sleepwalk.

TRANSLATED BY DYLAN MCGEE

A Tightwad Priest Crazy about a Boy. From *Stories from Tsuyu*, Volume 3, Story 8. (Department of Japanese Literature, the University of Tokyo)

JOKES WORTHY OF YOUR EAR

YONEZAWA HIKOHACHI

A Radish Fit for an Emperor

Miyashige in Owari was known for its daikon radishes, but the biggest one ever produced there was seven feet around and thirteen feet long! This was so unusual they decided to send it to no less a personage than His Majesty the Emperor himself. Try as they might, however, they could not get it to go up the stairs of the Great Hall. It was as if the radish had a will of its own. The courtiers were amazed. "I know why it won't go up. It's afraid the stairs of the *Great* Hall are a radish *grater*," said one. "That's it!" another said with a laugh. "This radish is the country's *gratest* coward!"

TRANSLATED BY JAY RUBIN

A Radish Fit for an Emperor. From *Jokes Worthy of Your Ear*, Volume 1, Story 1. (Department of Japanese Literature, the University of Tokyo)

A Certain Style of Face

Once, a bumbling samurai ran into a man he knew, somewhere near Kiyomizu Temple.

"Why, if it isn't old Sakuza!" he greeted him. "Tell me, how long has it been?"

The man was taken aback. "I don't know anyone named Sakuzaemon," he said.

The samurai peered closely into his face. "Well, I'll be. I beg your pardon," he said. And with that, he proceeded on his way.

Four or five blocks down the avenue, the samurai crossed paths with the very same man he had seen earlier.

"Listen, you've got to hear this! Just now, I ran into this fellow who was the spitting image of you. Boy, what a fool I made of myself!"

The man replied, "You've got me mistaken for the wrong man again. I'm the man you just met a few blocks down the street."

The samurai couldn't help running his mouth again. "Well, here I've gone and mistaken you for the wrong man twice. I swear, your style of face is sure popular in these parts!"

TRANSLATED BY DYLAN MCGEE

A White Mouse with Renal Vacuity

Once, a white mouse made its home in a medicine shop on Nijō Avenue in Kyoto. The shopkeeper was delighted, seeing this as a sign of good fortune; but little by little, sales began to slump. The shopkeeper's wife complained that no good had come to them since the white mouse took up in their shop, and the shopkeeper had to agree. He set a trap, using a small measuring box, and captured the little critter. When he inspected it closely, the mouse began to squeak.

"I am really not a lucky white mouse," it said. "I'm a black mouse. I suffer from a bad case of renal vacuity, and I've been stealing your foxglove pills and eating them. That's why my coat has turned white."

TRANSLATED BY DYLAN MCGEE

An Impromptu Performance

One evening after supper, a man set out to visit the grave of his late grandmother, remembering that it was the anniversary of her death. Meanwhile, the temple priest had just summoned his mistress and begun to indulge in a little drinking party, to dispel his boredom on this dreary day.

Festivities were in full swing by the time the man arrived at the rectory, throwing the priest into a panic. Fretting about how to hide his mistress from view, he shoved her underneath a massive cauldron in the kitchen.

Spotting the woman, the visitor said to the priest, "I say, what are you cooking up for us?"

The priest replied, "Oh, that. Well, it was so boring earlier that I thought we could have a performance of *Dōjōji*."

"Great idea!" the visitor replied. Tossing back a cup of *sake*, he chanted, "Here now, let's have a *daikoku* dance before the snake appears!"

TRANSLATED BY DYLAN MCGEE

An Impromptu
Performance. From
Jokes Worthy of Your Ear,
Volume 3, Story 4.
(Department of
Japanese Literature, the
University of Tokyo)

A Bather Kicks the Bucket

Once a man got into a hot washtub and, for whatever reason, rolled his eyes
and passed out right there in the water. A great commotion ensued in the
household, and the neighborhood quack was called in. He took the man's
pulse as he sat there in the tub, and gave a knowing look.

"Pull the stopper and drain the water," the quack instructed one of the
servants.

"All right, I've pulled the plug," the servant said.

"Good. Now put a lid on the tub and have him carted off to the
graveyard."

TRANSLATED BY DYLAN MCGEE

Piss-Poor in Arima. From *Jokes Worthy of Your Ear*, Volume 4, Story 13. (Department of Japanese Literature, the University of Tokyo)

Piss-Poor in Arima

No matter how hard up you are to make ends meet, there's always some way to get by on the bare essentials, even if it means going bare naked. Once there was a man who tried to come up with some new scheme for eking out a living. Seeing a bamboo rainspout, he got the idea to hollow out a bamboo stalk and make it into a pipe. Going to the Arima Hot Springs, he started making the rounds of the inns, hawking his services in a loud voice.

"Got yer piss pipe here! Drain your rain from the second story!"

A group of bathers called him over. "This we've got to try!" they said.

Standing outside in front of the inn, the man extended his device up to the customers on the second-story veranda.

"Hey, I can't aim into this!" one of them complained. "It's too narrow!"

"Right you are," the man replied, and with that, he produced from the breast of his kimono a funnel, which he proceeded to fasten to the tip of the pipe and guide back up to the veranda.

TRANSLATED BY DYLAN MCGEE

JOKES LEFT BY ROKYŪ

TSUYU NO GOROBĒ

A Peasant Plays It Safe

Two peasants were sowing seeds in their fields. One of the peasants, named Yotarō, called over to his neighbor in the adjoining plot.

"Say, Jirosaku! Fine farming weather we're having. What are you sowing?"

Jirosaku said something in reply, but not loud enough for Yotarō to hear.

"What was that?" Yotarō shouted back. "I couldn't make out a word you said."

Jirosaku walked over and whispered into his neighbor's ear, "I'm planting soybeans."

"What's with all the whispering? It's all right to raise your voice, you know."

"Because if I say it out loud, the pigeons might hear me!"

TRANSLATED BY DYLAN MCGEE

Like Father, Like Son—A Pair of Drunkards

One night, an old man came home boozed up on *sake.* He called out for his son, but there was no reply. He wasn't in his room.

"Don't tell me he's gone out carousing again. That sneaky little bastard!"

Just then the son staggered back home, drunk beyond description.

"Get over here, you moron," his father said. "Where the hell have you been, getting shit-faced like that? You keep this up and you're going to find yourself losing the inheritance on this house!"

"Quit your babbling, you old geezer," the son snapped back. "Besides, who wants a house that keeps spinning around in circles?"

Slurring his words, his father shouted back, "Why you little! What makes you think I'd even want to leave my house to some idiot who can't keep his face from going out of focus!"

It would be hard to find a bigger pair of drunks.

TRANSLATED BY DYLAN MCGEE

A Wild Boar Comes Back to Life

Once a hunter spotted a wild boar and aimed to shoot it, but got flustered and forgot to load his bullet. He fired off an empty charge. The spooked animal slumped over and died.

A meat buyer came by. The hunter figured it was as good a time as any, so he sold his game on the spot.

"Hold on, this boar hasn't got any bullet wounds on him," the buyer protested. "I can't tell when he died. How do I know this isn't just some stale hunk of meat?"

"I shot him just a moment ago," the hunter insisted. "But now that you mention it, he sure does look old."

When they turned to have another look at the carcass, the boar suddenly let out a squeal and righted itself on its hooves, tearing off for the mountains.

"Will you have a look at that!" the hunter exclaimed, pointing to the animal. "There's some fresh meat for you!"

TRANSLATED BY DYLAN MCGEE

Fickle Lovers Plot a Double Suicide

Through the land, love suicides are all the rage. Once a woman who lived near Osaka pledged her love to a certain man and suggested to him that they ought to commit suicide together. The man was put out by this request but sought to oblige the woman in any case, racing forth to Umeda Bridge for the fateful rendezvous.

"Things were crazy at home, and I wasn't able to find a short sword," he said upon arriving at the bridge. "What about you? Did you bring a shaving razor or something else sharp for us to cut our throats with?"

"No," the woman replied. "It didn't even occur to me."

"Well, then, you'd better go and fetch us a razor."

"All right," she said, and hurried back to her house.

Left there to think things over, the man decided that he didn't want to go through with this suicide after all and slipped away.

At length, the woman came back to the bridge, bringing a shaving razor. She called out for her lover but couldn't spot him anywhere.

"Don't tell me he's ditched me. That two-timing jerk! What's the point in killing myself for a loser like that?" she said, and returned home.

Some time later, the two ran into one another at Nihonbashi. With nowhere to hide, the man folded a tissue, perched it on his forehead, and called out, "Long time no see! Fancy meeting you in this life!"

TRANSLATED BY DYLAN MCGEE

JOKES TO BLOOM IN SUMMER HEAT

ANONYMOUS

One Hundred Tales of Food

One winter night, four or five friends met at a tavern, and one of them suggested that they tell a hundred ghost stories to dispel the boredom.

"But then what happens after the ghosts appear? There won't be anything to keep us entertained," the man alongside him protested. "Listen, how about we take the same principle of telling one hundred stories to make something appear, but instead of ghosts, we regale each other with stories about food? That way, after the hundredth go, we'll be visited by all sorts of things to eat. Now, that would really liven things up!"

The men were shown by the host to their seats. They settled in and began to tell their tales.

Around the time they got to the fiftieth story, an object came tumbling down from the ceiling rafters. Inspecting it, they found it to be a wooden bowl full of udon noodles.

"What have we got here? Now, that's the trick!" they said.

No sooner had they begun to eat than a barrel of *sake*, some five *shō* in capacity, dropped to the floor. After that came some broth to go with their noodles.

"I'd say we've done well for ourselves," one of them remarked, overjoyed.

They continued on with the storytelling. By the eightieth go, the house was seized by a thunderous roar, which reverberated above them and below them and in all four directions. Chills went up their spines as they anticipated what might be visited upon them.

A giant of a man, clad in an apron, dropped down from the ceiling. Drawing a note from his breast, the man said, "Here, this is the bill for the food you've been eating all evening."

TRANSLATED BY DYLAN MCGEE

One Hundred Tales of Food. From *Jokes to Bloom in Summer Heat*, Volume 4, Story 7. (Department of Japanese Literature, the University of Tokyo)

JOKES FOR SIDE STITCHES

TŌKAKU

Happy Being a Beggar

On the night of New Year's Eve, throngs of debt collectors were crossing Sanjō Bridge in Kyoto. Meanwhile, two beggars, a father and son, were sleeping under the bridge.

The son was stirred by the footfalls overhead. "I swear," he said, rubbing his eyes, "merchants really must have a tough lot in life. I mean, us beggars, we can sleep from dusk till dawn. But debt collectors, they don't know if they'll be able to get repaid what's owed them or not. If they can't, then they've got to run around till all hours chasing down deadbeats. Yep, compared with them, I'd say we've got it made—what with being able to sleep from dusk till dawn and all." All in all, the young man seemed pretty pleased with himself.

The man's father awoke from his slumber. "Good grief!" he scolded. "What are you babbling on about?"

"I was just saying, 'Look at those debt collectors. We've sure got it better off than them.'"

"And who do you have to thank for your life of ease?"

TRANSLATED BY DYLAN MCGEE

JOKES FROM THE GOD OF FORTUNE

ANONYMOUS

Ten-Thousand-Year Trunk

A samurai and his servant visited a shop with a great signboard out front that read, "Ten-Thousand-Year Trunks."

Ten-Thousand-Year Trunk. From *Jokes from the God of Fortune*, Volume 3, Story 2. (Tokyo Metropolitan Chuo Library)

"I'm here to buy a wicker trunk," the samurai said. "Show me your premium model."

"Please come inside," the shopkeeper greeted him. He then proceeded to bring out the finest trunk in stock.

Once they agreed upon a price, the samurai handed the shopkeeper some gold coins.

"Now I need you to notarize the bill of receipt with a seal of warranty," the samurai said, "to guarantee the trunk against damages for a period of ten thousand years."

The shopkeeper, though taken aback by this request, didn't miss a beat. "As you wish," he said. "We stand by the quality of our wares for ten thousand years, so I will be only too happy to issue you a warranty. However, please take care to ensure that the trunk is treated with a new coat of varnish every thousand years."

TRANSLATED BY DYLAN MCGEE

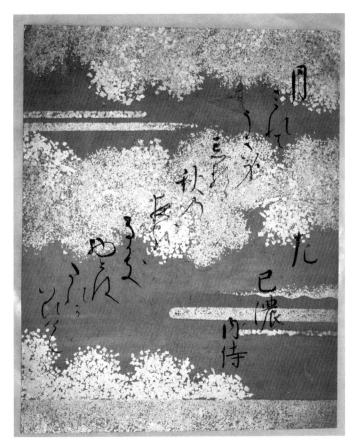

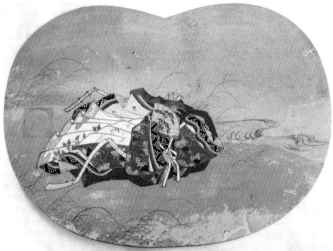

PLATE 1 Picture of Lady-in-Waiting Mino (Snake) and her accompanying poem. From Kanō Daigaku Ujinobu, illustrator, *The Poetic Competition of the Twelve Zodiac Animals* (ca. 1650). (Toru Takahashi Collection)

PLATE 2 As the prince lies dying, heirlooms of the Genji clan turn into a white pigeon and other creatures, including a dragon, come to visit him. The traveling monk by the prince's side is the god Hachiman in disguise. Iwasa Matabei's studio, from *Tales of Princess Jōruri* (twelve scrolls, seventeenth century). Designated as an Important Cultural Property of Japan. (MOA Museum of Art, Shizuoka)

PLATE 3 Actors wearing sedge hats leave a little theater while women watch them from a boat. Ihara Saikaku, *Saikaku's Hundred Linked Verses, Annotated by Himself* (hand scroll, 1692). (Tenri Central Library)

PLATE 4 European Christians are seen at the entrance of a church while some Japanese dressed in European clothes stand inside. Anonymous, *Southern Barbarian Screen*: two of six panels on a gold background (*Nanban Byōbu*, 1600). (Cleveland Museum of Art)

PLATE 5 The guest in the center is entertained by the courtesan, the assistant courtesan, and others. The room next door is a closet in which luxuriously thick bedding and a chest of kimono are kept. Hishikawa Moronobu, The interior of a Yoshiwara brothel (untitled red and black ukiyo-e, 1670s). (Sackler Museum, Harvard University)

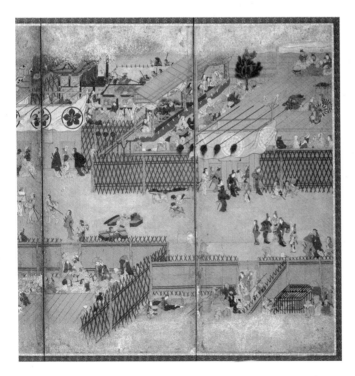

PLATE 6 The huts for puppet plays, sumo wrestling, dance, and storytelling surround a kabuki theater, at the entrance of which servants wait for their masters and others peek in from under the curtain. Anonymous, *Entertainment on the Shijō Riverbed* (two panels of a six-panel screen, 1620s–1640s). (Museum of Fine Arts, Boston)

PLATE 7 A street in the flourishing district in Sangenya at the mouth of the Kizukawa River in Osaka, later incorporated into the Shinmachi pleasure district in 1657. Anonymous, *A Pleasure Quarter at the Mouth of the River* (ten-panel standing screen, ca. 1640–1655). (Osaka Museum of History)

PLATE 8 The flourishing "cash only" clothing store featured clerks who represented departments within the store. Okumura Masanobu, *Large Perspective View of the Interior of Echigoya in Surugachō* (ukiyo-e, ca. 1745). (Museum of Fine Arts, Boston).

PLATE 9 The courtesan and her client who play the old woman and man in the nō play holding appropriate masks, a broom, and a rake as they stand in front of a pine tree that decorates the room's sliding screen. Ishikawa Toyonobu, *A Fashionable Parody of the Nō Play "Takasago"* (ukiyo-e of the beni-e category, ca. early 1760s). (Museum of Fine Arts, Boston)

PLATE 10 The nō chant could be one of the subjects that commoners' children studied at their small private schools. Kitagawa Utamaro, *Children's Nō Chant at School* (hand-painted hanging scroll, date unknown). (Hosei University Library and Hosei University Nogami Memorial Noh Theater Research Institute)

PLATE 11 Matabei (*left*), played by Nakamura Utaemon, is startled by the miracle he has caused, as his wife, Otoku, played by Nakamura Matsue, points at the magical image. The scene is from Tosa Shōgen Mitsunobu's house in a 1708 kabuki version of Chikamatsu Monzaemon's *jōruri* play, *A Courtesan's Soul within Incense Smoke*. Ryūsai Shigeharu, *Matabei the Stutterer* (ukiyo-e, 1829). (Waseda University Tsubouchi Memorial Theatre Museum)

PLATE 12 Superhero Kagekiyo frees himself from prison by breaking heavy bars, in a kabuki scene from a late production based on *Kagekiyo*, Chikamatsu Monzaemon's 1658 *jōruri* in five acts. Utagawa Kunisada II, *Ichikawa Ebizō in Kagekiyo Reborn from the Eighteen Plays of Kabuki* (ukiyo-e, date unknown). (Tokyo Metropolitan Chuo Library)

PLATE 13 As the courtesan Ōshū's old love letters are burned in an incense burner, her ghost appears in the smoke, in a scene from a song based on Chikamatsu Monzaemon's *A Courtesan's Soul within Incense Smoke*. Okumura Masanobu, *Actor Segawa Kikunojō I as the Courtesan Keisei Asamagatake, with Arashi Koroku I and Ichimura Takenojō IV* (ukiyo-e, 1736). (Museum of Fine Arts, Boston)

**P
A
R
T
XI**

Philosophizing the Ordinary

A Collection of Fallen Grains—Addendum

DAIDŌJI YŪZAN

These days Daidōji Yūzan (1639–1730) is best known for his *Code of the Warrior* (*Budō Shoshinshū,* posthumously published in 1828), a collection of highly moralistic and—considering the time at which it was written—anachronistic rules for samurai behavior. He was born one year after the Shimabara Rebellion and died 134 years before the first Chōshū campaign. In the ninety-one years of his life he saw no warfare of any kind. Nevertheless, his reputation is that of a military strategist. A lack of practical battlefield experience might have been considered something of a handicap in his chosen profession, but Yūzan seems to have been content to be an armchair strategist.

Little is known with any certainty about his life. His grandfather and subsequently, at least for a time, his father too had been samurai, but Yūzan was born into a household that had forfeited samurai status. He is said to have studied under Obata Kagenori (1572–1663), who had some battle experience, and a few others, whether or not they had. Just what Yūzan's status was is a mystery. It may be that until 1697, at the age of fifty-eight, he was one of the many figures, literate, smart, and ambitious, hovering on the outskirts of samurai society. In that year the daimyo of Aizu made him a vassal, giving him a modest stipend and, therefore, admitting him to samurai status. Unfortunately, he did not hold this position very long. Just three years later, for some unknown reason, he was summarily dismissed, and he spent the remaining thirty years of his life reminiscing about the good old days.

These good old days, as he described them in works written toward the end of his life, seemed to get better and better as they receded into the distance. *Code of the Warrior,* of course, with its idealization of samurai morality, is one. His reminiscences, written when he was eighty-eight years old and collected under the title *A Collection of Fallen Grains* (*Ochiboshū,* 1727), represent another. This work and its *Addendum* (from the fifth volume)—from which the following selections are taken—need to be handled with care. Yūzan writes with spurious authority of the "turbulent times" of the civil war period (in which Tokugawa Ieyasu finally unified the country), which ended thirty-nine years before he was born, so at best his judgments depend on hearsay. It is unlikely that samurai entangled in the exigencies of civil warfare were as loyal, upright, and frugal as those he describes, but this distorted image allows him to inject into his writing what, by this time, had become a common complaint—that samurai are not what they once were. They have become dependent on luxuries, they spend too much money, they get into debt, and they have lost their manly vigor. Take away the particulars of time and place, and we can see Daidōji Yūzan as yet another example of a universal archetype— the elderly scold.

ON THE MATTER OF FLOODS

Somebody posed this question: "There seem to be floods every year now, breaching dikes and ruining fields and paddies. Did things like this ever happen in the old days?"

So I responded: "Certainly, in the past in some years there were floods, but I cannot recall anything like these recent ones. People do not bother to see to it that dikes and riverbanks are well made. Of course these floods cannot be blamed on evil spirits. As a matter of fact, flooding was rare in the civil war period, and when it did happen, nobody was much affected by it. These days, frequent floods are related to our stable system of government, not to nonsensical theories about evil spirits."

Then came this question: "So floods were rare in the civil war period. But I cannot believe that we are to continue having floods just as long as we keep our style of government."

This was my reply: "Had civil war persisted, we would have had battles and skirmishes everywhere, with each side taking casualties, whether large or small. For example, if a thousand men were killed in a single engagement, probably a hundred or a hundred and fifty of them would have been samurai. The other eight or nine hundred would for the most part have been foot soldiers, pikemen, standard-bearers, or nondescript people without armor to protect them. But if samurai, safely armored, were to be hit with an arrow or a musket ball or struck with a spear or a sword, they would be only slightly wounded. In other words, as they say, the winning side wins, and the losing side loses, so those who lose suffer heavy casualties.

"When beaten samurai ride off in retreat, they know what their losses have been. Most of their dead—from the foot soldiers, pikemen, and standard-bearers down to armed grooms—are irreplaceable, because nobody else will want to join them. This being the case, it is difficult to hire even useless ronin as mercenaries. But if you then select capable peasants from your estate and force them into service as replacements for those killed, you will end up with fewer people working your land. Those few remaining, with so much land to manage, will neglect the more difficult of your taxable fields and instead cultivate productive plots outside your control. So distant upland areas are abandoned, produce no crops, and revert to grassland. Consequently, heavy rains are quickly absorbed, soon soaked up by grass and trees. This interrupts the normal processes of nature and causes a drop in river levels.

"But in peacetime, to manage a domain you need a large population, and it is simply not enough to have them work only on registered fields and paddies. You must have them clear hillsides to make fields, and cut brush at its base to prepare for cultivation. In that case even a small amount of rain carries topsoil into the rivers, and ultimately river bottoms are filled in, grow shallow, and their courses widen. So dikes and banks can often be breached.

"That was how things were seventy-seven or seventy-eight years ago. At that time I was stationed at Sōsenji, at Hashiba. An old peasant in his nineties, retired and living near the temple precincts, would come each morning and evening to the Sōsenji tea ceremony room. I heard him say that when he was a child, the Asakusa River was not as wide as it is now. At low tide the river course was quite narrow, so much so that children on the opposite bank and those on this side could throw stones at each other. Then, however, all of a sudden the river widened to its present shape. Of course such experience is not restricted to the Kantō region. When I was young and staying in a farmhouse at a place called Tsuda, near Takatsuki in Settsu Province, I had a good view of boats going up the Yodo River and was even able to tell how many men and women were on board. When I asked an old man of the household whether this would have been possible in the old days, he replied that when he was young (he was then eighty-six), he could make out the sails of river barges, but not the boats themselves. Then suddenly one day he was able to see them too. By this time the local dikes had been breached, with occasional overflows, so that now, he informed me, floods were a constant threat."

Then came another question: "On this matter of floods, I have been told that during the civil war period samurai, in need of servants, would bring peasants from their domains to act as vassals, resulting in a population decline in the countryside. Fewer peasants in the domain meant falling tax revenues and would leave samurai insecure and uncertain."

This was my reply: "It is hard to say whether the situation of samurai these days is like that of samurai during the civil war period. Peacetime warriors, whether they are important or not, base their reputations on how they present themselves. They decorate their houses with well-chosen ornaments. Wanting themselves, their wives, and their children to make a good appearance, they spend more than is wise to seem wealthy, and if their tax revenues are insufficient, they borrow, or buy on credit. What most distinguishes samurai of the civil war period from peacetime samurai is their houses. These were just shacks, their roofs serving only to keep out the rain, and they used hemmed grass matting as cushions. Because they did not entertain guests, they had no need of furniture. Their clothing, for their wives and children and themselves, was just padded cotton. When they went to the battlefield, they would drink their soup with unstrained miso and were used to eating small quantities of unpolished rice. In the morning and the evening, even when everything was quiet, they were not interested in good food. Their attendants behaved the same way. Other than demanding decent horses and someone to carry their spears they did not bother with unnecessary expense. For example, if the taxes from their estates fell short, they did not consider it any great hardship. When I was a young man, lower samurai would eat large helpings of inferior rice by mixing bran and salt water into it. On the battlefield they were accustomed to eating unpolished rice with brine. These days even samurai servants will not accept anything except white rice and malted miso soup. In fact, they think unpolished rice and tasteless soup are an insult."

WHAT BATHHOUSES WERE LIKE

Somebody asked this question: "They say that until the reign of His Excellency Daiyūin, officials from the magistrates' departments used to be summoned before the shogun, as they had been in the reigns of His Excellency Gongen and His Excellency Daitokuin, and each of them would be given direct orders. Have you heard of this practice?"

In reply I said: "Yes, I'm familiar with it. As an example, once during the reign of His Excellency Daiyūin the then town magistrate, Lord Yonezu Kanbei, ordered to appear before the shogun, was asked: 'Is it true that last night, on Kōji-machi Avenue, some guards from the Ushigome unit got into a fight with a local ronin?' 'I have not yet had a report on this,' Kanbei replied, 'but certainly these sorts of incidents should not be happening in town where they can be observed by ordinary folk.' The shogun, incredulous, then said, 'It definitely happened in Kōji-machi. Don't you know what goes on in your district?' To this Kanbei responded, 'Your Excellency is of course correct. There was most surely a brawl, but both parties left in a hurry, and by the time local residents arrived on the scene, it was over, and there was nothing to see. Because no officials were present, they decided there was nothing to investigate, and nobody has lodged a formal complaint.'

"Kanbei, now having been ordered to report on the details of the affray, left the castle and immediately began his investigation. The following day, on returning to the castle, he was called before the shogun for questioning. 'Last night I ordered the local people in for investigation, and indeed as Your Excellency was aware yesterday, the location was in front of the bathhouse at Kōji-machi. One side seems to have consisted of ten men, while the other was just one man. When both parties drew swords and began to exchange blows, they presumably realized that this was not a good place to fight. The group left, and when the local people arrived, they took the single man into custody. Because they restrained him without any difficulty, they said they felt no need to report the incident. This man, as Your Excellency said, is a worthless ronin. We know where he lives, and for the moment he has been placed under house arrest. The larger party seems to consist of foot soldiers from the Ushigome unit, but because the incident took place at night, nobody was able to recognize them. I await your instructions.'

"The shogun then said, 'It's obvious that the large group was foot soldiers. However, if there is any chance that a different group of foot soldiers were involved, you must look into it. In the meantime you are to make sure that the ronin you have in custody does not escape.' Kanbei then replied: 'I shall carry out your order as quickly as possible, but if the large group proves indeed to be foot soldiers then, after due consideration, both parties should receive the same punishment. However, the local gossip is that when this single ronin attacked them, the ten foot soldiers ran away. This is absolutely disgraceful behavior for bannermen, so I am sorry to say that in my opinion we should not proceed with our inquiries.' The shogun appeared extremely annoyed at this, so Kanbei, mortified, took his leave.

"Beginning with the next day, he was absent. He did not appear the following day either, pleading ill health. And so one morning a shogunal physician arrived to see how he was doing. As Kanbei received the physician with embarrassed gratitude for the shogun's generosity, the latter reported that, while on duty the previous night, he had heard the shogun say, 'Lord Yonezu

Kanbei is sick and has not been on duty. He is usually so healthy. I wonder what can be the matter? Go and see how he is.' 'So, I am looking in on you on my way home.' Kanbei burst into tears at this. 'I am so grateful. I did not expect this. I have been unwell recently and so have not come on duty. But since I feel better, I might return to work soon.' Having taken his pulse, the doctor said that in view of the shogun's kind concern, Kanbei might as well feel ready to attend that very day.

"The following day, Kanbei appeared before the shogun and said that he had recovered nicely and was grateful for the shogun's thoughtful consideration. He was then ordered to pardon the ronin who had been confined to house arrest for several days. As I think about such an example, I can say that Kanbei was certainly not the only one to be ordered before the shogun. Other officials were also called on occasion to be given instructions."

Then came another question: "What were downtown bathhouses like?"

I gave this answer: "I remember that during my youth bathhouses were being built here and there around town. Fires would be lit in the morning, then doused around four in the afternoon. During the day, until the seventh hour, bathhouse girls would scrape the grime from their customers, but then they would ready themselves for the evening, setting up a parlor inside the dressing room partitions, arranging gilded screens, lighting candles, changing their costumes, and attracting customers by playing the shamisen and singing. There were one or two such bathhouses near Kobikichō, and a foot soldier called, I think, Kurita Matabei, a member of the unit commanded by Lord Ishino Hachibei, got wounded in a fight in front of one of these bathhouses. This prompted an investigation, which concluded that such places were unsafe, and so fines were levied on them. Shortly after, all Edo bathhouses were ordered to be closed down. Just one, situated outside the main gate of Zōjōji Temple, was allowed. Employing bathhouse girls was prohibited."

ON THE ECONOMIC SITUATION OF SAMURAI

Somebody asked: "These days, nine or ten percent of samurai, from daimyo down through bannermen and their vassals, are stretched too thin financially, and you rarely see one well turned out. Was it like this in the old days?"

So I replied: "During the civil war period all samurai, whether they were of high status or low, were careful of their appearance. Townsfolk, farmers, and priests, though, were all shabby. Even samurai of low rank, in fact, dressed in such a way as to seem powerful during these civil war circumstances. This was especially so among the vassals of provincial lords, who paraded their authority to enhance their position by winning the respect of the common people. These, the townspeople and farmers of the domain, would never trade with other provinces during wartime, and their household servants were all dedicated to contributing to their lords' war efforts. Those commoners who thought only of their own glory were much disliked, and nobody would do business with them. Wealthy commoners, worried about keeping their gold and silver, wisely lessened their fears by commending their riches to the domain lord for his use. The domain's gold and silver was thereby concentrated in the hands of regional administrators. In view of these unsettling circumstances, the lord's retainers, generally lamenting the way of the world, felt that although their lives were safe today, they might well perish on the battlefield tomorrow. The domain samurai would have thought it disgraceful to borrow from others, promising to repay at the end of the year, when their future was unknown. So they would therefore live within their means, begrudging the spending of even the slightest sum.

"However, as circumstances are now, samurai whether they are of high status or low have become accustomed to the conditions of peacetime. They have become soft, craving luxuries and living far above their station. The salaries they receive from their lords can no longer sustain them, so they incur debts whenever they can, and do not worry about the interest these debts accrue. Gradually their obligations increase, so that ultimately they are trapped and ruined. With diminished resources they cannot repay their loans, placing their guarantors in an equally difficult position. It is unworthy of a samurai to cheerfully saddle others with their debts. The proverb says, 'Poverty makes you stupid,' and its meaning should be all the more understood in this age of peace and tranquility. In battle, those born into the samurai class dislike distinctions between rich and poor, and high and low. They abhor personal luxury. Those given salaries by their lord value frugality and simplicity and, conscious of their responsibilities, are not overly concerned about their appearance. All the same, they are also careful not to lose their dignity.

"Lately in particular, samurai, whether of high status or low, seem to be financially worn out. This is all due to the increase in the price of rice that took place during the Genroku era. Before that time a stipend of one hundred *koku* would fetch a hundred gold pieces. Thereafter it would bring upwards of two hundred, and that persisted for the next two or three years. This gave rise to the mistaken notion that such prices would continue forever, so people enlarged their houses, employed servants, and did things they had never done before. Because they were living beyond their means, their economic situation was greatly changed when the price of rice fell unexpectedly, and their incomes along with it. Hoping that perhaps things might improve by the end of the year, instead they found that the rice price fell still further. They piled up debts recklessly until they were absolutely ruined. When I was young, no daimyo was especially poor. If any one had been, his vassals would work hard to keep it a secret. Under such circumstances, the vassals themselves, too, if they were financially embarrassed, would do whatever they could to avoid humiliation."

ON THE MATTER OF DANCING GIRLS

Somebody asked this question: "Here in town these days girls are being brought together and taught dancing, popular ditties, songs from the stage, and shamisen. A great many people make their living this way. Was it like this before, or has it just begun recently?"

This was my response: "When I was young, no one would have wanted to be a dancer, no matter how much money one could make. No one but blind women used to play the shamisen; if a maid, for example, who was not blind was made to learn the art, it seemed to be an extraordinary thing to the world. Thus, two or three blind women, called *goze,* were hired for the women's quarters in daimyo households to perform on formal occasions, playing the shamisen and singing. It was probably from the middle of the Genroku era that somehow these *goze* came from everywhere to dance and play the shamisen. Suddenly girls all wanted to be dancers, and their parents, hoping for something better than a samurai with an income of only five hundred or a thousand *koku,* would aim to see them employed by someone with at least from five or seven thousand up to ten thousand *koku* and above, or even the lord of a province. So they would choose a teacher for them and have them learn to play, no matter how much it cost.

"I would not say that all of their employers would fall in love with them. But all the same, young men were charmed, would lose all sense of decorum, and, tipsy from too much *sake,* would behave indecently. Needless to say, those who were brought up with relaxed attention, and even those born into rigorously ethical families, may not be able to resist the combination of eros and *sake.* They will sicken and have no chance of living long. Confucius himself deplored those who indulge in debauchery.

"When I was young, whenever the daimyo wished to enter the women's quarters, a bell would be rung, and the senior ladies would order the young and pretty girls into the inner quarters so that the master could not catch them as they wandered around. But now, when did it start that a daimyo's daughter on her wedding day would have among her retinue some dancing girls and shamisen players as companions? A few days after the wedding, the senior ladies now organize entertainments with these dancing girls, and the young lords have come to think that nothing is more delightful. To be glad that the lord takes every opportunity to visit the women's quarters in the happy company of his wife is equivalent to poisoning the esteemed lord. This sort of thing has developed over the past thirty or forty years. It was unknown when I was a young man."

TRANSLATED BY HAROLD BOLITHO

The Country Zhuangzi

INDISCRIMINATELY SELECTED BY ISSAI CHOZAN,
A GENTLEMAN RESIDING IN THE EAST

The fashion of learning encouraged by the Kyōhō Reforms under the shogun Yoshimune (1684–1751) encouraged the spread of public lectures in addition to the so-called sermon books (*dangibon*), which popularized principles of Buddhism, Daoism, and Confucianism. *Country Zhuangzi* (*Inaka Sōji,* ten volumes in two parts, 1727) was one of the early widely read books published in Edo and continued to appear in a variety of versions until the mid-nineteenth century. The book presents the author's personal interpretations of Confucian thought of the dominant school, founded by Zhuzi (1130–1200), and of Daoism, particularly according to the master Zhuangzi (ca. BC 369–286). The two parts of the book consist essentially of parables featuring animals and plants, imitating Zhuangzi's rhetoric of paradox and explicating his thesis on the indeterminacy and changeability of life and the universe. And yet the author is not averse to Confucianism and, in fact, argues for a cohesive understanding of Daoism and Confucianism. These volumes contain stories that are chiefly in the form of dialogues, focusing more on ideas than on narrative action. The second part, however, includes stories of hell, indicating the author's inclination toward narrative fiction.

Three of the parables in the first part of *Country Zhuangzi* are presented here. The central text implied in "The Transformation of the Sparrow and the Butterfly" is the episode of Zhuangzi's own writing about a dream of being a butterfly. In his dream, Zhuangzi flies around freely as a butterfly, but he is not aware that he is Zhuangzi himself. As he wakes, he is back to the same old Zhuangzi. He poses the often-quoted question, "Did Zhuangzi become a butterfly in a dream, or did a butterfly become Zhuangzi in its dream?" Following Zhuangzi's model, "The Transformation of the Sparrow and the Butterfly" teaches that all beings, as changeable as they may be, are separate existences and that the form defines the content or the spirit.

Through a bullfrog's admonishing of a rat for its self-serving prayer to the gods and the Buddha, "The Bullfrog's Shinto" advocates an open attitude even toward one's enemies. The rat wishes for a total elimination of his mortal foe, the cat, while the bullfrog points out that cats will lose their whole raison d'être if rats behave themselves and give human beings no cause to hate them. The lesson is that one's desires are not to be fulfilled, because the desires themselves are formulated from a very narrow perspective. The translation given here is from the fable portion of the work. The last third, which is omitted in this translation, is a didactic sermon on the importance of keeping oneself clean inside and out before the gods and not mixing personal wishes in one's prayers.

"The Story of Sōemon" (Sōemon ga Den) describes the lazy eccentric Tamura Sōemon, a Daoist whose name suggests Zhuangzi by the use of the character "sō," which is the Japanese equivalent of the Chinese "Zhuang." In this story, Sōemon is accused of being perfectly useless as an educated individual, not easily identified as Confucian or Daoist. The polite but ironic response to this accusation suggests that his style of existence is, indeed, a true way of virtue according to Daoism. In the course of his unorthodox defense of himself, the accepted standards of accomplished gentlemen who maintain the golden mean are thoroughly satirized for their worldly ambition and self-display.

"Issai Chozan" was the pen name for Tanba Jūrōemon Tadaaki (1659–1741), a samurai who served three generations of lords in the Kuze clan, the rulers of Sekiyado Domain, not far from Edo. After his retirement in 1731, he took tonsure and devoted his last ten years to the education of the young as well as to writing on the subject of intellectual thought. In the "Seven Books by Chozan," which include *Country Zhuangzi, Art of Tengu* (1729), and *Country Zhuangzi Miscellanies* (1742), Chozan explicates the general principles of Daoism, Buddhism, and Confucianism, all of which he believed to be valid and interrelated. Although his cosmology and his sense of the self derive chiefly from Zhuangzi's teachings, he finds their commonality with the ontological and epistemological philosophy of the Zhuzi School of Confucianism and the principle of self-reliant enlightenment in the Zen brand of Buddhism. Reflecting the classical Chinese philosophy along with Zhuangzi's playfulness, Chozan's writings inspired the comic intellectualism among the writers of Edo. His technique of parable shed a strong influence on *gesaku,* which followed. Although his stance was far more didactic than that of later writers such as Hiraga Gennai, his use of irony set the tone for later *dangibon* and paved the way for the stronger expression of comedy and satire in *gesaku* that characterized the later Edo literature based in the city of Edo.

⌒(sj)⌒

PREFACE

The Breath of the Great Clod is what we call Wind. The Great Clod is this Heaven and Earth. All things born between Heaven and Earth come from this Wind—according to Zhuangzi.

When the people hear that all things that arise between heaven and earth do come from all directions as though on wind, they prick their ears and inch forward without knowing it. It is the people's taste to encounter the strange and mysterious; it is the people's mouths that have a fondness for empty words. We have wondered for some time how it would be to be able to direct people to the Way by speaking of the weird according to their tastes and by letting them enjoy their lives through the taste of words that come out of our mouths. *The Country Zhuangzi* is a book that can do it. A certain bookseller came to me and asked me to write a preface for it. Because besmirching paper with ink is my life's pleasure, why would I have declined? Whatever sense this book expresses, it does it through deliciously empty words. What makes us creep forward on our knees is its mystery and strangeness. Is it not the book's intention to have us follow the Way and take joy in our lives? This is a Zhuangzi, country style. It is indeed writing in the native syllabary from the brush of the great master.

> *The Ninth Month of 1727*
> *Composed by Ryūsankaku and*
> *calligraphy by Iida Hyakusen*

THE TRANSFORMATION OF THE SPARROW AND THE BUTTERFLY

One day a sparrow said to a butterfly, "In common parlance you are called a 'vegetable bug.' Long ago you wandered around the fields, unable to fly freely, finally attaching yourself to a plant leaf, where you hung wriggling. Now you are changed into a butterfly. You flit from flower to flower, trailing after their fragrances, and have a body capable of flight. How much more enjoyable life is for you now than it was before!

"Though I am a bird at present, have legs and wings and fly about as I please, it is said that we sparrows in the ninth month of the year must enter the sea and turn into clams. Now, if you look at those clams, you can see they don't have eyes or noses, legs or arms, and just sit covered in their shells and stick out their tongues from time to time, though eating what, I don't know. Even in the worst extremes of cold, all they do is tumble around through the ocean and dig holes for themselves in the sand. If I become one of them, what shall I do?

"If I had been born a clam from the start, I could accept this as what must be. But for a being that has received life once as a sparrow, that has known the pleasures of mountain and forest, then to be transmogrified, to bear the suffering of the ocean depths, to waste away or fatten at the whim of the tides' nutrients! How I will suffer, thinking back with fondness on former times! When I consider this now, all I can do is weep in distress. How lucky your fate, to rise from a mere caterpillar to your present state of freedom! What evil karma is mine, that I must descend from being a flying bird to become some strange creature!" Thus whimpered the sparrow through his tears.

Hearing this, the butterfly responded: "Such change is not a thing to mourn. It is neither downgrading for you nor an advancement for me! Energy gathers to become an object, and as it changes, the form changes. I, too, somehow: though it may be said that I changed from caterpillar to butterfly, I have no recollection of how it happened, not to mention any memories of the time when I was a caterpillar, though when I consider it now, I must certainly have pursued a normal caterpillar's existence.

"Long ago Zhuangzi dreamed he was a butterfly flying around, becoming in his dream one with the heart of the butterfly, not knowing he was actually a human. When he awoke and returned to being Zhuangzi, he wondered whether he was Zhuangzi who had become a butterfly or a butterfly who had become Zhuangzi. The principle of Change is thus.

"When you are transformed into a clam in the ninth month, you will no doubt act out of your Heaven-endowed nature and enter the sea without a second thought, as if you were slipping into a drunken slumber. Once you have become a clam, your present sparrow's mind will cease to exist, becoming of itself the mind of a clam. Even in the harshest cold, you will make your home in the ocean and not feel any chill; tumbling through the water will be a most natural way for you to get around.

"For the mind and spirit to change when the form changes is a constancy of principle. Principle exists not in form or appearance but in spirit. If there is already the spirit of a sparrow, then the sparrow principle exists. And when there is the form and spirit of the clam, the clam principle exists. The mind of a form depends on that form. When the form is destroyed, then the mind of this form is no more.

"Long ago there lived an old man. When he was on his deathbed and the head priest came to urge him to recite prayers to Buddha, the old man opened his eyes and said, 'All things are born from nothing and return to nothing. How can there be such a thing as transmigration and rebirth?'

"'What if by some chance there were?' asked the priest in return. 'What would you do then? Wouldn't it be better just to bend your principles and say some prayers?'

"The old man shook his head. 'Even if there were such a thing as rebirth, I wouldn't worry about it. Do you, honored priest, remember when you were in your mother's womb? Tell me, how did it feel when you were born?'

"The priest became angry and replied, 'Is there anybody who remembers this? Are you saying you do?'

" 'I don't,' said the old man. 'Since nobody remembers such a recent event as his own birth, how could anyone remember something as distant as a previous existence? And so, no matter what I might be reborn as in some future life, whether it be as an ant or a mouse, my present soul will cease to exist, and I will naturally assume the soul of the thing I am born as and live a suitable life as such. It is said that life is like a dream. The next world too is another life, and this life too will become as a dream. In that case, isn't it foolish to agonize now over something we cannot know as distinct from life? My only desire now is to die knowing that I am dying. This is true Buddhahood.' Hearing this, the priest withdrew, at a loss for words.

"Now yams are transformed into eels, and rotting grass into fireflies. Try asking an eel or a firefly if he knows the soul of the sweet potato or rotting grass. What is the karmic retribution of a yam and rotting grass? Yin and yang commingle and create form, and their spirit is active within this form, fulfilling the purpose of action and inaction, speech and silence. When the living spirit is expended and leaves its form, we call it death. Because the form contains the living spirit, it has the feelings of joy and anger, love and hate. After this form dies and the living spirit is no more, how can these feelings remain? A fire burns by consuming wood. When the wood is all burned up, the fire expires of itself. Though it may smolder for a while, it cannot be for long. But although we say the flame has gone out, yet it hardly means that the flame has been hiding in the flint and metal. You should take this to heart; it is not something that can be explained in words."

TRANSLATED BY DAVID SITKIN

THE BULLFROG'S SHINTO

There once was a fellow named Master Plain who, hearing word of an august shrine in our land, passed through to pay his obeisance. When he arrived, he found prostrate before the shrine's hall a man draped in dull gray, chirping meaninglessly and lost in a frenzy of prayer. Just then a bloated old tub of a fellow, dressed in a washed-out, rust-colored patchwork jacket, happened to appear from behind the hall. He called to the man prostrate in midprayer: "And what have we here! Strange mug, such shifty eyes, so very odd indeed!

A physiognomy that spells deep greed, nothing less—what exactly are you praying for?" To this the man replied, "Ah, shame—you've caught me in the act already! Sir, I am an aged rat. By birth so nimble—I hop across beams faster than men stroll the ground, and I've got some wicked strong teeth too. There isn't a thing I can't nibble through, and nowhere I won't go. I fancy anything: there's not a morsel I won't eat. A life of liberty but for that foul, fiendish feline who's kept in every house—harm's way for the unsuspecting rat! I pray to the gods and the Buddha, that they should intervene in one fell swoop and trounce every cat in the universe to death.

"The cat, you know, is a useless creature: he's felonious to the bone—look how he'll swipe that fish off the far edge of your tray or gobble up your prize canary, only to turn around and spread his droppings on the hearth. He'll even stay on to haunt you as a zombie-cat. Loads of grief, not an ounce of profit. My prayers are not so greedy, you see—I simply want deliverance from harm. And you, old man—who are you, and what brings you to pilgrimage here today?"

The man made his reply: "I'm the bullfrog under the porch. I seek nothing from the world. I do no harm to man's abode, and no one despises me. I'm as ugly as sin, so nobody dotes on me; I've no taste for fine food, and so it never strikes me to filch a meal. Squatting in the outhouse or under the porch, I eat what little bugs may come my way, and this suffices for a lifetime. What desires might prod me to pray to the gods? It makes sense for you to hate cats, since cats do you harm. But wait a minute—take a good look at yourself. The cat, as you say, is useless to men. But the fact that he's skilled in catching you leads folks to forgive the filched meals and keep him by their side. It's not that people love their cats—they hate you to the teeth. Petty men's minds are all the same—you've noticed the cat's unworthiness but forgot what a bane you yourself are to the world. If you're so nimble in nature and have such wicked strong teeth, why not climb a tall tree and chew on hard berries? If you have to fancy something, there are hills and fields brimming with bugs—and if you stuck to peoples' leftovers and grub that gets swept away, who would think to hate you and spend time raising pesky cats?

"And if you had a normal set of teeth, you wouldn't be able to pass through plugged-up spots, and as your peskiness shrunk, so men would come to hate you less. It's because of those teeth you brag about that folks can't keep you at bay, and that's why they raise cats, to snoop about aiming to catch you. Those fangs are hard proof that a petty man's talents will bring him to ruin. Rather than loathing pussycats and praying for miracles to the gods, I suggest a change of heart. If you stop pestering peoples' homes, no one will raise those worthless cats, and you can go on to lead a full, free life. You're not alone, you know—

The wise man turns out to be a bullfrog from the pond. "The Bullfrog's Shinto," in *The Country Zhuangzi*, by Issai Chozan. (Waseda University Library)

most folks fail to restrain themselves, blaming others instead; and when things get out of hand, they pray to the gods and plead to the Buddha. Such is the petty man's predicament. They say the gods refuse the insolent. 'All we need do is pray to the gods, and anything, good or evil, right or wrong, shall come true'—how foolish the mind of man!"

TRANSLATED BY ROBERT CAMPBELL

THE STORY OF SŌEMON

In his mad wandering not being affected by anything, in his stupidity having no usable wit, saying whatever he feels without concealment, loving books without remembering a word of them, he often naps through the day. When with the common people, he enjoys their company and their jests, but when that's over, he leaves without looking back. He rests above the muddy waters, at the foot of Bead Tree Mountain. You ask his name? He calls himself Tamura Sōemon, saying he comes from Sage Zhuangzi's seed dropped in China, which after many generations crossed over to Japan. Because he was born among the rice paddies, he called himself Ricevillage Zhuang-emon. There is a Confucian gentleman who always comes to visit him. One day this friend asked Sōemon, "To look at you, one could not give a name to what you are. You speak as if you believe in the way of the Sages, but in your actions there do not seem to be any deeds bad enough to constitute a crime such as what we learn from "Zisang's inattention to details," nor any good enough to hold up for praise. In the dank darkness of your mind, you idly keep on eating. Neither Confucian nor Buddhist, you just let your feelings run loose. You must be one of those people who are weary of the world. When you happen to take up your writing brush, you scribble out all sorts of nonsense, not a single kernel of truth to them. Though one might say that these are not things for deceiving the world and leading people astray, they are still useless superfluities. Fortunately, you read books. From now on you should reform your mind, follow the teachings of the Sages, take to heart the stories of the brothers Cheng Hao and Cheng Yi and of Zhuzi, and work to perfect your dignity and appearance. Then you can go and have your name known by others."

Sōemon replied: "It isn't that I'm not aware of the greatness of the Sages' teachings. How could I be one of those who leave the Path of Man and be content with self-neglect and self-abuse? Moreover, I don't think the delusive words of Zhuangzi, which are rather like 'Zisang's inattention to details,' are at all superior to those of the Sage. It's just that in terms of power there is strong and weak, in ability there is much and little. I myself am a small man of foolish temperament and of many infirmities. I know I cannot measure up to the moderation and preciseness of a gentleman who possesses dignity, decorum, virtue, and talent. If I can just reach an understanding of the uniformity of life and death, the consistency of fortune and misfortune, without losing my own individual personality due to human desire, then I will be happy.

"What leisure do I have to polish my speech and refine my behavior only to become known to people? On this earth each thing has its own feelings. Therefore, birds sing in the spring, crickets chirp in the autumn. Then why should I be such worthless gravel? Why should I keep quiet and have nothing to say? The good and bad, the gains and losses of the world are no concern of mine. All I do is express, under the pretext of describing things, what my heart feels. My jesting may cause people to laugh, but since I put my heart into my jesting, my real intentions should be understood."

TRANSLATED BY DAVID SITKIN

A Book of Everyday Morals

JIDARAKU SENSEI (YAMAZAKI HOKKA)

Among all the intellectual *kijin,* or eccentrics, of his time, Yamazaki Shunmei (1700–1746) stands out as a madman by his own declaration. Although he was also known as an Edo poet with the name "Hokka," he came to be better known by his self-derogatory appellation of "Jidaraku Sensei," or "Master Degenerate." Eccentricity was generally observed by others, while Jidaraku not only declared himself an eccentric but also acted out his strangeness in his life and his writings. Like many other educated madcaps, he has not been included in mainstream literary history.

Toward the end of his life, Jidaraku Sensei orchestrated his own "death" and funeral so that his writings could be published "posthumously." *A Book of Everyday Morals* (*Fūzoku Bunshū,* 1744) is a two-volume collection prefaced by a brief biography in which the "posthumous" author is described as a degenerate person, unmarried and having disappeared from the world after resigning from his off-and-on service as a samurai. "Hokka II," the imagined disciple, declares in the biography that his master has lived a life of satisfaction within his poverty, loving nothing but *sake,* tea, and napping. Credit is also given to him for never flattering the rich and the powerful. The introduction that follows says that Hokka was not a bad poet but that his prose "startled the gods and made even ogres cry." After Hokka's presumed death, while completely drunk, on the last day of the twelfth month of 1739, a burial was conducted at the Yōfukuji Temple in Nippori, to the north of the shogun's castle. Posing, again, as his own disciple, he erected a headstone, inscribing the "deceased" master's name. This same "Hokka II" remained the compiler of Hokka's "posthumous" writings.

The first volume of *Everyday Morals* opens with Jidaraku's invented genealogy, which supposedly originated from the Taira clan (or Heike clan, as it is commonly called) in the late Heian period. A description of his upbringing, the history of his service as a samurai, and his resignation from any work throughout his life is followed by the circumstances of his death and another, more detailed biography of Jidaraku written by "Hokka II." The inscription "Hokka II" put on the master's grave quotes him as saying, "Whether it is your soul or your body, whatever exists is vulgar. Whether it is your soul or your body, whatever dies is pure."

The collection includes short essays on eclectic subjects such as travel, smoking, likes and dislikes, Chinese poets, drunkenness, diseases, and cats and ghosts. One of the most engaging essays is on food, cooking, and eating, including a discussion of the seasons and their appropriate delicacies. His affectionate obsession with sizes, shapes, colors, and flavors of culinary materials and their scrutinous rules for preparation stand in opposition to widely spread, hypocritical efforts for political and social gain, which Jidaraku observes in disgust. What he seeks is an illusion of individualism as he imagines an individual identity that might exist completely free from the context of a corrupt social system.

The essay titled "Why I Call Myself Navel" (Mizukara Saijin to Yobu no Zei), translated here, is a typical example of the genre called mad prose (kyōbun). It identifies the navel as an organ isolated from all other parts of the body and one that does not come in a pair. And, most importantly, this organ is totally useless. Here is a metaphorical declaration of himself as an individual who does not belong to the whole and refuses to be made useful. In the foreword to "My First Pot of Rice Cooked in the New Year" (Shōgatsu Hajimete Meshi o Taku no Jo), Jidaraku realizes that he has not cooked rice for many days because of New Year's events. He is surprised to learn that his pots and pans agree with his principle of being independent by being free of any practical function. Those utensils appear in his dream to correct his misconception that there are occasions when serving a purpose is called for, the New Year's festivities being an example.

Jidaraku's heterodox philosophy is pronounced and further explored in *The Book of Toil and the Four Symptoms of Madness* (*Rōshikyō*, two volumes, published in 1747), the title parodying the homophonous *The Book of Laozi* (in Japanese, *Rōshikyō*), which referred to Laozi's *Dao De Jing*. "Shi" in the title means "four," but it probably refers to all four classes of people as designated by the shogunate and also echoes the word "death" (*shi*). In general terms, Jidaraku's notions of human life in relation to his political and social environment are very much Daoist, as they were among most intellectuals at his time. The idea of nonaction being superior to action and nonexistence closer to the truth than existence is at the bottom of Jidaraku's criticism of all the oppressive powers that surround an individual. Jidaraku denies any value in labor, for example, in opposition to doing nothing or taking a nap. Exertion of any kind, particularly efforts for achieving one's desires or obtaining comfort, is despised, for it is a way to submit to the general human obsession with social success, political power, monetary gain, and life's conveniences.

Clearly this type of worldview comes from Jidaraku's deep-rooted despair about the Tokugawa system with its strict rankings, policies, and ethics, buttressed by his personal grudges as an insignificant samurai. He equates the love of life with the love of death. Because one's heart, the central organ of his or her life, inspires a pursuit of pleasure, which in turn requires labor to attain it, one never achieves one's liberty without dying. The ultimate paradox in his thought is that death is a necessary condition for the pleasure of life. According to his philosophy, work of any kind, particularly the position of serving a lord as he has occasionally done, causes excruciating pain. While in service, one is compelled to say, hear, and do what one never wishes to by one's own judgment. A farmer's tilling, a monk's prayers, a priest's sutras, a doctor's treatments, a Confucian's readings, a nun's songs, a dancer's dances, and a samurai's martial arts are all laborious efforts at living, all of which do not bear the liberating value that death does. Jidaraku repeatedly describes the lives of the down-and-outs in order to highlight the ills of the superrich, who never cease their efforts to squeeze more money out of the poor.

Although Jidaraku isolates himself from his surroundings, particularly the world of the samurai, he is a representative of a mass of disgruntled samurai of the mid-eighteenth century. We can also say that the same element of frustration and denial can be seen in the writings of many eccentrics. However, Jidaraku's bitterness is far more intense than the others' and his philosophy of isolation and death marks him as an extreme case. His introverted approach separates him from another eighteenth-century eccentric, Hiraga Gennai, who imposed colloquial downtown speech on the language of politics and history, thereby turning his frustration as a jobless samurai into a political and economic issue for all of humanity.

⌒ (SJ) ⌒

WHY I CALL MYSELF NAVEL

From day one when Ying broke off from Yang, everything has had its opposite. To wit: heaven's got earth, up follows down, sun goes with moon, the stars join the sun, good opposes bad, mountains give way to rivers, sea turns into land, small faces big, and each corner has its circle. Old follows young, man goes with woman, straight hangs with crooked, darkness begets light. All born must die; each wise man hides a fool—and what once looked like back turns out to be front. Shinto gods oppugn the Buddha, and trees are different from grass. Metal ranks with stone, our heads hang over our arses, and feet face hands. Without backs there would be no bellies; eyes and ears pair off; the mouth comes complete with nose. Only a navel lacks its opposite.

What's more, each part of the body—eye, ear, nose, tongue, lip, hand, feet, hair, nail—is slave to his master the mind and knows not a moment's rest. Of these, only the navel has form but misses a proper function. As hard as his master may poke, he simply can't get him to do a chore: he's utterly useless. Of course you could point out one use—as measuring point for moxa remedies—but even this calls for no special genius on his own. He's the same sleeping or waking, the one part who won't budge an inch for his master. Since he won't work, he's always quiet, and in quietude lives a life of peace. In peace, illness never approaches him, and as long as he's bundled up in robes, he'll never fret over others who find him pretty or plain. Whenever his master feels regret, he can try to bite his navel, but it's so well placed he'll never reach it anyhow. So our little fellow skips the undue punishment.

By whose grace or by what fat stroke of luck do you owe your fortune, oh navel? The absence of your opposite makes perfect sense. I envy you so and have taken your name for my own: Master Navel. But tell me—how did you end up as lightning's favorite too? He's always on your tail—something I hardly envy!

MY FIRST POT OF RICE COOKED IN THE NEW YEAR

The boulevards are lined with festive stands of pine, and the voices of roaming singers rise from each corner. My neighbor's New Year stew has already come to a boil, but *chez-moi* it's cold rice left over from winter passed. New Year's Day rolls by, and I idle my way through the second; third and fourth days set, and I'm absent on the fifth, sixth, and seventh. Out and about eight and nine. The tenth finds me under the weather with last night's wine, and I can't even stand straight till the sun hits its peak.

I've come to my senses as the sun slips westward, and I try to count out the days: a hand's worth of fingers bend down and pop up straight again. Come to think of it, I haven't cooked rice once this spring—the serving crock sits listless, and the hearth is as cold as ice. A good look at the nature of things tells me these vessels may be inanimate, but they must know the difference between luck and despair. To be honed as a fine tool and used often—this must be what satisfies a vessel most.

"Sad, sad vessels, all strewn around my house—it's as if you'd been thrown away!" Mumbling to myself, I lie down once more. Just then the pot, the kettle, the serving crock, and all the other dishes hop out into the middle of the room and fall in line before me to sputter: "Your Lord's word is true but bears a lie as well. For it is our pleasure to lie idle, without being useful to anyone. We've no wish to debate the longevity of sharp or dull; but the more days one stays quiet, the longer life seems to grow. We may have joined the ranks of vessel-vassals, but who says that means we're never called to help? You use us as you need, and stop whenever there's no chore. To lack a constant chore is precisely our pleasure. Please, Lord, do not trouble yourself on our account.

"Having said as much, though, the year has changed and days fly by, and still you haven't used us once this spring. Servants in the house are expected to hail their Lord's health in the new year—we call this rite the 'Servants' New

The hermit speaks to utensils from his kitchen. "My First Pot of Rice Cooked in the New Year," *A Book of Everyday Morals*, by Jidaraku Sensei. (Waseda University Library)

Year Audience.' But we have yet to come in handy. By luck it is your pleasure to remain home today: we humbly place ourselves at your service."

I could barely make out these last words, when suddenly my dream burst, and I sprang up, shocked. It hit me on the head that these inanimate vessels must really feel this way. So I made up my mind to grant them their wish, and fetching some water, I prepared the rice and kindled a fire in the hearth. For who knows when this hearth will be rekindled, and all my vessel-vassals fall quiet again?

TRANSLATED BY ROBERT CAMPBELL

Source Texts and Modern Editions

This list is for readers who may wish to research the original texts from which the translations included in this volume have been made. Some of the works in the volume were handwritten and painted in forms of standing screens, hand scrolls, or albums. Each is held by one individual or institution. In our volume, many are reproduced in color inserts accompanied by captions that provide the sources, so those are not listed here.

For printed books that were bound in a number of volumes, volume numbers may be followed by the number of parts, because one volume sometimes stretched into two or more bound units. Printed books were often published in slightly different editions by separate publishers. Libraries that hold copies of the original or the oldest extant editions are given when possible. Some of the libraries that hold copies in relatively good condition are also listed, and more user-friendly ones are given preference. Although written copies of *jōruri* are extant because they were texts for chanting, kabuki were usually performed without a full written script. Likewise, songs were published as textbooks for practice, but copies from the period are hard to find.

The National Diet Library and the Waseda University Library offer extensive digital libraries, so the chances of reading texts online from those institutions are higher than at most libraries. The National Institute of Japanese Literature holds a very large number of texts on microfilm.

Some of the materials in the following list belong to special collections within the libraries, but the collections' names are omitted in favor of saving space. Each entry concludes with reference to an edition in modern transcription. All modern editions in the list were published in Tokyo except where noted.

Abbreviations of the Titles of the Modern Editions
HT = Hanashibon Taikei (Tokyodo Shuppan)
NKBT = Nihon Koten Bungaku Taikei (Iwanami Shoten)
NKBZ = Nihon Koten Bungaku Zenshū (Shogakkan)
SNKBT = Shin Nihon Koten Bungaku Taikei (Iwanami Shoten)
SNKBZ = Shinpen Nihon Koten Bungaku Zenshū (Shogakkan)

I. CHARACTERS AND MANNERS, HIGH AND LOW

Kanō Daigaku Ujinobu (illustrator), *The Poetic Competition of the Twelve Zodiac Animals* (*Jūnirui Uta-Awase E-Kotoba,* 6 pieces of paper bearing poems and pictures pasted on a single standing screen, ca. 1650). Owned by Toru Takahashi.

Ihara Saikaku, *Twenty Local Paragons of Filial Impiety* (*Honchō Nijū Fukō,* 5 vols., 5 parts, *ukiyozōshi,* Yorozuya Seibei, Edo, Okada Saburōemon, Osaka, and Chigusa Gohei, Osaka, 1686; illustration likely by Yoshida Hanbei). Held by the National Diet Library and Tenri Central Library. SNKBZ vol. 76, 1991.

Ejima Kiseki, *Characters of Worldly Shop Clerks* (*Seken Tedai Katagi,* 5 vols., 5 parts, *ukiyozōshi,* Kikuya Kibei, Kyoto, 1730). Held by the National Diet Library and Waseda University Library. Hasegawa Tsuyoshi, ed., Hachimonjiyabon Zenshū 11 (Kyuko Shoin, 1996).

II. EXPLORING JAPAN: TRAVELING THE FREEWAYS ON FOOT

Nakagawa Kiun, *Denizens of Kyoto* (*Kyō Warabe,* 6 vols., 6 parts, *kanazōshi,* Yamamori Rokubei, Kyoto, and Hiranoya Sahei, Kyoto, 1658). Held by the libraries of Waseda University and Tohoku University. Takemura Toshinori, *Nihon Meisho Fūzoku Zue,* Kyoto vol. 7 (Kadokawa Shoten, 1979).

Asai Ryōi, *Famous Places along the Tōkaidō* (*Tōkaidō Meishoki,* 6 vols., 6 parts, *kanazōshi,* publisher unknown, 1659). Held by the National Diet Library, the Tokyo Metropolitan Chuo Library, and Waseda University Library. Asakura Haruhiko, ed., *Tōkaidō Meishoki* (Heibonsha, 1979).

Kikuoka Senryō, *Glittering Highlights of Edo: Traces of Famous Places Old and New* (*Edo Sunago Onko Meisekishi,* 6 vols., 6 parts, *kanazōshi,* Wakanaya Kohei, Edo, and Yorozuya Seibei, Edo, 1732). Held by the National Diet Library and the libraries of Waseda University and Keio University. Koike Shōtarō, ed., *Edosunago Onko Meiseki Shi* (Tokyodo Shuppan, 1976).

Mukai Kyorai and Chine, *A Journey to Ise* (*Ise Kikō* combined with *Shijusō,* 1 vol., *Kikōbun,* 1686; first published by Ise Grand Shrine Office in 1850 in combination with *Nekorobigusa* in celebration of 150-year anniversary of Kyorai's death).

Held by the National Institute of Japanese Literature, the National Diet Library, and Waseda University Library. Shinsetsuan Ryūgai, ed., *Ise Kikō* (Hakubunkan, 1937).

III. THE MONSTROUS AND THE WEIRD

Anonymous, *One Hundred Tales from the Various Provinces* (*Shokoku Hyakumonogatari,* 5 vols., 5 parts, *kanazōshi,* Kikuya Shichirobei, Kyoto, 1677). The only complete copy held by the Tokyo National Museum. Tachikawa Kiyoshi, ed., *Hyakumonogatari Kaidan Shūsei,* Sōsho Edo Bunko 2 (Kokusho Kankōkai, 1987).

Tomikawa Fusanobu, illustrator and author, *The Bearded Lady of the Haunted House* (*Bakemono Hitotsuya no Higeonna,* 1 vol., *kurohon,* Tsuruya Kiemon, Edo, 1770). Held by Tohoku University Library and the National Diet Library. Kaji Seiko, ed., "Kusazōshi no Honkoku to Kenkyū," *Tokyo Gakugei Daigaku Kinsei Bungaku Kenkyū,* vol. 25, 2004.

IV. STAGING THE SUPERNATURAL: HEROISM IN KAMIGATA AND EDO THEATRE

Chikamatsu Monzaemon, "Matabei the Stutterer," Ukiyo Matabei scene from *A Courtesan's Soul within Incense Smoke* (*Keisei Hangonkō,* a *jōruri* play, Yamamoto Kyūbei, Kyoto, also published in Osaka, 1708). Held by the National Diet Library, the Tsubouchi Memorial Theatre Museum of Waseda University, and the University of Tokyo Library. Shuzui Kenji and Okubo Tadakuni, eds., *Chikamatsu Jōruri Shū* 2, NKBT vol. 50, 1959.

Anonymous, *Kagekiyo* (a one-act kabuki play composed for Ichikawa Danjūrō I, 1732; the existing script by Ichikawa Danjūrō VII, 1842). Held by Atsumi Seitarō. Gunji Masakatsu, ed., *Kabuki Jūhachiban Shū,* NKBT vol. 98, 1965.

V. LANDSCAPES AND SEASONS

Ihara Saikaku, *Saikaku's Hundred Linked Verses, Annotated by Himself* (*Saikaku Dokugin Hyakuin Jichū Emaki,* handmade scroll, 1692). Held by Tenri Central Library. Ebara Taizo et al., eds., *Teihon Saikaku Zenshū,* vol. 11 (Chuokoron-Shinsha, 1970).

Matsuo Bashō and Enomoto Kikaku, "The Peddler of Poems" (Shiakindo) from Kikaku, ed., *Empty Chestnuts* (*Minashiguri,* 2 vols., a *haikai* collection, Nishimura Ichirōemon, Kyoto, 1683). Held by the libraries of Hokkaido University, Tenri University, and Kyushu University. *Bashō Shichibu Shū,* SNKBT vol. 70, 1990.

Matsuo Bashō, Hamada Chinseki, and Suganuma Kyokusui, "Beneath the Trees" (Ki no Moto ni) from Chinseki, ed., *The Gourd* (*Hisago,* 1 vol., a *haikai* collection, Izutsuya Shōbei, Kyoto, 1690). Held by the National Diet Library and the libraries of Kyoto University and Tenri University. *Bashō Shichibu Shū,* SNKBT vol. 70, 1990.

Matsuo Bashō, Nozawa Bonchō, and Mukai Kyorai, "Throughout the Town" (Ichi-naka wa) from *The Monkey's Straw Raincoat* (*Sarumino*, 6 vols., 2 books, a *haikai* collection, Izutsuya Shōbei, Kyoto, 1690). Held by the National Diet Library, the Tokyo Metropolitan Chuo Library, and Waseda University Library. *Bashō Shichibu Shū*, NKBT vol. 70, 1990.

VI. NATURE AND SENTIMENTS

Tachibana Fukaku (Shōgetsudō), *Two-Needle Pine* (*Futaba no Matsu*, a *haikai* collec-tion, publisher unknown, 1690). Held by the libraries of Kyushu University and Tenri University. *Edo Tentori Haikai Shū*, SNKBT vol. 72, 1993.

Yosa Buson, ed., *The Jeweled Water Grass Anthology* (*Tamamoshū*, a *haikai* collection, Andō Hachizaemon, Kyoto, 1774). Held by the libraries of the University of Tokyo and Waseda University. Maruyama Kazuhiko et al., eds., *Buson Zenshū*, vol. 7 (Kodansha, 1995).

VII. LOVE AND EROS

Anonymous, *The Tale of Zeraku* (*Zeraku Monogatari*, 3 vols., 3 parts, *kanazōshi*, Ya-mamori Rokubei, Kyoto, late 1650s or early 1660s). Vol. 1 held by the Depart-ment of Japanese Linguistics, the University of Tokyo; vols. 2 and 3 held by Tobacco and Salt Museum, Tokyo; a combined single-volume edition held by Toyo Bunko Library. *Kanazōshi Shu*, SNKBT vol. 74, 1991.

Kon Hachirōemon, "Lovebirds' First Journey" (Hiyoku no Hatsutabi, *bungo-bushi–shinnai-bushi*, Yoshinoya Kanbei, Kyoto, and Izumiya Ichibei, Edo, date unknown). Okamoto Bunya, *Yūrishinnaikō* (Doseisha, 1967).

Hara Budayū, "Evening Mist over Mount Asama" (Yūgasumi Asamagatake, composed for a 1734 Edo production of kabuki *Keisei Asamagatake,* first performed in Kyoto, 1698, *itchū-bushi*). Nakauchi Choji and Tamura Nishio, eds., *Kokyoku Zenshū*, Nihon Koten Ongyoku Zenshū (Seibundo, 1929); and Okamoto Bunya, *Koshōhon Kō* (Doseisha, 1969).

Anonymous, "To Toribe Mountain" (Toribeyama, *katō-bushi–sonohachi-bushi–miyazono-bushi,* composed for the lovers' journey scene in a kabuki play by an anonymous playwright, published by Hachimonjiya Yazaemon, Kyoto, in 1706; it was later adapted as an independent song, which was published in *Miyazono Ōmuishu,* 1773). Kōno Tatsuyuki and Kuroki Kanzō, eds., *Genroku Kabuki Kessakushū*, vol. 2 (Waseda University Press, 1926).

Satsumanojō Geki, "A Puppet Master of the Floating World" (Ukiyo Kairaishi, *sonohachi-bushi–kato-bushi,* 1718). Nakauchi Choji and Tamura Nishio, eds., *Kokyoku Zenshū*, in Nihon Koten Ongyoku Zenshū (Seibundo, 1929); idem, *Nihon Ongyoku Zenshū*, vol. 11; and Sugi Masao, *Hōgaku*, Dentō Geinō Shirīzu 6 (Gyōsei, 1990).

VIII. PASSIONS AMONG MEN

Anonymous, *Mongrel Essays in Idleness* (*Inu Tsurezure*, 1 vol., *kanazōshi*, Takada Yahei, Kyoto, 1653). Held by the Rikkyo University Library and the National Institute of Japanese Literature. Haruhiko Asakura, ed., *Kanazōshi Shūsei* 4 (Tokyodo Press, 1983).

Urushiya Ensai, "How a Pledge of Undying Love Was Reborn" (Nisei to Chikaishi Sairai no En) from *Male Colors Pickled with Pepperleaf Shoots* (*Nanshoku Kinomezuke*, 6 vols., 6 parts, *kanazōshi*, 1702). Held by the National Diet Library and Rikkyo University Library. Fujitake Rokurō et al., eds., *Mikan Chinpon Shūsei* (Bunshinsha, 1933).

Anonymous, *Bad Boy Morihisa* (*Akushō Morihisa*) from *Virtuoso Vocal Pieces: Beating Rhythm with a Fan* (*Rangyoku Ōgibyōshi, utaibon,* publisher unknown, 1706). Original libretto held by the late Masayoshi Itō and copies held by the National Diet Library, the Waseda University Tsubouchi Memorial Theatre Museum, and Keio University Library. Geinōshi Kenkyūkai, ed., *Nō,* vol. 3, Nihon Shomin Bunka Shiryō Shūsei (San'ichi Shobo, 1978).

Anonymous, *The Male Players' "Takasago"* (*Yarō Takasago*) from *Virtuoso Vocal Pieces: A Stacked Pair of Sake Cups* (*Rangyoku Kumisakazuki,* sequel to *Rangyoku Ōgibyōshi, utaibon,* published by Kariganeya Shōbei, Osaka, Okada Denbei, and Nose Sajūrō, Kyoto, 1707). Handwritten copies held by the Nogami Memorial Noh Theatre Research Institute of Hosei University, and a copy held by the Tsubouchi Memorial Theatre Museum of Waseda University. Geinōshi Kenkyūkai, ed., *Nō,* vol. 3, Nihon Shomin Bunka Shiryō Shūsei (San'ichi Shobo, 1978).

IX. GOSSIP, REPORTAGE, AND ADVERTISING

Jōkanbō Kōa, "The Funeral Director's Blowout-Sale Circular" (Sōshichi Yasuuri no Hikifuda Seshi Koto) from his *Newfangled Spiels* (*Imayō Heta Dangi,* 5 vols., 5 parts, *dangibon,* Ōwada Yasubei and Ōsakaya Heisaburō, Edo, 1752). Held by the National Institute of Japanese Literature. *Inaka Sōji, Imayō Heta Dangi, Tōsei Ana Sagashi,* SNKBT vol. 81, 1990.

Asai Ryōi, *Stirrups of Musashi* (*Musashi Abumi,* 2 vols., *kanazōshi,* Nakamura Gohei, Kyoto, 1661, and Yamamoto Kyūzaemon, Edo, 1676). Held by the National Diet Library, the National Institute of Japanese Literature, and the libraries of Brigham Young University and Waseda University. Nihon Zuihitsu Taisei Henshūbu, eds., Nihon Zuihitsu Taisei, vol. 6 (Yoshikawa Kobunkan, 1972).

Iwamoto Kenjū, "Rounding Out the Snowman" (Yuki Korogashi no Ge) from Shōji Katsutomi, ed., *A Garden of Words from the Boudoir* (*Dōbō Goen,* 2 books [book 1 in 3 vols., book 2 in 1 vol.], *zuihitsu,* publisher unknown, 1738). Among many versions, the one that includes this essay is held by Robert Campbell. Two other versions are held by Chuo University. Hanazaki Kazuo, ed., *Dōbō Goen Shū* (published privately by Kinsei Fūzoku Kenkyūkai, Tokyo, 1991).

X. LAUGHING AT EVERYDAY LIFE

Anonymous, *Today's Tales of Yesterday* (*Kinō wa Kyō no Monogatari*, 3 vols., *hanashi-bon*, varying texts from early seventeenth century). Included in volume 3 of the original text is "A Fare Outcome" (untitled in the original). Held by the Tokyo Metropolitan Chuo Library, the libraries of Tenri University and Gakushuin University, and the Gotō Art Museum. Kotaka Toshiro, ed., *Edo Shōwashū*, NKBT vol. 100, 1966.

Anonymous, *Today's Book of Jokes* (*Tosei Hanashi no Hon*, 1 vol., *hanashibon*, late 1680s). Held by Tenri Central Library. Included in this work is "Supplicant and Cutpurse" (Goshō-Negai to Kinchakukiri no Kenka no Koto). Modern edition HT vol. 5, 1975.

Shoen Bushi, ed., *This Year's Jokes* (*Kotoshibanashi*, 1 vol., *hanashibon*, Bun'endō, Kyoto, 1773). Held by the National Diet Library. Included in this work is "Death Poem" (Jisei). Modern edition HT vol. 9, 1979.

Anonymous, *Hand-Rolled for Laughter* (*Tōsei Teuchi Warai*, 5 vols., *hanashibon*, 1681). Held by the Tokyo Metropolitan Chuo Library. Modern edition HT vol. 5, 1975.
   a. "A Young Man Learns Country Manners" (Zaigō ni Irimuko o Toritaru Koto)
   b. "A Pickpocket Delivers a Bundle of Joy" (Kinchakukiri no Onna San o Suru Koto)
   c. "A Shabby Dresser Gets Hung Out to Dry" (Sansuinaru Mono Sentakusuru Koto)
   d. "How to Love a Servant Girl" (Aru Hito Koshimoto o Chōaiseraruru Koto)

Shikano Buzaemon, *Stories Told by Buzaemon* (*Buzaemon Kuden-Banashi*, 3 vols., 3 parts, *hanashibon*, 1683). Held by the University of Tokyo Library. Included in volume 3 is "The God of Fortune" (Fuku Ebisu). Modern edition HT vol. 5, 1975.

Tsuyu no Gorō, *Jokes Told by Tsuyu* (*Karukuchi Tsuyu ga Hanashi*, 5 vols., *hanashibon*, 1691). Held by the National Diet Library. Modern edition HT vol. 6, 1976.
   a. "A Son Whose Labels Cut the Mustard" (Fudemamenaru Kakitsuke no Koto) from vol. 1
   b. "A Confession, Guessed Wrong" (Suiryō to Chigōta Koto) from vol. 1
   c. "Taking Care of Smallpox" (Hōsō no Yōjō) from vol. 2
   d. "A Tightwad Priest Crazy about a Boy" (Shiwaki Bōzu no Wakashugurui) from vol. 3

Yonezawa Hikohachi, *Jokes Worthy of Your Ear* (*Karukuchi Gozen Otoko*, 5 vols., 5 parts, *hanashibon*, 1703). Held by the Department of Japanese Linguistics, School of Humanities and Sociology, the University of Tokyo, and by the Tokyo Metropolitan Chuo Library. Modern edition HT vol. 6, 1976.
   a. "A Radish Fit for an Emperor" (Goshinmotsu no Daikon) from vol. 1
   b. "A Certain Style of Face" (Kao no Moyō) from vol. 1
   c. "A White Mouse with Renal Vacuity" (Jinkyo no Shironezumi) from vol. 2
   d. "An Impromptu Performance" (Sokuza no Nō) from vol. 3
   e. "A Bather Kicks the Bucket" (Saiwai no Hayaoke) from vol. 3
   f. "Piss-Poor in Arima" (Arima no Misugi) from vol. 4

Tsuyu no Gorobei, *Jokes Left by Rokyū* (*Rokyū Okimiyage,* 5 vols., *hanashibon,* published posthumously in 1707). Held by the Department of Japanese Literature, the University of Tokyo. Modern edition HT vol. 7, 1976.

    a. "A Peasant Plays It Safe" (Yōjinbukai Hyakushō) from vol. 1

    b. "Like Father, Like Son—A Pair of Drunkards" (Oyakotomoni Ōjōgo) from vol. 2

    c. "A Wild Boar Comes Back to Life" (Inoshishi no Yomigaeri) from vol. 3

    d. "Fickle Lovers Plot a Double Suicide" (Shinjū no Ōhazumono) from vol. 3

Anonymous, *Jokes to Bloom in Summer Heat* (*Mizuuchibana,* 5 vols., *hanashibon,* early eighteenth century). Held by Department of Japanese Literature, the University of Tokyo. "One Hundred Tales of Food" (Shokurui Hyakumonogatari) is from vol. 4. Modern edition HT vol. 7, 1976.

Tōkaku. *Jokes for Side Stitches* (*Karukuchi Heso Junrei,* 5 vols., *hanashibon,* 1746). Held by the Hosa Library. "Happy Being a Beggar" (Kojiki no Mijiman) is from vol. 2. Modern edition HT vol. 8, 1976.

Anonymous, *Jokes from the God of Fortune* (*Karukuchi Warai Hotei,* 5 vols., *hanashibon,* 1747). Held by the Tokyo Metropolitan Chuo Library. "Ten-Thousand-Year Trunk" (Mannen no Tsuzura) is from vol. 3. Modern edition HT vol. 8, 1976.

XI. PHILOSOPHIZING THE ORDINARY

Daidōji Yūzan, *A Collection of Fallen Grains—Addendum* (*Ochiboshū,* hand-copied, 11 vols., 1727; printed edition, 10 vols. in 5 parts, 1858). Held by the libraries of the University of Tokyo and the University of Tsukuba. Hagiwara Tatsuo and Mizue Renko, eds., *Ochiboshū,* Edo Shiryō Sōsho (Jinbutsu Ōraisha, 1967).

Issai Chozan, "The Transformation of the Sparrow and the Butterfly"(Suzume Chō no Henka), "The Bullfrog's Shinto" (Hiki no Shintō), and "The Story of Sōemon" (Sōemon ga Den) from his *Country Zhuangzi* (*Inaka Sōji,* 4 vols., 4 parts, *dangibon,* Izumiya Giheii, Edo, 1727). Held by the National Diet Library, the Tokyo National Museum, and the libraries of the University of Tokyo and Waseda University. *Inaka Sōji, Imayō Heta Dangi, Tōsei Ana Sagashi,* SNKBT vol. 81, 1990.

Jidaraku Sensei (Yamazaki Hokka), "Why I Call Myself Navel" (Mizukara Saijin to Yobu no Zei) and "My First Pot of Rice Cooked in the New Year" (Shōgatsu Hajimete Meshi o Taku no Jo) from his *Fūzoku Bunshū* (2 vols., 2 parts, *dangibon,* Nishimura Ichirōemon, Kyoto, and Nishimura Genroku, Edo, 1744). Held by Nakano Sanbin and the libraries of Kyoto University and Waseda University. *Inaka Sōji, Imayō Heta Dangi, Tōsei Ana Sagashi,* SNKBT vol. 81, 1990.

Contributors

HAROLD BOLITHO (1939–2010) was a professor of Japanese history at Harvard University. He also taught at the University of Melbourne and Monash University and conducted research at such institutions as the Australian National University, and the universities of Tohoku, Cambridge, Oxford, and Kyoto. His publications include *Treasures among Men: The Fudai Daimyo in Tokugawa Japan* (1974) and *Bereavement and Consolation: Testimonies from Tokugawa Japan* (2003).

STEFANIA BURK is a member of the Teaching and Educational Leadership faculty at the University of British Columbia in Vancouver, where she teaches Japanese literature and culture in the Department of Asian Studies. With her specialty in medieval Japanese poetics, her research has veered into the area of pedagogy and academic integrity, and she serves as Associate Dean, Academic, for the Faculty of Arts.

ROBERT CAMPBELL, director general of the National Institute of Japanese Literature, Tokyo, has taught at Kyushu University and the University of Tokyo. A specialist in Edo and Meiji literature, particularly Japanese poetry and prose in classical Chinese, he has authored and edited books and special journal issues in Japanese. He also brings his specialty in literary interpretation and teaching to a broader audience through frequent appearances on public and commercial media in Japan.

DAVID CANNELL, associate professor in the Institute of Global Affairs, Tokyo Medical and Dental University, holds seminars to train medical students in global scholarly participation. He taught earlier at Meiji Gakuin University and Sophia University,

Tokyo. A specialist of early Edo literature, he presented the paper "Field Dynamics in Genroku *Haikai* Poetry" in Tokyo in 2010.

CHERYL CROWLEY, associate professor of Japanese language and literature and director of the East Asian Studies Program at Emory University and the author of *Haikai Poet Yosa Buson and the Bashō Revival* (2007), is a specialist of *haikai,* calligraphy, and women's writing. Her articles include "Haikai Poet Shokyūni and the Economics of Literary Families" (2010) and "Calligraphy as a Resource in the East Asian Studies Curriculum" (2013). Her current research is on women poets in the Bashō School of *haikai.*

ALAN CUMMINGS is a senior teaching fellow in Japanese and the associate head of the Department of East Asian Languages and Cultures, SOAS, University of London. He also teaches as a guest lecturer at the University of Iceland. His research is in early modern Japanese literature and theatre, particularly kabuki. He has published *Haiku: Love* (2013) and several translations in the *Kabuki Plays on Stage* series. He is currently working on a monograph on Kawatake Mokuami.

CHARLES FOX, principal of Ritsumeikan Uji Junior and Senior High School and professor emeritus of Ritsumeikan University, Kyoto, has held visiting positions at the University of British Columbia, the Australian National University, and Harvard University. A translator of poetry by Kitahara Hakushū and fiction by Yasuoka Shōtarō and others, he has also produced and cowritten *Between Tides* (2017), a documentary by filmmaker Masa Fox on the descendants of the Ogasawara/Bonin Islands settlers.

MATTHEW FRALEIGH is an associate professor at Brandeis University, the author of *Plucking Chrysanthemums: Narushima Ryūhoku and Sinitic Literary Traditions in Modern Japan* (2016), and the translator of Ryūhoku's *New Chronicles of Yanagibashi* (2011 Japan-U.S. Friendship Commission Prize) and "Super Secret Tales from the Slammer" (2012 William F. Sibley Memorial Prize). He has been a visiting professor at Harvard University and Kyoto University. Since 2018, he heads the Association for Japanese Literary Studies.

C. ANDREW GERSTLE is a professor of Japanese studies at the SOAS University of London. A specialist of literature and popular culture of the Edo period, his publications include *Chikamatsu: Five Late Plays* (2001), *Kabuki Heroes on the Osaka Stage, 1780–1830* (2005), a book in Japanese on Edo-period erotic books for women (2011), and *Shunga: Sex and Pleasure in Japanese Art* (2013), as well as *Great Pleasures for Women and Their Treasure Boxes,* a translation of Tsukioka Settei's erotic book (2018).

TOM HARE is the William Sauter LaPorte '28 Professor in Regional Studies and professor of comparative literature at Princeton University. He studies Japan's classical drama and literature as well as portraiture and ancient Egyptian graphemics. His *Zeami: Performance Notes* (2008) received the Hosei University Noh Drama Prize in

Memory of Kanze Hisao in 2009 and the Japan-U.S. Friendship Commission Prize for the Translation of Japanese Literature in 2010.

HOWARD HIBBETT (1920–2019) was a professor of Japanese literature at Harvard University, a specialist and translator of Edo and modern Japanese literature, and also taught at the University of California, Los Angeles. Author of *The Floating World in Japanese Fiction* (1959, 2001) and *The Chrysanthemum and the Fish* (2001), translator of many works by Tanizaki Jun'ichirō and others, and editor of *Contemporary Japanese Literature* (1977, 2005), he received the 2018 Lindsley and Masao Miyoshi Translation Prize for his lifetime achievement in that field. He served as a member of the advisory board for this three-volume anthology.

SUMIE JONES is a professor emerita of Japanese and comparative literature and a residential fellow of the Institute for Advanced Study, Indiana University. She has held visiting positions at Harvard University, the University of Tokyo, Rikkyo University, and others. An author and editor on theory and practice of translation, she has translated crime stories from the Edo and Meiji periods. She received the 2019 Lindsley and Masao Miyoshi Translation Prize for her lifetime achievement as translator and chief editor of this three-volume anthology.

ADAM KABAT is a professor of Japanese literature at Musashi University, Tokyo. He has written extensively on monsters in the popular literature of the late Edo period and has published authoritative annotated editions in Japanese of major Edo books featuring monsters and ghosts. He has also written a textbook on how to read Japanese cursive script. His translations of modern Japanese fiction include *The Maid*, by Tsutsui Yasutaka (2010), and *The Voice and Other Stories*, by Matsumoto Seicho (1989).

ADAM L. KERN is a professor of Japanese literature and visual culture at the University of Wisconsin–Madison. Previously on the faculty at Harvard University, he has held research positions at the University of Kyoto, the University of Tokyo, and the National Institute of Japanese Literature in Tokyo. His writings include *Manga from the Floating World: Comicbook Culture and the* Kibyōshi *of Edo Japan* (2006) and *The Penguin Book of Haiku* (2018).

DYLAN MCGEE is an associate professor in the Graduate School of Humanities at Nagoya University, Japan, specializing in early modern Japanese literature, print culture, and comparative literature. In addition to various translations and articles on early modern Japanese literature, he is also preparing a monograph on the Daisō lending library of Nagoya that explores issues of reader reception, book circulation, and production of local literature.

SHINJI NOBUHIRO, professor emeritus of the University of Tokyo, has taught at Teikyo University and held visiting positions at Chulalongkorn University, Thailand; the Korean Institute of Foreign Languages; the Beijing Institute of Foreign Languages;

and the National University of Hanoi. He has edited two volumes of the Meiji Section appended to *SNKBT* (The New Anthology of Classical Japanese Literature) and co-edited volume 5 of a new collection of works of Sanyūtei Enchō (2013).

GREGORY M. PFLUGFELDER, associate professor of Japanese history at Columbia University, has authored, among other studies, a book in Japanese on the women's suffrage movement in Akita Prefecture (1986), which won the Yamakawa Kikue Prize, and *Cartographies of Desire: Male-Male Sexuality in Japanese Discourse, 1600–1950* (1999). His current work engages the construction of masculinities, the history of the body, and representations of monstrosity.

SHELLEY FENNO QUINN, associate professor of Japanese at the Ohio State University, teaches Japanese literature, language, and theatre. She trained in nō acting in Japan and played the lead in *Hagoromo*. Her interest in drama theory led to her *Developing Zeami: The Noh Actor's Attunement in Practice* (2005). Further research foci include nō's connectedness to other arts of narrative recitation ("Morihisa," 2013) and emergence and innovation in modern nō ("Kanze Hisao: Renaissance Actor," 2016).

ESPERANZA RAMIREZ-CHRISTENSEN, a professor emerita at the University of Michigan, is a specialist in classical Japanese literature with a particular interest in linked poetry, literary hermeneutics, Buddhist philosophy, and feminist critique. She also held a visiting position at Harvard University. Her publications include *Heart's Flower: The Life and Poetry of Shinkei* (1994), *The Father-Daughter Plot* (coeditor, 2001), and *Emptiness and Temporality: Buddhism and Medieval Japanese Poetics* (2008).

JAY RUBIN, a professor emeritus of Japanese literature, Harvard University, and formerly of the University of Washington, Seattle, is an award-winning translator of Murakami Haruki, Natsume Sōseki, Akutagawa Ryūnosuke, and other modern Japanese writers. His recent books include *Haruki Murakami and the Music of Words* (2012), *The Penguin Book of Japanese Short Stories* (2018), and a novel of his own in English, *The Sun Gods* (2015). He is currently translating modern Japanese versions of classical nō plays.

PAUL GORDON SCHALOW is a professor of Japanese at Rutgers University. His publications include a translation and study of Ihara Saikaku's *The Great Mirror of Male Love*, for which he received the 1990 Japan-U.S. Friendship Commission Prize for the Translation of Japanese Literature, and *A Poetics of Courtly Male Friendship in Heian Japan*, which was nominated for the 2007 Warren-Brooks Award for Outstanding Literary Criticism. In 2018–2020, he participated in a three-year *Genji* research project at Paris Diderot University.

DAVID SITKIN (1949–2005) was an attorney and translator specializing in law, science, and industry. Having pursued graduate studies in Japanese at the University of Hawai'i and at Waseda and Harvard, he taught English at Nagoya University and Japanese literature at Wittenberg University before moving on to the legal and translating professions. He was a contributor to Kodansha's *Encyclopedia of Japan* and Kairyudo's English textbooks.

HENRY D. SMITH II is a professor emeritus of Japanese history at Columbia University; he taught previously at Princeton University and the University of California, Santa Barbara. He is the author of *Hiroshige: One Hundred Famous Views of Edo* (1986), *Kiyochika: Artist of Meiji Japan* (1988), and *Taizansō and the One-Mat Room* (1994). He also edited and coauthored the series "Three Hundred Years of Chūshingura" in *Monumenta Nipponica* (2003–2006).

JOHN SOLT, poet, editor, and publisher, is a specialist and translator of Edo and modern Japanese art and literature. He has been a poet in residence and instructor at universities in Thailand. His publications include the prizewinning *Glass Beret: The Selected Poems of Kitasono Katue* (1996) and *Shredding the Tapestry of Meaning* (1999), later translated into Japanese. He compiled the twenty-six-volume *An Episodic Festschrift for Howard Hibbett* (2000–2010). His book *Poems for the Unborn* came out bilingually in Tokyo in 2019.

TORU TAKAHASHI, a professor emeritus of Japanese Literature at Nagoya University, is an expert on Heian courtly literature and arts. He has also taught at Sugiyama Women's University, Nagoya, as well as holding visiting positions at Indiana University and Charles University in Prague. His research in a large number of museums and libraries in Europe and the United States has enriched his books in Japanese, which chiefly concern the relationship between narrative and pictorial systems in literature and the other arts based on narratology and semiotics.

GLYNNE WALLEY, associate professor of Japanese literature at the University of Oregon, specializes in popular literature of the late Edo period. His book *Good Dogs: Edification, Entertainment, and Kyokutei Bakin's "Nansō Satomi hakkenden,"* about Bakin's *Eight Dogs,* was published in 2017. The first volume of his translation of *Eight Dogs* is forthcoming. He has also translated several contemporary popular novels, including the four books in Suzuki Koji's *Ring* series (2003–2006).

KENJI WATANABE, professor emeritus of Rikkyo University, academic dean of the Jiyu Gakuen College, and former principal of Rikkyo Niiza Middle and High Schools, has held visiting positions at Fu Jen Catholic University, as well as Indiana and Columbia universities. The author of a study of daimyo literary writings during the Edo period (1997), he is the chief editor of the 2006 edition of Fujimoto Kizan's encyclopedia of pleasure quarters (1678). His latest publication is an anthology of Yoshiwara courtesan reviews (2013).

STEVEN WILLS is an associate professor of East Asian history and the chair of the History Department at Nebraska Wesleyan University. His current manuscript project traces the impact of fire and the culture of firefighting in Edo-Tokyo from the 1650s to the 1950s. His work has appeared in *Flammable Cities: Urban Conflagration and the Making of the Modern World* (2012) and *Cartographic Japan: A History in Maps* (2016).

MARCIA YONEMOTO is a professor of history at the University of Colorado, Boulder. She is the author of *Mapping Early Modern Japan: Space, Place, and Culture in the Tokugawa Period (1603–1868)* (2003) and *The Problem of Women in Early Modern Japan* (2016). She is coeditor of the essay collection *What Is a Family? Answers from Early Modern Japan* (2019). Her present research project is a history of adult adoption in Japan from 1700 to 1925.

Permissions

Brigham Young University Harold B. Lee Collection

Cleveland Museum of Art

Harvard University Art Museums

Hosei University Library, Tokyo

Hosei University Nogami Memorial Noh Theater Research Institute

Keio University Library

Kyoto National Museum

MOA Museum of Art, Shizuoka

Museum of Fine Arts, Boston

National Diet Library, Tokyo

Osaka Museum of History

Tenri Central Library

Tobacco and Salt Museum, Tokyo

Tokyo Metropolitan Chuo Library

Tokyo National Museum

Toru Takahashi Collection

University of Tohoku Library

The University of Tokyo Department of Japanese Linguistics

The University of Tokyo Department of Japanese Literature

Waseda University Library

Waseda University Tsubouchi Memorial Theatre Museum

Index

Some of the names of persons that appear in the chronology, persons and subjects that appear in translated texts, and the titles of the books represented in this anthology are not included in the following.

INDEX OF NAMES

SUBJECT INDEX

TITLE INDEX